HARPERCOLLINS COLLEGE OUTLINE

Introduction to Sociology

Norman Goodman, Ph.D.
State University of New York at Stony Brook

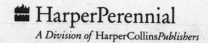

HarperPerennial
A Division of HarperCollins*Publishers*

To the countless numbers of students who were my partners in the mutual and exciting adventure of teaching and learning sociology.

An American BookWorks Corporation Project

Project Manager: Judith A.V. Harlan
Editor: Robert A. Weinstein

LIBRARY OF CONGRESS CATALOG CARD NUMBER 91-56007
ISBN: 0-06-467106-2

93 94 95 96 ABW/RRD 10 9 8 7 6 5 4 3 2

Contents

Preface

Introduction to Sociology is a part of the HarperCollins College Outline Series. It is intended to provide the student and general reader with a review of the essential elements of the discipline of sociology in clear, readable form. It can be used as either a review for or a supplement to many of the standard comprehensive textbooks or as a concise though integrated view of the field in conjunction with an anthology or instructor-selected set of relevant readings in the field of sociology.

Sociology is a diverse field. This book introduces the reader to its unique perspective, its key concepts, and its modes of exploring the social world as well as its explanations of social phenomena. The wide-ranging interests of the sociologist are made evident and examples are used to tie abstract ideas to concrete experiences. The focus is always on making the material accessible to the consumer—the student and general reader.

I would be remiss if I did not acknowledge the contributions of several key people to making this project a reality. Judith A.V. Harlan provided the absolutely essential professional discipline in the kind of delightful and supportive manner that kept this enterprise on track. Robert Weinstein provided invaluable and constructive scholarly and editorial criticism throughout the writing of this book. I am also indebted to Susan McClosky and Tannis McCammon, editors, and the fine secretarial assistance of Carole A. Roland for bringing this book to completion. Finally, my wife Marilyn deserves recognition for providing much needed love and support, as usual, during the complications this task necessitated in our joint life.

Norman Goodman
Stony Brook, New York
July, 1991

1

What Is Sociology?

In this chapter, we will explore the different perspectives of the social sciences, and of sociology in particular, in their attempts to understand and explain human behavior. We will examine the scientific basis of sociology, its origins, and its present form.

PERSPECTIVES

The Social Sciences

Sociology is one branch of the *social sciences*, a set of disciplines that examines the nature of human behavior and of human association and the resultant products of both. In order to appreciate how sociology contributes to an understanding of social life, it is helpful to understand the perspectives of the other social sciences.

Anthropology has two main branches. One, *physical anthropology* deals with the human being as a biological organism. In studying our biological roots, our ties to other species, and the biological variations among us it focuses on human fossils and artifacts. The second branch, *cultural anthropology* was once concerned with the nature and evolution of preliterate societies. More recently cultural anthropologists have turned their attention to modern industrial societies as well, in particular to the culture (see chapter 3) and social structure (see chapter 4) of neighborhoods and communities.

Economics is primarily concerned with how we produce, distribute, acquire, and consume necessary resources. While its main focus is on wealth, it also studies other kinds of resources such as food and energy.

Economists study, for example, influences on and effects of the unemployment rate, prices of basic commodities, and the total value of goods and services produced in a society (its GNP, gross national product).

Political science delves into issues involving the sources, distribution, and uses of power in society. It studies political processes in various groups and organizations. Political scientists are particularly concerned with forms and practices of government.

Psychology examines the bases and consequences of individual behavior, focusing on what leads the individual to behave in particular ways. There are many subfields in psychology, including the personality of individuals, the development of their cognitive abilities, and the biological basis of human behavior.

THE SOCIOLOGICAL PERSPECTIVE

There is no single sociological perspective; rather, there are several distinctively different "schools of thought" within sociology. But they all share a view of *sociology* as the scientific study of human social behavior and human association and of the results of social activities.

The basic premise of sociology is that human existence is social existence. We are linked to one another and depend on others for our existence. We influence and are influenced by others; indeed, our very sense of identity depends on this interaction, as will be discussed in chapter 6. Any attempt to understand social forms apart from individual action is doomed to failure. Sociology offers a rounded view of the human condition.

The sociological imagination. C. Wright Mills (1959) used the phrase "sociological imagination" to alert us to the need to broaden our vision. Individuals tend to see the world from their narrowly constricted view of themselves and their immediate social circle. Sociology, he argues, should focus attention on the wider social forces that affect individuals. To illustrate his point, he postulates that if one person is out of work, that circumstance could be seen as his or her "personal trouble," and efforts to help deal with that situation would focus on the characteristics of the individual. If, however, a million or more people are out of work, that is a "social problem" that suggests the operation of large-scale social forces and requires a social solution. The sociological imagination allows people to transcend their limited personal experience and to see their connections to others and to the institutions of society.

The utility of the sociological perspective. The larger picture provided by the sociological perspective encourages people to understand the social forces that structure their lives. It allows people to see how their personal experiences influence and are influenced by existing social arrangements and social constraints. Sociology enables people to understand the general by abstracting from the specific.

Émile Durkheim and suicide studies. The French sociologist Émile Durkheim studied rates of suicide of both societies as a whole and in selected segments of societies (e.g., Catholics and Protestants, men and women, married and single people). When he looked at the specific suicide rates, he saw a clear pattern: suicide is a function of the person's degree of integration into the social group. From this he fashioned a general explanation of suicide in terms of social integration that cuts across the specifics of religion, gender, marital status, and ethnicity.

Sociology also uncovers the latent (often unintended or unrecognized) aspects of social life. People who commit suicide are generally unhappy. Durkheim's research showing the relative consistency of suicide rates across social categories suggests that social as well as individual factors affect suicide. But because suicide is viewed as an individual act, the social dimension is often overlooked. By adopting a sociological perspective on suicide, Durkheim uncovered its social aspect—how the degree and type of social integration influence suicide rates.

Marriage. If people are asked why they married their spouses, they are likely to answer that they fell in love with them; that the spouse is the one and only person who could make him or her happy. However, there are also social norms that guide that decision, that define a limited set of individuals as potential marriage partners. Most people are generally unaware of these constraining social forces on what seems to be an intimate and personal decision. Sociology reveals these usually unrecognized social influences.

Sociology and Science

Sociology is the *scientific* study of social behavior and arrangements. While typically the notion of science suggests laboratories, measuring instruments, and algebraic equations, it actually refers to a general approach to gaining knowledge about any phenomenon.

THE ASSUMPTIONS OF SCIENCE

All organized "scientific" approaches to acquiring information about the world share certain assumptions. One assumption is that a world of reality exists independently of our perception or knowledge of it. For example, atoms exist even though we can't see them. In this sense, we "discover" laws of nature rather than create them.

Another of science's assumptions is that there is order in nature. Events don't happen haphazardly; they have preceding causes. Scientists also assume that knowledge about the world can be gained through systematic and objective observation. This is the hallmark of science: the systematic, disciplined, and objective observation of phenomena. Scientific truth can be tested empirically, that is, by careful, objective observation and measurement. The scientific method reduces the intrusion of personal values into the research process.

In short, science assumes the existence of an orderly world of cause and effect that can be penetrated by rigorous, objective observation and measurement. Values may intrude in the choice of what topics a scientist studies, but not in the method of uncovering knowledge. Ever cognizant of human fallibility, scientists often take a skeptical view of knowledge and demand evidence to support assertions.

THE TOOLS OF SCIENCE

Theories. Theories are systematic ways of explaining how two or more phenomena are related, especially in terms of whether one causes the other. Their major value is that they allow the scientist to go beyond the immediate factors under study and "generalize" to other phenomena having the same characteristics. For example, Durkheim found that the suicide rates of Catholics and Protestants differed, as did those of married and single people. He explained these findings in terms of a theory of social integration that now allows an understanding of suicide rates based on factors not originally studied by Durkheim.

Various hypotheses and data. Theories are made up of *variables*, traits or characteristics that change or have different values under different conditions. Theories link variables in ways that allow the development of *hypotheses*, statements about how two or more variables are connected or about how one or more variables will or will not change as certain specified conditions are altered. Hypotheses are tested by examining what they predict against empirical *data*, observable information such as facts and statistics.

Science, then, constructs theories, derives specific hypotheses from these theories, and tests the hypotheses by collecting and analyzing relevant data. The results are then used to evaluate the theory or theories that generated them. Theories can be abandoned, modified or accepted. The construction of theories and the confrontation of those theories with empirical data is a hallmark of modern-day science.

SOCIOLOGY AS A SCIENCE

Sociology is no less a science than chemistry or physics. It constructs theories to explain social life. *General theories* attempt comprehensive explanations, such as Talcott Parsons's (Parsons and Shils, 1951) "general theory of action" linking culture, social structure, and personality. Less comprehensive theories, or *middle range theories,* are "special theories applicable to limited ranges of data" (Merton, 1957:9). These are more common in sociology today; for example, Merton's theory of reference groups.

The scientific method is the foundation of sociology. Studies reported in the major sociological journals generally have the same formal structure as research in the physical or biological sciences. Some general theory is presented, along with a specific set of hypotheses to be tested. The relevant data are reported and analyzed, and conclusions are drawn from them about the appropriateness of the underlying theory.

The scientific status of sociology. While sociology is no less scientific than chemistry or astronomy, it does not seem to have the precision of either. In part that is because of its relative youth as a science. It has not had as much time to develop either its methodology or its theoretical conceptions. But more important, studying the behavior of people is not the same as studying the behavior of atoms or molecules or planets. People are more variable, and they change even while they are being studied. Also, sometimes reports of the results of a study cause people to change the behavior previously examined. These factors often mean that sociologists cannot generalize research findings as much as the physical or biological scientists can.

Sociologists confront another dilemma. While few people know much about the molecular structure of acids, most people consider themselves experts on the very things that sociologists study: crime, family life, social groups, and so on. Key concepts of sociological analysis are often framed in the language of everyday life, though the meanings of some words may be different. For example, *status* has a different meaning in sociology than it has in ordinary conversation. This confusion over words and the familiarity most people assume they have with the very substance of sociological analysis lead many to believe that sociology merely studies and states the obvious.

Sociology and common sense. Many "common sense" beliefs are simply untrue. For example, many believe that divorce is more common among middle and upper class couples than among lower class couples, or that most people on welfare really don't want to work. Both statements are false. Robertson (1987:9–10) lists twenty widely held "common sense" beliefs that sociological research has shown to be false.

The point is not that common sense is necessarily false but that sociology is a science. Sociology and common sense, therefore, need not be in conflict. In fact, common sense can be a rich source of hypotheses for sociologists. But sociologists go beyond the realm of common sense. They often take common sense notions about social life and subject them to rigorous testing that leads to their confirmation, rejection or refinement.

THE DEVELOPMENT OF SOCIOLOGY

Sociology is a relatively new science. While some sociological ideas go as far back as antiquity, the systematic attempt to understand and explain social behavior is less than 200 years old.

The Origins of Scientific Sociology

In general, people in stable societies are less likely to reflect on the social structures of their environment than people in unstable societies. The great upheavals of the fifth and fourth centuries B.C. in Greece and the seventeenth through nineteenth centuries in Europe led respectively to the development of Western philosophy and to consideration of the nature of "social order." Sociology developed in the early part of the nineteenth century as a response to changing social conditions.

THE FOUNDERS OF SOCIOLOGY

Auguste Comte (1798–1857). Auguste Comte, a French philosopher, is considered the founder of sociology, having coined the term in 1838 to define a particular method of studying society. Comte's aim was to use this new science to cure social ills. He became increasingly obsessed with this goal, and his work acquired a religious fervor. Comte focused on two specific aspects of society: order and stability, which he called *social statics* and social change, which he termed *social dynamics*. These, Comte believed, are the factors that hold society together and that instigate change.

The major factor promoting stability, Comte believed, is the common set of beliefs among societal members. Comte viewed social change as an evolutionary process that moves society toward better and better states. Though his specific views no longer play a significant role in modern sociology, his focus on social change and his insistence on a rigorous scientific methodology have had an enormous influence on other social thinkers, thus guaranteeing Comte a permanent place in sociological history.

Herbert Spencer (1820–1903). Comte's work was developed further by the English sociologist Herbert Spencer. Spencer attempted to explain social order and social change by comparing society with a living organism. Using this "organic analogy," Spencer saw society as a "system" composed of interdependent parts. In his view, sociology uncovers the key social structures and examines how they function to produce a stable society. In certain respects he was a forerunner of the "structural-functionalist" school of sociological thought, discussed later in this chapter.

Spencer was particularly interested in the evolutionary concept of the "survival of the fittest" and applied it to the study of how societies change. His approach, labeled *social Darwinism* led him to argue that if left free from government interference, society would weed out the "unfit" and allow only the best to survive and reproduce. This concept was used to support laissez-faire capitalism in both England and the United States.

Karl Marx (1818–1883). A German-born social philosopher and revolutionary, Marx spent many years doing painstaking historical research into the nature of society.

Like Comte, Marx was interested in studying social structures and social processes in order to improve society. His views became the basis for the "conflict school" of sociology, discussed below.

Marx believed that the fundamental "laws" of history could be found in the economic structure of society. He saw society as divided into two classes, those who own the means of producing wealth and those who do not; essentially, the "haves" and the "have-nots." This division, Marx believed, inevitably gives rise to "class conflict." Marx viewed the history of the world as a history of class struggle: lords against serfs, masters against slaves, capitalists against the proletariat.

According to Marx, the contradictions inherent in capitalism cause economic crises, which give rise to new social structures. This view, called *dialectal materialism*, assumes that the newly created structures will be an improvement on the older, more repressive ones. For this reason, Marx did not see conflict as bad but rather as a means of progress.

Marx's influence on sociology is still felt. While his view that economic factors are the most powerful influences on society is somewhat less accepted, most sociologists do grant their importance in social life.

Émile Durkheim (1858–1917). Durkheim's influence on sociology is not limited to his work on suicide, discussed above. Durkheim, influenced by Spencer and Comte, was especially interested in what holds society together; the problem of social order. His approach was essentially functionalist; he explored what function various social elements serve in the maintenance of social cohesion. He focused on the importance of shared beliefs and values ("collective conscience") and on collective ritual.

Durkheim believed that society is held together by the form of its social structure. In early society, which was less complex and less specialized than today's, people were linked because of their similarities. Most people did similar things; they were generalists. This sameness linked them through what Durkheim called *mechanical solidarity*. As society became more complex and differentiated, people took on specialized tasks that were necessary to each other. Durkheim called this kind of bonding through mutual support and interdependence *organic solidarity*.

Durkheim also contributed to sociological methodology. He argued that sociology must study social "facts" or forces that exist outside of individuals and constrain their behavior. He believed that people incorporate these constraining social influences into their identity, thereby transforming "social control" into "self-control" (see chapter 6).

Max Weber (1864–1920). German sociologist Max Weber has exerted enormous influence on contemporary sociology. He contributed both to the development of sociological knowledge and to sociological methodology.

Weber's main focus of study was social action. He was particularly interested in the values, beliefs, intentions, and attitudes that guide and direct our behavior. He developed a methodology, *verstehen* (understanding or insight), to uncover these underlying factors. Weber argued for a "value-free" sociology, the elimination of preconceptions and biases in the research process. In another innovation, he conceived of the *ideal type* the construction of a concept of a phenomenon that captures its essential elements and against which the real-world phenomenon might be compared.

An important aspect of Weber's work is in response to issues raised by Marx. Weber saw economic elements as but one of several important influences on social life. He attributed substantial importance to the social status derived from personal characteristics or esteem and to political power, the ability to influence the actions of others.

Weber's studies of organizations, especially bureaucracy, still influence research and theory in this area. He linked the rise of capitalism to the values and attitudes contained within the theology of developing Protestantism. And his research into various religions contributed an understanding of the roles of culture and social structure in theology.

Georg Simmel (1858–1918). Georg Simmel rejected the organic analogy of Spencer. He saw society as an "intricate web of multiple relations between individuals who are in constant interaction with one another" (Coser, 1977:178). The form that this interaction takes was the focus of Simmel's work. This approach, called *formal sociology*, could be used to study quite different spheres of social life (e.g., family interaction, business dealings, the legislative process). Simmel's ability to find common elements in the formal structures of these diverse types of interaction contributed to the further development of sociology.

Simmel's work led to research into "social types." His detailed analysis of the phenomenon of the "stranger" captured the subtleties and nuances of this social role. Contemporary discussions of the poor owe much to Simmel's descriptions of this social type. He saw the stranger as someone who is only marginally involved in a social group, technically a member but not fully accepted or integrated into it.

Contemporary American Sociology

Modern American sociology is built upon the theories described above. The earliest of these theories (Comte's and Spencer's) focused primarily on society, a large-scale social unit, and are called *macrolevel* theories. Other theories (facets of Weber's and Simmel's theories) deal with smaller units like the group and the dyad and are called *microlevel* theories. Many theories have both macro- and microlevel aspects. However, most contemporary theories in American sociology are primarily at either the macro- or the microlevel.

We will now look at two macrolevel theories—the "structural-functionalist" perspective and the "conflict" perspective—and at three microlevel theories—"symbolic interactionism," "ethnomethodology," and "exchange theory."

MACROLEVEL THEORIES

The structural-functionalist perspective. This theoretical orientation, defined in large part by the anthropologist Bronislaw Malinowski and the sociologists Talcott Parsons, Robert K. Merton and Kingsley Davis, is well known to the biological sciences, which use it to examine the structural aspects of organisms, their interrelationships, and the functions they perform for the organism as a whole.

The basic premise of this perspective is that *one can explain various phenomena, particularly social structures, in terms of their consequences (or "functions")*. Malinowski (1948), for example, explains the practice of magic among the Trobriand Islanders in terms of the sense of control it gives them over those activities that are both important and uncertain, like fishing on the high seas as opposed to fishing in the relatively safe lagoon.

An element in this perspective is the notion of *system*, the idea that *the various elements of society are related to one another in such a way that a change in one leads to changes in the others*. In the case of the Trobrianders, Malinowski argues that any analysis of this society must take into account the tie between the practice of magic and the economic impact of fishing on the entire community.

Parsons (1937; Parsons and Shils, 1951) was the foremost structural-functional analyst in American sociology. And like Parsons, most contemporary functionalists find Spencer's analogy useful in focusing on society's structural elements (e.g., social institutions, organizations, groups, social statuses) and their consequences (functions) for society as a whole.

In Parsons's view, society is a relatively stable, well-integrated social system whose members generally agree on basic values. Society tends to be a system in equilibrium or balance. Since any social change has widespread disequilibrating effects, change tends to be frowned upon unless it occurs slowly enough to allow the system time to adjust.

Merton (1957) refined and modified Parsons's functionalism. He points out that an organization can have both *manifest functions*, consequences that are known or expected, like the vote-gathering responsibilities of political machines, and *latent functions*, functions that are unintended or unexpected, such as the social service aspects of political machines in, for example, distributing food to the poor and helping them deal with the complexities of public welfare and public housing. Merton also points out that structures may have *dysfunctions*, negative consequences, as well as *eufunctions*, positive consequences. Further, a structure might be eufunctional for some part of society and dysfunctional for another part.

Not all social structures are functional for society, Merton argues; some can be eliminated with little significant effect. For example, Costa Rica gets by with no military institution. In other cases there may be *functional equivalents* to a particular social structure. For example, in the 1960s and 1970s many young people viewed communes as functional equivalents to the family. Today, some accept gay and lesbian couples as the functional equivalent of the marital couple, as is shown by their legal recognition as "domestic partnerships" in several major cities.

Critics of the structural-functionalist perspective point out both logical and pragmatic problems with this approach. They insist that some of the primary elements of the theory involve circular reasoning. To argue that a structure exists because it fills a certain need, and that because it fills a need it therefore must exist, adds little to our understanding, they point out. Further, they insist that the vagueness of the key terms *equilibrium* and *balance,* which were borrowed from biology where the consequences of a lack of balance (change in body temperature or blood pressure, for example) are clearly evident and measurable, does not add to our analytic power.

A third criticism, one with political implications, is that in viewing stability as all-important and decrying social change as disruptive, the structural-functionalist view is inherently conservative. Thus, functionalists are seen as supporting the status quo, the existing social arrangement. Critics argue that change is both necessary and desirable, that the American Revolution would not have occurred if the functionalist view had held sway, and that the civil rights and feminist movements would not be seen as beneficial.

One major alternative view to that of the structural-functionalists is "conflict theory," to which we now turn.

Conflict theory. The basic orientation of this perspective, derived from the work of Marx, *focuses on the conflict and competition between various elements in society*. The Marxist version looks at competition between social classes. Many contemporary conflict theorists (e.g., C. Wright Mills, 1956; Ralf Dahrendorf, 1959; and Randall Collins, 1974) focus on conflict between various racial, ethnic, and religious groups as well as on gender and class conflict. Conflict theorists note the seminal work of Simmel, who pointed to the divisive as well as to the consensual forces in society. Societies, he argued, have both associative (binding) and disassociative (disintegrative) pressures, and the relative weights of these pressures will vary at different times.

Lewis A. Coser, a major contemporary theorist influenced by Simmel, argues not only that conflict is inherent in society but also that under some conditions it serves very positive functions (1956, 1967). Conflict may help to clarify certain key values, Coser believes. Multiple group affiliations, which functionalists see as weakening consensus, are viewed by Coser as a mechanism for maintaining some level of stability by preventing a single axis of cleavage in society. Our belonging to different classes, ethnic groups, religions, and even genders keeps any one of these from dividing society into two mutually exclusive and continually warring camps. The social fabric is kept from being torn apart by divisive forces because of our varied and interconnected identities. Coser, in effect, blends aspects of functionalist analysis and conflict theory.

Whereas the functionalists decry change, conflict theorists tend to welcome it. Where functionalists see positive consequences of existing social arrangements, conflict theorists look for the winners and the losers, and assume both exist. In short, conflict theorists tend to have a more dynamic view of society and a more positive view of change.

Critics of conflict theory point to its tendency to focus on the divisive and conflictive aspects of social living, while ignoring the many harmonious and consensual processes that bind members of a society to one another. While functionalists have been accused of being politically conservative, conflict theorists have often been criticized for being politically radical, applauding if not fomenting change regardless of its consequences.

MICROLEVEL THEORIES

By and large, microlevel theories examine face-to-face interaction.

Symbolic interactionism. Though it was influenced by Weber, this school of thought is mostly indebted for its existence to the intellectual activities at the University of Chicago during the first third of this century, and particularly to the systematic thinking of the social philosopher George Herbert Mead. Symbolic interactionism starts with the premise that interaction is the primary social process. This interaction takes place through "symbols," representations that have agreed-upon meanings (see chapters 3 and 6). In fact, meaning derives from the interactions among sentient (thinking, feeling) beings.

Symbolic interactionists focus on the issue of identity, particularly the sense of self, which they argue is a social product. They analyze the social process through which identity develops, primarily meaningful social interaction (see chapter 6). They also focus on the nature of social interaction and how it occurs within a context of socially relevant understandings and considerations.

However, they point out that rather than being static, this social background is a dynamic process of shifting and emergent meanings that derive from the previous experience of the participants, from the social context of the situation, and from the relevant features of the specific interactional encounter (see chapter 7).

This perspective emphasizes individuals' active role in their own development. It does not see people as passive elements in society but rather as being selective and responsive to the social structures and processes in their lives. The individual occupies a more central role in this theory than it does in either functionalist or conflict theories.

Symbolic interactionism has been criticized for ignoring the more formal and organizational aspects of social life. How interpersonal interaction and a sense of identity is affected by large-scale social forces is not significantly accounted for in this perspective. Critics argue that symbolic interactionism overemphasizes the cognitive aspects of social life, ignoring (or underplaying) the rich emotional basis of human existence. The key concepts of this perspective, such as the "self," are seen as too imprecise and not capable of measurement and analysis.

Recent work in symbolic interactionism attempts to respond to the above-mentioned criticisms. Rosabeth Kantor (1977) and Sheldon Stryker (1980) have linked symbolic interactionism to the more organizational and structural aspects of society. Morris Rosenberg (1979) has attempted to subject it to systematic theoretical and empirical analysis. Much of the growing body of literature on the sociology of emotions has been contributed by symbolic interactionists.

Ethnomethodology. Rather than starting with the premise that there are shared, agreed-upon social meanings, ethnomethodologists study the processes by which meanings are created and shared. Ethnomethodologists derive much of their orientation from the work of Alfred Schutz (1962, 1964) and Harold Garfinkel (1967).

From the point of view of ethnomethodologists, there is no ordered social world unless the participants agree upon it. Together, people construct social reality. Ethnomethodologists study how people view order in the world, how they communicate that view to others, and how they understand and explain social regularities (e.g., "taking turns" in conversations). Much of ethnomethodological analysis examines the routine and mundane aspects of social life, such as telephone conversations. In fact, "conversational analysis" is a staple of ethnomethodological research.

Ethnomethodology reminds sociologists not to take for granted an ordered social world. It tries to clarify how social order is constructed and how people view it. Ethnomethodology, like symbolic interactionism, stresses the importance in research of taking a phenomenological point of view, of seeing the world through the eyes (and mind) of the respondent. Ethnomethodology has been criticized for its isolation from much of sociological analysis and for its failure to link up with the main currents of sociological thought.

Exchange theory. From this perspective, derived in part from economics and behavioral psychology, social life is a process of bargaining and negotiation. Interaction proceeds on the basis of a cost/benefit analysis. If the benefits derived from an interaction are greater than the efforts put into maintaining it, the interaction will continue. If not, it will be terminated.

The above crudely summarizes the basic idea of exchange theory as it was introduced by the sociologist George Homans in 1950. Since then, exchange theory has become more sophisticated. It now acknowledges the normative constraints on interaction—we are not always free to do what we want with others; there are customs and practices that circumscribe our actions. Issues of motivation (Gergen, 1969) and power (Emerson, 1962) have also been introduced into exchange theory.

Exchange theory is used to study transitory encounters as well as more enduring relationships, like friendship and marriage. It provides a different way of understanding the factors that sustain or weaken these relationships. It adds an experimental body of literature to the study of interpersonal relationships.

Critics of exchange theory insist that its basic assumptions are untenable. People are not always aware of the likely outcomes of maintaining or terminating a particular relationship, a necessary factor in determining likely costs and benefits. Furthermore, exchange theory assumes that much of life is guided by a "hedonistic calculus" whereby people seek to maximize pleasure and eliminate (or minimize) pain. But often people do things that maximize pain, or at least increase tension. Exchange theory does not account for acts of love or heroism, where the individual's goals (pleasures) are subordinated to the needs of others.

Sociology, then, has a rich heritage. Contemporary sociology has built upon that heritage and maintained a diversity that will continue to be a source of strength in the continual maturation of the discipline.

*I*n this chapter the focuses of the various social sciences were summarized. Anthropology deals with the biological basis of human behavior and with cultural evolution. Economics is concerned with the production, distribution, and acquisition of necessary resources as well as with consumption patterns. Issues of power in society are the province of political science, and psychology focuses on the determinants and patterns of individual behavior. Sociology is the study of human social behavior and association.

The chapter explored the nature of science, its assumptions, principles, and operating procedures. It then looked at how sociology follows the rules of science and why sociology has a legitimate claim to be considered a scientific discipline.

The chapter then examined the theoretical framework of sociology, from its early development by Auguste Comte to its present state. The work of some of the preeminent sociological scholars of the past was noted: Herbert Spencer, Karl Marx, Émile Durkheim, Max Weber, and Georg Simmel. Contemporary theories—the structural-functionalist perspective and conflict theory on the macrolevel, and symbolic interactionism, ethnomethodology, and exchange theory on the microlevel—were briefly summarized.

2

Doing Sociology: Methods of Sociological Research

The value of sociology depends not only on the theories it develops to explain human association but also on how well the theories conform to what actually goes on in the world. In other words, as a science, sociology depends on empirical research to test its theories. In this chapter, we will examine the logic of research as well as the process of conducting research. We will describe various research methods, highlighting some of the major problems involved in doing research.

THE LOGIC OF RESEARCH

Sociological knowledge rests on scientifically derived evidence. Sociologists acquire this evidence through a set of generally accepted procedures, a *methodology* , that directs their investigations and provides a way for others to verify the results.

Variables

In chapter 1, a *variable* was defined as a trait or characteristic that changes or has different values under different conditions. Age, sex, and social class are examples of the kinds of variables that sociologists typically use in their research.

INDEPENDENT AND DEPENDENT VARIABLES

In research, some variables influence other variables; these are called *independent variables*. The variables that are being influenced are the *dependent variables*. In a study of the effect of social class position on child-rearing practices, social class position is the independent variable, and child-rearing practices are the dependent variable. However, in a study of the effect of child-rearing practices on school performance, child-rearing practices are the independent variable, and school performance is the dependent variable. Child-rearing practices are the dependent variable in the first study and the independent variable in the second. Clearly, then, a particular trait or characteristic is not automatically an independent or a dependent variable. Which type of variable it is depends on its role in the specific research. The goal of research is finding out if, in fact, there is a relationship between the independent and dependent variables.

CORRELATION

A link between variables is often established by noting whether the two change together; that is, whether they are *correlated* . Establishing correlation is the first step in finding out whether one variable "causes" or influences the other.

Positive correlation. If the value of one variable increases (or decreases) while the value of the other variable also increases (or decreases), the two are said to be *positively correlated* . For example, sociologists have established a positive correlation between social class position and the number of years of schooling a person obtains: the higher the social class, the more years of education a person is apt to acquire.

Negative correlation. If, however, the value of one variable increases (or decreases) while the value of the other decreases (or increases), the two are *negatively correlated* . For example, negative correlation exists between the number of people in a group and the number of people who speak out in the group. The larger the group, the more the communication is dominated by a few individuals.

ESTABLISHING CAUSE AND EFFECT

The correlation of two variables is a necessary but not sufficient condition for determining that one variable "caused" the other. That is, correlation is a factor but not necessarily the only or determining factor.

Spurious correlation. Often, the link between two variables is a *spurious correlation*, one that is just coincidental. Sometimes the coincidence is accidental; this can be examined by using the probability theory that is the basis for the statistical analysis of the data under study. Sometimes the coincidence is caused by the correlation of the two variables with another variable; it may be this link that results in the observed correlation. For example, the number of violent crimes is correlated with the season of the year. More violent crimes occur in the summer than in the winter. Since more people are outside in the summer than in the winter, the rate of social interaction is greater, and the likelihood of confrontation and violence is higher. Summer doesn't cause violent crime, but it does lead to an increase in social interaction, which in turn is an important element leading to more violent crime.

Controls. Sociologists guard against accepting spurious relationships by using *controls*, various techniques of eliminating other factors that may confuse the relationship between the variables under study. The use of controls increases confidence that the observed relationship is a real and not a coincidental one.

Three elements must exist before the existence of a cause and effect relationship between two variables is determined: (1) the two variables must be correlated; (2) the independent variable must precede the dependent variable in time; and (3) there must be some confidence that there is no third variable related to the other two that may result in a spurious correlation. In short, correlation alone does not establish causation.

THE INTERCONNECTION OF THEORY AND RESEARCH

Theory Guides Research

Sociological theory and sociological research are not separate enterprises. Each is indispensable to the success of the other. The methods that sociologists use need to be appropriate to the theory they are examining. If a sociologist wishes to study how family conflict might have led to divorce, he or she is committed to a methodology that will allow the relevant individuals to describe their perceptions of the conflict and how it ultimately led to divorce. Census data is of no use for this purpose.

Theory does more than aid in selecting the particular method to use. It influences the choice of variables to examine and expectations about the relationships that might exist among the relevant variables. When Durkheim studied suicide, his theory of the relationship between suicide and social integration led him to define and then study variables that indicated different degrees of social integration. Without a theory, the researcher would be unable to choose intelligently among a wide assortment of variables to study or methods to use.

Research "Tests" Theory

Not only is theory indispensable to research, but sociological theory is useless without research. The relationships between variables suggested by a sociological theory need to be tested to see if in fact they exist. Durkheim's notion of the relationship between suicide and social integration would have remained merely idle speculation, no better or worse than other explanations of suicide, if he had not subjected it to the test of research.

The power of sociological theory rests both on its ability to specify relationships between variables *and* on the possibility of finding evidence to back up any such assertions. Both are essential to the sociologist: a sociological imagination, and sociological research techniques.

THE RESEARCH PROCESS

Research activities generally follow the pattern described in this section. Though the steps in the research process are not always followed in exactly the same way in every study (because the nature of the specific project may require some variation), the model described below serves as a basic illustration of the way research is typically conducted.

Defining the Problem

The first step in research is to select an appropriate problem to study. The particular focus of study may be an important question in sociology or it may be something that is of special and personal importance to the investigator. The basis for choosing a particular problem for study is less important than defining it carefully and in a way that can lead to scientific investigation from a sociological perspective.

Reviewing the Literature

Very few research studies focus on something completely new. Thus, it is necessary to find out what has already been discovered about the particular topic under investigation. The researcher begins by using the library, especially the computer search facilities and the specialized research indexes, to track down other research on the same topic. This review allows the researcher to avoid wasting time doing research that has already been done or going down blind alleys that have been marked off by others. It also permits the researcher to formulate a theoretical conception of the problem that ties it into existing sociological ideas and research. This review may also suggest relevant methodological approaches to the problem.

Formulating Hypotheses

The question under study must be phrased in a way that enables the researcher to obtain answers to it. Most often, the question takes the form of a *hypothesis*, an explicit statement about the expected relationships between variables. If the purpose of the study is to describe some social process or activity rather than to analyze the relationship among variables, there is still a need to frame questions that will guide the data collection phase of the research. The key problem here is to formulate a hypothesis (or guiding questions for descriptive research) that can be measured in appropriate ways; that is, to frame an *operational definition* of the central concepts.

Considering the Ethical Issues Involved

Though not all sociological research poses ethical problems, some do. Will the respondents be given anonymity or at least confidentiality? How can that anonymity or confidentiality be guaranteed? Will the actual research pose any risk to the participants? Will it cause them any mental anguish? What can be done to minimize risk or potential harm? These issues need to be considered very carefully *in the planning stages* of a research project. They are discussed further in the final section of this chapter.

Choosing a Research Design

The *research design*, the specific plan for collecting and analyzing relevant data, must be judged in terms of how it will help or hinder the researcher. There are several ways to collect and analyze appropriate data. Which procedure and analytic model are best will depend on what the researcher hopes to find out.

Collecting Data

A research project is no better than the quality of the data collected. Therefore, care must be taken to gather data appropriate to the questions raised in the research and in a form that makes it usable in answering these questions. The original data should be kept so that the researcher can use it to check issues that might arise later in the research.

Analyzing Data

Statistics help the researcher analyze the data collected by allowing him or her to arrive at appropriate interpretations. Information needs to be analyzed carefully so that the conclusions can withstand scrutiny. At this stage the data are often put into categories (for example, different social class levels or varying levels of job productivity) and examined for their interrelationships. This analysis will allow the original hypothesis to be confirmed, refuted or modified.

Drawing Conclusions

Once the original hypothesis is supported or refuted, the researcher can draw conclusions about the larger issues that framed the research: the theoretical conceptions or practical concerns that inspired the project. The research can add new knowledge, challenge the validity of what had earlier been accepted or modify what had previously been accepted as true. It can, and often does, raise new questions that need to be addressed by future research.

BASIC RESEARCH METHODS

Research methods refer to the actual ways researchers collect data. There are four basic research techniques: experiments, surveys, observations, and secondary analysis.

Experiments   Experiments provide ways to collect data under controlled conditions in order to establish whether there is a cause and effect relationship among the relevant variables. This approach draws on the methodology of the physical and biological sciences and especially on methods of laboratory research. In sociology experiments can be carried out either in the laboratory or in the "natural" or "field" environment.

LABORATORY EXPERIMENTS

Laboratory experimentation allows tight control over conditions that are not supposed to influence the research. Laboratory researchers can construct situations that fit their research designs. However, for many sociological issues the laboratory is an unnatural setting; results arrived at in the laboratory may not be applicable to the more usual settings in which the subjects typically find themselves.

FIELD EXPERIMENTS

In field experiments, sociologists study people in relatively ordinary circumstances. They then assume that their results will be appropriate to other individuals in similar situations. Because the setting is a "natural" one, however, the investigator has little control over factors that may be influencing the relevant variables in unidentifiable ways.

In short, the laboratory experiment provides control at the expense of being somewhat artificial; field experiment is closer to the real life experiences of the subjects but sacrifices control over factors that could have an unknown influence on the variables under study.

THE EXPERIMENTAL METHOD

The experimental method requires an *experimental group* of subjects that is exposed to some variable and a *control group* that is identical to the experimental group except that it is not subject to the *experimental variable*. Measurements taken in both groups before and after the introduction of the experimental (or test) variable can then be compared to see if the experimental variable had any effect. Since the two groups differ only in the introduction of the experimental or test variable, any differences between them on the "after" measure can be attributed to that variable. This technique is a powerful tool in uncovering cause and effect relationships. However, in such an artificial setting it is practically impossible to capture the important variables in many of the problems that interest sociologists. However, social psychology has used laboratory experiments quite effectively, and researchers in "collective behavior" (see chapter 22) have made good use of field experiments.

THE "HAWTHORNE EFFECT"

Another limitation of the experimental method involves the subjects' assumptions about the nature of the research and how those assumptions affect their behavior. The term "Hawthorne effect" derives from research done in the 1930s in the Hawthorne, New Jersey, plant of the Western Electric Company (Roethlisberger and Dickson, 1939). While studying the effects of various working conditions (increased lighting, more coffee breaks, different method of payment, and so on) on productivity, the researchers found that productivity improved even when they introduced negative factors (e.g., *reducing* the lighting). The researchers subsequently realized that simply focusing attention on the plant workers caused them to feel like a tightly knit group and increased their morale. The rise in productivity resulted from these positive feelings. The Hawthorne effect alerted researchers to the importance of considering the perceptions of the subjects, particularly their view of what the experiment is all about, in creating an appropriate research design.

Surveys

The most common research method used by sociologists is the *survey* , in which people ("respondents") are asked to respond to a series of questions about their characteristics, attitudes, values, behavior or perceptions of a situation or of events. Surveys can be used to obtain information (i.e., how many young people support capital punishment) or to explore the relationship among "facts" (e.g., whether youths who consider themselves religious are less likely to support capital punishment than are those who do not think of themselves as religious).

SAMPLING

Surveys are typically used to enable the researcher to make some statement about a *population*, the total group of people in whom the researcher is interested. Since it is neither practical nor economically justifiable to survey a large population, the researcher instead surveys a *sample*, a smaller group of individuals who are selected to be representative of the population. The way a sample is selected must ensure that it does truly represent the entire population. While there are many ways of ensuring this outcome, the most common technique is *random sampling*, which requires that every member of the population have an equal chance of being selected for the sample. The number of individuals needed for a sample does not need to be large, as long as it is representative. Typically, well-designed studies use a few thousand respondents to predict the outcome of national elections. Other more complicated techniques can ensure that types of individuals who form a small part (e.g., physically handicapped students) of the population (e.g., an entire high school) and thus might be missed in simple random sampling are in fact included in the sample. Whatever technical procedures are required, it is important that the sample be truly representative of the population.

QUESTIONNAIRES

A survey may involve the use of questionnaires, interviews or some combination of the two. A *questionnaire* is a series of specific questions or statements to which a person is asked to respond. Typically, the questionnaire is a written form on which the respondent checks, circles or fills in the appropriate responses.

Most of the time, the questionnaire provides a set of possible answers from which the respondent is asked to choose (a *closed-ended questionnaire*). To be effective, the questions must be phrased in simple and straightforward language. Frequently, this type of questionnaire is mailed to respondents; they are asked to complete the form and return it to the researcher. This procedure allows for a wider distribution of questionnaires than would be possible if they had to be administered face to face.

An *open-ended questionnaire* does not have a predetermined set of possible answers. Respondents are asked to answer general questions in their own words. The open-ended questionnaire can also be mailed to respondents, but it requires relatively sophisticated procedures of analysis. Open-ended questionnaires are similar in many ways to the interview.

INTERVIEWS

The *interview* asks general questions of respondents, allowing them to answer freely in their own words. The interviewer is able to follow up the answer to a particular question and thus to explore it in depth. Interviews are more flexible than questionnaires but are more difficult to analyze because of the different frames of reference respondents may use in answering the questions. Also, interviews require direct interaction of interviewer and interviewee. Interviews cannot be mailed to respondents as questionnaires can, making it a more expensive and more labor-intensive technique.

Analysis of interviews can be impressionistic and subjective, or the answers can be coded into a limited number of categories and then subjected to statistical analysis. Though difficult to analyze, interviews are a rich source of subtle information, especially on sensitive topics.

TELEPHONE SURVEYS

Questionnaires and interviews administered by telephone are becoming common tools of sociological research. They can provide a fast, efficient, and often economical way of reaching a large, far-flung, and diverse sample of individuals.

Observations

OBSERVATIONAL STUDY

An *observational study* is a way of examining the actions of individuals or groups by scrutinizing them, often intensively, but without questioning them or trying to influence their behavior. For example, parent-child interaction can be studied by observing families in the home (a field experiment) or from behind a one-way mirror in a research environment (a laboratory experiment).

Observational studies often focus on the content of relevant activities. They enable researchers to give rich descriptions of social processes in action as they try to understand cause and effect relationships.

Detached observation. In *detached observation*, the researcher remains outside what is being observed. Subjects may not even know they are being studied. By remaining outside, researchers are unlikely to influence what they are studying. However, their remoteness may limit their ability to see important events that are occurring. For example, it may be possible to study the behavior of a gang through detached observation, but only behavior that takes place in public. Secret meetings, planning by the group's leaders, and closed initiation ceremonies are not open to detached observation.

Participant observation. These limitations have led to the development of *participant observation*, a method in which researchers are active participants in the groups or situations they are studying. The classic participant observational study is William Foote Whyte's *Street-Corner Society* (Whyte, 1943), for which he "hung around" with a group of youths in the slums of Boston, observing their behavior and rituals. He got to know the group from the inside and thus acquired a rich and detailed understanding of what they did, and why. Though the youths knew they were being observed by a social scientist, they considered Whyte a member of the group and generally acted normally in his presence. On the negative side, participant observers risk becoming more participant than observer, losing the value of neutral observation.

Participant observation introduces ethical questions. If researchers are open about their research aims, they might influence the groups' behavior. However, not to disclose their research aims is a form of deceit and raises substantial ethical problems.

Secondary Analysis

Analyzing data that already exist is called *secondary analysis*. Government agencies publish all kinds of information that is useful for sociological analysis. One of the most widely used sources of data is the census, which provides information on population characteristics such as birth and death rates, marriage rates, types of households, age and sex composition, levels of education, trends in urbanization, and so on. These data have proved invaluable in research on the family, community patterns, migration, and other issues of sociological interest.

Sociologists also use statistics on economic enterprises, labor trends, patterns of health and illness, and housing construction to study social organization, changes in societal activities, and the "social and economic health" of society. Durkheim's famous study on suicide was accomplished using published statistics on suicide rates.

Diaries, letters, autobiographies, newspaper articles, and church records can also be rich sources of information for sociological analysis. Thomas and Znaniecki's (1918–1920) study of Polish peasants was based largely on these types of personal documents.

Secondary analysis has a number of advantages. It is usually less expensive to use than gathering original data. The quality of data collected by most government organizations is likely to be better than that of data collected by the individual researcher. Also, using secondary analysis assures that the researcher does not influence the processes, structures or actions being studied. A disadvantage of secondary analysis is the distinct possibility that the data were collected for reasons that are not directly relevant to the new questions being addressed. Also, in some cases the accuracy of the original data may either be suspect or unknown.

None of the research methods described above is without limitations. Each has advantages and drawbacks. The choice of research method depends on the nature of the problem under study; sociologists are likely to use the method whose limitations are least relevant to the focus of their analysis. If control of variables is important, then the experiment may be most appropriate. If having access to diverse views is important, some form of survey is most likely required. If information about key characteristics of large populations is relevant, secondary analysis of census data would likely be the method of choice.

PROBLEMS IN DOING RESEARCH

Competent research in the social sciences is difficult to carry out. Studying human behavior presents problems that are not ordinarily faced by the physical scientist. Some of these distinctive problems are technical; others are a result of the practical limitations of studying human beings.

Technical Difficulties

RELIABILITY

If the results of a study are to be accepted by the scientific community, researchers must believe that if they or others were to repeat the same study they would get similar results. That gives them confidence that what has been found was not an accident or a chance event. This consistency is called *reliability*. Reliability requires the use of identical comparable measures in research, much as consumers require a similarly calibrated scale when buying meat on subsequent days.

VALIDITY

A study must be more than reliable. The variables in the study that are supposed to represent a certain aspect of reality must in fact represent that reality. Measuring what is claimed to be measured is called *validity* . Some have challenged Durkheim's famous research on suicide on the ground that it lacked adequate validity. For example, while the suicide rates that Durkheim studied appear to be reliable, they may have been less valid than Durkheim suspected (Pescolodi and Mendelsohn, 1968) because the reporting of deaths as suicides may vary according to whether or not the communities in which the deaths occurred are highly cohesive. Durkheim did not appear to take this possible differential reporting of suicides into account, possibly reducing the validity of his findings.

Practical Difficulties

GETTING PEOPLE TO COOPERATE

Sociologists require the cooperation of their subjects or respondents. Participation in social research takes time, which many people find in short supply. Moreover, social research often involves personal and even controversial issues, and not everybody is eager to reveal personal thoughts to another. Thus, getting people to participate is a complex process of reducing the burden of participation and making it attractive to cooperate.

Sometimes the burden can be reduced by limiting the information required to less than what the researcher would ideally like to have. Such compromises are often necessary to accomplish the key goals of the research. Researchers can also lessen the burden on participants by submitting questionnaires that can be answered at the respondents' leisure, by telephoning a survey at a time convenient to respondents or by interviewing respondents in their homes rather than at a research site.

The attractiveness of participating in a research study is occasionally increased by a modest payment to cover any minor expense involved (e.g., travel costs to and from the research site, baby-sitting costs) or inconvenience caused. Most frequently, however, the attractiveness depends on whether the subjects or respondents view the research as important.

RESEARCH MAY CHANGE BEHAVIOR

People are aware of themselves as individuals. This self-awareness is of special concern in sociological research because people may alter their behavior in response to being studied. Knowing that their opinions on a particular topic are being studied, they may rethink and revise those views.

For example, a study of how parents discipline their children may lead parents to reevaluate and alter their methods.

Also, the very reporting of sociological research findings may alter the behavior of individuals, groups, and organizations.

In fact, the goal of policy-oriented research oftentimes is to change behavior. But when behavior is changed, the research results may no longer be accurate.

DIFFICULTIES IN PREDICTING BEHAVIOR

Human beings make choices in their behavior. These choices may involve situations about which people have insufficient knowledge on which to base an informed choice. Seeing situations as participants see them and being able to predict or understand their behavior is a difficult task. Researchers must constantly guard against the tendency to impose their own views on the participants; instead they should make every effort to view situations from the latters' perspective.

The Ethics and Politics of Research

Sociological research almost inevitably involves an ethical and a political component. The ethics of studying people was described above in connection with observational research. To what extent do people have a right to decide whether they should be studied? This problem is especially acute in observational studies because direct cooperation of the subjects is not always as necessary for observational research as it is for surveys.

The use of one-way mirrors, hidden recording devices, undisclosed participant or detached observation all raise ethical questions about the invasion of privacy. Current procedures established by the federal government require that subjects/respondents give "informed consent" to participation in research, thus eliminating this particular ethical problem.

Social research occasionally carries the risk of some harm to participants. For example, researchers' disclosure of sensitive information to participants' employers or spouses may cost participants their jobs or marriages. "Institutional review boards" required by the federal government help ensure that possible harm to research subjects/respondents is either eliminated or reduced to inconsequential levels by proper research design, or is adequately explained to the participants in advance of their consent to cooperate. These safeguards have sharply reduced the kind of ethical problems discussed above.

The use of research findings poses another type of ethical and even political problem. To whom does the sociologist owe primary allegiance? To the funding source? To the participants? To the scientific community? To society as a whole? These are not just idle questions. Should researchers accept funding to study the best way to induce people to purchase a clearly inferior product? Should certain topics (e.g., possible racial differences in intelligence) be off limits for study? Should the availability of the results of research be limited in any way? Should researchers be "punished" (through loss of grant funds, salaries, promotional opportunities, jobs) because of the issues they study or the results of their investigations?

The American Sociological Association (the major professional organization of sociologists in the United States) established a code of ethics to address some of these questions. The code provides a set of ethical guidelines that expresses the collective sentiments of the sociological community on these important matters. It is a standard to which all sociologists are held.

This chapter introduced the research process as an important element of the discipline of sociology. It emphasized the importance of defining the presumed cause (independent variable) and the effect (dependent variable) and established an appropriate link between them as central to sociological methodology. Theory and research go hand-in-hand. Theory suggests appropriate variables and research tests the accuracy of theory.

The research process often follows a set pattern. First a significant sociological problem is defined and the existing professional literature is examined to establish what is already known about the issue. In light of this knowledge, hypotheses about the relationship among variables are explicitly stated and an appropriate research design that will provide a clear cut test of the hypotheses is developed. Important ethical issues are not only considered, but often influence the type and form of data collection procedures to be used. These data are analyzed in light of the original hypotheses and appropriate conclusions drawn.

The basic research methods in sociology involve experiments either in the laboratory (less frequently) or in the "field," situations of everyday life. The experimental method of science is used to establish control groups as a baseline to contrast with experimental groups that are subject to some influence whose result is being examined. The main research method of sociology is the survey in which respondents are asked either through highly structured questionnaires or less structured interviews (in person, by mail or, increasingly, over the telephone) to respond to a series of questions about themselves, their attitudes, values, beliefs or behavior. It is important to draw a suitable sample to insure the appropriateness of drawing inferences about larger populations. Observation, either through the participation of the researcher in the activity or in a more detached fashion, and analysis of previously collected data (secondary analysis) are two other important methods of sociological research.

Sociological researchers face a number of problems in conducting research projects. On the technical side, they must insure that they are using reliable measures that will yield consistent results whoever carries out the research. Further, they need to be concerned with the validity of their measures, that is the extent to which they capture the reality supposedly being studied. On the practical side, it is often difficult to get people to cooperate in research. Moreover, research often changes the behavior under study and, along with the fact that individuals are aware of themselves and their actions and thus may alter either or both, makes it more difficult to predict human behavior than the action of atoms or molecules. Finally, there are considerable ethical and political dimensions to conducting social research and the researcher must take these into account in designing and carrying out a particular project.

3

Culture

In this chapter, we will examine the key concept of culture—what it is and how it both expands and limits human freedom. We will look at the components of culture and distinguish between "ideal" and "real" culture. Cultural diversity between and within societies will also be discussed, as will cultural relativism and ethnocentrism. From a general focus on culture, we will shift to a focus on American culture in particular. The chapter will end with a discussion of a new perspective, sociobiology.

WHAT IS CULTURE?

In ordinary conversation, the word *culture* often suggests some form of high art: opera, ballet, museums. A person with culture is defined as someone having refinement, sophistication, and a knowledge and appreciation of the arts. In this sense, culture is a characteristic of the individual. However, sociologists and anthropologists use the term in a broader way.

A Definition of Culture

There are many definitions of culture, ranging from the terse— "a distinctive way of life of a people, a design for living" (Kluckhohn, 1949)—to the enumerative—"that complex whole which includes knowledge, belief, art, morals, law, custom, and other capabilities acquired by man as a member of society" (Tylor, 1871). All definitions, however, share some common elements.

Culture is a characteristic of a society, not of an individual. Culture is all that is learned in the course of social life and transmitted across generations. In Ralph Linton's (1945) words, it is "the social heredity of a society's members."

Goodman and Marx (1982:85) saw *culture* as the "learned, socially transmitted heritage of artifacts, knowledge, beliefs, values, and normative expectations that provides the members of a particular society with the tools for coping with recurrent problems." Culture defines and makes available for a society's members the appropriate foods to eat, clothes to wear, language to use, values to hold dear, beliefs to guide behavior, and practices to follow. In short, culture shapes and structures social life.

Culture: A Human Invention

Culture appears to be a uniquely human characteristic. Other species do not seem to possess culture. Much of animal behavior is a function of instinct or derives from the specific learning of an animal during its life.

Why do humans have culture? In the course of evolution, many of the instincts that the human species shared with its mammalian ancestors were gradually "selected out," or lost. Nevertheless, humans flourished. Over time, humans developed into a large and complex species, in some sense the dominant species on earth. Why?

The short answer is "culture." Culture gave humans a better and faster method of adapting to physical, topological, and climatological change than would have been possible solely through biological evolution. The combination of anatomical evolution (brain development, the opposable thumb, bipedalism) and cultural development has brought the human species to its present highly developed state.

The relationship between culture and humans is reciprocal. Though we create culture (i.e., "inventing" language and values), we are also made "human" by it (see chapter 6). Much of what passes as "human nature" is in fact the product of a particular culture. Americans, for example, often see war, aggressiveness, and competition as innately human. Yet there are societies (e.g., the Arapesh of New Guinea) in which war is unknown and aggressive or competitive behavior virtually nonexistent.

Culture Limits Human Freedom

Culture restricts individual freedom. People are not free to do whatever they want. Laws, a cultural invention, prevent them from engaging in certain kinds of behavior (e.g., walking nude on a city street) and require them to act in particular ways (e.g., putting a token in the turnstile in the subway). Individuals cannot create their own language if they expect to communicate with others. Though biologically equal (while different), men and women are rarely equal culturally. In many societies men have higher social status and more power than women (see chapters 12 and 13). The same point might be made about the poor or minorities in most societies. Culture restrains unevenly.

**Culture
Expands
Human
Freedom**

At the same time, culture enhances freedom. Culture frees the individual from the controlling, predetermined behavior dictated by instinct. People vary their responses according to the situation; they make choices, limited though they may be. Even though culture is restricting, it often allows choice within an reasonable range of acceptable options. (For example, while walking nude on city streets is prohibited, the range of clothing one can choose from is quite broad.)

Culture frees us from having to continually reinvent the necessary aspects of social living. We do not have to constantly create a language with which to communicate or continually rediscover fire to keep us warm or to cook our food. Countless routine things we do every day and material items we need are provided through culture, thus freeing our time for creativity and exploration.

THE COMPONENTS OF CULTURE

Culture may be divided into two major components: material culture and nonmaterial culture.

**Material
Culture**

Material culture refers to all the tangible, concrete creations of society. These include the staple finds of archeological digs: clay pots, jewelry, weapons, and so on. Material culture also includes such diverse objects as television sets, airplanes, baseball stadiums, clothing, skyscrapers, and washing machines. In short, any physical manifestation of the life of a people is part of its material culture.

Material culture is passed on to succeeding generations. Some artifacts, like airplanes, are considerably modified; others, like bathtubs, undergo little or no change in their basic structure. Some, like the slide rule, are replaced by technological advances; others, like the hula hoop pass in and out of fashion. Whether substantially altered or not, the components of material culture become an important part of a society's physical environment.

**Nonmaterial
Culture**

Sociologists tend to focus on *nonmaterial culture*, the *abstract creations of society that are transmitted across generations*. These are the very heartbeat of social life.

KNOWLEDGE AND BELIEFS

The ideas we have about the world make up one important aspect of nonmaterial culture. These ideas are part of the cultural heritage of all societies. *Knowledge* refers to those conclusions based on some measure of empirical evidence. For example, the spheroid shape of the earth and the relationship between low birthweight babies and smoking during pregnancy are items of knowledge.

Beliefs, on the other hand, refer to conclusions that are not backed up by sufficient empirical support to be seen as unequivocally true. Two controversial examples of beliefs are: life begins at conception (see chapter 13) and capital punishment deters crime (see chapter 8).

The cultures of all societies embody ideas about the natural environment as well as about the world human beings have created. Moreover, all cultures have ideas about the many unsettled and ambiguous aspects of life and death, such as whether there is life after death, the meaning of human happiness, and the ultimate fate of the universe. These beliefs permeate the everyday existence of human beings everywhere.

VALUES

Values are abstract ideas about what a society believes to be good, right, and desirable. Values provide the context within which societal norms (see below) are established and justified. Values provide the basis on which we judge social action, thereby shaping the choices we make. In American society, for example, we strongly value work, and the "work ethic" influences our specific behavior.

Values are not just abstract conceptions; they are invested with considerable emotional significance. People argue, fight, and even die over values, such as "freedom." Values sometimes clash, as when some value the American flag as a symbol to be protected and respected and others value more the right to burn or desecrate the flag in protest of some aspect of United States policy. A value, therefore, is not necessarily universally accepted by a society, nor does it always have the same meaning in different societies. For example, democracies and totalitarian states interpret "freedom" quite differently. Moreover, within a society, values are often limited. For example, "free expression," which is highly valued by democracies, is often restricted during wartime; and even in times of peace, the laws of libel and slander and concern about causing "clear and imminent danger" limit people's right to say anything they want.

Values are not necessarily static; they can and do change over time. For example, values having to do with love, sex, and marriage have changed over the past several decades. Also, ongoing research shows that college students of recent years have come to see higher education as a means of acquiring financial security rather than as a way of developing a meaningful philosophy of life.

NORMS

Much of social life involves routine behavior. People awake and go to sleep at certain times, eat meals on a specific schedule, and dress in a particular way. This is not accidental. Our behavior is structured by *norms*, social rules and guidelines that prescribe appropriate behavior in particular situations. Norms also can shape the actions of people toward one another. "Norms of civility" define appropriate behavior toward others.

The framework of society's norms ("normative framework") is divided into folkways, mores, and laws.

Folkways. *Folkways* are the routine conventions of everyday life. They are the customary ways people act: waking up at a certain time, pouring milk onto cereal, keeping the lawn mowed, putting the garbage in the incinerator, dressing appropriately for the occasion, eating with the "correct" utensils. Folkways are actions of little *moral* significance; they are more often matters of taste. People are expected to behave in these ways; if they do not, they are likely to be thought of as eccentric, inconsiderate or strange but not usually as evil or bad. If people violate folkways, they are subject to gossip and ridicule, not beatings or jail.

Mores. *Mores* (pronounced "more rays"), however, are norms that are seen as central and significant to the functioning of society and to social life. Theft, a violation of the mos (singular of *mores*) of respect for private property, is a serious matter. It affronts societal conceptions of property distribution and trust. Patriotic values frame mores of how responsible citizens should behave. The recurrent debate about the desecration of the American flag raises strong emotions precisely because this behavior touches on central definitions of citizenship that are significant to society.

Taboos are mores that are proscriptive, that is, that define what should *not* be done. Societies generally have taboos about sexual and marital relationships between close relatives (the "incest taboo") and about eating human flesh. Violations of taboos and mores generally involve much more severe sanctions than do failures to adhere to folkways. These sanctions include imprisonment, exile, and even death.

The conceptual distinction between folkways and mores (first made by Sumner, 1906) is relatively clear. However, it is not always easy to distinguish specific behaviors as one or the other. The desecration of the flag provides a good example. For some, it is merely a violation of a folkway and merits no more than disapproval. For others, such an act is a violation of the mores of society and deserves severe punishment.

Laws. *Laws* are norms established and enforced by the political authority of the society. When these laws have been written down and codified, they are generally referred to as "enacted law." In some societies the law is handed down orally; this is referred to as "customary law" or "common law." In whichever form, law often applies to those behaviors seen as important to society. Much of the current debate about the appropriateness of laws that regulate any kind of sexual behavior between consenting adults is a consequence of differences between protagonists as to whether such behavior is really a matter of private "taste" or style (folkways) or of central concern to society (mores).

SIGNS AND SYMBOLS

Signs. *Signs* are representations; they stand for something else. There are two kinds of signs: natural signs and conventional signs (symbols). A *natural sign* has an inherent, built-in relationship with what it represents. For example, a particular odor is a sign that a skunk is nearby. There is an inherent relationship between the odor and the skunk. To give another example: when we see smoke, we know that some form of combustion is taking place. The two, smoke and combustion, are linked to one another. We did not create that relationship, but we do have to learn it.

Symbols. *Symbols* (or *"conventional signs"*), on the other hand, are not "natural"; they are arbitrarily created representations (words, gestures, objects, visual images) that acquire meaning through social convention. A flag, for example, is merely a piece of cloth with a certain shape, color, and design. Yet people die for it—not for the cloth itself but for what it represents, for the meaning ascribed to it. The flag is a symbol of a nation and embodies all the significance of that society. Weitman (1973) has shown that one can analyze the meaning that a society invests in its national flag as a way of understanding important aspects of that culture.

Language. *Language,* a socially constructed set of significant symbols, is the most important aspect of culture. The elements of a language have approximately the same meanings for those within the same linguistic community. Consequently, language becomes the main vehicle of communication between people. The wider the range of experience, the more symbols are needed to capture and to communicate it. Hence, the richness and variety of social life are linked to the richness and variety of language.

Gestures. People also communicate through *gestures*, movements of the body (or parts of the body, like the face and hands) that have socially agreed-upon meanings. In American society, making a circle with the right thumb and index finger, holding the three other fingers on that hand straight up, and moving the hand slightly means "A-okay; everything is fine." In other societies, the same gesture has different meanings. For example, in France it conveys the insult that one is nothing, a "zero." In Greece and Turkey, it suggests an undesirable sexual invitation. Gestures, like language, have meaning within a specific social context.

People communicate both verbally through language and nonverbally through gestures. In fact, face-to-face communication derives its richness and subtlety from the conjunction of verbal and nonverbal cues. Sometimes, however, the conjunction leads to confusion or to unwanted and unexpected interpretations of meaning. For example, some men accused of rape contend that while their victims' language said they didn't want to engage in sex, their gestures (tone of voice, facial expression, style of dress) said otherwise.

LINGUISTIC RELATIVITY HYPOTHESIS

Language does far more than enable people to communicate with others. The very nature of language, it has been argued, structures the way we perceive the world. This view, called the *linguistic relativity hypothesis*, was formulated primarily by two anthropologists, Edward Sapir (1929) and Benjamin Lee Whorf (1956). They contend that the language of a society directs the attention of its members to certain features of the world rather than to others. The classic illustration of this phenomenon is that whereas the English language has but one word for snow, the language of the Inuit lacks a general term for it. Instead, because distinguishing different forms of snow is so important in their daily lives, they have different words that describe different types of snow (e.g., fluffy snow, falling snow, damp snow, drifting snow). Thus, the usefulness of distinguishing among many types of snow has led to the creation of the words to name them and to their incorporation into the language of the Inuit.

The important aspect of the linguistic relativity hypothesis is its focus on grammatical structure, which Sapir and Whorf contend leads people to view the world in a particular way. For example, in some non-European languages (e.g., Chinese) the familiar separation of acting agent (subject) and action (predicate) does not occur (Tung-Sen, 1970). Instead, agent and action are bound together; the action is the actor and the actor is the action.

Together, according to Sapir and Whorf, the vocabulary and grammatical structure of a language determine how members of a society perceive the world. Today, most informed opinion accepts a "weak" version of the linguistic relativity hypothesis. There is general agreement that the vocabulary and grammatical structure of a society's language focuses its attention on certain facets of the world rather than on others and causes members to think in a particular style. However, the modified view of the linguistic relativity hypothesis holds that language is a "facilitating" mechanism. A particular language makes it easier to think and perceive in a specific manner, but it does not constrain people from seeing other facets of the world or from developing other ways of thinking. For example, when it serves their interests skiers can make distinctions between different types of snow just as Inuits can. Also, the dominance of the generic masculine form in grammar (e.g., chairman) is currently changing (e.g., chairperson) as our conceptions of the appropriate relations between men and women change.

"IDEAL" AND "REAL" CULTURE

Norms help structure behavior by defining culturally approved modes of action. Norms define the "ideal"; they specify what society says people *should* do, what they are *expected* to do.

But people do not always behave as they "should" or as they are "expected" to. For example, in American society, people generally subscribe to the norms of sexual fidelity in marriage. Yet between one-quarter and one-half of married men and women report some form of extramarital affair. Even so, those engaging in such actions often affirm the validity of the norms. They explain their behavior in terms of personal weakness or special circumstances ("my marriage is falling apart," "my spouse doesn't understand me and I need some love and affection").

Norms should not be confused with behavior. Norms specify socially desirable behavior, which may or may not be carried out. They are valuable insights into the forms of action that a society considers desirable, but they do not guarantee that those actions are actually being performed.

CULTURAL DIVERSITY

Culture differs both between and within societies.

Diversity between Societies

Anthropologists' reports indicate the considerable cultural diversity between societies. Societies vary in the ways they structure relationships among members (see chapter 13). But societies differ in their cultures as well. Variations in the material cultures of societies are evident in their different forms of dwellings and transportation. But it is in their non-material cultures that differences between societies are especially relevant to sociology.

Societies differ in their values and in the norms specifying appropriate behavior. Ruth Benedict (1934) described two polar opposites: a Dionysian culture of frenzied activity, heightened emotion, and individual aggrandizement through competition (the Kwakiutl of Vancouver Island in British Columbia) and an Apollonian culture of quiet reserve, sobriety, and moderation that emphasized the importance of the collective over the individual (the Zuni of New Mexico).

We can see similar differences in modern societies. The American culture's emphasis on the individual is considerably different from the socialist states' emphasis on the collective. Cultural differences are evident even between socialist states. Cuba is culturally quite different from the

Soviet Union. Both are quite different from the People's Republic of China. Also evident are cultural differences between capitalist states like the United States, Great Britain, and Japan. Certainly there are similarities across all societies. However, history, geography, climate, and social circumstances combine to distinguish societies from one another in many ways. For example, the cultures of island societies like Great Britain contain distinctive nautical elements lacking in landlocked countries like Hungary. The cultures of tropical countries are different from the cultures of countries in the temperate zone. Countries once dominated by France differ from those once controlled by Great Britain or Portugal.

The cultural diversity between societies demonstrates the flexibility and variability of human arrangements. Understanding and appreciating this diversity can lead to a healthy respect for the differences among peoples and for the ingenuity of the human species.

Diversity within a Society

Just as the cultures of different societies vary from one another, groups within the same society can also show variety, especially if the society is large, complex, and modern. These groups, called *subcultures,* can vary by social class, ethnicity, race, religion, and lifestyle, as well as by goals and interests.

SUBCULTURES

Subcultural patterns give a group a distinctive flavor and identity that makes it different from the overall society of which it is a part. The identity of a subculture may revolve around its ethnic heritage, whether it be Chinese, Italian or Polish. It could derive from a group's economic circumstance, as is true of the poor in the ghetto. The unique subcultures of New England and of the deep South are based on region and history. The drug subculture has its own patterns. In short, practically any moderate-sized group that has societal beliefs, values, norms, and lifestyles that are substantially different from those of the larger society can be considered a subculture.

A subculture often has a distinctive language. The language of scientists is essentially a subcultural jargon, as is the terminology of drug dealers or of jazz musicians. Distinctive forms of communication within subcultures provide a sense of identity, enable more precise communication between members of the subgroup, and shield this communication from outsiders.

The cultural mosaic created by subcultures can be seen as enriching a society. The United States, for example, has often seen its cultural diversity as one of its major strengths (although its strict immigration laws during most of this century show that not everyone holds this view). On the other hand, some societies (e.g., Japan) believe that subcultural variation dilutes the national culture and therefore discourage it.

COUNTERCULTURES

In some cases the cultural patterns of a particular subgroup are not just different but contrary to the patterns of the rest of society. *Countercultures*, as these subgroups are called, embody beliefs, values, norms, and lifestyles that are in direct opposition to those of the larger society. In the 1960s and early 1970s, for example, the "hippies" essentially challenged the fundamental American values of individualism, competition, and materialism. The growing neo-Nazi movement in Germany, the Ku Klux Klan in the United States, and the Moslem Brotherhood in Egypt have developed their own particular sets of cultural patterns that put them in opposition to the cultures of their own societies.

Sometimes, as was the case with the "hippie" movement in the United States, elements of the counterculture become absorbed into the larger cultural framework, and the distinction between the two is blurred. More often, however, the counterculture remains in sharp contrast to the larger society, as in the case with the Moslem Brotherhood in Egypt.

Cultural Relativism

The variety of cultural practices both within and between societies suggests that there is no single "best" cultural pattern. Such a conclusion is the basis of *cultural relativism*, the hypothesis that no cultural practice is inherently good or bad; each has to be understood in terms of its place in the larger cultural configuration.

This perspective leads the observer to refrain from passing judgment on unfamiliar practices. It presupposes a tolerance, and even respect, for cultural styles that may seem strange and even "unnatural." People tend to *evaluate* customs, practices, and behaviors in terms of their own, and often this evaluation takes on a moral tone that is tinged with considerable emotion. Cultural relativism guards against this.

Does cultural relativism mean that "anything goes," that there are no absolute standards? Does it call for condoning infanticide (the killing of children, often used as a population control mechanism) or brutality directed toward a minority group? Sociology, *as a discipline,* has no easy answer to these questions. As individuals, most if not all sociologists would deplore these practices. However, they would try to separate their preferences and moral views from their professional efforts to analyze the causes and consequences of a particular cultural practice. Taking a position of cultural relativism encourages people to take a more objective view of their own society and of its cultural practices. It provides a kind of distance from which to view the context of one's own life.

Ethnocentrism

The opposite of cultural relativism is *ethnocentrism*, the tendency to view one's own culture as morally superior to others and, thus, to judge other cultures by the standards of one's own. To be ethnocentric is to assume that one's own society does things in the only right and proper way (e.g., "America: Love It or Leave It"). The ethnocentric observer is therefore apt to perceive the practices of other cultures or subcultures as deviations, not just as differences.

Ethnocentrism is easier to maintain in relatively homogeneous, traditional, and isolated societies. In such societies there is likely to be little contact with different practices and little opportunity to see their utility and relevance within the framework of the culture in which they occur. When members of this kind of society are exposed to these variations, they are unlikely to have the range of experiences that would allow them to suspend judgment and to see a variation as merely different rather than as wrong.

AMERICAN CULTURAL THEMES

One of the earliest statements of American values came from a French visitor, Alexis de Tocqueville (1969; original 1835). He was particularly impressed by the informality and expressed equality he found in the United States, especially given his background in traditional European patterns of formality and status distinctions.

More recently, sociologist Robin Williams (1970) suggested that despite great cultural diversity in the United States, there are a limited number of basic values that comprise its cultural emphasis. A few of these values are described below.

Americans, Williams concludes, place great emphasis on *achievement and success*, especially in their occupational roles. They are highly competitive and see success as a measure of self-worth. *Activity and work* are also important to Americans. Americans are generally frenetic, busily engaged in some activity or another, especially involving the world of work. Occupational activities, especially for men but increasingly for women as well, are the center of their waking lives and of their conceptions of self.

Americans especially value *efficiency and practicality*. It is no accident that scientific "time and management" studies (Taylor, 1911) began in the United States. The only philosophical system indigenous to the United States is pragmatism, a philosophy that focuses on the practical consequences of a person's behavior. Americans are great believers in *progress*. They are generally optimistic about life, certain that things will get better.

Americans have a strong *humanitarian* side. They believe in doing good both as individuals and in groups —for example, through the considerable number of philanthropic organizations that they have created. They cherish *freedom* and *democracy*. They believe that individuals have the rights to express themselves freely, to pursue personal goals, and to increase individual happiness—though not generally at the expense of others.

However, Williams also notes the tendency of Americans to think in terms of social categories, which sometimes leads to *racism and feelings of group superiority*. Thus ethnocentrism is not unknown among Americans.

Other analyses of American values [e.g., Yankelovich (1978)] see changes on the way. They note an increasing attention to self and self-expression, a decreasing emphasis on work as the focal point of life, and an increasing concern with leisure activities. Clearly, American culture has undergone particularly rapid change over the past quarter of a century, and there is no reason to expect it to stop evolving.

CULTURE AND SOCIOBIOLOGY

In a major challenge to sociology and to the notion that culture forms human behavior, the entomologist Edward Wilson (1975) introduced a new discipline, *sociobiology*, the systematic study of the biological basis of human behavior. Wilson predicts that anthropology, psychology, and sociology will be absorbed by this new science because it better explains human activities on the basis of genetics than the other behavioral sciences do on the basis of culture or learning. He believes that all social behavior, including that exhibited by species other than human, is subject to the same processes of evolution that affect the species' physical characteristics.

Sociobiologists often use the example of parental protection of their offspring, usually explained on a cultural basis in terms of "altruism," to advance their argument. They contend that the reason parents in many species act in defense of their progeny has nothing to do with altruism. Rather, sociologists insist these animals are genetically programmed to act as they do because the survival of their offspring increases the chance that their own genes will be maintained in the collective gene pool.

Critics of sociobiology (e.g., Bock, 1981; Lewontin, Rose, and Kamin, 1984) say that the analogy between human and animal behavior (for example, comparing the mating rituals of animals with the courtship rituals of humans) is fundamentally flawed. They hold that the great diversity in human behavior argues against an explanation based on genetics. Encoded genetic programs, these scientists say, would cause a degree of uniformity in the social behavior of *homo sapiens* that clearly is not present.

Sociobiology, however, has forced sociologists to consider an important point that they have too often overlooked: biological factors must not be ignored in the examination of human social behavior. Biology not only sets some limits on what humans can do, but it probably also makes it likely that some cultural patterns will be more common than others (Barash, 1977). Thus, as often occurs in science, some of the more extreme claims of a new approach are rebutted, allowing new insights to percolate into established perspectives. Most social scientists reject the basic premise of sociobiology, but more and more are trying to understand precisely how biological forces influence social life.

This chapter examined the concept of culture in detail. It was pointed out that culture is a human development that restricts freedom to some degree but that also expands considerably humans' ability to deal with their environment. Aspects of material culture, such as artifacts, were discussed, as were the various components of nonmaterial culture—knowledge and beliefs, values, norms (folkways, mores, taboos, and laws), signs and symbols (language and gestures). The "linguistic relativity hypothesis," which states that language structures thought, was analyzed and was seen to need modification.

The difference between "ideal" and "real" culture was described. Attention was given to cultural diversity both between and within societies. This subject led to discussions of subcultures and countercultures and of the opposing concepts of cultural relativism and ethnocentrism.

The chapter also outlined Robin Williams's analysis of American cultural themes of achievement and success, activity and work, efficiency and practicality, humanitarianism, racism, and feelings of group superiority.

The chapter closed with a discussion of sociobiology as a major challenge to the cultural explanation of human actions. The arguments of both proponents and critics of sociobiology were summarized, and the insights and limitations of sociobiology were considered.

4

Social Structure

*A*ll *social life begins with society, the structure of human association. Humans are born into an already functioning society. Society is the hub of human existence; social life is societal life.*

The focus of this chapter will be the society itself: what it is, what it is made up of, and its various forms, as well as the theoretical perspectives from which sociologists examine it.

THE NATURE OF SOCIETY

Basic Features of Society

A major focus of sociological investigation is *society*, a collection of people who share a common culture (which they transmit to succeeding generations), a common territory, and a common identity, and who interact in socially structured relationships.

Sharing a common culture, territory, and identity binds people to one another. Common culture provides them with a shared "design for living," and common geographic territory provides a shared space in which to carry it out. These two combine to provide a shared sense of identity. This sense of communality is also produced by human interaction, much of which occurs through social channels. These channels of social interaction are among the structural elements—the building blocks— of society.

Social Structure: The Building Blocks of Society

Social interaction rarely occurs haphazardly. There is generally a pattern to our behavior. While culture determines some of the pattern much of it is also determined by the structural elements of society. In short, *social structure* is the recurrent pattern of relationships among the elements of society. Among these elements are status, role, groups, organizations, social institutions, and the community.

STATUS

In everyday speech, status refers to a level of prestige, wealth or power. However, when sociologists use the word *status*, they refer to a person's position in a network of social relationships. The status "mother" designates a member of the social network called "the family," as does "father," "daughter," and "son." Similarly, "principal" refers to a position in the school system, as does "teacher," "student," and "student aide." Each of these structural labels refers to a social network and defines a particular location or position within that network.

Some statuses are reciprocal: "mother" implies "child," "teacher" implies "students." Other statuses designate more diffuse networks; for example, "carpenter" refers to a position in the general occupational network of society rather than suggesting a connection with another specific status.

People have many social statuses (a person's *status set)*. Mother, daughter, pipefitter, Catholic, wife, student, friend, Italian-American, and woman might all apply to a specific individual. Some of these statuses are called ascribed statuses, ascribed statuses are *conferred on a person by society or by some group without the specific individual's input*, at least initially. People have little initial choice about their race, religion, ethnicity, sex, and even social class. These statuses are a function of the family into which one is born.

There are also *achieved statuses*, which *depend on qualities over which the individual has some control*. Marital (husband, wife) and occupational (pipefitter) statuses, as well as statuses in informal groups (friend, club president), are functions of individual choice, though social constraints can limit the options available to a person.

Culture in large and complex societies is also complex, but no individual is likely to be exposed to the entire range of cultural elements. What aspects of a culture people experience is strongly influenced by the social statuses they occupy. This is particularly true of infants and children, whose ascribed statuses expose them initially to only limited aspects of the larger culture. For example, infants born into Catholic families are usually not exposed to the values, norms, and beliefs of Muslim families. Girls (an ascribed status) are usually not socialized to the cultural values and norms that boys are. While people may change their religion, their social class, and even their sex, they are unlikely to do so during their early years.

Not all statuses within a status set are of equal importance. We often have a *master status*, a key status that has great weight (*in our social interactions and in our social identities*). Traditionally, a man's occupational status is central to his sense of self and to his dealings with others. In effect, a man's occupation is often his master status. This is changing for many men as they increasingly divide their time between career and family. Traditionally, a woman's family status has been her master status. However, as more women join the labor force, their work status is becoming increasingly important to them. Age is often a master status, "controlling" what persons are expected to do and how others are likely to react to them. The loss of a master status (e.g., when people retire or no longer have dependent children) can disturb the sense of identity people have built up over many years.

ROLE

Status is a positional concept; it locates a person within a social network. Role designates two different aspects of activities within a status. Ralph Linton (1936, 1945) initially defined role as all the things we expect of someone who occupies a particular status. Later on, he suggested that role is made up of the behaviors engaged in by an occupant of a particular status.

These two different emphases highlight the two important characteristics of role: expectations and behavior. Sociologists generally refer to *role prescriptions (expectations)* to define the social norms appropriate to a particular status. They use the term *role performance (behavior)* to refer to the actual behavior of the person who occupies a particular role. Brim (1960) expressed the difference between role prescriptions and role performance in terms of "deviance" (see chapter 8).

Roles versus status. Role and status, though related, are different. A person "occupies" a status, but "plays" or performs a role. Statuses make little sense without attached role prescriptions. A person's position in a social network is of limited value unless the "meaning" of that position is described by the role prescriptions. For example, to be a parent means to hold certain values (e.g., the importance of children) and to be subject to specific norms (e.g., the obligation to provide one's children with emotional, physical, and financial support). The position and the obligations go hand in hand.

But roles are not just obligations. Certain rights attached to a status are defined in the role prescriptions. For example, while office secretaries are obliged to show up on time and to do a competent job, they also have the right to a certain salary, to job protection, and to days off for sickness and vacation. Professors, while obliged to keep up with their chosen fields, to show up on time, and to be prepared for class, also have the right to a certain amount of respect, a certain level of work from students, and a certain amount of freedom to do research they deem important. Rights and obligations are interwoven within the role prescriptions that are attached to social statuses.

Role conflict. Role conflict results because the relationship between status and role is not one to one. That is, while the prescriptions attached to a status are usually in agreement (e.g., parents' status is in agreement with their obligations to take care of their children, to clothe them, and to feed them), sometime they are in conflict. The result is *role conflict.* For example, a "resident assistant" (status) in a college dormitory is supposed to provide "peer counseling" to fellow students (obligation) and, at the same time, is to report rule violations by students to college officials (obligation). The two role prescriptions of the resident assistant are thus in conflict, because the more the resident assistant enforces the college's rules, the less likely it is that he or she will gain the confidence necessary to be a successful counselor.

Role conflict also occurs when the role prescriptions associated with two or more statuses are contradictory. The committed student who is also a devoted friend experiences role conflict when a close friend asks for an important but time-consuming favor the night before a critical examination. Both role prescriptions are legitimate (studying before a critical examination and doing an important favor for a close friend), but satisfying one means not satisfying the other. Conflicts like this require people to evaluate and choose between legitimate demands.

Role strain. This occurs when efforts to meet the prescriptions embodied in a social status cause anxiety, stress, and strain. Unlike the prescriptions that cause role conflict, those that cause role strain are not necessarily contradictory. For example, an office supervisor is expected to maintain harmonious working relationships with fellow workers but also has the responsibility of evaluating them and determining their salary increases and promotions. While the two sets of expectations are not contradictory, meeting them often creates emotional and psychological strain for the supervisor.

GROUPS

A key concept in sociology is the "group" (see chapter 5). When sociologists use the term *group*, they mean two or more individuals who have a shared sense of identity and who interact in structured ways on the basis of a common set of expectations about each other's behavior. Groups are a distinctive feature of social life. Most activities take place in the context of groups whether these are families, teams, peer groups or work groups. Groups are everywhere; social life is group life.

Not all collections of individuals are social groups. People sitting together on a train are not necessarily a group. Members of a group have a sense of shared identity and a common set of expectations that structure their interaction another. Commuters on a train who notice each other every day, strike up conversations, define themselves as the "harassed commuters," and take the same seats every day are becoming a social group.

Social categories and social aggregates. Social categories and social aggregates are people who share a common characteristic (e.g., all redheads), *a similar status* (e.g., the "working class") *or the same situation* (e.g., attendees at a rock concert). Though people in the same social category are not necessarily a social group, they have the potential of becoming one if what they have in common becomes a basis of a shared identity and structures their interaction.

Social categories are convenient ways of describing people who share something in common and of indicating potential groups. But unlike groups, social categories and aggregates generally do not play a powerful role in social life. They are convenient statistical abstractions, not the socially constraining or facilitating forces that social groups are.

Organizations. An *organization* is *a type of group that is specifically created to carry out a particular task and that has a formal structure through which it attempts to accomplish that task.* (See chapter 5 for a more complete discussion.)

Organizations range in size from the very large (e.g., General Motors) to the very small (e.g., a school club). Regardless of size, an organization has formal rules and membership requirements that enable it to accomplish some end (e.g., the manufacture and sale of automobiles or the provision of a range of social activities for its members).

SOCIAL INSTITUTIONS

Many elements of a social structure are interrelated. That is, statuses, roles, and groups are not isolated from one another. Indeed, groups are composed of statuses, and organizations are made up of a series of interrelated statuses and even social groups. These elements of a social structure, in turn, help construct social institutions.

In order to survive, every society has to resolve certain recurrent problems. It must provide for the physical and emotional needs of its members, for the transmission of the society's common heritage across generations, and for the care of the young. Over time, societies develop stable and reasonably consistent cultural and structural configurations to attend to these problems. These are called *social institutions*.

Social institutions are marked by relatively stable clusters of values, norms, statuses, role prescriptions, social groups, and organizations that relate to a specific area of human activity. For example, all societies must have some system of producing, distributing, and acquiring the goods and services necessary for human survival. The social institution that deals with this problem is the economy (see chapter 17). While the form of the economic institution may vary across societies (e.g., market capitalism, socialism, communism, state capitalism), every society must develop some relatively consistent way of producing food, clothing, and shelter and of allocating these to its members. It does so through a variety of norms and values as well as through statuses, groups, and organizations.

Similarly, a society's need to provide its members with a basic set of intellectual and cognitive skills that will enable them to function in society is addressed through the social institution of "education" (see chapter 14). Any particular school (or school system) is just one part of a larger, more complex pattern we call the educational institution.

Functionalist View

According to functionalist theory, most societies have five major institutions. Two of these are the economy and education. The third, the family (as distinct from any specific family), is a social institution charged with the responsibility of caring for children and with transmitting the cultural heritage of society through socialization (see chapters 6 and 13). The fourth is the political institution, which is responsible for the organization and allocation of power among its members (see chapter 16). Religion is the fifth institution; it provides social cohesion through its concern with "ultimate values" (see chapter 15).

Characteristics of Institutions

Because institutions are configured out of interrelated cultural and structural elements, they tend to resist change. For example, the education institution has debated the issues of a voucher system, parental choice, and the neighborhood school for at least a quarter of a century, with little basic effect on the structure of education.

Institutions also tend to be interdependent. The major institutions of society tend to be based on and support similar norms and values and to have similar ends. For example, Americans' sense of individualism (see chapter 3) plays an important role in the United States' capitalist economic system (economy), in the checks and balances built into its political system (politics), and in Americans' freedom to pick their own marital partners (family). Upholding similar norms, values, and goals tends to make institutions interdependent; when change occurs in one institution, it is likely to occur in others as well. Functionalists tend to focus on the positive aspects of social institutions and the way institutions enable society to address recurrent concerns. Conflict theorists, on the other hand, criticize institutions for serving the ends of only some members of society. They look at the problems *caused* by the various social institutions rather than at those *solved* by them.

THE COMMUNITY

The *community* is a social group that shares not only an identity and a structured pattern of interaction but also a common geographical territory. This territorial sharing enhances the frequency and often the consequences of their interaction. Though community often refers to a relatively small and even isolated group of people who live together, it also can refer to modern urban society. For example, many major U.S. cities are seeing a resurgence of the idea of "neighborhood." In a sense, neighborhoods are communities.

Increasingly, the term community is used to refer to groups whose members do not have geographical ties with each other; for example, the "intelligence community" or the "scientific community." At the core of a community, then, whether or not its members share a geographical base, is a shared set of values and norms. Chapters 20 and 21, which deal with population and urbanization, will also contribute to an understanding the concept of community.

TYPES OF SOCIETIES

There are many kinds of societies. However, all societies can be classified into five basic types, depending on the technology they use and the subsistence strategy they adopt.

Hunting and Gathering Societies

The oldest subsistence strategy is *hunting and gathering* —hunting and fishing using simple tools made primarily of wood and stone, and searching for food. This form of subsistence is relatively rare today, being engaged in by perhaps only 300,000 people of the 5 billion on earth (Vander Zanden, 1990).

Since few environments are able to support large populations that depend on food acquired daily, hunting and gathering societies tend to be relatively small. Also, the search for adequate food requires nomadic wandering over large areas of territory. Because of this, the population density of these societies is low.

The economy of hunting and gathering societies is essentially at the subsistence level; members of the societies consume all they have. There is little trade among the different populations. Internally, most people perform the same tasks, with little if any division of labor based on age or gender. There is little social differentiation, and kinship ties are the primary form of social organization. Leadership tends to be informal and based on performance in hunting or food gathering.

Horticultural Societies

The development of plant cultivation between ten and twelve thousand years ago led to profound social changes. *Horticultural societies, based on the cultivation of plants*, gradually began to supplant hunting and gathering societies, particularly in the fertile regions of the Middle East and in Southeast Asia. Horticultural societies used a "slash and burn" technique in which they would clear a piece of land and burn the cut-down vegetation to make ashes for fertilizer. They would then plant crops, using simple tools such as digging sticks and, later, primitive hoes. Two or three years later when the soil became bereft of the nutrients necessary to sustain crops, the group would move on to a new area.

Horticultural societies were more efficient in providing food and other necessities than hunting and gathering societies. Through *cultural diffusion* (the spread of inventions, technology or aspects of nonmaterial culture from one social group to another) horticultural practices spread to Western Europe and China, creating a larger and more dependable food supply. The increased efficiency and the availability of surplus food allowed for some social differentiation; everyone need not be involved in the task of food production. Specialized statuses like the shaman (a person who performs magic and healing practices) and the artisan began to emerge. Political institutions began to develop, some taking the form of hereditary chiefdoms. Also, since accumulation of the necessities was not uniform, some people became more wealthy and thus more powerful than others.

Because of their greater geographical permanence, horticultural societies became quite different from hunting and gathering societies. They were larger, sometimes consisting of up to several thousand people. They were made up of more permanent structures, such as houses that were clustered in villages. Trade links between the villages developed. But increasing size and interaction with those who were different often led to animosity, leading to intertribal warfare and feuds.

Pastoral Societies

At about the same time that horticultural societies were evolving in fertile regions, hunting and gathering societies in more arid locations were evolving into *pastoral societies*. These societies, based on the domestication of animals, produced a more stable food supply than did hunting and gathering societies. Occasionally, societies would combine both horticultural and pastoral technologies to further increase the level and stability of food supplies.

Like horticulturalism, pastoralism led a society to grow. However, the amount of land needed to raise animals led to low population density. Pastoral societies tended to be nomadic because they needed to search for new grazing lands when the old ones no longer provided adequate nutrition. This wandering led to increased contact with other societies and resulted in trade between them. Contact with others also led to some intergroup hostilities and to the early development of enslavement of the captives.

Pastoral technology led to food surpluses. Specialized statuses, such as artisans, emerged, sometimes leading to institutionalized status inequalities (unequal value among societal members). Powerful leaders also emerged. The pastoral lifestyle also seemed to play a role in the development of religious beliefs based on supreme deities who took an active interest in everyday human affairs. These beliefs are consistent with the Judaism of the ancient pastoral Hebrews and with the religions that derived from it, Christianity and Islam.

Agrarian Societies

The "agricultural revolution" that occurred about 5,000 to 6,000 years ago led to the development of *agrarian societies*. These were *based on the large-scale cultivation of land, using the plow, and various draft animals*. Agrarian societies first emerged in the Middle East, but their technology diffused to other societies around the world.

Using plows and animals rather than first hand tools was a more efficient method of farming. Moreover, this efficiency enables people to stay in one place for long periods of time. Thus, permanent settlements began to develop. Later, farmers learned to make metal tools which were more effective than wooden and stone in breaking up and aerating the soil. Metal tools also enabled the development of irrigation, so necessary to large-scale agriculture. Large surpluses of food were produced, leading to the emergence of many specialized social statuses and distinct occupations. Over time, money rather than barter became the medium of economic exchange, which facilitated the growth of markets and trade. Trade led to the growth of large urban centers and, eventually, to the modern city (see chapter 21).

Social differentiation and, later, social inequalities became more pronounced and institutionalized. A specialized political elite emerged, often in the form of absolute hereditary monarchies. Similarly, social classes developed, in particular a growing economic elite who controlled the land worked on by a massive and dependent peasant underclass. The developing religions of that and subsequent eras increasingly conceived of deities in masculine form, enhancing gender stratification (see chapter 12).

With the development of an increasingly complex political, economic, and social structure, agrarian societies took a qualitative step away from the preceding societal forms. The complexity of these social structures increased the likelihood of their proliferation and further development.

Industrial Societies

It is only recently that the modern industrial society developed. The *Industrial Revolution* occurred initially in England in the mid-eighteenth century and then spread throughout the world. The result was the development of *industrial societies* that used complex, power-driven machinery to produce material goods. This technology produced goods so efficiently that it transformed most of the world's societies.

Mechanized production produced enormous surpluses of the basic necessities of life, leading to an accelerated creation of specialized social statuses, status hierarchies, and social inequalities. Paradoxically, mechanized production also resulted in less social inequality because it allowed for social mobility and reduced the importance of inherited social status (see chapters 9 and 10). The economic institution became increasingly differentiated as well as more prominent and powerful. The development of large-scale machinery meant that the central work place moved from the home to the factory and from the rural countryside to urban centers.

Industrialization also had a profound effect on education, the family, politics, and religion. The need for skilled and literate workers required that educational opportunities be extended to populations other than a small elite. The family lost its status as the center of economic production. A more educated population demanded and received more political rights. The moral authority of religion was diminished as industrialization increased differences in people's lifestyles, thus weakening their agreement on basic norms and values.

With industrialization came urbanization; people moved to where the jobs were, and that was in the cities. The overall standard of living rose, though not equally for all. The poor underclass grew. Industrialization's damaging effects on the environment became increasingly apparent (see chapter 20). Industrialization has brought many benefits, but it has also created a new set of problems for society to address.

Postindustrial Societies

Human society continues to evolve. A new type of society called *postindustrial* society, in which the main source of subsistence is the production of information and services rather than of material goods (Bell, 1973) emerged recently. The United States is regarded as the prime example of the postindustrial society. There, for the first time in human history, people are more likely to work in the service sector of the economy (e.g., sales, banking, machine repair, communications, education) than in agriculture or manufacturing.

However, agriculture and manufacturing do not disappear in the postindustrial society. They become more efficient because of increasingly sophisticated technology, which means that fewer workers are needed to maintain the same or higher level of output. Consequently, workers need to find other forms of employment and do so primarily in the service sector (see chapter 17).

Postindustrial society is primarily a knowledge-based and knowledge-producing society. Its focuses are on science and engineering and on education. Education provides the knowledge base for the scientists, engineers, and political decision makers in an increasingly technology-driven world. Economic institutions, while as important as ever, are much more dependent on these other spheres than they used to be.

Improved technology, communication, and transportation have led to increased mobility. Greater mobility has created a diversity of values and lifestyles in modern postindustrial society, increasing the possibility of greater equality between the sexes, greater tolerance for different lifestyles, and mutually enriching relationships between different subcultures.

Postindustrial society is still in a transitional stage. The prototypical example, the United States, continues its transformation into a postindustrial society. This transition creates problems for the different social institutions. For example, the educational system, which was basically developed for an industrial society, must adapt into one that better serves a postindustrial system. The family must adapt to changing gender roles, changing relationships among family members, and changing work roles. Thus the social structure of postindustrial society continues to change. The extent and nature of the changes it will undergo are not entirely foreseeable at this time.

A Sociocultural Evolutionary Approach: Gerhard and Jean Lenski

Much of the discussion of the different types of societies derives from the evolutionary views of Gerhard and Jean Lenski (1987). They see society evolving as a result of changing cultural knowledge, especially technology. Societies change as they develop more information about their environment and about how that environment can be "mined" for the use of their members. Usually the change is toward increasing complexity and technological sophistication.

Through either cultural diffusion or independent invention, most societies change over time. Once begun, change occurs at a relatively rapid pace. The driving engine for change, according to the Lenskis, is usually new technology, whether this is represented by hand tools to cultivate the land or by its replacement, machinery. The relationship between society and the physical environment is thus altered by new ideas, techniques, and tools.

Technological innovation usually limits the ability of the natural environment to shape the nature of society. As societies create and use technology, they assume increasing control over their destinies and are less at the mercy of the natural environment. Modern societies' dependence on fossil fuels, however, is a reminder that technological advances may also lead in some instances to a greater dependence on the natural environment.

A Structural-Functionalist Perspective: Talcott Parsons

UNIVERSAL FUNCTIONS

Talcott Parsons (see chapter 1), sees society as a social system, a set of structurally interrelated and interdependent parts that function harmoniously to maintain a stable society. In Parsons's view, these structural elements are the basic social institutions that exist in all societies. From this perspective all societies face similar problems. The institutions of society enable society to construct solutions to these universal problems. In essence, then, all social institutions serve the important functions.

Every society, Parsons argues, must provide for its own security and determine how it will allocate and use the power inherent in collective life. This function is at the heart of the *polity*, the political institution of a society. Every society must have some form of polity, though its exact nature may vary. Some societies are governed by an elected chief who serves for her or his lifetime; others by an absolute monarch; still others practice some form of democracy. Whichever form it takes, Parsons believes, each society has some system of government.

Parsons defines the *economy* as the social institution responsible for distributing the goods and services necessary to collective life.

Societies must reproduce themselves if they are to survive. This particular function, Parsons holds, is served by the social institution called *the family*. The family provides the socially approved means not only of sexual reproduction but also, through socialization (along with *education*), of social and cultural reproduction (see chapters 6 and 13). The family also satisfies the human need for intimate relationships.

Parsons argues that other institutions such as religion and medicine serve other important societal functions (see chapters 13 through 19).

THE *AGIL* PARADIGM

Parsons believes that there are four functions that all societies must carry out. This belief is the basis of his famous AGIL paradigm. The functions are adaptation, goal attainment, integration, and latency (later called pattern maintenance).

Adaptation refers to society's need to adapt to its physical environment, especially for its subsistence. This adaptation is the function of the economy.

Goal attainment refers to society's need to meet important goals, such as survival and good relations with other societies. The polity is charged with this responsibility.

Integration involves bringing the various elements of society together so that they function as a cooperative and mutually reinforcing whole. The family serves this end by linking individuals to one another through kinship bonds.

Latency (pattern maintenance) is the cultural sharing of general ways of thinking and believing. This function is achieved by the institutions of the family, education, and religion through their socialization activities and their fostering of satisfying relationships and common values.

THE EVOLUTION OF SOCIETY

Parsons sees society as a relatively stable social structure in which change takes place slowly and in an orderly fashion. Parsons also stresses the internal *differentiation* that takes place in society, especially the increasing specialization of society's component structures. Originally, the family was responsible for the four universal functions of society. As societies evolved, more specialized political and economic institutions developed. In today's postindustrial society, the internal differentiation extends far beyond that of horticultural or agrarian societies.

Parsons views *primitive societies* as roughly equivalent to what we have described as hunting and gathering and early horticultural societies. In these societies, there is little internal differentiation, and the family is the primary, if not sole, social institution.

Intermediate societies, roughly equivalent to late horticultural, pastoral, and early agrarian societies, superseded primitive societies. These societies have a modest amount of internal differentiation, consisting of a religious institution, early form of government, and an economic system. *Modern societies*, corresponding to industrial and postindustrial states, are the final stage of evolution, according to Parsons. In these societies, the five basic social institutions emerge as separate though interdependent spheres.

Parsons holds that internal differentiation results in more efficient social systems because the specialized institutions are better able to handle the recurrent and critical problems of society. For Parsons, then, differentiation equals progress, and social change; as long as it is moderate and orderly it is desirable.

Conflict Theory: Karl Marx

Marx did not see society as composed of harmoniously working structures that help meet a set of universal needs. In his view the institutions of society are instruments of control, not of problem resolution. Basic to control is the economic sphere. Those who own the means of production, the *capitalists*, are in a position to control and even exploit the *proletariat*, who provide the labor necessary to run the factories and other forms of economic enterprise.

Marx believes that the institutions of society are not equal and that the economic institution is preeminent. From it flows both political and social control. Marx held that there is little differentiation between the major institutions, despite its appearances to the contrary. In earlier societies the family was the principal institution; since the industrial revolution, that "honor" has gone to the economy. The other institutions serve the needs of the economic structure. Government, Marx argued, protects the capitalist class. Education's function is to provide trained and willing workers for capitalism; the family's function is to provide the tired and battered (male) worker with a place to be soothed and made whole for the next day of repetitive, meaningless work.

At the heart of Marx's analysis of society is his conclusion that the history of society is based on class conflict. The famous sentence from *The Communist Manifesto* (Marx and Engels, 1955; original, 1848) is clear on this point: "The history of hitherto all existing society is the history of class struggles." Society changes because the interests of the two classes, whether they are called masters and slaves, lords and serfs, bosses and workers, or capitalists and proletariat, are in conflict. Eventually, the subordinate class takes political and other forms of action to overthrow its oppressor.

SOCIAL CHANGE

Marx held that social change is neither easy nor automatic; it often brings hardship and difficulty. But, he believed, social change is inevitable once the working class recognizes that it is unnecessarily subordinated. Social revolution is the result, which leads to *socialism*, a more humane, egalitarian system in which no class is exploited. Thus, for Marx, fundamental social change comes not so much through evolutionary processes based on increasing technological sophistication but through revolution.

A Social Action Approach: Max Weber

Weber stresses the effect of styles of thought on social action. Ideas are primary motivators in social life, since how people think about something strongly influences how they behave.

For example, according to Weber, society has progressed from an earlier form in which "tradition," beliefs handed down from generation to generation, was the key element in collective life. This approach sanctified the past and often inhibited social change. Modern societies, on the other hand, exhibit a "rational" approach to the world, which Weber defines as a concern with efficiency and with the relationship of means to ends. This view looks forward to the future and both causes and welcomes change. According to Weber, then, rationality, efficiency, and means-ends calculations are the hallmark of modern society.

The stress on rational efficiency leads to the dominance of an organizational form known as *bureaucracy* (see chapter 5). Weber stresses that this organizational structure is necessary to provide the efficiency needed in modern society.

Weber proposes that Calvinist religious beliefs provided the critical background for the development of modern capitalism. Basic to Calvinist theology is the concept of *predestination*, the view that God has already selected people for salvation or eternal damnation and that nothing people do in this life can change their fates. Although one can never really know whether or not one will be saved, prospering in this world is taken as an indication of one's fate in the world to come. Calvinists believe that God would not allow the eternally damned to do well in the here and now. Thus, Weber argues, Calvinists stress the importance of success not so much because it is marked by material gain but because it both evidences and accomplishes God's will.

This viewpoint led to the traits that have become the hallmarks of capitalism—hard work, capital investment, and discipline. These traits are essential to the development of modern-day capitalism. Weber contrasts the Calvinist view with Catholicism, which stresses the importance of the next world over this one and the need to accept one's fate and to rely on the next life to provide the rewards for one's good works in this one.

Weber's analysis of the relevance of Calvinist beliefs to the development of a capitalist economic system demonstrates his belief in the impact of ideas on social change. Whereas Marx saw ideas as the result of social structure (particularly of one's place in the economic system), Weber saw ideas as the cause of the structures. Thus Weber and Marx have different and often conflicting views on the nature of social life. But the views of both stress social change more than the structural-functionalist viewpoint of Parsons.

This chapter has examined the social structure of society. The basic features of all societies were summarized: status (ascribed and achieved; master), role (role conflict and role strain), groups, social categories or aggregates, organizations, social institutions, and the community. Also discussed were different types of societies and how they evolved, from hunting and gathering societies, horticultural societies, pastoral societies, and agrarian societies to modern industrial and postindustrial societies. We looked at the technology and social organization of each type.

Several different theoretical perspectives of society were explored, beginning with the sociocultural evolutionary theory of Gerhard and Jean Lenski. Next summarized was the structural-functionalist view of Talcott Parsons which asserts that society's primary function is to meet basic universal needs. The conflict theory of Karl Marx, was discussed. Marx argued against Parsons's view that social institutions work together harmoniously for social benefit. He asserted that society serves the interests of the ruling class. Max Weber believed that changing ideas lead to social change. He illustrated his theory by analyzing how growing Calvinist religious beliefs paved the way for the development of capitalist society.

5

Social Groups and Organizations

In this chapter, we will explore the nature of social groups and organizations. We will discuss the various types of groups, how they are formed, and their structures and internal processes. We will also delve into formal organizations, noting the different forms they can take, and the links among organizations. Finally, we will analyze the concept of bureaucracy.

SOCIAL GROUPS

Human social life is group life. Individuals are involved in families, work groups, social or recreational groups, and school groups. A person is born into to a social group, gains his or her initial experiences in a social group, grows and matures in social groups, earns a living in a social group, and usually even leaves this world in the context of a group experience.

In chapter 4 a *group* was defined as two or more individuals who have a shared sense of identity and who interact with one another in structured ways on the basis of a common set of expectations about each other's behavior. While this is a useful general definition, there are in fact different types of groups.

Types of Groups

PRIMARY AND SECONDARY GROUPS

Contemporary sociologists, following the lead of Charles Horton Cooley (1902), make a distinction between primary and secondary groups. *Primary groups* are small groups in which members have close, personal, and enduring relationships. Because they are intimate and enduring, these groups are quite significant to the individual. In fact, Cooley called these groups "primary" because they are basic to the individual's social development. The family is the clearest example of a primary group. Primary group members typically spend considerable time together and share many activities and experiences. The relationships between members are deep because of the emotions invested in them. Members of primary groups often know a good deal about each other and care about each other's welfare.

A *secondary group*, on the other hand, is typically a larger, more temporary group that is brought together for some specific purpose or task and in which the relationships are relatively impersonal. These "secondary relationships" do not have the bonding power of "primary relationships." Secondary groups tend to be task-specific gatherings with few long-lasting effects on the individuals who compose them. Emotional investment in secondary groups is generally slight, and interaction between members tends to be focused on the activities that led to the group rather than on the needs, desires or concerns of the individual members. Members of secondary groups often have little personal knowledge of each other.

Some secondary work groups in which people are together for long periods of time may take on the characteristics of a primary group. The members might share confidences with one another, lunch together, arrange joint activities outside of work, and meet each other's families. The critical difference between primary and secondary groups is the degree to which the members have an emotional investment in the group and in each other, care about one another, and maintain long-term, rounded relationships with each other.

INGROUPS AND OUTGROUPS

Groups may also be divided into ingroups and outgroups. An *ingroup* is a group a person belongs to and with which he or she has a sense of identity and loyalty. It is contrasted with an *outgroup*, a group to which the person neither belongs nor has any sense of loyalty. People often have a measure of opposition and hostility toward outgroups. "We" are members of the ingroup, "they" are members of the outgroup.

The hostility between ingroups and outgroups serves to define the boundaries between groups. These boundaries may be geographical, such as those that define neighborhoods (and their resident "gangs"). They can also be cultural, as in the hostility between "natives" and "immigrants."

Ingroups and outgroups typically have little contact with each other. They often know very little about one another, and their mutual hostility is often based on stereotypes. These views, and the infrequent contact between the two groups, often reinforce the indifference or outright antagonism between ingroups and outgroups.

REFERENCE GROUPS

People are not always members of groups that are important to them or that influence them. These groups, called *reference groups*, are used by people to formulate, compare, and evaluate their own behavior.

Three functions of reference groups. Reference groups serve three functions. They serve a *normative* function when they define appropriate forms of behavior. A reference group may also serve a *comparative* function by providing either a model to imitate or a standard to judge the fairness of others' expectations of a person. Reference groups may also serve an *audience* function by evaluating the adequacy of the person's behavior.

Some reference groups may serve more than one of these functions. Parents, for example, ordinarily serve all three functions: they teach their children what to do and what not to do (normative function); they often serve as models for what children want to be and do (comparative function); and they show their approval or disapproval of their children's behavior (audience function). Similarly, friends often serve more than one reference function.

Reference groups are not always groups in the sociological sense of the term. The concept of reference group has been used to describe individuals or abstract ideas (for example, "freedom," "equality") that influence how people act or how they think of themselves. That influence can be either negative or positive; that is, it can help people determine what they do *not* want to be like as well as what they *do* want to be like. For militant anticommunists, traditional liberals are a negative reference group that they see as too soft and "fuzzy." They do not want to act the way liberals act; quite the contrary, they often wish to act in almost exactly the opposite manner.

How Groups Are Formed

Entrance into a group may be purely by chance. An individual is born into a certain family or attends a particular neighborhood school. However, individuals often choose to join specific groups. Two main factors seem to guide this choice: proximity and similarity.

PROXIMITY

The degree to which proximity, or geographical closeness, influences a person's involvement in a group cannot be overestimated. We form peer groups with those around us. We join *local* church groups.

Groups are composed of individuals who interact with one another. The closer geographically two people are, the more likely they are to see each other, to talk to each other, to socialize with each other. In short, physical proximity increases the likelihood of interaction and the kind of joint activities that result in the formation of social groups.

Festinger, Schachter, and Back (1950) investigated the pattern of social interaction in housing units for married students at the Massachusetts Institute of Technology. They found that the closeness of friendship depended on distance; those who lived in adjacent units were more likely to describe each other as close friends than they were those who lived farther down the hall. Also, friendships between those living in adjacent buildings were closer than those between individuals living farther apart. In short, proximity led to interaction, which played a role in the formation of friendship groups.

SIMILARITY

The creation of social groups does not depend solely on the physical proximity of their members. Another key factor in group formation is the similarity between individuals. As a rule, people prefer to associate with people like themselves. They feel more comfortable being with people with whom they share interests, beliefs, and values. They also tend to associate with others who have similar social characteristics such as race, religion, ethnicity, and class or who are similar in age, level of intelligence or other personal characteristics.

In a classic study of the formation of social ties that has been consistently confirmed over the years, Newcomb (1961) studied students in cooperative housing at the University of Michigan. He clearly demonstrates that the bonds that formed between the individuals in his study resulted primarily from their similar interests and values that were present at the beginning of their association. Similarity is also a major factor in selecting a marriage partner with whom to form the social group called the family (Belkin and Goodman, 1980).

Group Norms

Group behavior, like all social behavior, is considerably influenced by the norms operative in the group. As in the social world at large, activities within the group do not occur at random. Every group has a view of what is appropriate behavior for its members, and these norms guide group interaction.

THE FORMATION OF GROUP NORMS

Norms emerge through a gradual process of interaction among group members. An individual acts in a particular way, and others confirm the appropriateness or inappropriateness of the behavior or suggest (directly or indirectly) desired changes. Norms result from a cumulative process of group interaction.

The classic study of this process was conducted by Sherif (1966) using a perceptual test of the movement of a light. By requiring the subjects in the study to move from a situation in which they gave their judgments of the light's movements while alone to a situation that required them to announce these judgments publicly to a group of peers, Sherif was able to explore the actual formation of a group norm.

CONFORMITY TO GROUP NORMS

Since it is from groups that people generally derive many of the satisfactions of social life, groups wield considerable influence over the behavior of their members. Groups, generally, are less tolerant of behavior that deviates from their norms than is the case in the larger society. Pressure to conform is strong in small groups.

The classic study of conformity to group pressure was carried out by Solomon Asch (1952). He studied the pressure to conform to false judgments about the length of lines printed on a card. He found that about one-third of the subjects gave (an obviously) incorrect answer more than half of the time ("yielders"). They did so because they actually perceived the situation incorrectly, did not trust their own judgment or did not wish to go against the openly expressed views of others. Pressure to conform to group norms on values, attitudes, and other forms of social behavior is likely to be even greater. Later work (e.g., Middlebrook, 1974) indicates that Asch may even have underestimated the tendency of people to conform to group norms.

Group Structure

Groups are not random collections of individuals doing the same thing. Each group has an organization, a group structure.

STATUSES AND ROLES

Nowhere are the concepts of status and role more important than in the study of social groups. The members of a group often have different positions in the group (social statuses) and are expected to (and actually do) engage in different activities (roles). The mother (social status) in the family (group) is expected to engage (and actually does engage) in different kinds of behavior (role) than her children. The treasurer of a social club has a different set of responsibilities than the recording secretary.

In short, groups consist of interlocking statuses with their corresponding roles. The different statuses serve different aspects of the group's overall goals.

STATUS HIERARCHIES

Groups consist of interlocking statuses, but these statuses need not be equal. Some statuses may be seen as more important than others to the functioning of the group. Consequently, most groups have a "status hierarchy" in which some statuses are accorded more power and respect than others. For example, many groups have a chief officer (president or chair) who has more power to shape the group's activities than other members. In this case, the hierarchy is defined by the status positions (president or chair vs. ordinary members) and not by the personal characteristics of the members.

In some groups, however, differences in power and influence are not related to a person's position in the group's formal status structure. Some people are accorded more respect and influence than others because of who they are or what they do. Strodtbeck, James, and Hawkins (1957), for example, found that early in the deliberations of a mock jury, leadership was accorded to people according to their status in the world outside of this experiment and the first impressions they made. Later on, a third and key element became more important: the quality of people's performance in their jury role.

Later studies (e.g., Berger, et al., 1972) suggest that the external status characteristics that a person brings into a group do not diminish in importance over time but continue to influence that person's place in the group's status hierarchy. Personal characteristics and actions contribute to the development of differential power and influence in social groups and thus to the formation of hierarchies that affect the group's functioning.

BOUNDARIES

Groups have boundaries that mark off members from nonmembers. These boundaries serve to heighten members' interaction and to promote a group identity. The defined structure of the group establishes these boundaries.

Group Processes

Equally as important as boundaries and status hierarchies is group interaction. There are three central processes of group interaction: communication, conflict, and cohesiveness.

COMMUNICATION

Communication is probably the central activity of most groups. Members inform each other, reassure each other, shout at each other, correct each other. In short, they communicate information, feelings, and attitudes.

Communication between group members does not occur at random. A series of studies has focused on the nature of communication within groups. Bales, et al. (1951) finds that the pattern of communication is related to a person's status in the group. More specifically, Crosbie (1975) shows that communication within a group (especially a stable group) tends to flow between status equals or from a higher- to a lower-status person. Homans (1950) demonstrates how the nature of a group's activities contributes to the communication patterns between members. In situations involving task solving, communications are primarily between high- and low-status members; in social or recreational situations, communication is more likely to take place between status equals.

CONFLICT

Communication and members' interaction are not always smooth and pleasurable. Sometimes group members find themselves in conflict. Studying conflict in the family, a small group, Letha and John Scanzoni (1976) distinguish three different forms that conflicts can take. One kind of conflict can be either zero-sum or mixed motive. In a zero-sum conflict, a person either wins everything or loses everything. In a mixed motive conflict, neither person wants to win or lose all.

Another kind of conflict can be either personality-based or *situational*. *Personality-based conflicts* are caused by personal differences between the individuals involved; situational conflicts are caused by the social context the people are in (such as trying to divide up some scarce resource, like money).

Finally, conflict can be either *basic* or *nonbasic*. Basic conflict occurs over the fundamental norms of the situation, whereas nonbasic conflict involves the application of the agreed-upon norms to a specific situation. A group's argument over which team to challenge to a game of baseball would be a form of nonbasic conflict; to argue over whether they should be involved in athletic contests at all would reflect a more basic conflict.

In general, mixed-motive, situational, and nonbasic conflicts are more easily dealt with, since some form of compromise is more often possible. In the alternative forms, there is much more at risk: all or nothing, valued personality attributes, and fundamental aspects of the group.

Not all conflict is negative (Coser, 1956, 1967). Conflict can help clarify group goals and group boundaries. If handled properly, it can increase commitment and cohesiveness in the group. The key to the positive functioning of conflict is that it be normatively regulated (that is, that there be established and accepted rules for handling it).

COHESIVENESS

Cohesiveness, the degree to which members feel bound to one another, is also an important group characteristic. The more cohesive a group, the more likely it is that it will be stable and that the members will conform to its norms. Cohesive groups tend to do better at solving problems. In general, then, cohesion seems to be of great value to groups. One possible negative consequence of group cohesion is the tendency of cohesive groups to be less tolerant of differences and dissent.

Selected Issues in the Study of Groups

THE EFFECTS OF SIZE

The size of a group influences its structure and the interaction between its members. The smallest group, called a *dyad*, consists of two people and requires the active involvement of each member. Each must take account of the other if the group is to continue. In general, dyads involve more intense relationships and are less stable than larger groups.

The addition of a third person to a dyad creates a *triad*. There are several different possible relationships in a triad. There is also the possibility of a coalition of two against one, which brings about unequal pressure on the third person. However, if there is conflict between two members, the third can serve as mediator and try to maintain the harmony of the group. The triad is generally more stable than the dyad but still less stable than larger groups.

The larger the group, the wider the range of possible relationships between group members. Beyond a certain size, however, a more formal structure emerges to smooth group members' interaction. When a group contains more than about eight to ten members, it becomes virtually impossible for members to converse directly with one another. Some regulation of the flow of interaction is required, and some form of status structure emerges. Also, in larger groups talking *with* others is often transformed into talking *to* others.

There is no optimal size for all groups. Smaller groups tend to be more personal but less stable; larger groups tend to be less personal but more stable. The optimal size of a group depends on the nature and activities of the group.

LEADERSHIP

Most groups have a leader, a person who by virtue of personality, accomplishments or position plays a major role in affecting the activities of the group. A considerable body of research about leadership in small groups has identified two different types.

Instrumental leadership describes leaders who move the group toward accomplishing the goals of the group. The instrumental leader is task-oriented and focuses on the business at hand. Expressive leadership involves creating harmony and solidarity within the group. The expressive leader is concerned with group morale. Both kinds of leadership are necessary for stable and successful groups, though it appears that two different individuals tend to play these two different types of leadership roles in a group (Bales and Slater, 1955). Apparently, the task-oriented leader generates some degree of hostility in pushing a group to deal with its responsibilities and over time is unlikely to be perceived as very likeable.

Leadership "styles" also vary (White and Lippitt, 1953). Some leaders are democratic and attempt to elicit members' agreement on group action. Others are authoritarian and give orders that they expect to be followed. A third type is the laissez-faire leader, who makes no effort to direct or to organize the activities of the group.

There is no single leadership style that is effective in all situations, though it does appear that laissez-faire leadership is the least effective in most situations. In the United States, at least, democratic leadership seems to be the most useful in maintaining group morale and in solving group tasks. However, authoritarian leadership appears to be the most effective style in emergency situations in which there is little time for the consensus-building mechanisms used by democratic leaders.

GROUP DECISION MAKING

Decision making in a group rests upon the interaction of group members. Groups often require a degree of consensus, or agreement, before they will take any action. Also, groups' being composed of a number of individuals leads them to have at their disposal a wider range of knowledge, expertise, and skills than is generally possible for any single individual. Thus groups have greater resources to draw on in making decisions than do individuals.

Stoner (1961) found that individuals in groups are often more likely to make risky decisions than are individuals acting on their own. This "risky shift" has been attributed to a "diffusion of responsibility"; individuals in a group can spread responsibility for a decision to all the members of the group, and thus no single individual can be held accountable if the decision turns out to be wrong. This may lead to bold but risky decisions that individuals might be reluctant to make on their own. Also, the consensus-building process of the group may stifle dissenters and discussion of the negative consequences of the group's emerging decision.

However, if a group is highly cohesive, pressure to conform may lead to less-creative decisions (Callaway and Esser, 1984). Group members may censor their own ideas so as to reduce differences within the group, losing the value that different perspectives may contribute to solving a problem or taking necessary action. This type of reaction has been referred to as *groupthink*.

FORMAL ORGANIZATIONS

Modern society is a society of formal organizations. *Formal organizations* are large secondary groups deliberately created to accomplish a specific goal or set of goals. They are carefully designed and contain a formal structure of statuses and roles and smaller groups.

The Nature of Organizations

While each formal organization is unique (e.g., the Division of Motor Vehicles is different from a public university), they have certain similarities. These similarities reveal the general characteristics of all formal organizations.

PLANNING AND RATIONALITY

Deliberate and rational planning is one of the hallmarks of formal organizations. In some respects, it may be the most clearly defining feature of organizations. The design of formal organizations includes attention to *rationality*, an emphasis on the relationship between means and ends. Organizational structures are created to help the organization accomplish its goals. Rational planning requires a clear understanding of the organization's goals and of the kinds of activities and organizational structures that are necessary to reach those goals.

Not all organizations live up to the ideal of rational planning. Organizational actors (persons acting according to their organizational status) may not always carry out their responsibilities on the basis of a rational calculation of the appropriate means to achieve clearly defined ends.

FORMALIZATION

The formal structure of organizations sets them apart from other types of groups. In organizations, the relationships between activities as well as between organizational actors are highly structured. There is a precise description of duties of individuals and responsibilities of offices. Often, these formalized requirements are summarized in written documents that serve as the charter of the organization.

Bureaucracy

In large organizations, the variety of offices and responsibilities must be organized and coordinated for maximum efficiency. *Bureaucracy* is the formal administrative structure that is responsible for planning, supervising, and coordinating the work of the various segments of an organization. According to Weber (1978; original, 1921), there are several important characteristics of a bureaucracy, each of which is briefly described below.

SPECIALIZATION AND A DIVISION OF LABOR

In order to function well, each member of the organization has a specialized set of responsibilities. This *division of labor,* or persons carrying out their distinctive assigned tasks, leads people to develop special expertise in their jobs and makes the organization highly efficient.

HIERARCHY

The offices in a bureaucracy not only have their distinctive responsibilities but they are also organized into a *hierarchy*, in which each office is supervised by an office higher up in the level of authority. In most large organizations, this hierarchy has the form of a pyramid in which greater authority is accorded to the few at the top and less to the larger number at lower levels. Most people are aware of the hierarchy in their organizations.

RULES AND REGULATIONS

Most organizations have an elaborate set of rules and regulations that guides the behavior of employees. For the most part, these rules and regulations exist in written form and are the basis for many organizational decisions. The rules and regulations are intended to add an element of stability and predictability to the actions of the bureaucracy.

IMPERSONALITY

Bureaucrats are expected to treat each "client" of the organization as a "case" and not as an individual. The bureaucrat should be impersonal, taking necessary action on the basis of the organization's established rules and regulations or on the basis of precedent rather than personal feelings. Interaction with a client should also not be based on personal feelings but on the bureaucrat's official role.

FORMAL, WRITTEN FILES AND RECORDS

Organizational activities are expected to be communicated and recorded in written form and maintained as a permanent record to guide future action. Written records are essential for the organizational memory of bureaucracies. The typical complaint about "red tape" derives from this need for written records of all transactions. These documents are then available to the organization despite turnover or absence of personnel.

TECHNICAL COMPETENCE AND CAREERS

Employees are expected to have the technical competence to carry out their responsibilities. Weber points out that this is a sharp break with the past, when jobs depended largely on personal and family contacts, not on technical skill. While contacts still play a role in many bureaucracies, judgment of technical competence has become much more important. The development of "civil service examinations" was intended to provide a mechanisms for assessing technical competence.

Because of the criteria of technical competence, division of labor, and the hierarchal structure of organizations, employees can anticipate careers within the organization. Seniority and merit are associated with advancement; other factors such as family and personal connections are not assumed to be related to organizational efficiency and success.

ADMINISTRATIVE STAFF

Organizations often have specialized groups of employees who have no direct relationship to the explicit goals of the organization but who are responsible for its smooth operation. For example, while the bookkeepers and accountants in a manufacturing organization have nothing directly to do with producing the specific product, someone must keep account of the flow of money in and out of the organization so that raw materials can be obtained, necessary equipment purchased, and a price set for the finished product. Similarly, the administration in a university (e.g., president, deans) play no direct role in its primary teaching and research functions, but they perform managerial tasks without which the faculty would find it difficult to carry out their teaching and research responsibilities.

Alternative Perspectives

Weber presents a highly rational and objective view of the bureaucracies of formal organizations. He was the first to acknowledge that his model represents an *ideal type*, a "purified" model of a concept against which a real world example can be compared. Examining actual formal organizations has given rise to other perceptions of bureaucracies.

THE INFORMAL SIDE OF BUREAUCRACY

Most people know that bureaucracies do not always function in the precise, formal, and impersonal manner described above. Personal relationships form between members of an organization, occasionally leading to the use of other than the formal channels of authority. Rules are occasionally bent or even broken. Informal ways of taking action may supplant the existing formal machinery. Files are never entirely complete.

The formal structure of an organization is only an outline, a general framework, for structuring the activities of the employees. In their daily activities the members of an organization try to do those things that will, in their estimation, enable them to carry out their responsibilities; and many seek to do them in the easiest manner possible. Sometimes these goals require them to act differently than the way prescribed in the organizational manual. Occasionally, employees' friends and relatives use personal bonds that are difficult to ignore to request action not usually permitted by the formal structure. In short, people adapt to their circumstances despite the formal requirements of their jobs. They give bureaucracy a "human face."

SOME LIMITATIONS OF BUREAUCRACY

Along with an informal structure, bureaucratic organization also has some important limitations, even dysfunctions (that is, negative consequences).

Inefficiency. Bureaucratic rules and procedures are designed for the "typical" case, and efficiency depends on applying these rules to new cases. Whenever there is an atypical or unusual case (e.g., a taxpayer whose file was lost), the usual rules do not apply and efficiency is generally reduced. Because bureaucrats are used to systematically following established procedures, they often develop a "trained incapacity" to deal creatively and imaginatively with new or unique situations (Veblen, 1934). Inefficiency sometime derives from the hierarchal structure of bureaucracies. Employees in lower-level positions may conceal errors and mistakes from their superiors to avoid penalties. These "cover-ups" often make the bureaucracy less efficient because the errors are concealed and go uncorrected.

Goal displacement. Over time, people in bureaucratic organizations tend to forget the original goals of the organization. Instead, they focus their efforts on personal goals like doing the least amount of work, getting home early, and holding on to their jobs. Sociologists generally refer to this as "goal displacement."

Bureaucratic enlargement. Bureaucracies tend to grow and to enlarge their responsibilities ("bureaucratic enlargement"). More and more activities are seen as important to the bureaucracy. Today, universities are seen as responsible not only for the intellectual development of students but for their social and emotional growth as well. While this is probably an appropriate enlargement of the mission of universities, it does require additional staff and budget. Few bureaucracies shrink of their own accord.

Rigidity. Bureaucracies tend to develop a ritualistic rigidity, a preoccupation with rules and regulations. Merton (1968), discussing the "bureaucratic personality," and Whyte (1957), describing the "organization man," suggest that this preoccupation affects the personalities of the bureaucrats, stifling creativity and imagination. More recent research (e.g., Kohn, 1978) challenges this intriguing portrait of the bureaucrat, showing a more positive view of employees of bureaucratic organizations.

Oligarchy. Bureaucracies tend to develop into *oligarchies*, systems in which the many are ruled by the few. This point is stressed by Michels (1949; original, 1911) in his "iron law of oligarchy," which states that democracy and large organizations cannot exist together. Of necessity, large organizations need to concentrate power in the hands of a few. These powerful few are less and less accountable to those below them in the organizational structure, a situation that is incompatible with democratic equality.

Michels's view has not gone unchallenged. A number of scholars have pointed out that there are checks and balances that often limit the power of individuals high up on the organizational ladder. Boards of directors often serve as a brake on the power of chief executive officers. Competing forces within an organization often limit the absolute power of those in control. Periodic elections of public officials also serve to keep them from exerting absolute power. Thus, while there might be a tendency for power to accumulate at the top, that power is not unlimited.

Other Forms of Organization

The organization described by Weber is the most common today. However, there are other forms that large organizations take.

JAPANESE ORGANIZATIONS

Since its reconstruction after World War II, Japan has become a major economic power. Some have attributed this phenomenal economic growth to the particular organizational pattern of Japanese corporations that stems from a long tradition of giving priority to the group over the individual. In many Japanese corporations, the company and the workers make lifetime commitments to one another. The corporation takes major responsibility for the welfare of its workers. Promotion and salary increases are generally based on seniority, and workers anticipate spending their entire careers within the same firm.

The unit of responsibility in Japanese firms is not the individual worker but the small work group. The performance of the group and not of the individual is the focus of evaluation. Individuals gain different skills and experience over the years by being part of a number of these small work groups. Decision making is collective rather than oligarchic; that is, decisions are discussed and approved at all levels in the organization and not just handed down from above.

This pattern of organization is clearly different from the one usually found in the United States. In large part, the differences in organizational form stem from a basic difference between the traditional culture of the two countries. Japan has long stressed the importance of the group over that of the individual. Individuals see themselves as intimately tied to important social groups, and their identities are bound up with the identities of those groups. In the United States, on the other hand, individual autonomy has always been prized. Americans see themselves as having unique identities that are somewhat apart from the groups in which they function.

The Japanese take comfort from the security provided by the relationship between the individual and the corporation. It adds a desired element of stability and cohesiveness to their lives. Americans much prefer the freedom enabled by keeping their work and personal identities separate and being able to change their circumstances when they believe the situation requires it.

COLLECTIVISM

A new form of organization has emerged in the United States over the past quarter of a century, largely stemming from the social turbulence of the 1960s. These new organizations, which are nonbureaucratic and often involve the provision of social services, see themselves as offering an alternative to the "establishment" mentality of large formal organizations (Rothschild-Witt, 1979).

These organizations avoid the strict division of labor that leads to the development of narrow specialties. Members are encouraged to participate in a variety of tasks required by the collective. Individual initiative and creativity are stressed rather than strict preprogrammed rules and regulations. Authority is shared rather than bestowed as a result of hierarchal status; in fact, official titles are not the basis for respect or authority. "Clients" are treated as individuals rather than as cases or files. The activities of these collectivist organizations have a humanistic (person-centered) rather than a bureaucratic flavor.

This form of organization is better suited to small groups, since large companies lack the face-to-face personal contact so necessary to the operation of the collectivist organization. Also, these organizations spend much time building a consensus for group decision making and less time on actually providing services. There does seem to be a place in American society for the nonestablishment, collectivist organization that wants to provide a range of social and public services in an intimate way. These organizations should be seen as alternatives to large bureaucracies, not as replacements for them.

ORGANIZATIONAL REFORM

A number of large companies are experimenting with various facets of both the Japanese and the collectivist models, combining small intimate work groups with collective decision making authority. In some companies, workers have a seat on the board of directors and thus share some responsibility for overall corporate policy. Stock-sharing plans and other incentives inspire workers with greater commitment and loyalty to the company. These reforms are growing but do not as yet constitute a significant challenge to the traditional form of bureaucratic organization.

ORGANIZATIONS AND SOCIETY

Large-scale bureaucratic organizations simultaneously contribute to and reduce human freedom. Basing decisions and especially public policy on rationality and precedent rather than on personal whim enhances human freedom and encourages impartial justice rather than favoritism. On the other hand, bureaucracies generally give more weight to the past (precedent) and to the objective (generalized rules and regulations) than to the subtleties of a specific situation. In modern society, formal organizations show themselves to be both helpful and harmful to the human spirit. But, on balance, most scholars share Weber's view that bureaucratic organization decidedly enhances efficiency and productivity and thereby benefits most people.

This chapter discussed the different types of social groups that sociologists study: primary and secondary groups, ingroups and outgroups, and reference groups. Also analyzed was how groups form because of proximity of individuals and their common interests and views. Group norms were examined: how they are formed and how they pressure group members to conform. The aspects of group structure—statuses, status hierarchies, and boundaries— were also explored. Group processes (communication, conflict, and cohesiveness), the effects of size and leadership patterns on groups, and group decisionmaking were described.

The second half of the chapter dealt with formal organizations. Their characteristics such as planning, rationality, and formalization, were discussed. The elements of bureaucracy were analyzed: specialization, division of labor, hierarchy, rules and regulations, impersonality in dealing with clients, and the maintenance of formal, written files and records. Some of the limitations of bureaucracy were examined: inefficiency, goal displacement, bureaucratic enlargement, rigidity, and tendencies toward oligarchy. Other forms of organization were described, specifically the Japanese and collectivist models.

6

Socialization: Becoming a Social Being

*W*e all enter this world as potentially social beings. We are essentially helpless, dependent upon others for our most basic biological needs. The mature human being reading these words today is a result of an ongoing process of social interaction that has enabled him or her to develop an identity, a set of beliefs, and a range of skills that allow an active participation in society. We call this important process socialization. In this chapter, we will examine this critical social process and how it transforms the biological organism we call homo sapiens into a functioning social being, a participating member of society. We will first focus on the contributions of a person's biological heritage ("nature") and the supporting environment ("nurture") to the socialization process.

THE IMPORTANCE OF SOCIAL EXPERIENCE

Nature and Nurture   For almost two centuries scholars argued over whether our identity and how we behave are determined by our biological inheritance or by our social experiences. Typically, this issue was posed as "nature *versus* nurture."

NATURE

On the one side were the instinctivists, like Mcdougall (1908), who argued that human behavior is a result of *instincts*; that is, "inborn, fixed, genetically programmed patterns of action that are common to a species and not subject to variation with the experiences of the individual" (Goodman and Marx, 1978:120). By 1924 (Bernard, 1924) over 10,000 instincts had been identified as causes of social behavior. They ranged from the "aggressive" instinct that led to wars to the "affiliative" instinct that led to the establishment of society itself.

It soon became clear that instincts were an inadequate explanation for human behavior on two grounds. First, every time a form of behavior was identified, it was necessary to "discover" an instinct to account for it. Second, behaviors that were considered instinctive either were not found in some societies or were found to be the reverse of what had been expected.

NURTURE

The alternative view was that human behavior is a product of the social environment. Psychologist John B. Watson (1924), who argued the extreme environmental determinist view, took the position that human behavior and identity could be shaped in any way desired. Watson essentially said that if he were given healthy infants and complete control over their environment, he could raise them to be any kind of person he chose. In short, their biological inheritance (nature) was irrelevant and only the social world (nurture) determined their behavior.

NATURE-NURTURE

Today, there is general agreement that both nature and nurture contribute to the development of the person. Recent developments in the life sciences make it clear that biology plays an important part in human development. Just recently biologists isolated a gene that appears to be implicated in alcoholism. However, not all people who have that particular gene become alcoholics; and that is in large part because of their social context and social experience.

Most social scientists today acknowledge the joint contributions of heredity and environment to the formation of a person's identity and behavior. Increasing evidence comes from recent studies of identical twins demonstrating that identical twins (twins who share an identical genetic inheritance) do not have identical personalities; nor do they exhibit identical social behavior. Thus genetic inheritance alone cannot adequately explain human behavior. However, identical twins are often more alike than fraternal twins (twins who share only some genetic inheritance) and are considerably more similar than non-twin siblings. Clearly, then, inherited genetic factors play a role in human development. The veritable explosion of knowledge in biology, especially in genetics, will increasingly show the ways nature and nurture intersect to make us the kinds of persons we are.

The Effects of Childhood Isolation

One way to explore the contribution of social context to the development of a person is to study those individuals whose social contact during childhood was lacking or severely restricted.

FERAL CHILDREN

From time to time there have been reports of children raised in the wild by animals. While many of these reports are often unreliable, there have been several cases (e.g., Singh and Zingg, 1942; Malson, 1972; Lane, 1976) that have been documented to some degree. In all these cases, the children were barely recognizable as human. They could not speak, walked either on all fours or hunched over, reacted to humans with fear or hostility, and ate their food by tearing at it as wild animals would do.

The authors of the reports about these children were often not trained social scientists; further, we do not know what kinds of lives these children had before they were abandoned or lost in the woods. However, these reports do suggest some of the effects of a lack of significant human contact on the socialization of the young.

CHILDREN RAISED IN ISOLATION

There have been three celebrated cases of children who were raised in relative isolation from human social contact. Two of the children, Anna and Isabelle, were reported by Kingsley Davis (1940, 1947, 1948). Both girls were born out of wedlock and kept in isolation by their maternal grandfathers, though Isabelle was isolated with her mother, who was a deaf mute. Both girls were about six years old when they were discovered. They could not speak, walk or keep themselves clean. They were apathetic and quite indifferent to their surroundings. Anna died of jaundice after four years without having learned more than a few words and phrases, some rudimentary aspects of self-care, and how to follow simple directions. Isabelle, who was treated by a team of physicians and psychologists, fared much better. After about two years of intensive work, she apparently reached a normal level of development and was able to go to school. It is not clear whether Isabelle's better performance was due to a better biological inheritance, her isolation in the company of her deaf mute mother or the excellent attention she got after she was found. A third child, Genie (Curtiss, 1977; Pines, 1981), shared some of the experiences of both Anna and of Isabelle. Genie was isolated at the age of two and found when she was thirteen. Her initial condition was similar to that of Anna and Isabelle, and she received care similar to that of Isabelle. Though she improved somewhat, she did not develop to the level of other children her age the way Isabelle apparently did.

All three cases demonstrate the importance of human contact in developing those characteristics we define as normal in human beings. Furthermore, studies of children in orphanages and similar institutions (e.g., Spitz, 1945; Dennis, 1960, 1973; Yarrow, 1963; Bowlby, 1969; Rutter, 1974) showed them to be physically, socially, and emotionally retarded when compared with their peers raised at home. These deficits tended to persist even after the children left the institutions.

These research studies seem to show that "normal" human development requires human care and human contact, the opportunity to see and learn from others, and the close physical contact of other human beings.

THEORETICAL PERSPECTIVES

The process of socialization has been studied from a variety of different vantage points. Three particular perspectives stand out as particularly detailed and interesting ways of examining socialization: psychoanalysis, cognitive theory, and symbolic interaction. A brief introduction to each approach follows.

Psychoanalysis: Sigmund Freud

Sigmund Freud (1856–1939), a research scientist and physician, developed psychoanalysis as a way of exploring the content and mechanisms of human mental life. His training led him to appreciate the importance of biological factors (nature) and of social experience (nurture) to the development and maintenance of human personality.

FUNDAMENTAL HUMAN NEEDS

Freud believed that there are universal human needs or drives that help guide and shape human behavior. One is *eros*, the "life instinct," which Freud believed explains people's need to form attachments or bonds with others. The other is *thanatos*, the "death instinct." Freud saw this drive as the basis of our aggressive bent. These two drives are often in opposition, and the drama of human life is a consequence of this conflict.

THE STRUCTURE OF PERSONALITY

In Freud's view, personality is composed of three elements: the id, the superego, and the ego. The three have separate roots and functions, but their interaction is the substance of mental life.

The *id* is the storage bin of our universal biological drives, which often demand immediate satisfaction. It is largely unconscious and operates on the "pleasure principle": it wants what it wants when it wants it. From the psychoanalytic perspective, the human infant is primarily an id; it is a bundle of biological needs that require immediate satisfaction. These demands are not always honored because of the demands of social living and the nature of reality.

The former is represented in personality by the *superego*, which is similar to what we call the conscience. It is initially formed by the prescriptions and prohibitions of the child's parents. As the child grows older and is introduced to a widening circle of social influences, contributions to the superego expand.

In many ways, the id and the superego are similar. Both are demanding, relatively inflexible, and often not in contact with reality. Often they are in opposition. The id wants something and the superego constrains it because of social norms. The task of mediating this conflict falls to the third element of personality, the *ego*.

The *ego* is that part of personality that is in contact with reality. It mediates between the often unrealistic demands of the id and the occasionally restrictive requirements of the superego; it also tries to adjust both to social reality.

In essence, the personality contains within it (the id and superego, respectively) the same conflict, discussed earlier, that exists between the individual and society and between nature and nurture.

THE DEVELOPMENT OF PERSONALITY

Human personality develops through a series of unfolding, universal, biologically based, and age-linked stages that Freud called "the stages of psycho-sexual development." The stages derive from the attachment ("cathexis") of the libido, which is the sexual energy derived from the life instinct, to various parts of the body. This cathexis sensitizes the particular area, making it particularly pleasurable to touch, stimulation or manipulation; that area then becomes the focus of interest.

The first stage, occurring during the first year of life, is the *oral stage*, in which the infant seeks gratification through oral activities such as sucking and biting.

The second stage, which takes place during the second year, is called the *anal stage*. At this time the central issue is bowel and bladder control.

The *phallic stage* occurs from about age three to five and is the period of initial sexual focus. This is the time of the *oedipal conflict*, named for Oedipus, the Greek legendary figure who killed his father and married his mother. In psychoanalytic theory, this conflict refers to the child's tendency to form a strong emotional attachment, with sexual implications, to the parent of the opposite sex and to develop a hostile rivalry with the same-sex parent. This conflict is resolved by the child's withdrawing the strong attachment to the opposite-sex parent and identifying with the same-sex parent, though this withdrawal has always been more pronounced in boys than in girls in Freud's writings. One consequence of this resolution is appropriate gender-role learning, an issue that is discussed in chapter 12.

In the *latency stage*, from about age five to puberty, sexuality recedes in importance. The focus is on the development of physical and intellectual skills.

The *genital stage* results from a resurgence of sexual energy, probably due to the hormonal changes of puberty. In contrast to the earlier phallic stage, the scene is now set for a more mature sexuality involving the sharing of sexual pleasure with another.

These stages of development are seen as the universal biological heritage of the human species. However, the response to the cathecting libido is also important for the development of personality. Thus for Freud, personality depends on the interplay of our biological characteristics and social experience, though he did place considerably more emphasis on biological factors.

The intertwining of nature and nurture is also the hallmark of the theories of Erik Erikson, a psychoanalyst who extended many of Freud's original ideas. Erikson incorporated the growing body of sociological and anthropological knowledge into psychoanalytic theory. He introduced into Freud's stages of psychosexual development a greater awareness of and accounting for the social context, redefining the process as one of psycho *social* development. Erikson also focused on socialization as a continual process throughout life and described additional stages of adult development.

Cognitive Theory: Jean Piaget

While Freud focused almost exclusively on the emotional aspects of socialization, Jean Piaget (1896–1980) directed his attention to the area of cognitive development. Though he and Freud differed in their emphases, they shared the view that the developmental process proceeds through a universal series of stages that are rooted in biology.

At first Piaget studied cognitive development by carefully observing his own children. He concluded that the process of development occurs in four stages.

THE SENSORIMOTOR STAGE

The first stage, the *sensorimotor stage*, occurs during the first year and a half of life. During this period, children learn through their senses, mainly through physical contact with the world. They push, poke, touch, kick, and bite objects in their environment. At this time, children cannot use symbols or engage in higher-order thinking. Their world is their direct physical experience of their surroundings.

THE PREOPERATIONAL STAGE

It is in the second stage, the *preoperational stage*, which occurs from about the age of eighteen months to seven years, that the ability to use symbols (particularly language) begins to develop rapidly. Children begin to understand, at least in a rudimentary way, things they cannot see or touch. They are increasingly able to distinguish between reality and fantasy. However, they have an egocentric view of the world; they find it difficult to see from the perspective of another. To understand that a friend is crying because of the child's refusal to share a toy is simply not possible, certainly in the earlier part of this stage.

THE CONCRETE OPERATIONAL STAGE

It is in the *concrete operational stage*, between the ages of seven and eleven, that the next important development occurs: the ability to use logic and to appreciate alternative perspectives. Logic allows children to understand the nature of cause and effect. However, their thinking still tends to be tied to identifiable, concrete objects and events rather than to abstract ideas. They also begin to understand the perspectives of others and to see the possibility that there may be alternative points of view: this is a major step forward in social development.

THE FORMAL OPERATIONAL STAGE

The fourth and final stage Piaget called the *formal operational stage*, which begins at about the age of twelve. Children (shortly to be called adolescents) begin to think abstractly. Not only can they conceive of the *possibility* of alternative views, but they can now actually imagine what those views are. This ability to think abstractly allows them to transcend the limitations of time and space. They can truly envision a future and places they have never seen.

Piaget believed that the exact ages at which children go through these stages vary from child to child and even from society to society. However, he insisted that the sequence of stages is rooted in our biological inheritance and is universal and unchangeable. Later investigators (e.g., Kohlberg, 1969) have used a "cognitive-developmental" approach similar to Piaget's to study the stages of moral development. Recently, feminists (e.g., Gilligan, 1982) have criticized this approach, arguing that it enshrines a distinctively masculine view of morality and moral development (and, by implication, cognitive development as well).

Symbolic Interaction: George Herbert Mead

Because of his ability to synthesize the views of others and to organize them into a relatively coherent theoretical framework, George Herbert Mead (1863–1931) is considered to be the founder of the school of thought called *symbolic interaction*. Mead was a social philosopher who shared with the psychologist John B. Watson the view that the environment is a critical element in human action. Originally, in fact, Mead termed his approach "social behaviorism." However, unlike Watson, Mead placed considerable weight on understanding the cognitive processes that lead to observable behavior.

Mead explored the development and organization of the self. He was interested in its role in such polarities as freedom and control, change and stability, creativity and conformity. The self became the central feature of the symbolic interactionist approach to socialization.

THE DEVELOPMENT OF THE SELF

The self grows out of social experience because of the individual's ability to view her or his actions from the perspective of others. This is made possible through language (a system of significant symbols; see chapter 3), which allows us to be both object and subject at the same time. As we speak to others, we hear what we say just as they do; and we can react to those statements just as others do. In those situations we are both the subject (the "acting" person), and the object of action (one of the "receiving" persons). In essence, Mead argued that it is by "taking the role of the other" and reflecting back on ourselves as objects that we develop a self. This view of the self emphasizes social context over biology.

In contrast to Freud and Piaget, Mead did not see this process as occurring through a series of age-linked stages. Rather, he viewed the self as becoming increasingly more complex as a result of an ever-widening circle of social experience. He did, however, distinguish between development that occurs before and after the effective use of language.

PREVERBAL PERIOD

In the "preverbal" period, children, whose interaction with others is rudimentary, do not distinguish between what is the self and what is not the self. Gradually, through the interaction of others who apply labels to the child and to the environment, infants come to make this distinction. Communication, too, depends on others "interpreting" (actually assigning meaning to) the actions of the infant and labeling them by means of verbal symbols.

VERBAL PERIOD

As children develop the ability to understand and to use symbolic communication (language and gestures), they enter more actively into their own development. In this "verbal period," children's cognitive abilities are increasingly developed through social interaction.

Play. Mead labeled the early form of this interaction *play*. Through play, children learn to take the role of another, though in a relatively simple fashion. They may play the role of a mother offering a bottle to an infant and then switch to the role of the infant and accept the bottle. In this way, children learn that there are different social roles, each having a different perspective.

The Organized Game. Mead called the next step the *organized game*. During this stage, children develop the ability to see the connection among multiple roles and to view the roles they are playing as part of a system of roles. Mead liked to use the example of playing baseball, which teaches children that the position they are playing is linked to the other positions on the field; and that to play their position well they need to know those other positions as well.

In developing this ability, children learn to take the role of multiple others and to reflect back on their own actions from the perspective of this role. This reflected view of the child's own behavior plays a critical role in the development of the social self.

Generalized Other. Mead suggested that in a later stage of development, children are able to look back at themselves not only from the vantage point of a specific other person or role but also from the perspective of the "community" as a whole. As a consequence, they are able to understand the "rules" that govern their actions and the actions of other participants, whether the "game" is baseball or life itself. In the case of children's games, actions are governed by specific rules. In the game of life, the rules are what sociologists refer to as norms and values (see chapter 3).

Mead called this perspective the role of the *generalized other*. It frees us from the influence of specific others and leads us to do what we believe is proper and correct rather than what a parent or another individual believes is right. It provides for some measure of stability in and social control of our behavior because it is guided by community standards.

THE NATURE OF THE SELF

Cooley (1902) wrote about the "looking glass self," our conception of ourselves that is derived from our response to what we think are others' perceptions of us. This view of ourselves affirms the importance of taking the role of the other in forming the social self.

Mead thought of the self as interacting phases called "the me and the I." The *me* is the social phase of the self. It is the internalized social order that promotes stability, predictability, and social control. Working jointly with the "me" is the *I*, the novel, creative, unpredictable phase of the self. The self is essentially a dialogue between the "I" and the "me." The "me" is a social product, while the "I" has an unclear relationship to social experience.

The self, then, is truly a product of the interaction of the unique individual and the social context. Each of us perceives and interprets the social context differently. Hence, the social reality of one person need not be the same as the social reality of another.

The "I" and the "me" account for the self as subject ("I") and as object ("me") and for the joint importance of freedom ("I") and control ("me") and of change ("I") and stability ("me").

AGENTS OF SOCIALIZATION

Socialization is a complex process that involves many individuals, groups, and social institutions. In a way, these elements may be seen as routes through which society is involved in socialization; they are, in essence, agents of society. In this section, we will discuss some of the main characters in this continuous drama.

The Family

The single most important agent of socialization is the family. The family is the first and most continuous social world for the infant and child. It is where the first and most long-lasting intimate social relationships are established. Communicative ability, primarily through the learning of language, occurs initially in the family. And it is in the family that the infant and child is introduced to key elements of the culture.

The family is largely the entire social world of infants and young children, the main arena of their experience. Equally important from a sociological point of view, the family provides the child's initial social identity in terms of race, religion, social class, and gender. General life chances, health, longevity, amount of education, and type of occupation are powerfully influenced by the family into which the child is born. Kohn (1963, 1969, 1976, 1977), among others, has shown that parent-child interactions differ by social class, partly because of the different values that middle and working class parents wish to instill in their children.

The School

This social institution has direct responsibility for instilling in the individual the information, skills, and values that society deems important for social life. Not only "reading, 'riting, and 'rithmetic," but honesty, dependability, and punctuality are part of the school's socialization agenda. The school provides a social setting that is quite different from that of the family.

Family relationships are intimate. People treat family members differently than they treat non-family members. Though parents may be warm and kind to all children, they are expected to and generally do have a special feeling and relationship with *their* children.

In school, the teacher is supposed to treat all children alike. Moreover, the teacher's actions are guided by what the child does rather than by who the child is. Teachers are not supposed to have "special relationships" with some students. Though this does occur, it is not considered appropriate.

In school, children are introduced to formal systems of evaluations: grades and report cards. This is in marked contrast to the informality of family practices and constitutes a new and often difficult experience for many children. Young children also learn many skills of interpersonal interaction. They learn what it means to share with others, to take turns, to accommodate to comparisons with peers. In short, this new social world for children contributes substantially to their socialization.

The Peer Group

Before they enter school, most children enter the world of the peer group. This arena is different from that of the family in several respects. First, by definition the peer group is composed of status equals, that is, children of the same age and general social status. Second, social position in the family is automatic; in the peer group it generally has to be earned. Third, in the family (as in the school), socialization is often deliberate and planned; in the peer group a good deal of socialization takes place without, it appears, any deliberate design.

The peer group shares with the school the important function of loosening the child's bonds to the family, which initially are all-encompassing. Both school and peer groups provide additional and sometimes alternative models for behavior as well as new norms and values. Consequently, children must also learn how to deal with conflicting views among those considered to be important—those whom sociologists refer to as "significant others."

The Mass Media

The agents of socialization discussed above are all involved in interactive and personal contact. This is not true of the mass media, which are various modes of communication intended for large audiences (e.g., radio, television, motion pictures, newspapers, magazines, books, and, especially today, videos, records, cassettes and compact disks). The media influence socialization by providing additional and alternative role models as well as social norms and values.

Perhaps the most influential mass medium today is television. A positive view of television is that it provides an excellent medium of instruction (e.g., "Sesame Street") and an entertaining way of expanding the horizons of children by exposing them to places and events they may not be able to experience first hand (e.g., "Wild Kingdom"). The negative view of television stresses the unreality and overly simplistic nature of many programs and especially their frequent depiction of violence. Only recently has television provided a more rounded picture of the kinds of people who make up our society, especially members of "minority" groups, and moved somewhat away from stereotypical portrayals.

Videos and music play an increasingly important role in the socialization of the young. Currently there is a movement to label potentially offensive or controversial records and tapes (just as movies are labeled) to control access to them by the young.

Other Agents   In addition to the family, the school, the peer group, and the mass media, socialization is also carried out by religious institutions, neighbors, recreational organizations, communities, and so on. All of these contribute to the person's view of the world and her or his perceptions of what is desirable and undesirable behavior. In some cases, their influence may be significant.

SOCIALIZATION THROUGH THE LIFE COURSE

Most of discussion above deals with socialization during infancy and childhood. However, socialization is a lifelong process. Though it doesn't end with childhood, socialization after that time is not quite the same.

Developmental Socialization   *Developmental socialization* refers to a continuation of the socialization that began during childhood. This type of socialization builds on prior learning. Formal education, for example, is largely a matter of developmental socialization.

Resocialization   Occasionally, we experience *resocialization*, the uprooting and restructuring of basic attitudes, values or identities. *Voluntary resocialization* may be seen in cases of religious conversion or in those individuals voluntarily undergoing psychotherapy. In both cases, the person's aim is to replace her or his present identity with a new one and, occasionally, to replace existing values and modes of behavior.

Resocialization can also take place on an involuntary basis, such as when the authorities commit people to prison or to mental hospitals. In cases of *involuntary resocialization*, what is often required is what Goffman (1961) calls a "total institution." This environment enables the person to break sharply with the past and gives the resocializing agents considerable control over the person's day-to-day, and even minute-to-minute, activities.

The Need for Socialization after Childhood   As we mature, we take on different statuses and play new roles (Brim and Wheeler, 1966). Since these statuses were unavailable to us earlier (e.g., occupational statuses, marital statuses), we were not able to learn the requirements of the new roles. Additional socialization experiences, such as formal occupational training or on-the-job training, fill the gap. Even with respect to marital and parental roles, earlier learning is often insufficient and further developmental socialization is necessary.

Socialization after childhood is occasionally required when rapid social change alters the norms. For example, the role associated with the status we term "woman" has undergone considerable change over the past generation. Conceptions of appropriate gender role behavior learned in childhood twenty years ago are not as useful today. New norms, values, and behaviors are required for the modern woman. This is accomplished through continuing socialization.

Finally, much of what we learn in childhood consists of general and abstract norms and values that often need to be modified when put into practice later. For example, we teach our children to be honest. Later they have to learn to temper that honesty, on certain occasions, with tact.

Changes in the Content of Socialization

What we learn during childhood often differs from what we learn after childhood. During childhood we tend to learn general norms and values. After childhood, there is a greater emphasis on clear, observable behavior. The person knows what to do, and the focus now is on how to do it. Often, people must synthesize various bits of specific learning acquired from school and jobs in working out behaviors that will accomplish their goals.

Idealism is often associated with the young; realism with adults. While idealism doesn't have to disappear with age, it does often have to confront reality. One of the difficult aspects of socialization in later life is dealing with the world in a realistic way without abandoning one's ideals. We transform the question from "Why is this being done?" to "What is the best way to do this?" For example, many in the environmental movement during the past two decades have learned how to integrate an idealistic vision with economic and social realities. Socialization after childhood requires a shift from dependence to autonomy and then to influence over others (Goodman, 1985:82–83). But before we can accomplish these important transitions we must learn the necessary skills.

SOCIALIZATION AND FREEDOM

The nature of socialization raises the question of whether successful socialization restricts individual freedom. Wrong (1961) holds that socialization is never complete. Drawing on the work of Freud, Wrong points out that human beings are "social without being fully socialized."

Mead took a balanced view that people give up some freedom in the course of social living, but in return gain the benefit of social intercourse. Within the self, the "I" and the "me" represent a balance between the needs of society and the needs of the individual. The symbolic-interactionist perspective is that the "I" and the "me" are not inherently in conflict, nor are the individual and society. (The psychoanalytic perspective is that the "id" and the "superego" *are* in conflict.) The "I" and the "me" function jointly as the self; the individual and society are two sides of the same coin. While conflict may occur between the two elements, they are not inherently in opposition. The one does not automatically and completely restrict the freedom of the other.

People are often able to select and recombine their different socialization experiences in individual ways. There is rarely an all-embracing process of socialization that completely stifles the individual's freedom. People are free to choose and to act on that choice. In fact, our legal system is based on the premise that people have individual responsibility and individual freedom of choice. To the extent that we understand the process of socialization we are able to exert substantial control over our lives.

The focus of this chapter has been on the process of socialization. The age-old argument about whether nature or nurture is more important in human development was first explored, and the contributions of both theories were pointed out. Some of the devastating effects of social isolation on human development were then summarized.

The different theoretical perspectives that have been used to study socialization were examined. To summarize: psychoanalysis sees human development as a series of genetically determined stages of unfolding psychosexuality and postulates that personality is made up of the id (biological drives), the ego (reality), and the superego (the conscience). Jean Piaget's theory of the biologically based stages of cognitive development was also explored. The contributions of George Herbert Mead, through the development of symbolic interaction, were noted, particularly his thoughts on the development of self through a series of social stages.

The various agents of socialization—the family, the school, the peer group, and the mass media—were discussed. Finally, various aspects of lifelong socialization and resocialization were detailed.

7

Social Interaction and Social Networks

Social interaction is an ongoing feature of all societies. It is the substance of social life. In this chapter, we will examine how the presence of others affects behavior. We will also examine various theoretical perspectives on social interaction. How reality is constructed during social interaction and the important role played by communication will also be explored. Finally, the structure of social interaction and the resulting social networks will be analyzed.

THE NATURE OF SOCIAL INTERACTION

People "deal" with each other every day. They talk with one another, embrace one another, touch one another. This interaction is at the heart of social life. *Social interaction* refers to people's mutual and reciprocal influence. It implies that individuals take each other into account in their daily behavior, that their behavior is affected by the presence of others. The others exert their influence either by being an "audience" to the behavior or by being "co-actors," co-participants, in it.

Audience Effects

The very presence of others affects behavior. The principle of *audience effects* explains how individuals' work is affected by their knowledge that they are visible to others. In an early study, Zajonc (1965) demonstrates that the presence of others tends to increase the speed at which people perform an activity. However, it also increases the most typical kind of behavior for an individual in that situation. If people are learning a new task (typing, for example), the audience effect will likely result in their typing at a faster rate than if they were alone; but, since errors are typical in learning situations such as this, the presence of others will also increase the frequency of typing mistakes. These results suggest that people should practice new activities alone (to reduce error frequency), but rehearse learned tasks in the presence of others.

Co-action Effects

Not only do people act in the presence of other, but they also act jointly with others. The principle of *co-action effects* describe the influence on people's behavior of others' involvement with them in a similar action. In an early study Sherif (1936) demonstrates the influence of others' involvement in the task of judging the apparent movement of a stationary point of light. Individual judgments were substantially affected by the public judgments expressed by the other co-actors in the experiment.

Focusing on a more socially relevant issue, Darley and Latane (1968) studied bystanders' lack of involvement in emergencies. They demonstrated that subjects in the experiment were considerably less likely to take any action when confronted with a potentially dangerous situation (e.g., smoke coming out from under the door of an adjoining room) when other actors in the situation (actually trained assistants) failed to respond to the impending problem. Apparently, the situation was one in which there was a *diffusion of responsibility*. The presence of co-actors led to a sense of shared obligation for any action, and when the others took no action, the experimental subjects did not feel that they had any special responsibility to do anything.

In short, social interaction, either through the mere presence of others or through joint action, has a significant effect on behavior.

THEORETICAL PERSPECTIVES

Studies on social interaction examine behavior at the micro level. They focus on the mundane actions of people as they go about their daily lives. Four major theoretical perspectives have been used to study social interaction: symbolic interaction, dramaturgy, ethnomethodology, and social exchange. All but dramaturgy were considered briefly at the end of chapter 1.

Symbolic Interaction: Aligning Actions

The key assumption of the symbolic-interactionist approach is that people do not respond directly to the world around them. Rather, they assign meanings to aspects of their environment and then act toward these aspects in light of the assigned meanings. For example, people do not respond to a chair simply as pieces of wood put together in a particular way but rather in terms of their understanding that it is something to sit on. Thus, meaning that organizes the individual's actions is the critical element in the symbolic-interactionist perspective.

DEFINING THE SITUATION

W. I. Thomas (1931) called this important act of attributing meaning in a social context *defining the situation* . He pointed out that the meanings people attribute to the world around them lead them to act in particular ways. For example, paranoid individuals' usually mistaken belief that others are plotting against them leads them to take defensive action. Thomas put this simply: "If men [people] define situations as real, they are real in their consequences." People may rush out to the supermarket to horde food on hearing that there is an impending strike of truckers who bring food to these stores. The information may or may not be correct; however, if people believe that the information is accurate, they will take whatever action they believe is necessary to protect themselves.

How people define situations influences how they will interact with one another. In general, people align their actions with those of others. That is, they try to fit their behavior to the behavior of others so as to accomplish their own ends. This fitting together of "lines of action" gives social life much of its organization. From a symbolic-interactionist perspective, this coordination of action does not automatically flow from the social structure in which people are embedded, as structural-functionalists have argued, but instead from people's need to "negotiate" an order to their lives through common definitions of situations that allow for, and sometimes require, joint action.

In short, social interaction is a series of trial and error actions that test the definitions of the situations held by other actors in the same context. Differences in the definitions may require the actors to revise the meanings they initially attributed to the situation, if the social interaction is to proceed successfully. This adjusting of situational definitions occurs through tentative steps that are influenced and guided by the responses of others. Their response may confirm the current meanings or require them to be reformulated. This entire process is a necessary part of human social interaction.

Dramaturgy: Staging Action

Dramaturgy, as put forth by Goffman (1959), derives from symbolic interaction. If meaning in life is a social construction (not given in nature, but needing to be created and interpreted), the theater (where everything is "staged") is an appropriate model for illustrating social interaction. The use of the language and conceptual framework of the theater to examine social interaction is what Goffman meant by the *dramaturgical approach.*

Individuals play different roles, often in different situations. The concept of role is central to drama. Varying situations suggest the different scenes in which actors are involved. Also, actors also often play to different audiences. For example, some politicians are personally opposed to abortion but respect the law as currently interpreted. In speeches to women's groups such as the National Organization for Women, these politician may emphasize the need to support the current law, while in a speech to a fundamentalist religious gathering they may focus on their personal opposition to abortion.

FRONT- AND BACKSTAGE

Some of the activity involved in putting on a play is not intended for public consumption. For example, rarely is the public invited to see rehearsals. In general, the public is allowed to see only the finished product, and only that action takes place on the stage, not in back of it or in the wings.

In short, there is a *front stage*, where the action that takes place is available to all, and there is a *back stage*, hidden from all but those involved in the "production," where much of the preparatory and supportive activity takes place. Consider a formal dinner party. Usually, the guests are not allowed in the kitchen ("backstage"); they are restricted to the more public areas of the living room and dining room ("front-stage"). Only the most intimate friends are given access to back stage areas, and even they are not always granted such privileges.

PRESENTATION OF SELF

An important element in all social interaction is *impression management,* through which a person adopts an identity or provides identities for others, thereby influencing the outcome of social interaction. Goffman describes this process as a *presentation of self,* the "self" being the identity a person adopts and about which he or she attempts to gain agreement from others in a situation. Presenting different identities in different situations is not a form of dishonesty, unless the person doesn't believe in the identity being presented. Throughout life people are taught to act in ways that are appropriate to the situation. Individuals learn to behave differently in the presence of strangers than they do when they are with close friends or family members. Part of maturing involves learning both the various aspects of our identities and the appropriate ones to display in various situations.

Presenting a particular view of the self often has the effect of limiting others' range of action. For example, if others accept a person's presentation of self as a friend, they are obliged to treat that person as a friend and not as a stranger. Friends are accorded certain privileges that are not available to strangers. In this way, the actions of others are indirectly limited by the identity put forth—to the extent that it is accepted by the others.

ALTERCASTING

Altercasting is a more direct way of limiting the range of behavior of others (Weinstein and Deutschberger, 1963). Here, the other (alter) is presented with (cast into) a particular identity that will constrain behavior. For example, if the other is defined as and accepts the identity of a close friend, it will be difficult to deny a request for a loan, since asking for money is appropriate in such a relationship.

In both forms of impression management, the participating individuals are likely to support the identities offered. Often, all have a stake in maintaining the smooth flow of the interaction in which they are involved. Like good actors in a play, they would like to get through the performance with a minimum of difficulty. Supporting each other's presented identities promises to achieve just that.

The dramaturgical approach attempts to combine a structural view of social interaction with the more flexible approach of symbolic interaction. In other words, while the social structure provides "scripts" that make social life somewhat ordered and predictable, people are capable of improvising, especially in relatively unfamiliar or unusual situations. Life is therefore a blend of predictable order and flexible innovation.

Goffman's perspective has been criticized for appearing to say that people are dishonest in the way they attempt to manage impressions and control access to backstage regions. Goffman makes the point that dishonesty results from presenting a self in which one doesn't believe. People's identities have different facets, and which facet they present depends on the social context.

Also, denying access to a variety of backstage areas is not only a routine part of social life, it is also used to maintain some semblance of privacy—something most people would agree is necessary. In short, Goffman's approach doesn't presuppose a cynical view of human behavior; however, such a description might be appropriate in certain circumstances.

Ethno-methodology: Exposing the Rules

Symbolic interactionists focus on the importance of the meanings people attribute to the social world around them. Dramaturgists add the notion of the individual's sensitivity to the setting of social interaction. The ethnomethodological approach directs attention to the often unanalyzed rules that guide and structure our interactions with others. The focus of this perspective is on the procedures by which people make sense out of social reality. Ethnomethodologists are concerned with common sense understandings of the world.

ASSUMPTIONS

All people have certain expectations about the reality about them. They expect that automobile drivers will stop at a red traffic light; that at a movie theater, the person behind the counter will take their money and give them a ticket that allows them to enter the theater; that when they are talking to someone, the other will wait until they are finished before starting to talk. These routine, taken-for-granted assumptions, according to eth-nomethodologists, smooth the path of social interaction and make social life easier. But how do they arise? How do members of the society come to share them and to rely on them in their daily interactions?

Ethnomethodologists attempt to uncover these underlying assumptions that form the basis of social behavior. One way they do this is by examining what happens when one of these rules is violated. In a classic experiment, Garfinkel (1967) had students act as guests or boarders instead of sons or daughters when they were at home. The students addressed their parents as Mr. and Mrs., politely requested second helpings at the dinner table, and displayed gracious "visitors'" manners. These actions resulted in the complete disorientation of family members, who demanded explanations for their children's surprising behavior.

In short, the violation of normal expectations revealed the presence of a set of rules that governed social interaction but about which the participants were only dimly aware. Only their violation brought them to the surface so that they could be examined.

Social Exchange: Cost/Benefit Analysis

Social exchange has its roots in behavioral psychology and economic analysis. From this perspective, social interaction is a series of exchanges that have both costs and benefits. At a minimum, people expend time and energy in social interaction; these are seen as costs of the activity. Presumably, people also derive benefits from these interchanges, such as joy, affection, jobs, and enhanced self-esteem.

From a social-exchange view, a cost/benefit analysis is essential to understanding social interaction. It presumes a rational approach to maintaining social relationships. There is a presumption that individuals understand the costs involved in their social transactions and the benefits that might be derived. They are then in a position to judge whether they derive some "profit" (benefits minus costs) from the exchange. If they do not, the interaction can be forgone or terminated; if they do, it can be continued.

DISTRIBUTIVE JUSTICE

Homans (1961) introduced the concept of *distributive justice*, the notion that people expect to receive benefits in social interaction that are roughly proportional to the costs they have incurred. This idea is central to the social exchange model. Blau (1964) has argued that people get the relationships they deserve. If individuals want to maintain a particular relationship or social interaction (because it offers certain benefits), they must be prepared to offer their partners in the enterprise what they (the partners) wish in order to persist in the enterprise. In short, if people wish to receive, they must also be prepared to give.

The early work of Homans (1950, 1961) and Gouldner (1960) highlights the importance of reciprocity in social exchange, the assumption that social norms require that a favor be returned by a favor. This view assumes that social interaction involves some kind of social balance sheet. Benefits given must at some point be reciprocated at similar, though not necessarily identical, value. Reciprocity is seen as an essential norm of social life and an important guide for social interaction.

THE SOCIAL CONSTRUCTION OF REALITY

From a sociological, and especially symbolic-interactionist, point of view, people create and shape the nature of their own social worlds. This process is referred to as the *social construction of reality* . Each society constructs its own version of the world, its "truths." In some societies the guiding forces of the world are seen as supernatural; in others they are the impersonal forces of nature. Some individuals structure their lives around their belief in a personal deity, a god who knows their every thought and action and who responds to them in terms of this knowledge. For others no such supreme being exists. Different versions of reality are not limited to weighty issues like religion. They also come into play in everyday events in people's lives.

Defining the Situation

Earlier in this chapter, Thomas's concept of "defining the situation" was discussed. Thomas argued that people act in terms of their conception of reality. For example, there was a time when the earth was generally considered flat, and thus no one sailed to its "end." The idea that the earth was flat led to behavior based on that belief. Our knowledge that the earth is not flat and that it wasn't flat even when people believed it was flat is irrelevant to our understanding of people's behavior at that time.

On a smaller scale, social interaction is guided by how people define a situation. If they believe that the other participants are hostile to them, they will behave with that in mind. They will create a mini environment, a social reality, that conforms to their definition of the situation.

The Process of Social Construction

Sociologists' understanding of how reality is socially constructed was advanced significantly by Berger and Luckmann (1963), who concluded that the process takes place in three stages.

PEOPLE CREATE THE CULTURE

This notion was discussed earlier in chapter 3 in the context of material and nonmaterial cultures. People create the material artifacts of a culture, such as automobiles, television sets, airplanes, clothing, and washing machines, as well as its nonmaterial elements, such as norms, values, and cognitive beliefs.

CULTURAL CREATIONS BECOME REALITY

After a while, these cultural creations are seen as a positive, natural, and inevitable part of the social landscape. They are taken for granted by most people; few today look up in astonishment when airplanes fly overhead or are surprised to see flush toilets in homes.

PEOPLE ABSORB THIS REALITY

The socialization process (see chapter 6) causes individuals to adopt their culture's perception of reality. As a consequence, few question the source or validity of these beliefs or the inevitability and usefulness of the material culture. Robertson (1987:161–164) shows how even the basic concepts of "space" and "time" are changing social constructions. For example, the geocentric view of the solar system (the idea that the earth is the center of the solar system) gave way to a heliocentric view (the sun is the center of the solar system), and the concept of the atom as the smallest unit of matter gave way to the more recent understanding of subatomic particles. Even perceptions of distance changed when technology advanced from sailpowered boats to turbine-driven boats and from propellered airplanes to jet planes to spaceships. Conceptions of time are socially constructed (Zeruvabel, 1981). What, after all, is "natural" about a "week" or an "hour"?

At a more intimate level, social interaction itself is part of the process by which social reality is created and shaped. Each participant in a situation has a particular definition of it. Through social interaction, these differing definitions are negotiated, and some agreement is reached, if the interaction is to be maintained (what Goffman called arriving at a *working consensus*), about the nature of social reality in the relevant circumstance. Thus in everyday behavior individuals construct and reconstruct the social reality in which they function. The ethnomethodologists, it will be recalled, continually focus attention on this important social process.

COMMUNICATION AND
SOCIAL INTERACTION

Communication (see chapter 3) is the vehicle for social interaction. People talk to each other, smile at one another, touch one another. Social interaction must be transacted through some medium, and that medium is communication. Hartley and Hartley (1961:16) wrote:

> The importance of communication in the study of social processes would be difficult to overemphasize. Because communication is the means by which one person influences another, and in turn is influenced by him, it is the actual carrier of social process. *It makes interaction possible* [emphasis supplied].

Social Networks: The Structure of Social Interaction

STRUCTURED SOCIAL INTERACTION

Social interaction does not occur completely at random. Most interchanges occur as a consequence of some existing relationship between individuals. These connections may be built into the statuses people occupy and the roles they play (see chapter 4). Directly relevant is Merton's (1957:368–384) concept of the *role set* , the set of relationships a person has as a consequence of occupying a particular social status. For example, the elementary school teacher is automatically involved in a set of relationships with students, parents of students, fellow teachers, and school administrators. These relationships constitute a structure of social relationships that the person automatically inherits by becoming an elementary school teacher. The characters of the relationships may vary from one teacher to another, but all teachers are bound into this set of relationships by virtue of their occupation.

Individuals occupy multiple statuses (see chapter 4) and thus are involved in a number of role sets. These role sets and status sets often determine social interaction. Individuals interact most often with relatives, co-workers (or fellow students), and friends. While some interaction occurs by accident (for example, when someone strikes up a conversation with a fellow vacationer), most occurs along these structured channels.

SOCIAL NETWORKS

Social interaction can also result in new social relationships. A person's web of social relationships is called a *social network* . Social networks are composed of relationships of differing degrees of intimacy and connection. Some of the relationships are relatively close and important (e.g., friends); these have the characteristics of primary ties. Others may be secondary (e.g., acquaintances); these involve more casual and superficial bonds.

The web of social relationships. Network analysis is a distinctly sociological way of examining social relationships. It is based on the notion that structural patterns of relationships are more important than the personal characteristics of the individuals involved. Network analysts argue that they can provide explanations for events that are not otherwise easily understood. For example, Granovetter (1973) has demonstrated that the failure of a particular community to organize and protect itself against an unwanted urban renewal program was not because its members were uninterested, apathetic or incompetent. Rather, he argues, their inability to stop the program stemmed from the particular kind of networks that existed in the community. The community under study was made up of a number of small, self-contained networks; there were few links of communication between them. Thus communitywide organizing became difficult, and the leverage that such a comprehensive effort might have had was never available. Network analysis focused on the community structure that prevented its organizing despite the motivation of individuals in the community.

The characteristics of networks. Networks have certain characteristics whose examination enhances an understanding of social behavior: density, reachability, and range.

Density refers to the percentage of all possible links that might be created among network members that are actually established. People's sense of "community" often depends on the degree to which they are involved in dense networks. In such networks, many people are "connected" to others, have some sort of relationship with a number of others, and feel the support that such dense links confer.

Networks can also be described in terms of their *reachability*, which refers to the number of links between any two individuals in a network. The higher the density, the greater the reachability, since in a high–density network there are more links to any individual than in low networks. In a 1967 study, Milgram showed that people live in a smaller, denser world than they generally realize. Subjects in the Midwest were given the names of people on the East Coast whom they did not know. The subjects' assignment was to see to it that these people received a booklet that the subjects had been given. To achieve this, each subject was to send the booklet, along with a target person's name, to someone he or she was personally acquainted with. This person, in turn, was to send the booklet and name to someone he or she knew, and so on until the booklet reached someone who knew the target person. On average it took only about five to eight links to complete the task. This ingenious experiment made it clear that national networks exist. Because of them, many people are within relatively easy reach of each other—though they often don't realize it.

It is also possible to characterize networks in terms of their *range*, the number of direct contacts that any individual has within a specific network. Range is also related to density. The more dense a network, the more likely any individual is to have a relatively wide range of links. Individuals with a wide range are often seen as important; they have the "contacts."

The use of social networks. Social networks have been used in various types of sociological analyses. They help the analyst get at the web of intricate social relationships that are the heart of social life. One dramatic use of network analysis involved disentangling the complex process by means of which individuals go about finding a job. In general, network analysts have found that network ties are of considerable importance in the job-seeking process. Their studies support the observation that "it is not what you know, but who you know that counts."

In a 1973 paper, Granovetter focused on the strength of ties in networks. The strength of a tie depends on the "amount of time, the emotional intensity, the intimacy (mutual confiding), and the reciprocal services which characterize the tie" (p. 1361). Granovetter demonstrated that contrary to expectations, strong ties are not necessarily better than "weak" ties. Weak ties give people more freedom of action than strong ties. Strong ties create substantial social pressures on the individual and hence are more restricting. Even in communities, strong ties within separate networks may limit community integration and increase fragmentation.

Granovetter argues that networks are complex social structures that serve as a link between micro- and macro-levels of analysis. In Granovetter's words (1973:1360):

The analysis of processes in interpersonal networks provides the most fruitful micro-macro bridge. In one way or another, it is through these networks that small-scale interaction becomes translated into large-scale patterns [e.g., diffusion, social mobility, political organization, and social cohesion], and that these, in turn, feed back into small groups.

The presence of others affects behavior differently if the others are merely an audience rather than co-participants in social interaction. In the first case, they often merely speed up the existing behavior. In the second, they have a wider effect: they allow for a diffusion of responsibility that may lead to nonaction.

Four different theoretical perspectives on social interaction were described. Symbolic interaction defines the meaning of the social situation and aligns the actions of the co-participants. Dramaturgy deals with the staging of action—creating the social setting in which interaction takes place and the management of impressions (presentation of self and alter-casting) during the interchange. Ethnomethodology aims to expose the underlying rules and often unstated assumptions that guide social interaction. Social exchange focuses on a cost/benefit analysis of social interaction; we remain in only those situations in which the benefits outweigh the costs.

The importance of the social construction of the reality within which interaction takes place was discussed. This social construction includes the creation of culture, its incorporation into the overall reality, and the learning and acceptance of that reality. Communication as the major vehicle for social interaction was mentioned.

The structure of interaction was the last issue in this chapter. The role set is an important element in organizing social interaction. The result of this structure is the social network, the web of social relationships. Networks have density, reachability, and range. They are an increasingly useful analytic tool in sociology, particularly in linking micro- and macro-levels of sociological analysis.

8

Deviance and Social Control

---

*T*his chapter focuses on both legal and social deviance and on various explanations for each. The types and frequencies of crimes, and the components of the criminal justice system will be described and the social implications of deviance assessed.

WHAT IS DEVIANCE?

Most people conform to the norms of society most of the time. They do so because of the socialization process they have experienced and because of the structures of social control (e.g., laws, police) in society. But what about those people who do not conform? What causes their behavior, and how should society respond to them?

Legal Definition

All societies condemn certain behaviors. Murder, rape, incest, treason, and theft are generally considered reprehensible in most societies. In advanced industrial societies, these actions are prohibited by formal legal codes and there are penalties for engaging in them. Such actions are called *crimes* ; that is, they are considered *legally deviant*. In addition to these more serious crimes, many societies also consider other behaviors to be violations of legal norms; these include such actions as disobeying traffic laws, disturbing the peace, carrying a concealed weapon, and, more recently, entering, modifying or erasing computer records of others.

Juvenile delinquency refers to the violation of legal norms by those who are below the age at which the law treats people as adults. In addition to laws defining certain acts as crimes no matter who commits them, there are others that are specifically related to age. "Ungovernability" and "truancy" are among the behaviors that will bring young people but not adults into contact with the police and the courts.

Criminal deviance exists across the world, despite the fact that the specific legal norms defining unacceptable behavior may vary from one society to another. In the United States, criminal law is enacted by the various states as well as by the federal government. Thus what may be a crime in one state (for example, purchasing a hand gun) may not be considered a crime in another. What is considered deviance in the legal sense, then, varies not only from society to society but also from area to area within large industrial societies.

Social Definitions

Crime is easy to define as a deviant form of behavior. More difficult to define are those forms of behavior that are considered to be *socially deviant*, that is, that violate social norms but not the legal code. To give two examples: until recently, wearing earrings was considered inappropriate for men. And, in the 1960s and 1970s, many young men broke with convention and defiantly wore their hair long, and youth in general dressed in distinctly more casual clothes (often old jeans and T-shirts) than was considered appropriate. In the context of the times, such behaviors were considered to be socially deviant; they did not conform to the general norms of society but were not a sufficient threat to the social order to be defined as criminal.

Explaining Deviance

Explanations of why people engage in deviant acts have ranged from the biological and psychological to the more sociological. These different explanations stem from different assumptions not only about the causes of human behavior but also about how deviant behavior might be changed. Consequently, these different perspectives will be discussed separately.

BIOLOGICAL AND PSYCHOLOGICAL EXPLANATIONS

At one time, supernatural forces were thought to be the cause of deviant behavior. People acted in irrational ways because they were possessed by the "devil" or by "bad spirits." In the nineteenth century, this explanation gradually gave way to what was considered a more "scientific" approach, based on the knowledge of biology at that time.

The foremost explanation of this type, though not the first, was put forth by Cesare Lombroso (1876; 77), a physician who worked in Italian prisons. He subjected prisoners to all sorts of physical measurements and determined that they had distinctive physical features: low forehead, protruding jaw, prominent cheekbones, large ears that stuck out, and considerable bodily hair. In short, Lombroso believed that criminals were "atavistic," that they were biologically underdeveloped from an evolutionary perspective. The work of Lombroso was seriously flawed. Using more carefully designed research, Charles Goring (1913), a British psychiatrist, found that the characteristics Lombroso attributed to criminals were also present in noncriminals. Goring argued that there are no essential physical differences between the criminal and noncriminal populations.

Nevertheless, the idea that criminals are a distinct physical type continued to crop up. In 1949 Sheldon argued that "body type" was related to criminality. He described the criminal as likely to be a *mesomorph* (muscular and athletic) rather than either an *ectomorph* (tall, thin, and fragile) or an *endomorph* (short and fat). The general outlines of Sheldon's position were supported by the research of the Gluecks (1950), though they argued that body type is not a direct cause of criminality. In their view, mesomorphs have a personality type (insensitive to others and likely to react to frustration with aggressive behavior) that might lead them into criminal acts. Thus, they concluded, the relationship between physical characteristics and criminality is an indirect one.

Recently some investigators have argued that violent criminal behavior may result when a person has a chromosomal pattern containing an extra male chromosome (XYY) rather than the standard number (XY). The XYY pattern was found to be more prevalent among male criminals than among males in the general population. But the number of subjects studied was too small to establish a link between the presence of an extra male chromosome and criminal behavior with any degree of confidence. Recently Wilson and Herrnstein (1985) concluded that biological factors have a negligible effect on criminal behavior and that the social environment plays a key role in either facilitating or inhibiting any influence biological characteristics may have on such behavior.

SOCIOLOGICAL EXPLANATIONS: MICROLEVEL THEORIES

Differential association. The key idea behind *differential association theory* (Sutherland, 1940) is that criminality is learned in the course of socialization. Through interaction with "significant others," individuals develop the kinds of beliefs, attitudes, and values that make them more or less willing to conform to social norms. Whether or not people engage in criminal acts largely depends on the nature of the influence and the amount of time they spend with others who support and model deviant behavior.

In differential association theory, criminality is a routine outcome of the presence of a deviant subculture through which people learn norms and behaviors that lead them into antisocial acts. This explanation is a straightforward use of learning theory in the context of socialization. What distinguishes the criminal from the noncriminal is not the process of socialization but its content; *what* is learned, not *how* it is learned. All people may learn values and norms that might be termed antisocial; what matters is the frequency of contact with these values and norms, as well as their intensity. Another factor is age. Young people have little experience with which to evaluate or put into context these ideas and behaviors. They are more vulnerable to all kinds of influence, including those leading to delinquent behavior.

This theory has also been used to explain the persistence of criminality in particular communities or neighborhoods (Shaw and McKay, 1942). Once deviant subcultures develop, their values, attitudes, norms, techniques, and behaviors become available to others in the community through their being modeled by criminals. Moreover, these values and behaviors are transmitted to future generations through socialization. In this manner, particular communities become breeding grounds for criminal behavior for generation after generation.

While the notion that criminal behavior is learned like any form of behavior has gained wide acceptance, differential association theory has been viewed as incomplete. Nowhere does this theory address the issue of why certain activities get defined as criminal. Any comprehensive theory must address that issue as well.

Control theory. Walter Reckless and his colleagues (1956) focused on the issue of why, even in high-crime areas, some youths do not become delinquents. They argue that a person's development of a "good" self-image serves to "insulate" him or her from the surrounding delinquent subculture.

The more general point of *control theory* is that criminal behavior results from a lack of internal control by the individual and of appropriate and effective external control by society. Central to this view is the idea that what needs to be explained is not deviance but "conformity." Conformity is seen to result from internal and external control mechanisms. But what are these mechanisms of social control?

Building on Durkheim's theory, control theorists argue that community integration and strong social bonds lead people to accept and conform to the norms and values of their community. Hirschi (1969) advanced the idea that strong social bonds have four defining characteristics.

Attachment involves substantial links to particular individuals in the community. Connections to specific others induces people to take the feelings and concerns of these others into account, making them more likely to act in "responsible" ways.

Commitment, or people's investment in society, tempers their behavior. In the 1960s, one rallying cry of those promoting social change was "don't trust anyone over thirty." The belief underlying this slogan was that people over the age of thirty were likely to have families and full-time jobs, giving them a stake in the existing system and thus making them less likely to wish to change it. They were more likely than younger people to conform to existing social norms and values.

Involvement in and with nondeviant activities and people, Hirschi argued, leaves less time for delinquent behavior.

Shared *belief* systems bind together members of the community and strengthen their resistance to deviant actions.

While control theory is a useful supplement to differential association theory in its highlighting of the importance of internal controls and of the social integration of the community, it too is incomplete. Control theory, for example, seems unable to explain *white collar crime*—criminal activities (e.g., embezzlement) by high-status, seemingly "respectable" people who are well integrated into their communities. Nor does it help explain the behavior of those well integrated into deviant subcultures, where the strong social bonds and social norms are not viewed favorably by the larger society.

Thus the issue is not only community integration but also the nature of that community's belief system. Strong community ties within a deviant subculture may well contribute to deviant behavior. Control theory doesn't address why people engage in one form of deviance rather than another. Finally, the lack of integration of individuals into their community may be either a cause or an effect of their deviant behavior. In short, control theory plays a part in the explanation of deviance but cannot stand alone.

SOCIOLOGICAL EXPLANATIONS: MACROLEVEL THEORIES

Structural strain. Some explanations of deviance focus on large scale social forces. One such theory stresses Durkheim's concept of *anomie*, which refers to a situation in which the typical norms that guide behavior are no longer appropriate or effective. The effect of anomie is to reduce society's ability to structure appropriate behavior. On this basis, Merton (1938) argues that deviance arises from a *structural strain* that results from the lack of a clear relationship between culturally supported *goals* and societally provided *means* to attain those goals. The effect of this mismatch is that while individuals learn through the process of socialization what the society expects of them (its goals), they are often unable to accomplish those aims because of the lack of adequate means. For example, in the United States, people are expected to be successful occupationally and financially. But not all people can be "successful" in those terms. Some individuals without the means to attain either higher education or specialized training are less likely to be "successful." This condition leads to a sense of anomie.

Merton defines four types of deviant adaptations. In one, *innovation*, a person accepts the standard cultural goals but does not accept the socially sanctioned means of obtaining these goals (e.g., the person using "insider information" to trade in stocks and bonds). Another, *ritualism*, refers to situations in which persons who do not accept or seem to understand the cultural goal still act in socially approved ways (e.g., the stereotypical bureaucrat who is more intent on making sure that all the proper forms are filled out than on achieving the purpose of the forms). *Retreatism* describes the situation of the person who has abandoned both the culturally approved goals and the means (e.g., the vagrant, the drop-out). Finally, *rebellion* is a mode of adaptation whereby the person fails to accept culturally approved goals and means and substitutes other goals and means (e.g., the revolutionary, or Rosa Parks, the civil rights protester).

According to structural strain theory, the source of difficulty is in the social structure and culture, not in the individual. Thus it is particularly useful in explaining deviance in the lower class (see chapter 9), in which socially acceptable avenues for success are less available. Also, structural strain theory more effectively explains specific deviant behaviors (e.g., those involving theft) than deviance in general. However, it is less helpful in understanding noncriminal social deviance or "white collar" crime.

Capitalism and conflict theory. The roots of conflict theory are derived from the Marxist view that *capitalism*, an economic system characterized by private rather than government ownership of the means of production, distribution, and exchange of wealth, is the source of crime. Since control over necessary resources is not equally distributed, capitalism induces people to engage in criminal behavior either to obtain what they believe they should have (the "exploited" worker) or to maintain or expand what they have acquired (the capitalist). This conflict stems directly from the competitiveness built into capitalism, with its stress on profits, and from the inability of workers to attain the income necessary to maintain at least a minimal level of existence.

Quinney (1974; 1980) argues that capitalists control the legal system; they define as crimes anything that would threaten the privileges and properties they have accumulated through capitalism. From this perspective, even those crimes that seem petty (e.g., gambling, drinking, engaging in illicit sex) are viewed as threatening the values of hard work and sobriety that underpin a capitalist structure.

Similarly, Spitzer (1980) points out that control over the legal apparatus by capitalists allows them to use it to control those who threaten the functioning of capitalism. For example, he argues that since those who steal threaten the property of the rich, that behavior is likely to be defined as criminal. Further, he proposes that capitalists also play a key role in defining as socially deviant those who will not supply the labor needed to make the capitalist machinery hum or who do not show proper respect for authority, an important requirement in hierarchal capitalist organizations. On the other hand, those whose behavior supports or exemplifies the capitalist approach (e.g., the rugged individualists involved in competitive athletics) are held up as the models with which the deviant is contrasted.

The conflict approach to deviance suggests ways in which the economic structure of society influences the political sphere, especially in defining certain acts as criminal or otherwise deviant. Like the structural strain theory, it locates the source of deviant behavior within the social structure and not within the individual.

However, it too has certain limitations. Conflict theory assumes that the rich are all-powerful; that they are free to define anything they wish as criminal or deviant. This approach ignores consumer or worker protection laws that restrict the freedom of action of capitalists.

Also, the "capitalist" class is not in complete agreement on what its interests are and how to protect them. If this were not true, it is unlikely that there would be antitrust laws that restrict some companies from controlling events to their liking.

Another problem with conflict theory is that it ignores deviance in societies that do not have substantial inequality. Crime and deviance exist even in socialist countries that have sharply reduced inequalities among their members.

Like the other theories about the causes of crime, the conflict perspective adds to our knowledge about deviance but is not a complete explanation.

Labeling theory. One of the most popular explanations of deviance today is *labeling theory*, which sees deviance as the inability to categorize certain actions as appropriate or inappropriate. While similar to the conflict theory of deviance, it is based less on the economic sphere than on the power of individuals or groups to label behavior.

The basic argument put forth by labeling theorists (e.g., Lemert, 1951; Erikson, 1962; Becker, 1963) is that no behavior is inherently and automatically deviant. Deviance requires definition. Different societies (and different groups within a society) label different acts as deviant. In the United States, for example, walking the streets in tattered clothing mumbling about the glory of God will likely subject a person to ridicule or earn him or her a stay in jail or a mental institution. In other societies, the same act might inspire respect because of its religious nature.

Equally important to this theory is that while all people occasionally engage in acts that are defined by their society (or group) as deviant, these deviant acts are not always observed, or if they are observed they are seen as temporary misbehaviors. This is called *primary deviance*. What is critical to labeling theory is not the act itself, but *secondary deviance*, its public labeling as deviant and the offending person's consequent acceptance of a deviant identity. This acceptance may be regarded as a *stigma*, a potent negative view that substantially changes a person's sense of self and thus leads her or him into a "deviant career" (Goffman, 1963). An act of secondary deviance can also lead to a *retrospective labeling* of a person's past identity to make it conform to the present identity.

Labeling theory has been used to explain both criminality and social deviance. The issue of identity is essential to the labeling perspective, which has roots in symbolic interaction theory. The deviant act is less important than its being labeled as deviant. In turn, that label affects the person's sense of identity, which may lead to further deviant acts.

Labeling theory links micro and macro approaches to deviance. The definitions of deviance reside in cultural definitions (macro). But the applications of those definitions take place through face-to-face interaction with others and play a significant role in individual identity (micro). This approach is useful in exposing deviance as a *social* process rather than a *moral* process—some people have the power to enforce their views of appropriate behavior on others. It is also a useful way of looking at behaviors defined as violations of both legal and social norms.

Labeling theory has some limitations. Research shows that some criminals engage in criminal practices (e.g., shoplifting) even though they are not caught and never subjected to an identity based on secondary deviance (Gove, 1980). For some, being labeled a deviant is a powerful incentive to change the behavior rather than continue it. Finally, there are people in jail (e.g., rapists, contract killers) and in various types of mental institutions because their behavior is a threat to themselves or others and not because their actions have been arbitrarily defined as wrong by those in authority.

Crime

Crimes are violations of legal codes. Some are more serious than others. Some actions defined as crimes in one society may not be in another society. In the vast United States, what is considered criminal behavior might vary from state to state. However, it is possible to classify types of crimes in ways that permit analysis of crime in different locations and at different times.

TYPES OF CRIME

There are many ways to categorize criminal behavior. For example, the Federal Bureau of Investigation (FBI) uses what it calls *index crimes* to examine the frequency and distribution, and changes in both, of serious crimes in its annual *Uniform Crime Reports for the United States*. The seven index crimes are murder, rape, assault, robbery, burglary, larceny, and automobile theft. Clearly, a number of important crimes (e.g., drug possession, stock manipulation) do not show up in the FBI reports. Consequently, sociologists tend to use a scheme that is more theoretically focused to describe different types of crime.

Crimes against the person (crimes of violence). These are crimes that involve violence or the threat of violence against persons. They are the crimes that contribute to the growing unease in American society, the feeling of many that they are not safe in the streets or even in their own homes.

Violent crimes include *homicide* ("the willful killing of one human being by another"), *aggravated assault* ("an unlawful attack by one person on another for the purposes of inflicting severe bodily harm"), *forcible rape*, and *robbery*.

Crimes against property. Some crimes involve the taking of something of value that belongs to someone else. These crimes include *larceny-theft* ("the unlawful taking, carrying, leading, or riding away of property from the possession of another"), *automobile theft*, *burglary* ("the unlawful entry of a structure to commit a crime"), and *arson* ("any willful or malicious burning [of] or attempt to burn the personal property of another").

"Victimless" crimes. Some offenses are acts that have no apparent victim, no one to lodge a complaint as would the victim of a theft or an assault. Crimes without apparent victims include *gambling, public drunkenness, prostitution, illegal drug use, homosexuality between consenting adults,* and *adultery*. Not all of these are crimes everywhere; for example, gambling is legal in Las Vegas and Atlantic City.

White collar and corporate crimes. Earlier, white collar crime was defined as violations of the law by middle and upper class individuals in the context of their jobs. Some of these crimes could be categorized as "crimes against property" (e.g., *embezzlement* and *fraud*), but their close connection to the everyday work activities of the criminal seems to warrant separating them. These crimes also include *false advertising claims, stock and bond manipulation, price-fixing, price-gouging, anticompetitive action to form monopolies, environmental pollution,* and *selling ineffective or harmful food or drugs*. These activities began to be considered crimes around the latter part of the nineteenth century; before that, most corporations (and individuals) pursued their business interests in a relatively unrestricted manner.

CRIME STATISTICS

The statistical accumulation of information about crime has been very useful in clarifying the characteristics of criminals. It also has allowed criminologists to examine the kinds and frequencies of criminal acts over time and in different places.

Characteristics of criminals. It is surprisingly difficult to identify the types of persons who commit crimes. Many crimes go unreported, often because victims do not want to be identified or caught up in the bureaucracy. In fact, the United States Department of Justice estimates that there might be three times as much crime as is reported. Most statistics on criminals pertain to those who have been caught, and in some cases only to those who have been convicted. In short, the data on criminals are such that characterizations of the kinds of people who commit crimes must be tentative.

Age is related to crime. Criminals tend to be relatively young; most are in their teens and early twenties. This age group accounts for more than 40 percent of all violent crimes and about half of all crimes against property. White collar crimes, on the other hand, are more likely to be committed by those who are considerably older.

Gender is also related to crime. Men are about four times more likely than women to commit crimes against property and about nine times more likely to commit violent crimes. This difference between crime rates is due to several factors. Some crimes are automatically linked to gender; rape is basically a male offense and prostitution a female offense. Also, law enforcement agents are often more reluctant to label women criminals than they are men. As men's and women's rights become more equal, the difference in their crime rates might decline (Adler and Adler, 1979).

Social class plays a role in crime. A higher proportion of criminals are from the lower class than from the middle and upper classes. However, victims of crimes also come disproportionately from the lower class. Furthermore, people from the lower class are more likely to be arrested and convicted than those from the other social classes. Social class is also a factor in the different types of crime committed. "Street" crimes (e.g., robbery, assault) are more likely to be committed by criminals from the lower class. White collar crime, on the other hand, is more frequent among those from the middle and upper classes.

Race is overwhelmingly implicated in crime. African Americans are much more frequently arrested than their proportion in population. In 1986, when they constituted about 12 percent of the population, they accounted for about 28 percent of arrests for all serious crimes, 33 percent for crimes against property, and 45 percent for crimes against the person (U.S. Federal Bureau of Investigation, 1987). However, the majority of all criminals are white. There is also a relationship between social class and race that affects the crime rate. African Americans are more frequently arrested and convicted than are whites. Also, African Americans are less likely than whites to commit white collar crimes. Yet these statistics are not factored into the FBI reports that are used in statistical analyses of crime.

The variety and frequency of crime. Data on the frequencies of the major forms of criminal behaviors are based on reported crimes; however, as stated above, many crimes go unreported. Also, since these data are based only on those categories used in the FBI's *Uniform Crime Reports*, i.e., on index crimes, there is inadequate information on national rates of white collar and victimless crimes.

Crimes against property occur almost ten times more often than crimes against people. Among property crimes, larceny-theft is by far the most recorded act, followed by burglaries and then by auto thefts. Aggravated

Type of Crime (FBI Index)	Number Reported
Crimes against the Person	
Murder and nonnegligent manslaughter	18,980
Forcible rape	87,340
Aggravated assault	725,250
Robbery	497,870
Total:	1,327,446
Crimes against Property	
Burglary	3,073,300
Larceny-theft	6,926,400
Motor vehicle theft	1,102,900
Total:	11,102,600

Table 8.1 Frequency of Different Types of Crime, 1985.

Source: U.S. Federal Bureau of Investigation, Uniform Crime Reports for the United States, 1985, Washington, D.C.: U.S.G.P.O., 1986, Table 1, p. 41.

assault and robbery are the two most frequently committed violent acts, followed by forcible rape and homicide. (See Table 8.1)

Increasing crime is evident over the past ten years, both for property crimes and violent crimes. What has led to this increase? In part it is due to the effects of drugs and the greater availability of guns. However, a worsening economic situation, an increase in the rate of homelessness, and the increasing acceptance of violent images in the media also play a role in the rising crime rate. Also, the social climate in the country influences the amount of crime, as does geographical location.

Crimes are more frequent in metropolitan regions than in smaller urban, suburban, and rural regions. Though the sheer numbers of people in metropolitan regions have contributed to this difference, even the *rates* of crime, which take population into account, show the same effect. Wealth is concentrated in metropolitan regions making them attractive targets of criminal behavior; these areas also have higher concentrations of youth and drug users, who are more likely to commit crimes. Also, the anonymity of the metropolis weakens the kinds of social controls that serve to reduce crime in more tightly-knit communities.

Crime varies between societies as well as within a society. The United States has one of the highest crime rates among the industrialized societies of the world. Several factors have been suggested as explanations. Emphasis on individual success, high rates of social and geographical mobility (which reduces social controls), and great disparities of wealth are among the known factors.

THE CRIMINAL JUSTICE SYSTEM

There are many elements of society that play roles in identifying and dealing with crime. Taken together, these make up the *criminal justice system.*

The police. The individual's initial point of contact with the criminal justice system is typically the *police*, the social agency charged with maintaining public order by enforcing the law and acting to prevent crime. The police must ultimately be selective in their activities. In some communities, they may stress deterrence as well as enforcement; in others, the sheer amount of crime overwhelms them and only enforcement is possible. Even then, they often focus on only the most serious crimes. Additionally, social and economic considerations influence how the police carry out their mandated role.

The courts. Those arrested are brought into contact with another element of the criminal justice system, the courts. Here, those charged with crimes begin their involvement in an *adversarial system* , in which lawyers for the defense and for the government (the prosecution) battle to establish the legitimacy of their position on the guilt or innocence of the accused. Increasingly, because of the high volume of cases, this process results in *plea bargaining*, a negotiation to reduce the level of the criminal charge in return for an admission of guilt to the lesser charge.

For many, plea bargaining undermines the basic philosophy of American justice of presumed innocent until proven guilty. However, the impossible work load of the courts is generally considered adequate justification for entering into a plea bargain.

Probation. Persons convicted of a crime do not necessarily go to prison. One alternative is *probation*, in which they remain "free" but are subject to a number of restrictions for a defined period of time. Typically, they must not have any contact with known criminals or possess weapons; they must maintain their roots in a community and show responsibility through gainful employment. Probationers report to a probation officer, an agent of the court, on a periodic basis to ensure their compliance with the conditions of their parole. Recently, technological advances have been used to monitor compliance. For example, electronic devices (often in the form of a bracelet) can be worn by probationers to signal their location.

Probation for those involved in less serious crimes and for those who seem less likely to be involved in further criminal behavior is an alternative to prison. Currently, because of overcrowding of the jails, it is used more frequently.

Correctional institutions. A person convicted of a crime and not placed on probation is placed in a correctional institution. There are various forms of correctional institutions, including jails for those awaiting trial and maximum security prisons for those convicted of serious violent crimes. Correctional institutions serve several different functions.

Incarceration is the confining or locking up of criminals. Incarceration is used both to punish the criminal and to protect society. However, prisons are notorious for the crime that takes place *within* them. Drug abuse, robbery, aggravated assault, homosexual rape, and murder occur in prisons.

Retribution is another punitive function of incarceration. Most people believe that criminals should be punished for their behavior. Revenge for wrongdoing is seen as restoring a moral balance for the injury suffered by victims.

Deterrence, the notion that punishment prevents crime, is another rationale for imprisonment. However, imprisonment apparently does *not* serve as a deterrent to the convicted criminal. Considerable research has shown that about two-thirds to three-quarters of all released convicts become *recidivists* within four years; that is, they are rearrested for additional crimes after leaving prison. In fact, prisons can be training grounds for learning or improving techniques of criminal behavior; they also serve as places where people in the criminal subculture can make contact. Nor is it clear that imprisonment deters others from committing crimes.

Rehabilitation, the attempt to reform offenders and make their behavior conform to general social norms, is the final reason offered for imprisoning criminals. Rehabilitation includes psychological counseling, educational programs, and vocational training and guidance. Rehabilitation has not proved to be very effective, as evidenced by the high rate of recidivism. However, this lack of success is partly due to the relatively low investment in rehabilitation programs during or after the prison term. Only about 4 to 5 percent of the budgets of correctional facilities is devoted to rehabilitation.

Parole. Some prisoners are released from prison before the end of their maximum sentence on the condition that they behave themselves and remain under the guidance and custody of a parole officer. Like probationers, parolees are subject to restrictions and must report regularly to their parole officers. Actions that violate the conditions of the parole will send a parolee back to jail to serve out his or her original sentence. Theoretically, prisoners are selected for parole because they do not seem as likely to commit crimes upon their release.

THE CAPITAL PUNISHMENT CONTROVERSY

The death penalty is a continuing source of controversy in American society. Capital punishment was struck down by the Supreme Court in 1972 and restored in 1976 with the qualification that the trial courts consider whether there are any "mitigating" circumstances, conditions that would justify a less severe punishment.

Those who support capital punishment argue that it is an appropriate moral retribution for a terrible act, that it serves as a deterrent to others who might consider committing the same crime, and that it protects the society from the particular individual who committed the crime.

Opponents of capital punishment counter by pointing out that one moral wrong does not justify another and that the death penalty does not act as a general deterrent because most murders are crimes of passion, not rational acts of which the killers calculate the consequences. Also, comparing the murder rates in states with and without capital punishment does not support the conclusion that the death penalty acts as a deterrent. Further, the limitations of any judicial system make it almost a certainty that some innocent people will be convicted of capital offenses and therefore put to death. Also, there is an apparent bias in invoking the death penalty when the defendant is African American rather than white, male rather than female, and poor rather than rich or when the victim is white.

THE SOCIAL IMPLICATIONS OF DEVIANCE

Sociologists do not see deviance as an attribute of the person; it is the label conferred on a particular behavior through social processes. When these processes are codified and enforced by the state, we call their violation a "crime." Other less clearly formulated social definitions often cause various forms of behavior to be seen as "peculiar," "odd-ball," "different," or "crazy." These behaviors often lead people to avoid the person associated with them or to insist that the offending person's actions be restricted in some way.

Social Stigma

A number of forms of noncriminal deviant behavior carry with them a social *stigma*, a potent negative identity. In our society, mental illness carries such a stigma, as do gross physical deformities, disabilities, and even medical disorders (e.g., AIDS). Compulsive behavior, whether it involves gambling, using drugs or eating, is often defined as deviant and therefore stigmatizes the person engaging in it. In short, unconventional people are seen as deviant. Defining unconventional people as "deviant" rather than as "different" seriously affects how others treat such individuals and, inevitably, how persons so defined come to view themselves.

Deviance and Society

Durkheim (1938; original, 1895) points out that deviance exists in all societies. He argues that far from being abnormal, deviance is a necessary feature of all societies and serves several important functions. Social definitions of deviance mark the *boundaries of permissible behavior*, thus clarifying what the society thinks is right and proper action. Labeling acts as deviant also *strengthens the moral force of the behavior* seen as socially acceptable. Also, society's response to deviant behavior often *enhances social solidarity* by unifying people behind that response.

Deviance may also serve society by leading to social change. Deviance demonstrates alternatives to existing norms and values. For example, according to Merton, innovation is a form of deviance that can be seen as not only positive but also as absolutely necessary if a society is not to stagnate. Those defined as deviant at one point in time may become the heroes of the future. The people who fought to give women the right to vote were seen as deviant at the time, but today we take women's right to vote for granted and praise those who battled to bring it about.

Deviance, then, is behavior that is different from the ordinary or traditional. Whether that behavior is applauded or condemned depends on who is making that judgment; it also depends on the particular era in which the behavior occurs. Deviance, in short, is the result of a social process.

Crime and juvenile delinquency result from violating laws and are two forms of legally defined deviance. Social deviance, on the other hand, refers to actions that violate social, though not necessarily legal, norms.

There have been numerous explanations of deviance. Biological and psychological explanations have been put forward by Lombroso and more recently by Sheldon and the Gluecks. They argue that certain physical characteristics are associated with criminality, sometimes directly (Lombroso and Sheldon) and other times indirectly (the Gluecks) through others' response to the person. Today, little credence is given to theories espousing any direct relationship between physique and crime, and evidence about its indirect relationship is still subject to dispute.

Sociological explanations of deviance focus on both the micro- and macrolevels. On the microlevel, differential association theory focuses on a person's interaction with deviants and her or his consequent socialization to deviant values, norms, and behaviors. Control theory highlights the lack of adequate control mechanisms on the part of the individual and society to help people avoid the available opportunities for criminal behavior. The strengths and limitations of these theories were explored.

Structural strain theory deals with the macrolevel. It suggests that the lack of articulation between cultural goals and available structural means to attain these goals leads to different forms of deviance: innovation, ritualism, retreatism, and rebellion. Conflict theorists, on the other hand, argue that the inequities of the capitalist economic system cause crime. Labeling theory focuses on the importance of certain acts being defined as deviant and the consequent labeling as deviant of those found engaging in such behavior. It stresses the social construction of deviance. The usefulness and limitations of each of these theories were explored.

The various types of crime, defined largely by the FBI, were described and their relative frequency reported. Crimes against property occur about ten times more frequently than crimes against people (crimes of violence). Crimes also occur more frequently in metropolitan areas than anywhere else, and in the United States more frequently than in practically any other society. Criminals tend to be in their teens and early twenties, male, and—except for white collar criminals—from the lower and working classes. There is little information on white collar and victimless crimes since these are not indexed by the FBI.

Various aspects of the criminal justice system were described. These include the police, the courts, probation, various types of correctional institutions, and parole. Also discussed were the arguments for and against capital punishment.

Finally, the social implications of deviance was examined. Being defined as deviant often leads to social stigma, which affects both self-image and treatment by others. The role of deviance in defining the moral boundaries of society, in strengthening the moral force of permissible behavior, and in enhancing social solidarity was also noted.

9

Social Stratification

*O*ne fundamental problem in all societies is how to distribute resources. It is this topic, the distribution of societal resources—social stratification—that is the focus of this chapter. We will discuss the various forms and theories of stratification. Finally, we will focus on the social institutions and processes that serve to maintain a society's stratification.

SYSTEMS OF STRATIFICATION

Every society distributes its resources unequally. One person may have more wealth or power than another. These differences between individuals reflect *social inequality* and may result from one person's working harder than another or choosing a job or career that wields more power than another's.

Distinctions between entire social categories rather than just individuals are referred to as *social differentiation*. When people in these different social categories are ranked in some hierarchal order that gives them differing access to social resources, the result is *social stratification*.

In effect, the differently ranked social categories constitute layers or "strata" in society, much as geological layers or strata of rock make up the earth's crust. Those in similar strata share similar *life chances*, such as the level of education they are likely to attain, the level of health they are likely to enjoy, and the standard of living they are likely to possess.

Social stratification is a characteristic of society, not of its individual members. While its form may vary, all societies except the most technologically primitive have some system of stratification. In each society, the system is justified by an ideology that is especially embraced by those who benefit most from it. This system, with its ideological support, is transmitted to future generations through the process of socialization.

Caste

A *caste system* is a "closed" system of stratification in which position in determined by the family into which a person is born; change in that position is not usually possible. *Ascribed statuses* (those assumed by persons at birth—e.g., race, sex—and over which they have little control) determine a person's caste position.

Often a caste position carries with it a specific occupation. Members of one particular caste might be shoemakers, members of another might be butchers. These occupations are embedded in the caste and are passed down through the family to succeeding generations. Because of this generational transmission of status, people tend to marry those at the same social level. This process is called *endogamy* (see chapter 13). The ideology supporting a caste system often derives from religious beliefs provides it with a strong basis. In fact, in some societies this religious base has led to the belief that contact between members of different castes can lead to *ritual pollution*, or the rendering as "unclean" of a member of a higher caste because of contact with a member of a lower caste.

Though the number of societies with caste systems has diminished, two prime examples—India and South Africa—stand out.

INDIA

India has four main castes and several thousand subcastes. Despite the attempt of the British to do away with the caste system during their rule over India, they never succeeded in doing so. Even though the caste system was officially abolished in 1949, two years after India became independent, it is still a powerful force in Indian society, especially in rural areas. Occupations and marital opportunities in rural India are almost exclusively related to caste. The anonymity provided by large numbers of people in urban areas weakens caste as a factor in social relations, though it still plays an important role.

SOUTH AFRICA

South Africa's system of *apartheid* is another form of caste. Essentially there are four castes: whites, blacks, "coloreds" (people of mixed race), and Asians. By birth, persons are assigned to one or another of these four castes. From that point on, their life chances are determined. Where people can live and work and whom they can vote for are all functions of caste. At the present time, negotiations are underway to unravel the system of apartheid.

Class

A *class system* is a form of "open" stratification in which the position a person has through birth can be changed. In essence, an individual's position in a class is based on *achieved status* (e.g., marital and occupational status), which is acquired, at least in part, through his or her own efforts and decisions rather than through the accident of birth.

The openness of a class system leads to *social mobility* (see chapter 10), the movement of individuals up or down in the class structure. Because of social mobility, classes are not as sharply defined as castes. The boundaries between classes are somewhat blurred, and even the number of classes is not always clear. Also, the criteria that determines whether people belong to one class rather than to another are flexible.

Like caste, class strongly influences an individual's life chances. Those in the higher classes generally have greater access to society's resources, such as education, jobs, and health care. However, through social mobility a person's life chances at birth can be changed.

Class is multidimensional; i.e., there are several factors that contribute to it, such as wealth, power, and social prestige. In a complex class structure, an individual may not possess all the attributes of any given class. For example, a person who has great social prestige (e.g., an entertainer or a star athlete) may have little power. This possible *status inconsistency* is another reason why class boundaries are not very sharply defined.

GREAT BRITAIN

One of the most frequently cited examples of a class society is Great Britain. In that country, there is a clear *upper class* made up of individuals whose families have had wealth, prestige, and occasionally power for several generations. There is also a relatively large and diverse *middle class*, which is made up of individuals who have earned reasonable wealth from business and the professions, and, at the low end, from white collar clerical (e.g., bookkeepers) or service (e.g., sales clerks) jobs. Below that, there is the large *working class*, whose members often earn their livings in the manual trades (e.g., coal miners). Still further down in the hierarchy is the *lower class*, which is made up of individuals who either do not work at all or whose low incomes are supplemented by the government.

The class system plays a significant role in British society. Social relationships, access to jobs, and entrance into universities are often influenced by a person's class background. Even the different accents of British speech reflect class position. The potency of the class system in Great Britain is partly a result of its feudal past, when practically all the land was owned by the nobility (who constituted the upper class) and was worked by the peasants. The Industrial Revolution changed Great Britain from an agrarian society, in which status was based on land ownership, to an industrialized society, in which those engaging in commerce amassed large amounts of wealth and power. The development of the crafts and the professions served to separate the wealthy upper class from the peasants and the growing body of factory and mine workers. These constituted the middle class. The steadfastness of British tradition helps maintain these class distinctions, however subtle they might occasionally be.

Classless Societies

Is it possible to have a modern industrial society without social classes? The certainty that just such a society was possible led in Russia to a revolution in 1917 against the czarist agrarian society.

Careful study of the Union of Soviet Socialist Republics (U.S.S.R.), has shown, however, that the revolution failed in its aim to establish a classless, communist society. In a 1984 study, Lane determined that the U.S.S.R. was stratified into four classes. First, there were the high government officials. Below them were the intellectuals, professionals, and lower-level government officials. Following them were the manual workers; and last were the peasants, who worked the land. Thus while theoretically it may be possible to have a classless society, the most thoroughgoing attempt to create one did not succeed. Given the recent break-up of the communist system in Eastern Europe, it seems unlikely that the world will witness a revival of a similar attempt in the near future.

THEORIES OF STRATIFICATION

Various theories have been offered to explain the existence of stratification systems in practically all societies. These different views are generally based either on a structural-functionalist view of society or on a conflict view.

A Functionalist View: Kingsley Davis and Wilbert Moore

The Davis-Moore functionalist view was put forth in 1945; it asserts that some form of stratification is inevitable and socially necessary. In this view, society is composed of a complex system of statuses and roles. If society is to function well, those statuses must be occupied by the most qualified people. The most important positions often require extensive and difficult training (e.g., to become a physician). Consequently, few people will wish to expend the time, money, and labor required. In that case, society must develop some system of unequal rewards to encourage those with the necessary talent to undergo the required training.

This system of unequal rewards is precisely what is meant by social stratification. If anybody in society could fulfill any position, then a system of unequal rewards would not be necessary. But, Davis and Moore argue, this in not the case. Talents and abilities are not equally distributed in society. Nor are all positions equally desirable. Thus a stratification system serves to motivate those with the necessary skills to occupy the necessary statuses and to perform well the requirements of those positions.

The original Davis-Moore theory (which has been modified and refined since its introduction in 1945) sets out the basic functional explanation of why a stratification system is necessary and nearly universal. However, it has not gone unchallenged. Tumin (1953) argues that the functional importance of any position in society is difficult to establish precisely. How much more important to society is a physician than a garbage collector? More than the difference in their average incomes? And how would a society make that determination?

Tumin also argues that whatever justification for stratification there might have been at one time, systems of stratification tend to perpetuate themselves to the point that they are now counterproductive. Those in higher positions tend to pass them down to their children, thus denying those from different backgrounds, but with equal or superior talent, the chance to compete for the higher positions. Such a situation harms both the individuals denied access and society by depriving it of the most talented person for any particular position. In short, Tumin argues that the Davis-Moore theory that society is a *meritocracy* in which there is a relationship between the qualities of individuals and the rewards they earn does not reflect reality. The success (or lack of it) in acquiring social rewards in one generation is transmitted by families to future generations, thereby limiting an unrestricted matching of talent and rewards required in a democratic and efficient society.

A Conflict Theory: Karl Marx

Marx argued that there are only two fundamental classes in society: those who own the means of production (the nobility in feudal societies and the *capitalists* or *bourgeoisie* in industrial societies) and those who do not (the serfs or peasants in feudal societies and the *proletariat* in industrial societies). He argued that stratification is not inevitable or even necessary if the means of production is owned collectively rather than by a small number of individuals. In Marx's analysis, capitalism as an economic system (see chapter 17) is responsible for producing social stratification. Capitalism, according to Marx, encourages workers to produce more than is necessary for their own or the owners' needs, leading to what he called *surplus wealth*. The capitalist uses that surplus to make a profit rather than giving it back to the workers who produced it. Marx argued that the system of stratification produced by capitalism is therefore inherently exploitative; owners' profits always come from the labor, and at the expense, of workers.

There have been a number of criticisms of Marx's theory. Since Marx's time, there has been a rapid rise of the middle class in industrial societies, rendering his two-class view obsolete. Furthermore, in modern industrial societies the ownership and management of the means of production is often divided, and the widespread selling of stocks, including to individual workers or to workers' pension plans, has blurred the sharp line between classes that Marx had drawn. Also, the tremendous growth in the power of unions has changed the balance of power between owners and workers considerably.

Despite these criticisms, Marx's view of social stratification continues to influence sociological thought on this issue. A number of sociologists (e.g., Domhoff, 1983) have argued that power is still concentrated in the hands of a small economic elite and that labor unions still have to battle for anything the workers need. Victory in those battles, they point out, is hard to come by.

A Multi-dimensional View: Max Weber

The most important attack on Marx's view of social stratification came from Max Weber (1946). Weber believed that Marx's analysis of social stratification as based on economic inequality (social class) is too limiting. Stratification, Weber contends, is a multidimensional concept. There are three separate and distinct spheres into which people can be differentiated: the economic, the social, and the political. A person can rank high on one dimension and low or intermediate on one or both of the other two.

ECONOMIC SPHERE: CLASS

Marx focused on only one dimension, economic *class*. Weber believed that class should not be seen as a simple division into neat categories (for Marx, just two). Instead, Weber argues, people's economic position should be seen as a continuum ranging from high to low.

SOCIAL SPHERE: STATUS

People have different amounts of social prestige or honor (what Weber calls *status*). The clergy have high prestige but generally lack the wealth that would place them high on the economic, or class, scale. Successful entertainers are often revered and granted considerable prestige; however, they cannot automatically turn that prestige into any real political power.

POLITICAL SPHERE: PARTY

The third dimension, which Weber calls *party*, refers to political power. Power may or may not depend on an economic base. People have worked their way into positions of power by rising within government without the benefit of great personal economic wealth. Superstar athletes rate very high on the economic and status dimensions; however, only rarely are they able to convert their social and economic standing into political power.

Weber's analysis of stratification has influenced generations of social scientists. His critics point out that in practice a person's standings in different dimensions of stratification often go together. Political power is related to economic power. Those who have money call the shots in the political sphere. Witness the many accusations of conflict of interest when members of Congress appear to be influenced by contributors to their campaign funds. However, even Weber's critics generally accept the multidimensional nature of stratification. It has become commonplace in sociology to base a measurement of people's *socioeconomic status (SES)* on some combination of factors, including wealth, power, and prestige. In this way, the variety of elements that make up a person's standing is captured.

An Attempted Synthesis: Gerhard and Jean Lenski

Despite the criticisms noted above, both the functionalist and conflict approaches contribute to an understanding of social stratification. Gerhard and Jean Lenski (Lenski, 1966; Lenski and Lenski, 1987) have used their analysis of the evolution of society (see chapter 4) to try to combine the functionalist and conflict approaches into a single unified theory of social stratification.

In their view, the lack of surplus food in hunting and gathering societies makes it virtually impossible for any segment of the population to accumulate more resources than any other. Everything that is produced is consumed. Thus, unequal distribution of societal resources is unlikely. However, as societies evolve because of increasing technology (see chapter 4), the surplus resources that become available are often unequally distributed. This unequal distribution results in stratification, which is solidified through the power that accumulates to the "haves" and is passed on to succeeding generations through families.

As technology improves and societies become more industrial, greater surpluses may result. These tend to be distributed to a larger segment of the population. In this way, the effects of stratification tend to be reduced in more industrially advanced societies. It is true, however, that in large modern societies the effects of stratification may be sharpened in its large urban areas because of factors that will be discussed in chapter 11. Also, the criteria for membership in the social classes becomes more complex, blurring to some extent the differences between them.

In short, the Lenskis believe that some degree of social stratification is inevitable because skills, talents, intelligence, and other personal attributes as well as societal resources are not likely to be equally distributed. However, not all societies are equally stratified. The nature of a particular society has some effect on its degree of stratification. Highly industrialized societies and those without marked external threats are likely to be less stratified than other types. The Lenskis also suggest that societies whose cultural values stress the importance of "free will" may be highly stratified and that the nature of societal leadership may influence the stratification system.

MAINTENANCE OF
THE STRATIFICATION SYSTEM

Stratification systems persist. India's caste system survived British rule and continues today despite having been officially abolished when India gained independence. Class systems existed in socialist societies despite an official ideology to the contrary. The persistence of systems of stratification results from the influence of social institutions and social processes.

Social Institutions

Several societal institutions serve to support the existing stratification system. In essence, these institutions tend to legitimize the dominant groups.

THE ECONOMY

Stratification is based on the unequal distribution of societal resources; most frequently these involve economic goods and services. In many societies, some form of money is the medium of exchange that allows people to acquire the necessary goods and services. The differential allocation of these resources both defines and contributes to social stratification. When unequal economic resources are transmitted to future generations, as they often are, the existing stratification system is maintained.

THE FAMILY

The mechanism through which the differential allocation of societal resources is transmitted to subsequent generations is most likely to be the family (see chapter 13). Most people understand that someone with the name of Rockefeller is likely to be a member of that elite family and to have inherited some part of the economic resources, political power, and social prestige that goes with the name. Families, particularly those with considerable resources, arrange to pass those resources on to subsequent generations.

A less obvious form of maintaining the existing stratification system involves the effects of socialization on those in different social classes. Different social classes tend to raise their children to act and think differently, to have different levels and kinds of education, and to have different types of jobs or careers. Kohn and his colleagues (e.g., Kohn, 1969; Kohn and Schooler, 1983) argue that differential socialization in the middle and working classes leads to different kinds of personalities that are linked to class-based occupations. Families, then, transmit their class position directly through the transmission of wealth and property and indirectly through their socialization practices.

Also, socialization leads to the development of a set of values and beliefs that often supports the existing system of stratification. This "ideology" is a powerful force for continuity.

RELIGION AND IDEOLOGY

As was mentioned in the discussion of the Indian caste system, stratification is often accompanied by a set of religious or ideological beliefs that justifies and supports it. Earlier in Western Europe, feudal monarchies solidified their power by asserting the "divine right of kings," the belief that the king (and the monarchical stratification system) was created and blessed by the appropriate god. The caste system is supported by a belief in the innate moral inferiority of the lower castes. In modern industrial societies, the supporting ideology focusses on a person's merit, hard work, superior talent, and equality of opportunity.

Ideological beliefs maintain the stratification system. Particularly in modern societies, these beliefs deflect attention from the structural and cultural supports for the stratification system and explain it in terms of the characteristics of individuals. Persons well placed, in this view, are where they are because of their own efforts or talents; persons less well off have only themselves to blame.

THE POLITICAL ORDER

The state also helps maintain the existing stratification system. It does so through its control over the legal system, ensuring the passing and application of laws that support an existing system of unequal distribution of resources. For example, laws can be used to encourage or discourage, require or forbid the transmission of substantial amounts of inherited wealth by individuals and families to succeeding generations. In general, the relevant laws are made by those who benefit from the existing class system; thus they are unlikely to allow legislation to change the situation.

The state also has a monopoly on power and coercion that can be used to maintain the existing stratification system. The maintenance of apartheid in South Africa is a clear example of the state using the coercive power of its military and police to maintain the desired caste arrangements.

Often, the use of the legal system goes hand in hand with the coercive power of the state—used or implied—to maintain the status quo, the existing arrangement. However, in large and complex societies, power may be sufficiently dispersed to allow some change (see chapter 16).

Social Processes

Structural support for the existing stratification system is often joined by selective social processes.

COOPTATION

Cooptation involves bringing people into the system who might threaten its continuity or very existence. By giving them a "piece of the action," the hope is that they will at a minimum not work to change the system and, at a maximum, actively help to maintain it.

The trick in coopting people, Selznick (1948) argues, is to give them the trappings and burden of responsibility without granting them real power to effect any substantial change. In a way, some forms of student involvement in the governance of educational institutions may be seen as cooptation. Despite the presence of students on committees (including executive committees) and their being "consulted," effective power often remains exclusively in the hands of the administration. The same cooptive elements may be seen with respect to the participation of faculty in the governance of many educational institutions.

Efforts at cooptation are often focused on the leaders of the opposition, those who have the power to rally critics and threaten change. They may be wined and dined, given elaborate explanations of why the current situation is the best (at least under present conditions), and invited to membership in the circles that exercise a measure of power.

This process of cooptation may be clear and direct, as when industries include a limited number of union members on their boards of directors. It may be indirect, taking a form such as allowing the growth of the middle class, as has happened in many industrial societies, which reduces the likelihood of the kind of revolutionary turmoil and change Karl Marx anticipated. Allowing the middle class to grow essentially coopts the proletariat by allowing it the advantages of middle class life afforded by the existing system, thus ensuring its cooperation in maintaining the status quo. Piven and Cloward (1977) provide a detailed analysis of the cooptation of several of the "poor people's movements."

THE PRINCIPLE OF CUMULATIVE ADVANTAGE

Those well placed in the system of stratification not only reap considerable material benefits but also gain additional predominance through their position. They are often able to pass these advantages on to their children, other relatives, and friends, who can then use these benefits to even further advantage. Thus beneficial placement in the stratification system has a cumulative advantage.

This phenomenon ties directly into Merton's conclusions about science as a social institution. In discussing the reward system in science, Merton (1968) coined the phrase the *Matthew effect*, drawing upon the Gospel of Matthew ("For unto every one that hath shall be given, and he shall have abundance"), to refer to the tendency of those with already established reputations in science to reap rewards more easily than those less well known. In other words, if one is well placed in the system, other rewards are more likely to be available. This led Merton to see in the field of science a stratified reward system based on prior success.

Merton applied the idea of the Matthew effect more broadly to describe what he called the *principle of cumulative advantage*, referring to a similar phenomenon in social institutions. Cumulative advantage serves to maintain and even strengthen existing differences in the allocation of societal resources—the essential underpinnings of a system of social stratification. Children of famous entertainers (e.g., Michael Douglas, son of Kirk Douglas) or politicians (Joseph Kennedy, son of Robert Kennedy) like to claim, perhaps justly, that they have achieved standing in their chosen professions on the merits of their own abilities. However accurate those claims may be, there is no doubt that they start out with the advantage of name recognition and contacts that those with "ordinary" parents lack.

In short, social institutions tend to be a conservative force in society; they support and maintain the existing social arrangements. This is especially true of the stratification system. Furthermore, there are relevant social processes that complement the institutional support for the existing stratification system. The joint effect of these structural and cultural forces is to make the stratification system one of the most stable elements in society.

This chapter discussed the different stratification systems that societies use to distribute their resources. A caste system is a closed form of stratification. Caste is allocated at birth, often justified on a religious basis, and can seldom be changed. India and South Africa are examples of such systems. A class system is relatively open. While people are born into a class, they can change it. Great Britain is an example of this form of stratification. The issue of whether there could be a classless society was explored, and it was suggested that it seems unlikely.

Several different theoretical explanations of stratification were analyzed. The functionalist view of Davis and Moore asserts that because society needs to fill key positions with people who have the necessary abilities and training, social resources will always be unequally allocated. Therefore, some form of stratification will be inevitable and socially necessary. Conflict theorists argue that there are only two fundamental classes: those who own the means of production and those who do not. Members of the first group control society and distribute its resources to benefit themselves. Criticisms of both the functionalist and conflict views were presented, and the multidimensional view of Weber was elaborated. He argues that there are three bases of social stratification—economic wealth, social prestige, and political power—and that they all must enter into any analysis of stratification. The Lenskis attempt to synthesize the functionalist and conflict views of stratification. They believe that stratification needs to be examined in terms of the evolution of society. They maintain that some degree of stratification is inevitable in all societies but that its form and extent is influenced by the nature of the society itself.

Social institutions generally serve to maintain the existing stratification system. The economy is one of the main bases for stratification. Often the already-unequal allocation of economic resources to a given family is transmitted to future generations. In this sense, the economy and the family work together. Families also reproduce the stratification system by the way they socialize their children into the appropriate values, attitudes, and careers. Religion and ideology tend to support the existing system, especially in caste systems. The political order is often influenced by the economic order and uses the legislative or coercive power of the state to maintain the stratification system.

Not only social institutions but also social processes operate to support the existing stratification system. Two major processes were discussed. Individuals who might threaten the system—particularly leaders of opposition groups—are often coopted, or brought into the system in ways that benefit them and reduce their opposition. The other process is that of cumulative advantage, what Merton called the "Matthew effect." Those benefiting from the stratification are often able to use those benefits to further advantage, thereby heightening the unequal allocation of societal resources.

10

Social Class and Social Mobility in the United States

In this chapter, we will focus on the nature of social class in the United States. We will examine the various dimensions of social class as well as the methods of identifying the different social classes. Brief portraits of the social classes will be presented and the significance of social class in the life of Americans will be examined. Finally, the issue of social mobility will be addressed.

DIMENSIONS OF INEQUALITY IN THE UNITED STATES

Weber argues that Marx's focus on economic factors rendered an incomplete explanation of social inequality (see chapter 9). Weber insists that political power and social prestige are two other dimensions of social differentiation and stratification. This more complex view is clearly appropriate to any analysis of social stratification in the United States.

Economic Resources

Two elements make up the economic resources of the American population: income and wealth.

INCOME

The term *income* refers to salaries, wages, and earnings from investments. In the United States, income is unequally distributed in the population. In 1986 the median family income (the point at which half of the families have incomes below this amount and half above) was $29,460 (U.S. Bureau of Census, 1987a). However, in the same year the richest 20 percent of American families received 43.7 percent of all income, or more than double what they would have if income had been equally distributed. By contrast, the poorest 20 percent received 4.6 percent of all income in the United States, or less than a quarter of the amount based on an equal distribution. The top 5 percent of all families earn as much income as the lowest *forty* percent.

Those with the highest incomes are likely to derive most of it from investments rather than from salaries or wages. In 1985, 17,000 Americans reported incomes of over $1 million; only about 16 percent of this income was derived from either salaries or wages. The remainder came from earnings based on business profits, stocks, bonds, and other investments that produce income from rents, interest, dividends, bonuses, and capital gains. For example, in 1984 the chairman of NCR (a major corporation) had a base salary of just over $1 million and also received an additional income of $12 million for various activities.

The Matthew effect (see chapter 9) seems to apply to income distribution as well as to scientific reputation. Those who have shall be given more. High income provides surplus capital that can be invested to produce still further income. Those with low incomes have little disposable funds to invest and thus must depend almost exclusively on their salaries and wages.

The gap in income between the rich and the poor has increased over the past decade. Tax changes that took effect during the Reagan administration led to an average annual loss of about $400 for those with incomes below $10,000 and an average annual gain of about $8,300 for those with incomes above $80,000 (Sawhill and Palmer, 1984).

WEALTH

The difference between the incomes of the rich and the poor is small when compared with the difference in their *wealth*, which is defined as the total value of the money and valuable goods that a person or family controls. These assets include items like stocks and bonds and personal property like real estate, cars, and boats. It has been calculated that the top 12 percent of American families controls about 38 percent of the assets of the country (U.S. Bureau of the Census, 1986).

The inequity is even greater than the above figures suggest, since the assets owned by the poor consist largely of items like cars that tend to decrease in value over time, whereas the assets of the wealthy (such as real estate and stocks) are more likely to increase in value over time. In fact, those families in the lowest 20 percent of the wealth distribution have slightly more financial liabilities than assets, giving them a negative net worth.

Wealth in the United States is quite concentrated. About 20 percent of American families control over 75 percent of the country's wealth. The top 5 percent, sometimes called the "superrich," own about one-half of American wealth. A *Forbes* (1987) survey of the wealthiest 400 Americans showed that the three richest individuals jointly have as much wealth (approximately $15 billion) as about 500,000 "average" members of the population.

One major factor in the disparity in income between the haves and the have-nots is family inheritance. In 1986 all of the 90 families with assets of over $500 million and 168 of the 400 individual worth over $180 million, inherited either all or part of their wealth (*Forbes,* 1987). The disparity in the assets owned by the rich and the poor is maintained and even increased by the ability of the wealthy to pass on their accumulated assets to future generations.

Political Power

Economic resources are not the only things that are distributed unequally among the population. *Power*, the ability to influence the actions of others, is also allocated differentially. *Political power* refers to the ability to influence governmental action, and it too is not wielded equally by all people. To a large extent, political power is linked to economic resources. Those who command economic power often have a greater influence on governmental action than those who do not. This is evident in the frequent scandals involving government officials (e.g., members of Congress and presidential aides) who are accused of "selling" influence to those who can afford it in exchange for personal and political contributions.

Perhaps the best example of how economic leverage can be translated into political power is the tax code. Favorable tax legislation is often sought by those with great economic resources. Termed "relief" by some, "loopholes" by others, special provisions reduce the likelihood that the tax system is "progressive"—that is, based on the principle that the more you earn, the more you pay. Every year a small number of extremely wealthy individuals pay little or no taxes, and some highly profitable corporations such as Boeing and General Electric often pay no taxes at all.

Economic resources are not the only basis of unequal political power. When this country was founded, only white propertied adult men were allowed to vote. It took a civil war to make African Americans full citizens with all the attendant political rights, and even that progress had to be supplemented by additional major legislation in 1965. Women received this right only in the early part of this century and young adults (ages eighteen to twenty-one) even more recently.

If political power were equally distributed, those holding high political office would represent more or less a cross section of the population. This is clearly not the case. Most members of Congress and state legislatures are white, Protestant, middle-aged men with considerable personal or family wealth. This also holds true to those appointed to positions of political power. Brownstein and Easton (1983) show that 95 percent of the top officials appointed by President Reagan when he took office in 1980 were men and that 98 percent of them were white. Almost half of them were earning over $100,000 at the time of their appointment, with a substantial minority earning over $200,000. However, this situation seems to be changing rapidly as more women and minority-group members are elected or appointed to positions of political power.

Prestige

The third dimension of stratification in Weber's analysis is *prestige*, people's social standing or the amount of "social honor," esteem or respect they are accorded. In the United States, differences in prestige are less extreme than are differences in wealth, income, and political power. Americans are remarkably more informal and less status conscious than people in most other countries. Except in the armed forces, there is little automatic deference of somebody deemed socially inferior to someone seen as socially superior. In contrast to the British, for example, Americans do not bow or curtsy to their head of state.

OCCUPATIONAL PRESTIGE

Occupation is important for the income it provides. But it also plays a key role in determining both social and economic standing. Research into the prestige of different occupations has been a staple of American sociological study for most of this century. Consistently, certain occupations (e.g., medicine, law, banking, college teaching) are highly esteemed by most Americans. These occupations often require considerable skill, talent, and training. Yet they are not always among the highest paying positions in the occupational world. Business executives earn considerably more than either college professors or most bank officers, but they do not have the same high level of prestige. And star athletes and entertainers have high prestige and income, but these are rarely translatable into political power.

In general, *white collar* occupations (those that involve mental activity more than manual labor and are relatively free from extensive supervision; e.g., architecture or the ministry) have greater prestige than *blue collar* occupations (those that involve considerable manual labor and are often closely supervised; e.g., restaurant work or garbage collecting). In all of the studies of occupational prestige (e.g., National Opinion Research Council, 1987), white collar positions consistently capture the highest levels.

FORMAL EDUCATION

In addition to being nonmanual and involving less supervision, the more prestigious occupations also tend to require a considerable amount of formal education. Higher levels of education lead individuals into higher occupational positions and shape a way of thinking and a style of life that are often highly esteemed. In the United States in 1987, about a quarter of the population had less than a high school education, while almost 40 percent went no further than high school. About 36 percent had some college or university education, while slightly more than half of these at least completed college with some going on to graduate or professional schools. The higher individuals climb on the education ladder, the more esteem they are likely to be accorded. Education has specific occupational effects as well (see chapter 14 for more about education).

THE AMERICAN CLASS SYSTEM

Identifying Social Classes

The task of identifying and describing the different social classes in the United States is more difficult than it appears. Two major factors contribute to the complexity: the multidimensional nature of social class (see above) and the different ways the issue can be approached.

THE MULTIDIMENSIONAL NATURE OF SOCIAL CLASS

There being three different bases of social inequality suggests that an individual may not have the same position on each. Some individuals may rank high on social prestige and low on their income (e.g., the clergy); others may rank high on both (e.g., famous entertainers or "superstar" athletes).

These different dimensions of social differentiation make it difficult to place any particular individual in a specific social class. However, they do not substantially affect the study of the class *system* in the United States.

UNCOVERING SOCIAL CLASS

There are three general methods that have been used to examine the class structure of American society.

The *reputational method* was used by Warner and his associates (Warner and Lunt, 1941, 1942; Warner, 1949) in the first detailed social-scientific explorations into the stratification of modern communities. Researchers using this approach ask individuals in a community to identify its social class structure (class being understood as a social group made up of people with common attributes) by describing the differences between status groups in their community and placing particular individuals into these categories. This approach is particularly valuable when used in small groups or communities where most people know each other and in predicting patterns of association within that community. Most such association takes place within the same class.

The *self-placement method* is another technique that involves subjective judgment. Respondents are asked to identify the class to which they believe they belong. In this method, social class is viewed as a social category into which people locate themselves with others having similar characteristics. Until fairly recently, women tended to claim their husbands' class positions as their own, though that has begun to change (Simpson, Stark, and Jackson, 1988).

Unlike the reputational method, this approach can be used with large populations since people are asked to place only themselves and not others. Because of its subjective nature, the self-placement method has also been particularly useful for examining political behavior. Who people think they are influences how they will act or vote.

The *objective method* is the final way of assessing social class. In this technique, social class is viewed as a statistical category into which the researcher places people based on objective indicators presumed to reflect class position. The three most common indicators used in this approach are type of occupation, amount of income, and level of education. Typically, this method attempts to capture the multidimensionality of social class—what sociologists refer to as socioeconomic status (SES). This method is the easiest and simplest to use, which explains its popularity.

The various methods of assessing social class generally yield similar though not identical results. Which one to use depends on why the analysis is being done and what situation is being studied. In general, all three methods have identified five social classes.

Portraits of the Different Social Classes

THE UPPER CLASS

The upper class is quite small, usually about 3 to 4 percent of the population. It consists of the richest and most powerful people in the community. Often their wealth has been in the family for several generations, and this continuity in combination with economic resources confers considerable power. At the national level, the upper class has had great influence on domestic policy and foreign affairs. Most members of the upper class are highly educated, many having attended elite colleges and universities. They are most frequently white Anglo-Saxon Protestants.

Some investigators have pointed out differences within this class. The elite of this group, about 1 percent, are the "aristocracy" of the country. Their wealth has been largely inherited, and they form a relatively close-knit circle; they are "society." The names Rockefeller, Kennedy, du Pont, Whitney, and Vanderbilt are frequently associated with this group. The remaining 2 to 3 percent of the upper class represent those with new wealth.

They are in the upper class because of what they have accomplished, whereas the elite are included because of who they are.

THE UPPER-MIDDLE CLASS

This class, about 5 to 10 percent of the population, consists mainly of business and professional persons with relatively high incomes (between about $50,000 and $100,000 annually). A large number are white Anglo-Saxon Protestants. They, too, are likely to be well educated, though they have not necessarily attended the elite colleges and universities. They have all the external symbols of success such as good jobs and nice homes in good locations, and they travel extensively. Members of this class tend to be quite active in political and community life.

THE LOWER-MIDDLE CLASS

Comprised mainly of those in less well-paying white collar jobs (about $20,000 to $50,000), this class makes up about 30 to 35 percent of the population. In this class are owners of small businesses, teachers, middle-level managers, and sales representatives. Members of the lower-middle class are very concerned about proper and respectable behavior. They are often the backbone of the communities in which they live, supplying much of the labor for its voluntary social service and charitable activities.

THE WORKING CLASS

In general, the members of this class (about 40 percent of the population) are in blue collar occupations or low-level sales or clerical jobs, with annual incomes of between $15,000 and $25,000. Their income makes their economic position quite vulnerable; they are affected by even minor economic fluctuations. Slight downturns in the economy, illnesses or unemployment cause the working class considerable strain. The members of this class are less well educated than the members of the classes "above" them, often having only a high school education or less. They tend to live in less desirable neighborhoods and have less influence over events that affect them than members of the upper, and middle classes.

THE LOWER CLASS

Sometimes called "the poor," members of this class constitute about 20 percent of the population and have annual incomes of less than $15,000. Contrary to popular belief, most of the poor in the United States are white. Other members of the lower class include African Americans, Hispanics, and other "minority" groups. The unskilled, the unemployed, the homeless, those dependent on welfare, and residents of deteriorating urban neighborhoods or poor rural communities belong to this class. The poor are often perceived to have caused their own impoverished condition through either laziness or lack of skills or ambition. Seen as the "dregs" of society, many often accept that description of themselves and sink further into the kinds of activities (or lack of activities) that led to that perception in the first place.

THE SIGNIFICANCE OF SOCIAL CLASS

If people's social class positions were merely categories useful for statistical or research purposes, the concept would be important only to social scientists and some government agencies. However, social class position has an important effect on the lifestyle and life-chances of each and every person. Social class is related to how healthy individuals are, how long they live, the kinds of education they receive, and the kind of family life they lead.

Health and Longevity

HEALTH

There is a direct relationship between socioeconomic status and health. About twice as many middle and upper class individuals report their health as excellent compared with those in the lower class; about five times as many lower class individuals rate their health as fair or poor (National Center for Health Statistics, 1987).

These differences arise from several factors. The poor are more likely to live in a less safe and less healthy environment. They are less likely to be able to afford the kind of nutrition that promotes health or the quality and frequency of medical care that is required for good health.

Socioeconomic status is also related to mental health problems. Those at the lower end of the socioeconomic scale are exposed to considerable stress. More important, they generally lack the control over their environment that would allow them to deal effectively with that stress (Kessler and Cleary, 1980). Consequently, they are more likely to suffer from emotional problems and less likely to recover from them quickly.

LONGEVITY

Middle and upper class individuals live longer than those in the working and lower classes. In fact, that difference shows up immediately: infants born into poverty are about 50 percent more likely to die during their first year of life than those born into more wealthy families. The conditions that lead to differential longevity are the same ones that lead to differential physical and mental health.

Family Life

Lower class families tend to have more children than middle class families; married couples in this class also have a higher divorce rate. Family life in the lower class is thus more hectic and less stable than it is in the middle and upper classes.

The pattern of family life also differs by social class. There is a much sharper and more traditional separation of men's and women's roles in the lower and working classes. Despite considerable changes substantial differences in gender roles still exist in all social classes (see chapter 12).

Modes of disciplining children in lower and working class families are more likely to involve some form of physical punishment. In the middle class, discipline is more commonly based on the emotional attachment of parent and child and takes the form of attempting to reason or persuade or of withholding love.

Even the goals of child rearing are marked by differences among the classes. Middle class parents, expecting their children to take jobs requiring creativity and flexibility, more often attempt to instill a sense of individual autonomy and initiative in their children. Lower and working class families are more likely to believe their children will have jobs requiring them to follow rules and procedures; thus they focus on instilling in their children a sense of obedience to authority.

Education

Level of education both reflects and contributes to class position (see chapter 14). The more education individuals have, the more likely they are to attain higher class status. The higher individuals' class status is, the more likely their children will acquire higher levels of education.

Initially, a college or university education was the exclusive province of the wealthy. More recently, education has become seen as necessary to elevate one's social position (see chapter 14).

Personal Values and Attitudes

Those in the middle and upper classes are likely to experience a sense of control over their lives. Thus they are more willing than those in the lower and working classes to *defer gratification*, to put off immediate pleasure in favor of more long term benefits.

Working class individuals are more likely to focus on the present than on the past or the future. Upper class individuals tend to have a strong sense of the continuity of the past, and both they and those in the middle class share a future orientation as well because of their perceived ability to influence it. The social liberalism of the middle and upper classes is a product of the kind of education they have received, while their economic conservatism relates directly to their eagerness to protect their economic interests. The social values of the working and lower classes are a product of their education and upbringing, which stress obedience to authority rather than flexibility and tolerance for diversity. Members of these classes perceive economic liberalism as more likely than conservatism to improve their inadequate economic circumstances.

The upper class stresses the importance of "breeding" (good manners and style) as well as of being "cultured" (being well versed in art, literature, and music). But these characteristics are to be understated, discreetly exhibited, muted. The upper middle class, especially its uppermost level, similarly values being cultured and stresses ability and achievement as well. The lower middle class places emphasis on the appearance of respectability: being neat, clean, moral. Survival is often a key goal of the working and lower classes: making an adequate living and gaining some small measure of pleasure in life, often through spectator activities such as going to the movies, watching television or going to a ballgame.

SOCIAL MOBILITY

Forms of Social Mobility

One of the differences mentioned earlier (see chapter 9) between an open (class) and a closed (caste) stratification system is that in the former, individuals are socially mobile—they can change their social positions. There are several different forms of social mobility.

VERTICAL AND HORIZONTAL SOCIAL MOBILITY

Vertical social mobility refers to a change from one social position to another of either higher or lower rank. For example, a gas station attendant who goes to night school and becomes a sales executive exhibits upward vertical mobility. On the other hand, a bank officer who is laid off and becomes an insurance agent becomes an example of downward vertical mobility.

Horizontal social mobility refers to movement from one social position to another of approximately equal status. A bank teller who becomes an insurance agent demonstrates horizontal social mobility. The difference in status between these two positions is minimal.

INTER- AND INTRAGENERATIONAL SOCIAL MOBILITY

Sociologists are particularly interested in *intergenerational social mobility*, or change in the social position of children relative to that of their parents. A lawyer whose father was a truck driver has achieved upward intergenerational social mobility. On the other hand, a schoolteacher whose father was a physician has experienced some measure of downward intergenerational social mobility.

Intragenerational social mobility refers to change in the social position of individuals during their lifetimes. The gas station attendant who becomes a sales executive is an example of upward intragenerational mobility; the bank officer who becomes an insurance agent exhibits downward intragenerational mobility. Both are forms of vertical mobility. An insurance agent might become a travel agent, exhibiting horizontal intragenerational mobility.

Individual Factors in Social Mobility

Most studies of the factors that influence social mobility focus on intergenerational mobility. One of the most important of these studies examines the *status attainment model* (Blau and Duncan, 1967). Resting squarely within the functionalist tradition, the study highlights the individual factors that contribute to a person's social mobility. Its focus on individual factors such as education and occupation underplays the importance of structural factors in social mobility.

SOCIAL CLASS

The higher the social class of their parents, the higher the social class individuals are likely to attain. Clearly, families transmit wealth, levels of education, values and attitudes that affect their children's class position.

EDUCATION

Education provides people with the skills, values, attitudes, and contacts necessary to obtain the kinds of jobs that define their social status and the careers that signify upward social mobility.

OCCUPATION

The jobs individuals have determine their salaries, where they will live, their opportunities for advancement, and important contacts for future jobs. They affect people's patterns of leisure activities, providing further opportunities for developing those interests, values, and contacts that are helpful in rising up the class ladder.

RACE AND ETHNICITY

Racial and ethnic discrimination has clearly limited some people's ability to be upwardly mobile (see chapter 11). For example, Blau and Duncan (1967) found that even African Americans with high levels of education are not likely to attain the same level of occupational positions as whites. Members of certain ethnic groups were for many years restricted from the highest levels of occupational achievement, which limited their social mobility. Though this has changed considerably since the Blau and Duncan study, such differences still exist (see chapter 11).

GENDER

Women have similarly had restricted mobility because of discriminatory attitudes and practices (see chapter 12). Even when they have been allowed into traditionally masculine occupations, women have often not been able to advance to the highest levels with the same frequency as men. This, too, is changing, but gender differences still persist.

OTHER FACTORS

A number of personal factors have been shown to be associated with social mobility. Physical attractiveness, interpersonal skills, health, intelligence, and even height and weight play a role in social mobility. Luck, being in the right place at the right time, is also often involved.

Structural Factors in Social Mobility

In addition to personal qualities of individuals, social structure also influences social mobility. To the extent that there is economic growth, increasing numbers of new higher status positions are created, and more opportunities for social mobility become available. Also, technological advances increase the status of existing positions. For example, the status of some clerical jobs has been enhanced through the increased use of computers; people holding some of these positions are described as "information processing specialists" and earn higher salaries. Some individual factors in social mobility may be viewed in structural terms as well. For example, discrimination and restricted opportunities for women and members of minority groups are partly a function of social structure. As such, they demonstrate the blending of individual and structural influences on social mobility.

Social Mobility in the United States: Myth or Reality?

The opportunity to improve one's social position is part of the American creed. Americans take for granted that considerable opportunity for individual advancement exists. Do the facts justify these beliefs? By and large, the answer is yes. Several research studies (e.g., Blau and Duncan, 1967; Hauser and Featherman, 1978) have shown that almost 80 percent of men show some intergenerational mobility, most of which is upward. However, much of the upward mobility has been caused by structural changes in the society; specifically, an explosion of new white collar occupations and an expansion of existing white collar jobs.

A close look at upward intragenerational mobility shows that rather than imitating the Horatio Alger myth of moving from "rags to riches," most of it has been relatively small in magnitude. Sales clerks have become floor managers, not regional vice presidents.

Not all categories of individuals experience the same degree of social mobility. As indicated above, African Americans traditionally have less social mobility than whites (Pomer, 1986). The same has been true for women. Once again, recent changes have reduced the differences in rates of mobility between whites and blacks and between men and women.

The overall rate of social mobility in the United States is about the same as it is in most industrialized societies (Bendix and Lipset, 1967). However, downward social mobility from middle and upper class status in the United States is less frequent than in many other countries (Fox and Miller, 1965). On the other hand, there seems to be more mobility for the working class in the United States than in other industrialized societies. This mobility of the working class contributes significantly to the view that the United States is the "land of opportunity." This perception, in turn, increases the emphasis on individual achievement and fuels constant immigration to the United States.

Recent Trends in Social Mobility in the United States

Throughout most of its history, the United States has enjoyed a geographical and economic expansion that facilitated social mobility. Even the Great Depression of the 1930s had only a temporary effect on widespread social mobility. More recently, however, economic growth has slowed considerably. Not only have jobs not been expanding at the same rate that they did in the past, but also many industries (e.g., the steel industry) have severely declined. Thus the opportunities for social mobility have not been increasing at anywhere near the same rate that they did in the past.

Equally important, the standard of living of many Americans has dropped in the past decade or two. Between 1955 and 1973, the median family income in the United States rose by about 65 percent; however, between 1973 and 1986 it declined by about 2 percent (U.S. Bureau of the Census, 1987).

The consequence of these changes has been to slow the rate of social mobility in the United States in recent years. Moreover, this has lead to a decrease in the traditional confidence that Americans have had in their ability to better themselves. World trends in economic restructuring are somewhat complex; certain areas of the world are expanding while others are contracting or barely holding their own. Right now, the United States' place in these trends is not clear. Thus it is impossible to determine whether the rate of social mobility in the United States will continue to slow down, remain constant or return to its former relatively high level.

*S*ocial class is a multidimensional concept. Social class position is influenced by economic resources, political power, and social prestige. While these various dimensions of social class often go together (the wealthy have more political power and prestige than the poor), they need not do so.

Social class in the United States has been studied by asking members of a community to identify its class structure (the "reputational" method), by asking them to identify the class to which they believe they belong (the "self-placement" method), and by researchers placing individuals into predetermined social classes according to certain criteria—usually occupation, income, and education (the "objective" method).

Brief portraits were provided of each of the five major social classes in the United States: a tiny upper class, a relatively small upper-middle class, a much larger lower-middle class, a slightly larger working class, and a somewhat smaller lower class. The descriptions were based on the typical income and occupations found in each of the classes.

Also discussed were the effects of social class on health and longevity, on family life and child rearing practices, on the level of education likely to be attained, and on personal values and attitudes.

Finally, both intergenerational and intragenerational vertical and horizontal social mobility were explored. Individual factors leading to social mobility—social class, education, occupation, race and ethnicity, gender, and a variety of personal and interpersonal characteristics—were examined, along with structural factors such as the expanding economy and technological advances. Changing opportunities for social mobility in American society were considered. It was concluded that considerable social mobility has been and continues to be possible, but that it is more incremental than dramatic.

11

Race and Ethnicity

*I*n this chapter, we will examine race and ethnicity as a basis of social inequality. We will explore the pattern of interaction of key racial and ethnic groups and provide brief descriptions of several minority groups in American society. Contemporary issues of affirmative action and the effects of racism and social class on discrimination will be explored.

BASIC CONCEPTS

Race and ethnicity are powerful words in American and most other societies. Their meanings often differ according to who is using them.

Race

Among biologists and anthropologists, race has often been taken to refer to a collection of people who have a common biological heritage and who pass it on to subsequent generations. In this sense, race is often defined in terms of some set of physical characteristics (e.g., skin color, hair texture, nose shape) that has resulted from the evolutionary adaptations that various populations have made to their physical environments.

RACIAL CATEGORIES

While the number of races and subraces defined in biological terms is very large, anthropologists at one time tried to bring some order to this area by using three main racial categories: *Caucasoid*, having light skin and wavy, straight or curly hair; *Mongoloid*, having yellowish skin and a characteristic fold of skin around the eyes; and *Negroid*, having dark skin and woolly hair. However, sociologists have pointed out that because different populations have interbred (married and had children with people from other races) for thousands of years, there is no such thing as a "pure" race. Thus, to define race strictly in physical terms would be inaccurate and confusing.

Sociologists tend to view *race* as a category of people considered to be similar because they share common physical attributes. It is the belief that those with similar physical characteristics should be lumped together that is important. "Race," then, is socially constructed rather than biologically determined. For example, there are many people categorized "Negro" whose skin color is lighter than that of many people classified as "Caucasian." Social definition rather than biological fact is the hallmark of the sociologist's conception of race. Beliefs about race, rather than "facts," influence race relations in the United States and elsewhere.

Ethnicity

Whereas race refers to physical characteristics, *ethnicity* focuses on cultural elements. Members of an *ethnic group* share a common cultural heritage that marks them as distinct. These cultural features often include national origin, language, religion, dietary preferences and practices, and a sense of a common historical heritage.

As is evident, ethnic characteristics differ from racial characteristics in that they are learned and transmitted across generations through socialization. Race, on the other hand, is indexed biologically and transmitted genetically. Though the two are conceptually different, they often are linked. For example, Asian Americans are seen not only as a racial group because of their distinctive physical features but also as an ethnic group if they maintain their traditional cultural characteristics.

Ethnicity can more easily be changed than the distinctive physical characteristics of race. It is easier for people to avoid being labeled with an ethnic group identity than with a racial identity. Typically, the children of immigrants adopt the culture of their new country and try to avoid being labeled as a member of their parents' ethnic group.

Minority Groups

In homogeneous societies, where most if not all the members have a common background (as in small preindustrial societies), the issue of minority groups does not arise. However, in heterogeneous (culturally diverse) modern society, the concept of the minority group has become increasingly relevant. A *minority group* is made up of people who share a common set of cultural or physical characteristics that marks them as different from the dominant group and for which they often suffer social disadvantages.

As in the case of race and ethnicity, minority group membership is an ascribed status. Change is sometimes possible, but it is not always easy. Furthermore, minority group status often fosters strong ingroup identification, a self-consciousness as a member of a distinct group, especially when its members are subjected to unequal treatment.

Not all minority groups are smaller than the dominant group. For example, in South Africa the smaller white group has for decades completely dominated the numerically much larger black population, denying them access to wealth, education, and political power; sociologically, it is the black population that is the "minority group." Even in the United States, women, who constitute slightly more than 50 percent of the population, have some of the characteristics of a minority group.

Not all minority groups suffer automatic discrimination. In some societies (e.g., Switzerland), the rights of minority groups are scrupulously protected. They are enshrined in law and followed in practice.

Prejudice

Prejudice is an unsupported generalization, a prejudgment, about a group or category of people. Prejudice involves a belief such as "African Americans are lazy and shiftless," "Jews are money-hungry" or "women are emotional." Consequently, it often leads to negative feelings about those social categories. While it is possible to have a favorable prejudice, the concept is almost always used to describe negative attitudes.

SOURCES OF PREJUDICE

Social scientists have devoted considerable attention to trying to understand the basis of prejudice. Five major explanations have been offered.

Stereotypes, inflexible views of a class of people that resist change even in the face of evidence that suggests their falsity, are a source of prejudice. These general categorizations do not permit the prejudiced individual to see the wide differences that exist among people who may be in the same social category. All members in that category tend to be seen as alike.

Authoritarian personalities have been described as having a distinctive set of traits—conformity, intolerance, and insecurity—that results in their being prejudiced (Adorno, et al., 1950). These individuals, seen as a product of cold, distant, and disciplinarian parents, tend to be narrow in their views, anti-intellectual, and inflexible. They do not like differences, especially those that may cause some question about their own characteristics, activities or group affiliations.

Scapegoating refers to placing blame for one's own failings and limitations onto others less powerful (Dollard, et al., 1939). This occurs especially when individuals are frustrated but cannot vent their feelings against the real source of frustration because it is too powerful or to uncertain. A prime example of this is the scapegoating or blaming of Jews in Germany for the economic difficulties that followed from World War I.

Culture sometimes provides a set of normative attitudes against a particular class of individuals. Ethnocentrism (see chapter 3) often provides the cultural basis for prejudice.

Social conflict may provide the basis for prejudice. Conflict between peoples often leads to prejudice against the opposition so as to justify the hostility. Protestants and Catholics in Northern Ireland exhibit clear prejudice for one another as a result of their continual conflict. Another cause of prejudice is economic conflict, as between African Americans and poor whites in the South and between large numbers of "Gastarbeiters" (guest workers imported by several European countries to take menial jobs) and the poor in those countries.

Not all people who are prejudiced act on their beliefs. Prejudice is a state a mind, not a particular form of action; though it often forms the basis for behavior.

Discrimination

Prejudice refers to people's attitudes and beliefs, discrimination to their behavior. In short, *discrimination* is the unequal treatment of people based on their membership in a group or social category. Traditionally, discrimination refers to behavior that harms the object(s) of discrimination.

REVERSE DISCRIMINATION

Recently, the term *reverse discrimination* has been used to refer to the providing of special advantages to individuals just because they belong to certain social categories. This concept, which will be discussed later in this chapter, has political implications and remains controversial. The term *discrimination* in this book is used in its traditional meaning.

The relationship between prejudice and discrimination is complex. People can be prejudiced without actually discriminating against a member of a minority group because of their fear of legal constraints, social pressure or their own stronger sense of social justice. An example of this is a member of a country club who dislikes Hispanics but votes to admit them to membership out of a sense that discrimination is wrong. Others may discriminate without being personally prejudiced, as in the case of employers who may not hire women for key positions for fear of offending some important clients who are prejudiced (e.g., Mobil Oil's concern for its operations in Saudi Arabia).

INSTITUTIONAL DISCRIMINATION

Discrimination need not be personal. *Institutional discrimination* refers to actions that may not have been intended to be discriminatory but have that effect nonetheless. For example, in the United States, poor housing and health care and generally inferior education have resulted in many African

Americans being unable to attain positions of authority, wealth, and influence in the corporate world. In some cases, denial of good occupational opportunities has rested less on personal prejudice and discrimination by individual employers than on the discriminatory practices woven into the very fabric of society, but the result has been discriminatory nonetheless.

PATTERNS OF RACE AND ETHNIC GROUP INTERACTION

Interaction between racial and ethnic groups may take a variety of forms. Simpson and Yinger (1985) have identified six basic patterns.

Assimilation

When a minority group modifies its distinctive characteristics and ways of life to conform to the pattern of the dominant group, sociologists refer to this pattern as *assimilation*. Most often, this change is voluntary and involves speaking the language of the dominant culture and changing ways of dress and even family names. This pattern is quite characteristic of the children of immigrants.

Sometimes, however, assimilation is forced on a minority group. For example, recently Bulgaria tried to eliminate the ethnic identity of citizens of Turkish descent, who are about 12 percent of the population, by having them change their Islamic names to Slavic ones and by eliminating any references to them in Bulgarian history books.

The United States has a mixed pattern. On the one hand, it emphasizes its role as a "melting pot," assimilating the various and diverse cultures of immigrants into its common culture. On the other hand, it also contains large pockets of unassimilated cultural diversity. Assimilation and maintenance of traditional patterns have coexisted within American society for at least a century.

The pattern of assimilation discussed above refers to changes in cultural practices and identities and is primarily applicable to the analysis of ethnic groups. Racial assimilation is more difficult because of the difficulty of changing the physical characteristics that form the basis of defining racial categories. Racial assimilation depends largely on racial intermarriage, which reduces the distinctiveness of racial categories.

Pluralism

The pattern in which all racial and ethnic groups retain their distinctive identities and enjoy relatively equal social standing is called *pluralism*. American society exhibits some characteristics of pluralism. Most major cities have distinctive neighborhoods that reflect the pluralistic nature of their citizens. Up to a point, the law protects the rights of the different ethnic and racial groups. However, the refusal to permit Mormons to practice polygamy (marriage to multiple spouses; see chapter 13) is a demonstration of the limits to pluralism in the United States.

Perhaps the most successful example of pluralism is found in Switzerland. There, large ethnic groups of French, Germans, and Italians live in relative harmony and equality. Most Swiss speak at least two of the country's four national languages; thus all are able to communicate with each other. Also, its small size and relative economic stability have contributed to making pluralism work in Switzerland.

Segregation

Segregation involves the physical and social separation of the different ethnic and racial groups. Segregation may be either voluntary or involuntary. Voluntary segregation occurs in most major cities in the United States. Different ethnic groups have created distinctive cultural environments in which they feel comfortable and practice their own culture. Voluntary segregation occurs even outside large cities, as with the Amish in Pennsylvania.

Segregation, however, is often involuntary. The foremost example is the system of apartheid in South Africa. There, blacks and whites live and socialize in completely separate and segregated worlds. Until recently blacks were allowed into white areas only to work, and when their work was over they had to go back to their own communities. The establishment of separate "homelands" for blacks, where they lived and carried out their social life, effectively segregated them from white South African society.

The United States is not immune to this pattern. Up until the 1960s, official segregation occurred in the South and unofficial segregation in the North. In the South, not only were residential neighborhoods segregated but also public facilities including restaurants, bus terminals, bathrooms, and even water fountains. Today, despite the illegality of overt discrimination, racial segregation in American cities is still quite widespread (Calmore, 1986), even though a majority of African Americans would prefer to live in integrated neighborhoods (National Opinion Research Center, 1987:171).

Domination

In the social pattern called *domination*, the dominant group uses its power to maintain control over minority groups, granting them little power or freedom. This pattern is evident in the Soviet Union's long-time domination of the Baltic states of Estonia, Latvia, and Lithuania—though this is currently changing. While in this particular instance domination does not involve segregation, the two often go hand in hand (e.g., South Africa).

Increasingly, world opinion makes it difficult to maintain open domination and repression of cultural minorities.

Population Transfer

One solution to intergroup differences is *population transfer*, the removal of one of the contending parties. For example, in 1972 all Asians were ordered to leave Uganda, a black African country in which they had lived for generations. Hostility between Hindus and Muslims in India led to the creation of two separate countries, India and Pakistan, in 1947 and to the resettlement of vast populations.

Cypress is similarly divided between those of Turkish and Greek origin. And Lebanon is divided into Christian and Muslim areas, and the Muslim areas are further divided between Sunni Muslims and Shiite Muslims.

Annihilation

Clearly the most extreme pattern of relations between different ethnic and racial groups is for one, the dominant, to annihilate or eliminate the other, the minority. *Genocide* is the extermination of one class of people by another; this was the Nazi's "final solution" to the perceived problem of Jews in Germany. The horrible extermination of 6 million Jews in Europe during World War II is not the only example of this pattern. Much of the colonization of Latin America and Africa by the European powers beginning in the sixteenth century depended on eliminating the native populations and taking their resources and their land. During the nineteenth century in the United States, many newspapers called for the annihilation of entire tribes of Native Americans.

RACIAL AND ETHNIC DIVERSITY IN THE UNITED STATES

Historically, the dominant group in U.S. society has been made up of white Anglo-Saxon Protestants (generally referred to as WASPs), those emigrating to these shores from Great Britain. Although no longer a numerical majority (they are about 25 percent of the population), they have largely shaped the nature of American society and hold key positions in its power structure. Nonetheless, the United States is both seen and actually is a land of considerable racial and ethnic diversity.

African Americans

Outside of a few African countries, the United States has the largest population of "blacks" in the world. They are about 12 percent of the population and have been the most visible and vocal minority group in recent years.

The first blacks were brought to the United States by the Dutch in 1619. They were either slaves or indentured servants who were required to work for a specific period of time to pay for the cost of their passage.

The first law legitimizing slavery was passed in Virginia in 1661, and it was not until Lincoln's Emancipation Proclamation in 1863 and the passage of the Thirteenth Amendment in 1865 that slavery was officially abolished nationally, though the northern states began to outlaw it starting in 1780. However, "Jim Crow" laws in the South preserved racial segregation and second-class citizenship for African Americans until the 1960s. Informal racial separation still persists today.

Most African Americans lived in the mostly rural South until World War I, when many migrated to northern cities in search of jobs. At the same time, large numbers of newly arrived European immigrants were in direct competition for the same jobs. This economic conflict resulted in continued discrimination against African Americans, this time without the legal support it had in the South, but just as demoralizing and destructive.

Although *Brown v. Board of Education,* the 1954 Supreme Court case that resulted in the formal desegregation of public education, was an important event in the history of race relations in the United States, the 1960s were the real turning point. During this decade the civil rights movement helped both to overturn segregation laws in the South and to pass civil rights bills reducing overt discrimination in employment and in access to public facilities. The Voting Rights Act resulted in the election of more African Americans to major political office.

Recently, the picture is mixed. More and more educated young African Americans have gained the education and skills necessary to attain better jobs. Consequently, there is a growing middle class. On the other hand, many, if not most, are still either unemployed or trapped in low-paying, dead-end jobs. The flight of many whites to the suburbs has left many African Americans marooned in deteriorating city slums, which are breeding grounds for crime and drug abuse. Economic pressures have reduced governmental funds for public services (especially for health, education, fire and police security, and mass transportation) that most affect those in the inner cities.

Despite the acknowledged gains of the past three decades, the quality of life of African Americans is still worse than that of whites and even of a number of other minority groups.

Hispanic Americans

Hispanic Americans are quite diverse in ethnicity and culture. Though many have their roots in Spanish culture, most have mixed Spanish, African, and Native American ancestry. Hispanic Americans comprise at least 6 percent of the population of the United States. Their exact population is uncertain because of the large number of "undocumented aliens," otherwise known as illegal immigrants.

The population of Hispanic Americans is growing very rapidly for two reasons: (1) the large number of Hispanic American women of child-bearing age, and (2) the high rate of legal and illegal immigration caused both by the proximity of Latin American countries to the United States and by the many Hispanic American families that encourage friends and relatives to immigrate and smooth the way for newcomers. It is quite likely that as their numbers increase, Hispanic Americans will overtake African Americans in the next few decades as the largest minority group in the country.

MEXICAN AMERICANS (CHICANOS)

Concentrated largely in the Southwest, Chicanos are the largest of the Hispanic American groups. Many Chicanos are descendants of the first Mexican settlers in the United States, but others are of more recent origin. Mexicans have always been seen as a convenient, inexpensive, and plentiful source of labor, especially for the large farms in the Southwest. Many are migrant farm laborers. However, the mechanization of agriculture has reduced the demand for farm workers, causing Chicanos to migrate to more urban locations, where the jobs are presumed to be.

The urban environment, however, has not been hospitable to Chicanos. Many live in urban ghettos ("barrios"), where they have about two-thirds of the average income of whites. As is common in urban slums, relatively few get the necessary education to improve their lot; only about one-quarter of Chicanos have completed high school. Chicanos have maintained their language and ethnic identity and exert considerable pressure to have bilingual education (in both English and Spanish) provided in the public schools.

PUERTO RICANS

Puerto Rico was ceded to the United States in 1898 after the Spanish-American War, and Puerto Ricans were granted U.S. citizenship in 1917. About half of the 2 million Puerto Ricans in this country live in the barrios of "Spanish Harlem" in New York City. They too have tried to maintain their language and ethnic identity, which, coupled with their typically dark skin, has caused considerable prejudice and discrimination against them.

Many Puerto Ricans have not fared well in the United States. Their average family income is about half that of Americans as a whole. Of the large number who go back to Puerto Rico after a stay in the United States, many intend to return sometime in the future.

CUBAN AMERICANS

Cuban Americans are the third largest group of Hispanic Americans in the United States; there are about half as many Cuban Americans as there are Puerto Rican Americans. The bulk of Cuban Americans came to the United States as a result of the 1959 Cuban revolution led by Fidel Castro. Most took up residence in Miami, close to home. Unlike the other two groups of Hispanic Americans, these immigrants were mainly from the middle class; they were well educated, and many were professionals. They adapted well to their new environment and became a potent political and economic force in Miami. Their average income is considerably higher than that of the other two groups and is almost equal to the general average in the United States.

A second wave of Cuban immigrants arrived in 1980. Known as the Mariel boat people, many of these were poor and unskilled; some had recently been released from prisons and mental institutions. Lacking the educational and occupational skills of the earlier Cuban immigrants, many in this group have not thrived. They have been received with considerable hostility, even from the earlier Cuban arrivals, who see them as a threat to the gains already made.

Asian Americans

Although numerically quite a small group, about 5 million people (2 percent of the population), Asian Americans have done quite well economically. Both their average educational level and their average income are higher than those of Americans as a whole. They make up the fastest-growing minority group in the United States at the present time. The group is made up of about equal numbers of people of Chinese, Japanese, and Filipino ancestry. These are joined by increasing numbers of Koreans and Vietnamese.

CHINESE AMERICANS

The first Asian immigrants arrived in the United States at about the time of the California gold rush in 1849. Tending to settle on the West Coast, they constituted cheap and plentiful labor for Americans pushing west. In the latter part of the nineteenth century, a severe depression caused immigrants and Americans alike to compete for scarce jobs. Having few legal protections, the immigrants fared poorly.

To combat the effects of discrimination, Chinese Americans in urban areas set up self-help organizations and kinship networks. However, these close-knit networks both discouraged assimilation and encouraged the Chinese to preserve their language and ethnic identity.

World War II marked an important change for Chinese Americans. Because of the shortage of labor, they were able to obtain better jobs, thus beginning the voyage of assimilation into the American culture. Without the earlier restrictions that generally limited them to working in laundries and restaurants, Chinese Americans began to enjoy considerable social mobility. However, many Chinese Americans have not achieved the same degree of success as the group as a whole and remain trapped in the ghettos of urban Chinatowns. The recent flare up of gang warfare and violence in New York's Chinatown highlights the variation in the quality of life within the Chinese American community.

JAPANESE AMERICANS

The Japanese immigrated to the United States somewhat later than the Chinese and remained largely on the West Coast. Because the Japanese had greater prior contact with Americans than did the Chinese immigrants, they were able to assimilate more easily. Also, they were more likely to engage in farming instead of competing for scarce urban jobs. However, the hostility that resulted from their attempt to buy farm land led to the imposition of legal restrictions against them.

Most devastating to Japanese Americans was their treatment by the United States after Japan's bombing of Pearl Harbor on December 7, 1941. Over 90 percent of all Japanese Americans were "relocated" to military internment camps, complete with barbed wire and armed guards. The United States government justified these actions by contending that these Japanese Americans could be undercover agents for Japan. Most concede now that the forced relocation of Japanese Americans was an act directed against a whole category of people and that it was probably motivated more by racism than by serious security considerations.

After World War II, Japanese Americans began to flourish. Their traditional emphasis on education and hard work paid off. They had more education than the average American and a much higher average family income. However, Japan's recent economic success has reawakened some old hostilities that may again be directed toward Japanese Americans.

FILIPINO AMERICANS

Filipinos were considered American subjects from 1898, when the Philippine Islands became an American possession, until they gained independence in 1935. Large numbers of Filipinos began to immigrate to the United States in the 1920s to meet California fruit growers' demand for cheap labor. Changes in the immigration laws in 1965 led to a doubling of the Filipino American population in the following decade. This rate of growth suggests that they may soon become the largest Asian American group. Most are well educated and have settled in urban areas, where they can put their considerable job skills to good use.

Native Americans (Indians)

No minority group in the United States has been treated as poorly as Native Americans. Their lands were taken by the government, and vast numbers were killed during the drive for westward expansion. Their culture was destroyed, and most were herded onto reservations and treated as "wards" of the state (that is, as children who could not take care of themselves). Approximately two-thirds of all Native Americans currently live on or near reservations. They have substantial unemployment—greater than 50 percent in some areas. Few Native Americans acquire the education necessary to obtain better, more stable jobs. Less than 40 percent have completed the eighth grade. Their rate of alcoholism is about eight times higher than the national average. The suicide rate for Native Americans is double that of Americans as a whole.

Recently, Native Americans have become better organized and more militant. Some tribes have demanded the return of or compensation for the lands taken from them, many of which contain vast resources of oil, water, and minerals. Many Native American communities are pressured from within to resist assimilation and to preserve their traditional cultures. The resurgence of interest in Native American culture throughout the United States may aid that effort.

White Ethnics

The term "white ethnics" has been used recently to refer to white Americans whose descent is from European areas other than Great Britain. They are the "non-WASPs." White ethnics are a diverse lot. Among them are the Italians, Poles, Scandinavians, Germans, Armenians, Greeks, Irish, and many more. They tend to congregate in separate communities or urban neighborhoods. Examples are South Boston, which is largely comprised of Irish Americans, and the North End of Boston, which is densely populated by Italian Americans. Polish Americans are concentrated in and around Chicago, Scandinavian Americans in Minnesota, and German Americans in Pennsylvania. While white ethnic groups have always been marked by a sense of cohesiveness, they experienced a surge of ethnic awareness and pride after other minority groups, especially African Americans, began to enjoy social and political gains as a result of the civil rights movement of the 1960s. In some people, this ethnic pride represented a form of backlash caused by the preferential treatment that African Americans and Hispanic Americans began to receive at that time. In others, however, ethnic pride simply represented a renewed interest in ethnic identity and culture. To realize the strong presence of ethnic pride in American life, one need only consider the number of ethnic groups who each year mount major parades in New York and many other large cities. Many groups feel that their pride is justified by the substantial progress they have made in moving from the factories and sweatshops that were the work places of their parents and grandparents to better-paying, more stable, and higher status jobs.

Large numbers of immigrants arrived on these shores during the late nineteenth and early twentieth centuries. Many of these immigrants desired nothing more than to be assimilated into American culture. They often insisted on their children speaking only English in the home, and they changed their names to sound more "American."

CONTEMPORARY ISSUES IN RACE AND ETHNIC RELATIONS

Racism

Racism is the belief that one racial category is inherently superior to another. The ideology of racism provides the moral basis for discrimination. The history of Western colonialism is based on racism. The populations of the colonized areas, often perceived to be at a lower stage of evolutionary development, were defined as biologically inferior. Consequently, it was not considered necessary to treat them with the ordinary civility required among equals.

Adolf Hitler's political philosophy centered around the alleged superiority of the "Aryan" race (supposedly composed of Caucasians of non-Jewish descent, of which the tall, blond, light-skinned, blue-eyed man was considered the ideal) and its right to rule the world. The notion of a pure "Aryan" race is a biological fiction; such a race does not exist. (Hitler himself was short, dark-skinned, and dark-haired.)

Racism has played a major role in the history of the United States. Africans were brought here as slaves and treated as inherently inferior beings. As large numbers of Asians came to this country, they met similar attitudes. Native Americans were routinely treated as inferiors. All these cases of racism seem to be based on economic factors. It appears that racism has often served the economic interest of the dominant population. Those deemed inferior could be given (or, as in slavery, compelled to perform) the menial, low-paying jobs that, given a choice, most people are unwilling to do. The ideology of racism—inherent inferiority—provided the justification for this exploitation. It took a Civil War, constitutional amendments, and legislation to do away with legally supported racism in the United States.

Besides the personal form described above, racism has an institutional form. *Institutional racism* refers to organizational practices that have the effect of treating racial groups unequally. Institutional racism is often evident in the subjective hiring process, which often disqualifies those who are different, including racially different, because they "don't fit in" or are not "one of us."

Affirmative Action

The societal response to personal and institutional racism has been to develop a policy of *affirmative action*, which is the practice of setting goals and timetables for increasing the number of minority group members in such organizations as businesses, government offices, and educational institutions. Despite the belief of some that affirmative action leads to the hiring of less-qualified or underqualified individuals, affirmative action does not require nor does it usually lead to such action; it is intended to ensure that those formerly excluded are now included in the mainstream of economic, social, and educational life. The exact form of affirmative action required varies by circumstance.

Not all people accept the concept of affirmative action. Some have seen affirmative action as *reverse discrimination*, or prejudicial action against the interests of white people who themselves may have no history of prejudice or racial discrimination. Proponents of affirmative action argue that the government has a right and responsibility to act against *institutional* racism and discrimination with *institutional* remedies. The debate continues today.

Race, Ethnicity, and Social Class

In an important book entitled *The Declining Significance of Race*, Wilson (1978) argues that the plight of African Americans has become less a matter of racial discrimination than of social class, though he acknowledges that the two are deeply intertwined. He focuses his analysis on the economic changes required to improve the lot of African Americans. Wilson continues his structural study of inner city African Americans in his more recent book (Wilson, 1987), *The Truly Disadvantaged: The Inner City, the Underclass, and Public Policy*.

Wilson's work has often been misinterpreted as saying that race is no longer a factor in American society. He believes that racial discrimination still exists but that social class has become increasingly important. While there has been a dramatic increase in the size of the African American middle class, it is still a proportionately smaller group than among Americans in general. Whereas the African American middle class is estimated to be about 20 percent of all African Americans in the United States, the middle class encompasses between 35 to 45 percent of the entire population. Also, even when African Americans and whites in the same social class are compared, the latter have higher incomes and a better quality of life (Landry, 1987).

African Americans thus seem doubly handicapped. They suffer from racism, personal and institutional, and the effects of their class position. The same is apparently true for some Hispanic Americans and for Native Americans, though not for Asian Americans, who are more likely to have a higher social class position than members of the other minority groups discussed above. When economic conditions improve, competition between different groups, and hence discrimination, is reduced. On the other hand, when economic conditions worsen, the reverse occurs.

*T*he issue of race and ethnicity has been discussed in this chapter. Though race has certain physical markers, it is basically socially defined. Because of constant interbreeding, there are no "pure" races. Ethnic groups are defined in terms of cultural rather than physical differences. Minority groups are a feature of American society and often serve as the basis for prejudice (an attitude about a particular category of individuals) and discrimination (a pattern of behavior that results in the unequal treatment of members of a particular category).

The various patterns of racial and ethnic interaction in society were identified: assimilation (becoming like the dominant group), pluralism (retaining group distinctiveness and equality between all groups), segregation (physical and often unequal separation), domination (majority control over minority groups), population transfer (removing one of the groups), and annihilation (e.g., genocide).

Several minority groups in the United States were briefly described. The important issue of racism was explored in both its personal and institutional forms. Society's response to institutional racism has been to develop affirmative action programs, despite the opposition of some who call this policy reverse discrimination. Finally, the relative contributions of race and social class to discrimination were discussed, with the conclusion that both still play a role.

12

Gender and Age Stratification

*S*ex and age are the two most universal bases for social stratification in all societies. In this chapter, we will discuss the relationship between the biological concept of sex and the sociological concept of gender. We will examine the differences between men and women and the source of those differences. The issue of sexism, and responses to it, will also receive attention.

The role of age in American society will also be analyzed. Ageism, as a counterpart to sexism and racism, will be explored. Biological and psychological as well as social and cultural aspects of growing old will be discussed.

SEX AND GENDER

In all societies, men and women are treated differently. Societal expectations for behavior vary by sex. But what is this characteristic on which these differences are based?

Sex: A Biological Designation

Sex is a biological concept that is the basis for the division of the human species into females and males. Sex is determined at conception, when both parents contribute equally to the twenty-three pairs of chromosome that are the child's biological inheritance. One of these pairs determines the child's sex. The mother can contribute only an X chromosome to this pair, whereas the father may contribute either an X or a Y chromosome. If the father contributes an X to the mother's X, the resulting embryo will have an XX pair and be female; if he contributes a Y to the mother's X, it will have an XY pair and be male.

The chromosomal differences lead to different tissue and organ development. The basic structure of a developing embryo will be female unless testicular tissue produces the hormone testosterone, which leads to the development of male genitals. Thus with one rare exception, everyone is biologically either female or male. The exception is the *hermaphrodite*, the rare person who has some combination of female and male genital organs.

BIOLOGICAL AND SECONDARY SEX CHARACTERISTICS

Biologists distinguish between *primary sex characteristics*, the genitals necessary for human reproduction, and *secondary sex characteristics*, the different physical attributes of males and females (such as wider hips and larger breasts for females and more extensive bodily hair and greater upper body strength for males) that are not directly related to reproduction. Both serve to mark the differences between females and males.

Gender: A Social Designation

Female and male are concepts that are applicable to human and to other animal species equally. On the other hand, the terms *men* and *women* refer only to humans, because these signify *gender*, the social and cultural traits that different societies assign to males and females. Gender is socially defined, whereas sex is biologically determined. Societies assign varying characteristics to females and males; however, nature does not vary the basic characteristics of female and male.

The differences between the concepts of sex and gender are important. Except as a consequence of transsexual surgery, biological sex differences between females and males are not subject to change. However, gender differences are social constructions and are subject to social change. The way American society, for example, defines appropriate "feminine" behavior can be changed. In fact, it has been changing quite dramatically for more than a half century.

HOW DIFFERENT ARE MEN AND WOMEN?

Biological Evidence

Both sexes have female and male hormones, though females have more of the former and males more of the latter. Though it is not scientifically valid to apply the results of animal studies to human beings, there is evidence that increasing the levels of male hormones leads to increased aggressiveness and sex drive in some animals. However, the effects of hormones on the behavior of either females or males vary considerably both between individuals and for the same individual at different times.

As a rule, males are taller and heavier than females and have greater muscular strength. To some extent, these differences contribute to the ability of males to dominate females. However, from another point of view, females can be seen as the more durable sex, for while more males than females are conceived, more of them die before birth and at younger ages throughout the life cycle. Though there are about 140 males conceived and 106 born for each 100 females, this gap disappears by the time they reach their mid-twenties and are actually reversed (85 males for each 100 females) after the age of sixty-five. Also, more malformed male infants than females are born, and, apparently, there are more hereditary defects among males. Females also seem to have a greater tolerance for pain and to be more resistant to disease than males.

In short, there is ample biological evidence of differences between males and females. Some of these differences favor females; others favor males.

Psychological Evidence

It is evident that there are typical differences in the behaviors and personalities of men and women. Men, as a rule, tend to be more aggressive and more active. They exhibit greater mathematical ability and greater skill at spatial visualization. Women, on the other hand, are more likely to be nurturant, that is, concerned about and inclined to take care of others. They are more emotional and verbal.

While there is no disputing the existence of these and other differences between men and women, it is very difficult to determine whether they have a biological basis or are learned. Studies of adults are of little help because by adulthood biology and learning are so intertwined that it is almost impossible to disentangle them. Investigators have focused on infants in whom little learning has taken place, when sex-relevant differences, it is presumed, can be ascribed largely to nature.

A number of studies have shown just such sex-linked differences in infancy. For example, male babies are more active than female babies, while female babies smile more frequently. However, even in these studies it is not always easy to attribute these differences simply to biology. A growing body of evidence suggests that from birth, boy babies and girl babies are treated differently. Boy babies generally receive rougher treatment than girl babies; for example, they are more often bounced on the knee. Their parents are also more tolerant of their restlessness. Girl babies are generally handled more gently and treated more affectionately. These differences in treatment begin within the first few weeks of life.

Another way of studying sex differences is to examine cases of sex "misassignment," where a person of one sex is mistakenly taken for and treated as a person of the other sex. This has occasionally happened, for example, when there has been a genital deformity at birth and a biological boy (lacking a penis) is raised as a girl; or when a girl whose clitoris (internal genital organ) is enlarged and taken to be a penis is raised as a boy. Money and Ehrhardt (1972) have shown that children can be raised to be either gender, irrespective of their biological sex.

There seems to be agreement that there probably are basic biological predispositions that account for differences in behavior in females and males. However, there is considerable variation within as well as between each sex group; many of these predispositions can be canceled out through cultural learning. Moreover, the differences in behavior that do exist involve relatively insignificant activities that do not justify social stratification by sex (Hyde, 1985).

Cross-Cultural Evidence

Another research approach is to look at the evidence from different societies. If gender differences are solely a function of biological sex differences, there should be no variation across societies in *gender roles*, the patterns of behavior, rights and obligations defined as appropriate for each sex. If substantial differences in gender roles do exist, it suggests that they are caused more by culture than by biology.

ALLOCATION OF SOCIETAL TASKS

A number of anthropologists (e.g., Mead, 1935; Murdock, 1937) have studied the allocation of societal tasks on the basis of sex. In general, three clear patterns emerge from these studies. First, sex is a major basis for allocating social tasks. In most if not all societies, men and women are assigned different social roles. Second, a limited number of tasks seem to be consistently assigned to one sex rather than to another. Women are universally responsible for child rearing and domestic care, activities that center around the home. Men are assigned tasks that require intense physical activity and travel away from the home, such as hunting and fighting.

Third, beyond this limited number of consistently sex-linked tasks, there is considerable cross-cultural variation in gender roles. In other words, what is considered appropriate female behavior in one society may be performed by males in another. For example, Murdock (1937) found that in fifty-four societies, the task of "preparing and planting soil" was "always" or "usually" performed by men, in fifty-seven societies it was performed by women, and in thirty-three societies it was performed equally by men and women.

The cross-cultural evidence suggests, then, that there are some consistent cross-cultural patterns in social roles that are linked to sex differences but that these are neither predominant nor inevitable; considerable variation in social roles also exists.

MARGARET MEAD'S APPROACH

Perhaps the most dramatic description of the cultural influence on behavior often thought to be exclusively sex-linked is found in the work of Margaret Mead (1935). She studied three societies in New Guinea. Two of them showed considerable similarity in the behavior of men and women. In one, the Arapesh, *both* men and women were cooperative, unaggressive, and emotionally warm. In another, the Mundugumor, who were headhunters and cannibals, *both* men and women were selfish, aggressive, and insensitive to others. In short, Arapesh men and women exhibited what is generally considered to be "feminine" behavior, and Mundugumor men and women displayed typical "masculine" behavior.

In the third society, the Tchambuli, there were in fact differences between men and women, but they were the opposite of what are considered typical gender roles in American society. Women were dominant, wore no ornaments, and were unemotional; men, on the other hand, were submissive, emotional, gossipy, and nurturant toward children.

GENDER ROLES

*Traditional
Gender Roles
and
Stereotypes*

Women in the home and men outside would be an accurate summary of traditional gender roles of the past. Men were seen as responsible for working outside the home and earning the income necessary to support the family. They were the main contact between the family and the outside world. They were also supposed to be the authority figure and the disciplinarian of the family. They were expected to make the key family decisions.

It was their destiny to participate significantly in the life of society, especially its political activities. Politics and higher education were considered exclusively male preserves.

Women, on the other hand, were expected to focus their lives around the home and children. Their main tasks were child rearing and home care. In their spare time, they would engage in voluntary and charitable activities in their communities.

In short, gender roles became stereotypes: the husband/father as the dutiful provider and the wife/mother as the contented homemaker taking good care of her husband and children. Personality stereotypes developed that paralleled these roles. Women were expected to be affectionate, sensitive to others, and caring. They were considered dependent, emotional, passive, and conformist. They were not expected to be too knowledgeable about anything mechanical, athletic or political. Given their focus on the home and children, they would not need to know about the complexities of the outside world; they could passively rely on their husbands.

Men, on the other hand, were expected to be assertive (if not aggressive), self-reliant, competent, and knowledgeable in a range of areas that would enable them to be successful in the "outside" world. Their occupational roles took priority over their family roles; though such emphasis may not always have been preferred, it was generally considered good for the family.

Gender Roles and Stratification	**GENDER INEQUALITY**

A Functionalist View. The initial position of functionalists is that if all or most societies exhibit a pattern of male dominance, then it must be functional and beneficial, at least to some degree. The allocation of different tasks to different roles, a division of labor, is seen as highly efficient (see bureaucracy; chapter 5). Since biological sex differences already distinguish men from women, most societies capitalize on it.

Because human infants are helpless they must be nurtured for some time. Before the advent of formulas and bottles, breast feeding was essential for survival. The very act of breast feeding is itself a nurturing and supportive act that requires the mother to stay with the infant, often close to home. Thus, the functionalists (e.g., Zelditch, 1955) argue, it is efficient that she be responsible for the child and the home, while freeing the husband to deal with the larger world outside.

Functionalists maintain that this division of labor is still an efficient one (Parsons and Bales, 1955). Families need specialists: an *expressive* leader who is concerned with its internal relationships, and an *instrumental* leader who connects the family with the outside world. While it is not necessary that women be the expressive leaders and men the instrumental leaders, the earlier division of labor rooted in biology was an efficient system and thus easier to continue. Equally important, the two spheres—home and the outside world—have traditionally carried different amounts of prestige, the former not commanding as much respect as the latter. Thus men playing the instrumental role are accorded higher prestige and authority than women playing the expressive role.

This view was generally accepted until recently, when critics began to attack it for being outmoded. Given modern conveniences, longer life spans, and fewer children, among other changes, women no longer have to devote their lives to the expressive, internal relationships within the family.

Also, the changing economic and social climate argues against inflexible roles for either men or women.

A Conflict View. To the conflict theorist, the functionalist argument is simply a way to justify the power of the dominant group. However the differences in power between men and women may have begun, they have been maintained because those benefiting from these differences have little reason to change the situation (Collins, 1985).

Conflict theorists argue that the source of gender role differences is rooted in economic inequality. Since men, in their traditional roles, are seen to make a greater economic contribution to society than women, they are accorded greater prestige and power. In societies where women and men make relatively equal contributions to the economy of society, there is considerably less gender inequality. Blood and Wolfe (1960) demonstrate that even in the United States a woman's power in the family is directly related to her economic contribution.

Today, functionalist and conflict theorists are in less disagreement than they were in the past. Many conflict theorists accept the idea that the traditional division of labor by sex may have been functional at one time. Also, a growing number of functionalists understand that the traditional roles are no longer as functional as they once might have been.

Contemporary Gender Roles

Gender roles today are more flexible than they were in the past. While many traditional conceptions of gender roles persist, considerable variation is permitted and even encouraged. More women are in the labor force, and the word *househusband* has entered into the language. More and more organizations have provisions for "parental", rather than "maternal" leave for childbirth and initial child care.

WORK

In recent years there has been a remarkable change in the economic base of gender inequality. Whereas in 1900 only about 20 percent of women worked outside the home, in 1987 the figure was about 55 percent—and about three-quarters of them worked full time. More than half of all married women are in the labor force. About two-thirds of married women with school-aged children and a little more than half with preschoolers are working; the numbers are considerably higher for divorced women.

Men and women continue, however, to show differences in the types of jobs they hold. Women still predominate in what have been considered "feminine" jobs: clerical, sales, and service positions. Men are more likely to be in the professions, managerial positions, and the skilled trades. Though the situation is changing, traditional sex segregation is fairly common in the occupational world. And women earn slightly less than two-thirds the income of men in comparable jobs, though the discrepancy has been decreasing.

EDUCATION

Colleges and universities used to be exclusively for men. That situation, too, has changed. Increasing numbers of women have been entering institutions of higher learning; in fact, at the present time more women than men attend these institutions. The same is true, to some degree, for postgraduate education. More women than men earn master's degrees, though men are more likely to receive Ph.D. degrees, which are considered stepping stones to high-level professional careers. This also is changing fairly rapidly.

The increased presence of women in the labor force did not end sex segregation there, and the same is true for institutions of higher learning. Women still take different courses of study than men. They are less likely to pursue programs in science and engineering and more likely to focus on the humanities and social sciences. Even though increasing numbers of women are enrolling in business programs, most degrees in business still go to men. These differences often reflect the different socialization experiences of men and women.

POLITICS

Women in the United States received the right to vote only in 1920. Until fairly recently, it was rare for women to hold major elective or appointive office. That situation, too, has changed, but more rapidly at the local than at the national level. There are now a considerable number of women mayors and some female state governors. A number of women serve in the Congress, and a woman, Geraldine Ferraro, has run for vice president of the United States. But though the political power of women is increasing, it is still not commensurate with their numbers in the population.

HOUSEWORK

Increasing numbers of husbands share household duties. However, the home is still seen primarily as the province and responsibility of women. Husbands' household tasks tend to center around the family car, finances, the lawn, and repair work. So while many wives and husbands share household tasks, the sharing is often not totally equal, and many women find themselves having to do most of the child care, cooking, and housework as well as their outside job. Hochschild (1989) has termed this "the second shift."

The full effect of the changing nature of gender roles, however, has yet to be felt. Clearly, men are increasingly likely to share child care and housework with their wives. The transmission of new conceptions of gender roles through socialization (see chapter 6) will likely result in an increase in the number of men who are willing to accept household responsibilities in the future.

GENDER ROLE SOCIALIZATION

Family. Gender roles are learned in the course of socialization. In the family, children are treated as either boys or girls. Boys have traditionally been expected to be active, rough, and independent. Girls have been taught to be gentle, caring, and dependent. Some of this learning has been direct, as when boys are treated more roughly than girls; some of it has been more indirect, as when children observe the gender behavior of their parents. Though families today are less likely to use stereotypical blue clothes for boys and pink for girls, there is ample evidence that the two sexes are treated differently (Major, 1981).

Peer groups. The peer group also plays a role in gender socialization. Peer group activities of boys and girls differ significantly (Lever, 1978). In middle childhood (the pre-teen and early teen years), boys often engage in team activities, like sports, in which competition and rules are extremely important. Girls, on the other hand, are often involved with fewer peers in less organized, more spontaneous activities that have less stringent rules (e.g., jump rope, talking, and singing). This difference decreases in later childhood and the teen years.

Schools. Until fairly recently, schoolbooks usually portrayed boys and girls in stereotypical gender roles. For example, boys in stories were active and girls passive; girls played with dolls, boys with trucks and soldiers. Men and women were portrayed in stereotypical parental roles. Growing awareness of and pressure on the publishing industry have led to considerable change in the portrayal of gender roles in textbooks and school materials.

High school curriculums have generally reflected traditional gender roles. Boys took shop and science, girls home economics and literature. Again, greater awareness and social pressure have led to change. Increasing numbers of teachers and guidance counselors advise students to take courses of study that interest and will be useful to them, independent of gender stereotypes.

Mass media. The mass media—films, books, magazines, and especially television—are important agents of socialization (see chapter 6). Nowhere have the traditional gender role stereotypes been reinforced more than in the media (Busby, 1975). Until quite recently, men were usually portrayed as tough and fearless law enforcers, brilliant scientists, expert physicians, and skilled lawyers. They took charge of situations, except in their homes, where they were flummoxed by simple challenges such as operating a dishwasher and making a grilled cheese sandwich. Women, on the other hand, were generally merely decorative. They looked pretty, deferred to men, and were often the targets of comedy. Their activities centered around the home.

These stereotypical portrayals began to change during the late 1980s, and increasingly women are being portrayed in responsible positions, as active agents in life instead of as passive, attractive bystanders.

Goffman (1976) demonstrates the effects of advertising practices on gender role socialization. Like television, print advertising was once more guilty than now of portraying men and women in ways that reinforced traditional stereotypes. Men were made to look taller, and therefore more powerful; women were often shown lying on a bed or sofa or sitting on a floor—a subordinate place.

SEXISM

Ideology

Changes in traditional gender roles did not occur without a struggle. Earlier practices reflected what has come to be called *sexism*, the view that one sex (usually the female) is inherently inferior to the other. Sexism is similar to racism in that it refers to an entire category of individuals, is based on physical attributes, and restricts the social and economic opportunities of its objects.

The ideology of sexism is rooted in the belief that men are naturally superior to women. The belief systems of most of the world's major religions support this view, whether in the Old Testament ("Blessed art Thou, O Lord our God, King of the Universe, that I was not born a woman"), the New Testament ("A man is the image of God and reflects God's glory; but woman is the reflection of man's glory"), and the Koran ("Men are superior to women on account of the qualities in which God has given them pre-eminence").

Institutional Sexism

Sexism is similar to racism also in that as well as being personal it also has an *institutional* form. In other words, the belief in the inherent superiority of males is woven into the social fabric and affects the social and economic opportunities of women whether it is personally intended or not.

Some see institutional sexism as more destructive than personal sexism. Individuals who are prejudiced against women and discriminate against them can be confronted and their views and actions possibly changed. But institutional sexism, like institutional racism, is more pervasive and less easy to deal with directly at the personal level. For example, police and fire departments have traditionally excluded women from their ranks, though some women are undoubtedly capable of performing these jobs. Governmental affirmative action programs that address racism (see chapter 11) also try to remedy the results of sexist hiring practices.

Sexism is embedded in the very language of our society. For example, when gender is unknown or immaterial, the masculine form is used. Linguistic practices like this show how pervasive yet subtle sexism is. For several years writers and publishers have been experimenting with different ways of eliminating sexism in language.

Responses to Sexism

FEMINISM

One response to sexism has been the rise of *feminism*, a social movement (see chapter 22) organized to eliminate sexist attitudes toward women. Feminism challenges the view that traditional conceptions of gender roles are natural and necessary to an effective society. Feminists argue that gender stratification restricts the educational and occupational opportunities of over one-half of the population and point out that this is not just discriminatory, it is dysfunctional for society, which needs as many skilled and educated people as possible, whether they are men or women, to perform necessary tasks.

Feminists also battle against sexual harassment wherever it occurs. Women report unwanted and uninvited sexual advances, especially from those in authority at work or in school, with some frequency. *Acquaintance rape*, forced sexual intercourse by a man who is known to or engaged in a social activity such as a date with the victim, is of growing concern. Feminists have pushed for laws and procedures to protect women from these destructive practices.

RESISTANCE TO FEMINISM

Feminism is resisted by those who embrace the traditional view of the appropriate roles for men and women. Some men oppose feminism because it threatens their dominance and control. Some women also oppose feminism, especially those who have incorporated the traditional view of gender roles into their own gender role behavior and derive satisfaction from it. Others resist feminism in the mistaken belief that all its proponents are man-haters who seek to set men and women against each other. Still others don't oppose feminism but point to "sexist" practices that disadvantage men (e.g., the frequent presumption that in divorce children should be awarded to the mother). But supporters of feminism have grown in number and influence over the years.

A Symbolic Interaction View

Activity (substitution) theory (Friedman and Havighurst; 1954), an alternative to disengagement theory, points out the importance of a high level of social activity to the personal satisfaction and sense of self among the elderly. Drawing heavily on symbolic interaction theory, activity theory emphasizes the sense of self that derives from the statuses people occupy and the roles they play. The elderly are no different from younger people; they should not be treated differently. Proponents of this view also stress the differences among elderly people. Some may want to disengage; others will not. No one action will be suitable for all the elderly.

Critics of this viewpoint argue that activity theorists do not really come to grips with the reality that some elderly do suffer from health and other problems that would warrant their disengagement from difficult and stressful roles.

Responses to Age Inequality

The elderly have become a much more politically active group over the past quarter of a century. Taking their lead from the various political movements of the 1960s and 1970s, several organizations have formed to promote the interests of the elderly. In 1972 Maggie Kuhn, a church administrator, founded the Gray Panthers, an organization of young and old who are dedicated to changing society's treatment of the elderly. Perhaps the most politically potent of these organizations is the American Association of Retired Persons (AARP). It has a large membership and a newsletter and is quite influential in national and state politics.

Political pressure from these and other groups has been highly effective. The federal government and many state governments have passed laws forbidding forced retirement because of age. Social Security payments are now tied to levels of inflation, and a national health care program for the elderly, Medicare, has been created. Many of these advances are the results of direct and organized action taken by the elderly themselves.

The chapter began by distinguishing between sex as a biological concept and gender as a social and cultural creation. Some representative biological differences between men and women were summarized, as was the view that one sex is "weaker" than the other. Psychological evidence of the differences between men and women were discussed. Studies of infants and other societies were described to explain the biological roots of gender differences. By and large, it was decided that differences between men and women are more a result of cultural learning than of innate biological factors.

Traditional gender roles—woman at home, man at work—became stereotypes and reinforced the separation of the sexes. The functionalist view is that the traditional gender roles merely capitalize on a basic biological difference between men and women. Conflict theorists, on the other hand, see these stereotypes as a form of stratification, that is rooted in economic factors.

Gender roles have been changing over the past several decades. More women are in the labor force than ever before, even mothers of young children. However, sex segregation still occurs in the types of jobs held. Also, more women are enrolled in colleges and universities, and they are more likely than ever before to be active in politics. More husbands share child care and household responsibilities. An attempt was made to show how socialization in the family, the peer group, schools, and the mass media contribute to traditional ideas about gender roles. It was pointed out that within the last decade more emphasis has been placed on flexibility in roles.

Personal and institutional sexism, as a counterpart to racism, were discussed. One response to sexism has been the growth of feminism, a social movement to eliminate sexist attitudes toward women. Objections to feminism are based on an eagerness to retain existing privileges and to play out culturally learned gender roles, misconceptions of what it is, and a concern that it is limited to eradicating discrimination against women.

Age as a basis for social stratification was also discussed. American society has been aging during this century, leading to the growth of a new specialty, social gerontology, to deal with the problems of aging. The biological changes that take place with increasing age were discussed, as was the misconception that all elderly people are sick, frail or bedridden.

The myth of the automatic deterioration of the intellectual and mental capacities of the elderly was shown to be inaccurate. A detailed discussion was provided on some of the social and cultural changes (e.g., work, retirement, economic base) that take place in old age. The social isolation of some elderly people was mentioned, and the growing problem of elder abuse was described.

The issue of ageism was discussed. The functionalist argues the necessity of providing for the disengagement of the elderly from positions of responsibility. Conflict theorists, on the other hand, dispute the argument that disengagement is at the heart of age stratification. They point to the economic benefits to those in control of excluding the very young and the old from the labor market. The importance of activity for the elderly's conception of self, derived from symbolic interaction theory, was described as another alternative to disengagement theory.

Finally, it was pointed out that a number of recently formed organizations promote and protect the interests of the elderly. They have become increasingly influential and caused the passage of important and beneficial legislation.

13

The Family

The family is the most fundamental institution in all societies. Because we tend to be so immersed in families, it is easy for us to take them for granted. In doing so, we risk not fully understanding their importance. However, when the existence of the family is threatened, we become more aware of it. That is the case today, when the utility of the family as a key social institution is being questioned and dire predictions abound about its ultimate demise.

What is this social institution that creates such profound concern? How universal is it? Is it really functional, either for society as a whole or for the individuals who compose it? What generalizations can we make about the contemporary American family and its future? In this chapter, we will address these questions in light of contemporary knowledge about the family.

KINSHIP: BASIC CONCEPTS

Kinship is "a structured system of relationships, in which individuals are bound to one another by complex, interlocking and ramifying ties" (Murdock, 1949:2). In essence, kinship defines a social network. The key element of kinship is the family.

Family
    The *family* is a relatively permanent social group of individuals connected by ancestry, marriage or adoption. In our society, we are mostly familiar with one particular version of the family, the nuclear family, and to

some degree with a second, the extended family. A third major family structure also exists: the polygamous family.

THE NUCLEAR FAMILY

The *nuclear family* consists of two adults of the opposite sex who maintain a socially sanctioned sexual relationship, along with their own or adopted children (Murdock, 1949). Today, the predominance of this form of relationship is being challenged by the increasing recognition of single-parent families, childless/childfree families, and "domestic partnerships" of gay and lesbian couples in relationships that are the functional equivalents of marriage.

There are, moreover, two types of nuclear families. One is the *nuclear family of orientation*, the family into which we are born and in which we occupy the status of child. It is through the members of this family that we derive our initial orientation to life; hence its name. Another is the *nuclear family of procreation*, which is the family we create through marriage and in which we hold the status of adult. This family is often referred to as the "conjugal" family because of the centrality of the marital bond. Since it can be viewed from these two perspectives, then, each family can be said to be composed of two nuclear families.

Most people, therefore, are members of two nuclear families. Since these two social groups provide somewhat different experiences, people are subject to two sets of expectations and responsibilities. Ordinarily these do not conflict. On occasion, however, they may conflict, for example, when adults try to balance their responsibilities to their children and to their aged parents. Both have claims on time, energy, and resources. Balancing these responsibilities has become an increasing social problem, especially because of the increased lifespan of our population. The new term *sandwich generation* describes those mature adults who are increasingly "sand-wiched" between the needs of their aging parents and their developing children.

THE EXTENDED FAMILY

The *extended family* consists of two or more nuclear families linked by the parent-child tie, which includes the bonds of siblings. For example, you, your parents, and your grandparents comprise an extended family. The link in this chain is your parents, who are tied to your grandparents as their children and to you as your parents. The extended family is occasionally referred to as the "consanguineal" family because of the "blood" ties that bind them.

THE POLYGAMOUS FAMILY

One type of family not legally permitted in U.S. society (with the exception of the Mormons in an earlier time) is the *polygamous family*, which consists of two or more nuclear families linked by the marital tie. In some societies a person may have more than one spouse. When a woman may have two or more husbands, it is called *polyandry*. When a man may have two or more wives, it is called *polygyny*. Families comprised of a person, his or her multiple spouses, and their children are called the polygamous family (the general term covering either or both kinds of plural spouses).

Marriage

Whereas the family refers to a social group, *marriage* refers to the socially approved arrangement by means of which a family is created. It is in essence a set of customs, beliefs, and norms that socially defines the way that men and women can affiliate to create a family. It often entails a set of social, economic, and sexual obligations between partners.

A CROSS-CULTURAL PERSPECTIVE

The family is a universal social institution. It is instructive to compare how it is formed and structured and how it functions in different societies around the world.

Establishing Families

Although the ways in which families are created differ across societies, there are some universal regulations that restrict the selection of a partner and certain typical practices that people follow in selecting a partner.

PARTNER SELECTION REGULATIONS

Two basic and universal regulations guide partner selection. The first is *exogamy*, the rule that defines the class of individuals who are not acceptable as marriage (or sexual) partners. The most common form of this rule is the "incest taboo," which specifically prohibits close relatives from marriage to one another. Though there are occasional exceptions for royal families in a few societies, the incest taboo is a universal phenomenon. Exogamy, and specifically the incest taboo, forces the development of useful alliances outside the nuclear family and encourages social and cultural diversity.

The second regulation is *endogamy*, which specifies the class of persons with whom marriage is both permissible and encouraged. In many societies, particularly very small societies, the endogamous boundary coincides with the boundary of the society itself. In large, complex societies like the United States, the endogamous rule applies to those with similar social backgrounds of race, religion, ethnicity, and social class. Thus endogamy encourages group (or subgroup) solidarity.

Exogamy and endogamy function jointly. Together they define what family sociologists call the "field of eligibles," the pool of socially sanctioned potential marriage partners. In our own society, we are encouraged to select a marital partner from the field of eligibles. However, there is no longer the legal compulsion to do so that existed, at least for race, until fairly recently in some states. Even the moral force that urges selection from the socially defined field of eligibles has declined in recent years, as evidenced by the increasing rate of intergroup marriages.

PARTNER SELECTION PRACTICES

The actual procedures a person follows in selecting a partner vary considerably across the world. In general, however, there are four major practices used to acquire a marital partner.

One of the rarest forms is *marriage by capture*. In societies where there is a shortage of women, one means of correcting this imbalance and providing an appropriate number of wives is to capture them from other societies. There are just a few reported cases of such a practice. More common, however, is *marriage by purchase*. Many societies practice this form of mate selection. Sometimes the purchase involves a "bride price" or "bride service" on the part of the man or a "dowry" on the part of the woman or her family.

A fairly universal selection practice is *marriage by arrangement*. In this form the families of the man and woman arrange the marriage for them. Most societies consider marriage to be an important *social* bond, so important that it cannot be left to the judgment of the relatively immature young.

Finally, the most familiar practice is called *marriage by consent of the principals* or *conjugal courtship*. In this form mate selection is left to the two individuals themselves. In the United States, we generally consider this to be the only proper means of choosing a marital partner. However, this is not a universal view.

Types of Marriage

There are two basic types of marital arrangements: monogamy and polygamy.

MONOGAMY

Monogamy, marriage between one man and one woman at a time, is the arrangement we know best. It fits well with the relatively equal numbers of men and women of "marriageable age" in most societies, and hence allows each person a potential marital partner. Given the present high rate of divorce and remarriage in the United States, the system we have has been called "serial monogamy."

POLYGAMY

We have earlier mentioned *polygamy*, or plural marriages, and two of its forms: *polyandry*, marriage of one woman to two or more men; and *polygyny*, marriage of one man to two or more women. There is a third, relatively uncommon, form: *group marriage*, whereby two or more men are collectively married to two or more women. Some marital arrangements established on communes in the 1960s and 1970s approximated this marital form.

While monogamy is the most practiced form of marriage, it is not the most preferred form in the world; polygyny is (Murdock, 1949). However, since polygyny often requires substantial wealth and social status, it is likely to be practiced by only a few in the societies that permit it. Given the relatively equal number of men and women in most societies, and the relatively few individuals who can support plural households, most marriages are monogamous.

Patterns of Descent

How do we trace our ancestry? How do we determine who are our kin? Different societies around the world answer these questions differently. There are two major ways in which descent can be traced.

UNILINEAL DESCENT

Unilineal descent traces descent through only one parental line. *Patrilineal descent*, the most frequent form around the world, traces only through the male line. *Matrilineal descent* traces heritage only through the female line. Property, names, and resources of various kinds are passed down either from father to son or from mother to daughter, respectively. Patrilineal descent was more common in preindustrial pastoral and agricultural societies because men provided more of the necessary resources for the family. In horticultural societies, where women provided more of the family's necessities, matrilineal descent was more common.

NON-UNILINEAL DESCENT

Non-unilineal descent traces inheritance through both the male and female sides of the family. The system in existence in the United States (and in most industrial societies) is called *bilateral descent*, which traces descent equally through both the men and women on the father's side and both the men and women on the mother's side. One other non-unilineal descent system, *double descent*, is a straight linear combination of the matrilineal and patrilineal descent systems. Heritage is traced through the men (but not the women) on the father's side and the women (but not the men) on the mother's side.

Lineage is important in most societies. It often determines eligible marital partners as well as the distribution of property and other resources.

Patterns of Residence

Societies around the world differ in the customs that determine where newly created families establish residence. The decision as to whose family, if either, to reside near reveals the distribution of power between men and women. Residence contributes to that power by increasing the family's likely involvement in the marriage, especially child rearing. Residence patterns involve considerations of economic security and mutual protection. Thus the norms of residence are critical elements of a society. Four patterns are evident from anthropological reports.

Patrilocal residence, the most common pattern, occurs when two people marry and establish residence near or within the residence of the man. *Matrilocal residence* situates the new couple near or with the woman's family. *Bilocal residence* allows the new couple to choose between living with or near either family. The most familiar pattern to us is *neolocal residence*, where the new couple establish their own home regardless of the locations of nuclear families. This pattern reduces the opportunities for economic help and security but increases the opportunities for establishing a degree of independence.

Patterns of Authority

How power and authority are distributed within the family also varies across societies. The most common pattern is *patriarchy*, where family authority is vested in the man. Where this authority is vested in the woman, the pattern is called a *matriarchy*. When legal and moral authority is vested in both the man and the woman, we have an *egalitarian* system.

Few societies have a matriarchal system. Men have tended to dominate the family. However, the patterns are shifting in many societies, especially in the United States, as a result of the increasing numbers of women in the work force and of single or divorced female heads of households.

Marriage and family patterns are but one part of a society's culture. American society places great emphasis on the importance of the individual, perhaps best evidenced by the Bill of Rights. Given this important cultural value, it is not surprising that marriage and family patterns in the United States are weighted toward the individuals involved. In other societies, the importance of the group may overshadow the needs of the individual, and their marriage and family patterns will reflect that importance. While the patterns of other societies may seem strange to us at times, some of our patterns will seem equally strange to them. In short, marriage and family patterns both reflect and influence the general values of the society.

A THEORETICAL ANALYSIS OF THE FAMILY

The family has been the focus of intense analysis. Structural-functionalists have looked at the positive functions of the family. Conflict theorists, on the other hand, have tended to focus on the family's dysfunctions.

Universal Functions of the Family: A Functionalist View

The main analysis of the family from a functionalist view derives from the work of Murdock (1949) and Parsons and Bales (1955). This perspective argues that there are certain functions that the family serves in all societies, making the family central throughout the world.

REGULATION OF SEXUAL ACTIVITY

Every society places some restrictions on the sexual activities of its members. By and large, these limitations restrict sexual activity to the marriage and family system, whether this is monogamous or polygamous. The incest taboo is another restriction that involves the family.

REPLACEMENT OF SOCIETAL MEMBERS

The restrictions on sexuality are largely aimed at providing a mechanism for replacing societal members from generation to generation. No society can survive unless it can reproduce itself. Limiting sexual activity to the family provides an important way to do this.

SOCIALIZATION

The family is the agent not only for biological reproduction but also for social/cultural reproduction (socialization). Through the family, the society reproduces with reasonable continuity its social and cultural heritage. Though there are other agencies involved in the socialization process, none is a more powerful or more continuing influence than the family.

SOCIAL PLACEMENT

The family provides each individual with an initial social identity. These family-derived statuses give the person a legitimate position in society, a social standing that significantly influences later life experiences.

INTIMACY AND COMPANIONSHIP

The family provides both the initial and the ongoing social contexts in which the human needs for affection, warmth, and nurturance are met. The intimate nature of family life is especially suited to providing the necessary emotional support.

Dysfunctions of the Family: A Conflict Perspective

Conflict theorists do not see the family as the bastion of warmth, nurturance, and companionship described by the functionalists (e.g., Collins, 1985; and Engels, 1902, original, 1884). Instead, they take a radically different view, stressing the dysfunctional aspects of family life.

THE SUBORDINATION OF WOMEN

Friedrich Engels, a collaborator of Karl Marx, argued that the family subordinated women by making wives essentially the property of their husbands. Through childbearing and child rearing, women were kept in the home while men were free to organize society and participate in key social decisions.

VIOLENCE IN THE FAMILY

Conflict theorists note that a significant amount of violence occurs within the family. They point not only to rising levels of domestic violence, such as spouse and child abuse, in today's society but also to the statistics from earlier times indicating that a substantial portion of homicides in the United States were committed by family members, usually a spouse.

PERPETUATES THE STRATIFICATION SYSTEM

The functionalist view addresses the family's role in shaping social placement, without judging the desirability of the result. The conflict view suggests that in perpetuating the existing system, the family suppresses changes that might occur through unrestricted social mobility. Children of upper and middle class families tend to acquire more education, get better jobs, have higher incomes, be more healthy, and live longer than children from working class families.

DELEGITIMIZES VARIANT LIFESTYLES

The predominance of the traditional nuclear family tends to devalue alternative family structures and lifestyles. When a society prefers a nuclear family with the husband as key decision maker and the wife as domestic caretaker it makes other possibilities more difficult, whether it is that of the woman who wants to delay or forsake marriage for a career, of the man who wishes to spend more time with his family and less time on the job, or of those who choose a different sexual lifestyle.

In short, the conflict theorists argue that to define the traditional family as a model for all is in the best interests neither of society, because it stifles creativity and change, nor of the individual who may gain greater happiness and security in other types of arrangements.

THE CONTEMPORARY AMERICAN FAMILY

There is no question that the contemporary American family is considerably different than it was just a generation or two ago. We turn now to today's family in the United States.

General Characteristics

The American family is monogamous; we marry only one person at a time. And while there is more intermarriage today, and certainly more tolerance than before, we are also for the most part endogamous, generally marrying someone of the same race, religion, ethnicity, and social class. The selection of a marriage partner is primarily by individual choice and consent—conjugal courtship—rather than by other means. New couples generally establish a new home (neolocal residence) though economic considerations have led some young people to require help (including the sharing of a home) from parents. We have a bilateral descent system. Authority patterns in the family are increasingly egalitarian, though some families still have patriarchal (and in some subcultures, matriarchal) overtones.

A number of the functions originally performed by the family have been assigned to, or are at least shared with, other social institutions. Socialization, for example, is shared with the school, especially preschool and day care centers. Safety, security, and health are essentially the responsibility of the police, the courts, the medical profession, and government-sponsored health programs. The basic functions of intimacy, sexual regulation, and social placement are still largely in the hands of the family. In essence, the number of functions served by the family in the United States has diminished over the past century, making it a more specialized institution than it once was.

The marriage rate increased from 1976 to 1985, though it has decreased slightly over the last few years. The age at first marriage has been increasing over the past thirty years. As practically everyone knows, the divorce rate has been going up. All these trends seem to suggest a substantial change in contemporary American marriage and family patterns: marriages are contracted later in life, and more of them are being dissolved than before. Does this signal the demise of the family? Not according to most Americans, who overwhelming tell pollsters that they intend to get married. Moreover, the remarriage rate remains high. Taken together, all these trends suggest a considerable change in the American family, but not its disappearance.

The Importance of Romantic Love

Americans have generally considered romantic love to be an essential consideration in the decision to marry. What distinguishes romantic love from love of parents, friends, liberty, God or even an ice cream sundae is passion and a form of caring (Turner and Helms, 1988). Passion refers to the "fascination" that lovers have for each other, their preoccupation with one other, and a feeling of "exclusiveness" that makes their relationship take priority over other relationships. There is also an element of "sexual desire," the wish for physical intimacy with one other. Caring refers to the desire to give the utmost for the other, to sacrifice for the other, and to be a champion for the other.

Why is romantic love so important? Goode (1959) writes that it provides important emotional support. Love helps young couples loosen the bonds to their parents. It provides an incentive for marriage, the socially approved form for the satisfaction of emotional and sexual needs.

Though love is a cultural product, to most it seems to be a natural phenomenon. Love is a central element of books, plays, movies, television shows, and music. Although there are pragmatic considerations that affect both the decision to marry and the success of the marriage, most Americans cannot conceive of marriage without romantic love.

Parenthood

One of the greatest challenges to a marriage is parenthood. However, most Americans assert that they want to have children, and the majority of these would prefer to have two children (N.O.R.C., 1987:234). Children change the nature of the marital relationship, transforming it from a marriage to a family. Most new parents have received no real training for this important responsibility, although this is changing. Increasing numbers of young people are taking courses in high school or college that deal with family life. These courses have a pragmatic focus, introducing the students to the specific requirements of being a parent.

There is an important shift in parenthood today toward greater joint responsibility. More fathers are sharing more of the responsibilities of child rearing with their wives than has been true in the past. In part, this is because of the large numbers of women, including mothers of young children, are in the work force. Increasingly, parents are learning how to redistribute the tasks of parenthood to take into account their different skills and schedules, their other responsibilities, and, most important, the needs of the children.

Despite all these challenges, most parents find that children bring joy into their lives. They find that being parents broadens and enriches their lives and gives them increased contact with others, including social institutions such as the schools.

Dual-earner Families

The modern American family is increasingly a dual-earner family, where both partners work outside the home. Most husbands have always been in the labor force. Today more than half of all women are as well, and almost two-thirds of all mothers with children under the age of eighteen also work outside the home (U.S. Bureau of Labor Statistics, 1987). This increase is largely due to the influx of middle class women; there have always been large numbers of working class women employed outside the home. In addition, changes in societal values have increased career opportunities for these women, as have difficult economic conditions that require two incomes where one used to be sufficient.

Dual-earner families must make mutually satisfactory arrangements to share domestic and child care responsibilities. The growth of day care and preschool centers has helped parents, but these are relatively few in number and are generally available only to those who can afford the services. The number of "latchkey" children (children between the ages of five and thirteen who are unsupervised before or after school) remains high. Addressing these challenges is becoming a higher priority of policy makers. A difference in income has affected family decision making. Early studies by Blood and Wolfe (1960) showed that women shared in family decision making in proportion to the degree that they worked and contributed income to the family. Women who worked full time outside the home had more power than those who worked part time. Both had greater influence over family decisions than those who did not work outside the home at all. Today, more families are contending with issues of equity independent of whether and how much income is brought into the family (Spitze, 1988).

Family Violence

An increasing amount of violence is taking place within the family. Some of the increase is the result of people's greater willingness to report such cases to the authorities. However, there does seem to be an actual increase in the amount of family violence today.

Typically, abuse has been seen as a working class phenomenon. Actually, spouse and child abuse occurs in all social classes, though the likelihood of abuse increases with financial problems and unemployment. Most, though not all, of the victims of spouse abuse are women. About 2 million women are abused each year. Historically, abused women have had few alternatives to remaining with their violent husbands. Often there were children who may have been endangered by the violent spouse if the victim left. Further, some women had no economic alternative to staying. In the past, and even today in many places, the criminal justice system was hesitant to get involved in what it deemed a domestic dispute or a private family matter.

Currently, the increasing number of support groups, greater sensitivity on the part of police and the courts, and increased public awareness provide abused spouses more alternatives. There are now shelters that provide temporary homes for victims until they find more permanent quarters for themselves and their children. More police systems have instituted a "pro-arrest" policy, treating spouse abuse like any other kind of assault and battery.

Child abuse too has increased. About 2 million children are abused each year. As with spouse abuse, men are primarily responsible. In many cases, the abusers themselves were abused as children, perpetuating a cycle of violence. Courts are increasingly turning to treatment programs to break this cycle.

Marital Dissolution and Reconstituted Families

The high divorce rate in the United States is partly the result of our relatively high marriage rate. However, the major reasons for the increase in the divorce rate have to do with changes in American society.

Increasing emphasis on personal happiness and fulfillment has led many to leave relationships they find less than fulfilling. Increasing geographic and social mobility, combined with a weakening of community bonds, has undone many of the social restraints on marital dissolution. Women's greater participation in the labor force has allowed them to be economically independent. Dual-earner families have additional burdens that strain a marriage. There is less social stigma attached to divorce than in the past. Finally, the easing of divorce laws and the establishment of "no-fault" divorce have played significant roles.

WHO GETS DIVORCED?

Divorce is more likely among those who marry early, especially those marrying in their teen-age years. It is also more common among those in the working class than in the middle class. In part this is the result of the financial strain that is more likely to occur in working class families. Previously divorced people have higher subsequent divorce rates than those in their first marriages. The more dissimilar the social backgrounds of the marriage partners, the more differences are likely to emerge, and consequently the more likely the couple is to divorce. Finally, divorce is more common among those who are geographically mobile, in part because of the loss of the stabilizing influence of community bonds.

DIFFICULTIES DUE TO DIVORCE

Divorce often brings pain to marriage partners in addition to that which led to their separation (Spanier and Thompson, 1984). Divorce can bring feelings of personal failure and loneliness as well as financial hardship. Weitzman (1985) found that the after-divorce standard of living *dropped* substantially for women but *rose* for men.

Issues of child custody complicate many divorces. While typically women are awarded custody of the children, an increasing number of men are seeking more child care responsibility. *Joint custody*, in which the child may live with one parent but spend considerable time with the other, is becoming more common. In some situations, the child's time is divided equally between the two parents. Joint custody enables the child to maintain a relationship with both parents. However, this arrangement may be quite difficult for the parents especially in the case of a particularly nasty divorce.

In the past, divorce was seen as extremely harmful for the children. Present research seems to indicate that children are better off if unhappy parents divorce than if they stay together in an atmosphere of anger, bitterness, violence, and hate (Spanier and Thompson, 1984).

REMARRIAGE AND RECONSTITUTED FAMILIES

About three-quarters of divorced women eventually remarry, as do more than four-fifths of divorced men. This high rate of remarriage attests to the importance of marriage in American society. The demise of a marriage is often attributed to that particular marriage, not to the institution of marriage.

Remarriage creates a *reconstituted* or *blended* family made up of two parents, at least one of whom brings to this new family unit one or more children from a previous marriage. Interpersonal relationships in these families are extremely complex. Who is responsible to whom? Who provides discipline? Nurture? What are the responsibilities of the noncustodial biological parent? What authority does he or she wield? There is little societal agreement on appropriate family roles and responsibilities within these families. But as the number of blended families increases, more social definition of the appropriate norms, roles and social conventions are likely to be established.

The Variety of American Families

There is no single model for the contemporary American family. Middle class families have a higher standard of living than working class families, which affects how they function. Affluence brings a higher level of security; poverty and unemployment add strains. Class differences often influence the interpersonal dynamics of family life. Middle class couples are more likely to have flexible definitions of gender roles. They are more likely to spend their leisure time together. They tend to be more communicative with one another, which derives in part from the greater verbal skills learned through their higher level of education and their participation in jobs that often require and reinforce verbal skill.

Cultural traits of racial and ethnic groups also influence family styles. For example, the historic removal of black men from the family during slavery has led over time to a reduced presence of men in contemporary African-American families. Substantial migration from the rural south to the cities of the north led to the presence of large numbers of African Americans who lacked the industrial skills necessary to make an adequate living. Racial prejudice and discrimination further deepened their economic insecurity.

One-parent families are much more common in the African American community than elsewhere. Rates of illegitimacy and births to teenagers are considerably higher among African Americans than among whites. Much of this is the result of the intersection of race and class, as these more negative features of family life are more common among African Americans living in poverty, cut off from the mainstream of middle class economic and social life. Leaders in the African American community have recently recognized that these difficulties are a threat to the future of their group.

They are devoting considerable energy to the problems of early marriage, births to single women, drug use, poor education, and limited employment opportunities. Their success in solving these problems will show them to be the result of poverty and hopelessness, not of race.

THE FUTURE OF THE FAMILY

Alternative Family Forms

The past several decades have seen many alternative forms of intimate relationships take root in American society. Indications are that these forms will survive well into the future.

COHABITATION

Cohabitation refers to the sharing of a household by an unmarried couple. This is not a new practice, but its frequency has increased sharply, as has its social acceptance. The number of cohabitants has increased from about one-half million in 1970 to about two-and-a- half million today, a five-fold increase. However, cohabitating couples represent only about 5 percent of all U.S. households.

Cohabitation is particularly frequent among the young, especially college students, and in major metropolitan regions. It is less common among those who profess to be deeply religious. Most cohabitating couples do not have children. Most cohabitators eventually marry, though not necessarily to the first person with whom they cohabit. Though initially cohabitation was viewed as an alternative to marriage, today it is often viewed as a stage in courtship leading to marriage.

SINGLE-PARENT FAMILIES

In 1960 about 8 percent of all families had only one parent; today more than 20 percent do. Most of these families are headed by women. This increase is a consequence of the high divorce rate and the increasing rate of births to single women where the newborn is not given up for adoption. A growing, though still numerically small, number of couples are choosing to have children without getting married. If the present trend continues, within the next twenty to forty years close to half of all families could be headed by one parent.

Today there is much less social stigma attached to single-parent families than there was at one time. However, these families tend to be more impoverished than two-parent families. The phrase "feminization of poverty" generally refers to women heads of single-parent families. There have been conflicting studies about the effects on children of single-parent households.

SINGLEHOOD

Though the United States has the highest marriage rate in the world, a growing number of people are choosing what Peter Stein (1976) calls "creative singlehood." About one-quarter of all households consist of people living alone or with nonrelatives. For many, singlehood is a temporary stage on the way to marriage or remarriage. For some, though, it is a chosen lifestyle.

Another class of singles is made up of those who are widowed or divorced and do not remarry. Most of these are older women. While some of them are single by choice, a number are without a partner because of demographic factors: there are too few available partners in the socially appropriate age range.

GAY AND LESBIAN RELATIONSHIPS

American society, like most, has generally looked down on homosexual relationships, seeing them as a threat to marriage and to the stability of society. However, this social form has recently gained a modest measure of tolerance if not acceptance. Though still not legally viewed as a marriage, a gay relationship has been recognized in some major cities as a "domestic partnership" and given some aspects of the legal status of families.

Gay and lesbian couples exhibit many of the same patterns of family life as heterosexuals (Blumstein and Schwartz, 1983). These couples share notions of romantic love and make the same pragmatic arrangements of domestic life that heterosexuals do. In many respects, their interpersonal family dynamics are indistinguishable from those of "straight" families. With artificial insemination, children from previous marriages, and growing access to adoption, more gay and lesbian couples are experiencing the joys and challenges of parenthood.

CHILDLESS/CHILDFREE MARRIAGES

An estimated 5 percent of all married women indicate a desire not to have children; improved contraceptive technology has increased their chances of remaining childfree. The limited amount of present research suggests that couples choosing this route tend to be highly educated and career oriented; many are first-born children. For many, the decision not to have children evolves during the course of marriage rather than being present before marriage.

The Abortion Controversy

Few family issues have caused more divisiveness in the United States than the issue of abortion. Abortion was illegal in the United States until 1973, except under very limited conditions. In *Roe v. Wade,* the United States Supreme Court declared that women had a constitutional right to abortion. This right is not absolute, and as the fetus develops the state is given an increasing role in the decision to abort.

The Supreme Court decision did not end the long-standing controversy over abortion. Many groups, declaring themselves "pro-life," organized to oppose abortion. Proponents of abortion rights also organized, joined by those who, though they might think abortion morally wrong, believe that the decision to abort should be left to the woman acting on the advice of her physician. This alliance defined itself as the "pro-choice" movement. The two groups tend to attract different kinds of activists (Luker, 1985). Those involved in the pro-life movement tend to have less education and income, to be less likely to be married or to have children, and to have a more traditional view of the proper roles for men and women than activists in the pro-choice movement.

At the root of the controversy is a clash of values that cannot easily be resolved. While there are religious, scientific, moral and political aspects to the abortion controversy, much of the dispute centers around the privacy of family decisions. The controversy is not only about abortion itself but also about society's views of sexual relations, family size, and family relationships.

CONCLUDING COMMENTS

The traditional nuclear family made up of a husband who works outside the home, a wife who takes care of the family, and dependent children is no longer the role model. Moreover, the family no longer performs many of the functions that it once did. Does this mean that the family is a dying institution? Probably not. While the family of the future may not resemble the traditional nuclear family, it will still be recognizable. It will probably be smaller, family roles will be more flexible and even interchangeable, and there will be more single-parent families. But it will still consist of one or more adults and at least one child, and it will continue to be responsible for the socialization of the young and for meeting the human need for intimacy and companionship. In these regards, the family will continue to be the cornerstone of modern society.

In this chapter the nature of the family was examined. The concept of kinship was explored, particularly the different types of families: the nuclear families of orientation and procreation, the extended family, and the polygamous family forms (polyandrous and polygynous). Endogamy and exogamy were described as regulations guiding the selection of socially approved marriage partners; also discussed were the various practices used to acquire a marital partner: marriage by capture, marriage by purchase, marriage by arrangement, and the form practiced in the United States, marriage by consent (conjugal courtship).

The different forms of marriage—monogamy, polygamy (polyandry, polygyny, and group marriage)—were described, as were the different patterns of descent (patrilineal, matrilineal, bilateral, and double), residence (patrilocal, matrilocal, bilocal, and neolocal), and authority (patriarchy, matriarchy, and egalitarian).

Two opposing views of the family were described: the functionalist view that it is important because it serves basic social needs, and the conflict view that it is disadvantageous to women and to the possibility of social change. Issues involving the contemporary American family were examined, especially romantic love and parenthood, the growing problems faced by dual-earner families, and domestic violence. Divorce and remarriage received attention, as did alternative forms of family relationships (cohabitation, single-parent families, singlehood, gay and lesbian relationships, and childless /childfree marriages). The controversial issue of abortion was also summarized.

14

Education

In this chapter, we will examine education as a key social institution of modern society. We will explore functionalist and conflict views of the place of education in American society. We will also look at the characteristics of the American educational system and the current issues it faces.

EDUCATION AND SOCIETY

Education plays a key role in society. Functionalists see it as useful in allocating social roles and fostering change. Conflict theorists, on the other hand, see it as means of perpetuating the existing, unfair stratification system. We will examine both these views in some detail.

The Functions of Education: A Functionalist View

Functionalists see education as a necessary and desirable social institution in facilitating the activities of society. Education, they argue, performs a number of essential societal functions.

SOCIALIZATION

In modern society formal education supplements the family's role in socializing the young. The complexity of contemporary societies requires more specialized training for the young than can generally be provided solely by the family. This training requires specialists who have the necessary technical knowledge and can transmit that knowledge to the inexperienced.

Since basic language and mathematical skills are indispensable to modern society, they are an integral part of the school curriculum. Today's rapidly changing knowledge base mandates that schools not only provide students with the basic facts but also teach them how to continue learning so as to adapt to change. Teaching how to think is a fundamental part of the educational system, functionalists maintain.

Schools teach not only facts and thought processes but also societal norms and values. These are taught both directly and indirectly. Schools generally teach basic facts about the social and political nature of society. For example, civics classes inform students about the structure of government and the political process. They also focus on the fundamental obligations of citizenship. Routine affirmations of societal loyalty are promoted by encouraging students to recite the pledge of allegiance and to sing the national anthem.

Societal norms and values are also taught indirectly. Respect for others, obedience to authority, honesty, neatness, and being on time are part of the "hidden curriculum." The use of a grading system also teaches students that personal achievement and competition are important.

Even school-based nonacademic programs promote socialization. Athletic programs emphasize personal development and hard work as well as both cooperative and competitive behavior. School clubs and societies teach interpersonal and other skills.

SOCIAL INTEGRATION

Schools serve as a melting pot for individual differences. They play a major role in the assimilation of immigrants (see chapter 11). In the schools, immigrants—especially their children—learn the language, technical skills, and social norms necessary to smooth their passage into the life of their new society.

Schools tend to emphasize conformity and to discourage deviance. The cooperative child who follows instructions and does what the teacher says is prized by most teachers and is rewarded for that behavior. Those who have their own ideas about what to do tend to upset established routines; they are often seen as deviant and can suffer for these actions. Even the creative child is occasionally seen as difficult, though most teachers welcome such a child.

Schools also provide a setting for the development of peer groups. Children of similar ages are brought together; they share activities and experiences that often become the basis of friendships. The school is frequently the setting for many of their common extracurricular as well as academic activities.

SOCIAL PLACEMENT

Education, along with the family, serves as a main pathway into the structure of society. In contrast to the family's initial provision of ascribed status, many achieved statuses (particularly occupation) depend, at least in part, on a person's educational background. In effect, schools serve to sort individuals into the statuses available in society.

Functionalists see education as a response to the growing occupational specialization that results from industrialization. The school system is crucial in meeting the economy's demands for trained workers. It provides individuals with the technical and social skills they will need to do their job satisfactorily, whether they are going to be factory workers, sales clerks, lawyers or airline pilots.

Education also provides social mobility (see chapter 10). Education can help a person move up the social ladder. In this respect, education enabled the expansion of the middle class in the last century.

CULTURAL INNOVATION

To the extent that the educational system does its job, it increases the number of educated and intelligent individuals in society. These individuals are then able to provide the innovation necessary for social progress to take place.

The formal educational system leads to cultural innovation in yet another way. At the highest levels of education (universities), faculty not only teach but they are also expected to engage in scholarly activities and research.

Most scientific and medical research is conducted at universities. Many artists, musicians, and writers have or have had appointments at universities. Thus many of the major scientific and cultural advances in society have come from the scholarship and research of university faculty.

LATENT FUNCTIONS

The educational system also serves several latent (that is, unintended or unrecognized) yet nevertheless important functions. Many of the peer relationships developed in schools become the basis of life-long friendships. Important career or job contacts often stem from connections in or with particular schools. And a fair number of marriages develop from relationships begun in schools.

School also plays an important role in child care. Before the recent growth in preschool programs, many women who wished to work could not do so until their children began attending school because they did not know or could not afford anyone to leave the children with. Their children's attendance in school freed them to get jobs, take courses or pursue a variety of social, intellectual, and recreational interests.

In another vein, adolescents who are in school are not on the job market, thus reducing the competition for jobs.

An Alternative View: Conflict Theory

Conflict theorists see the educational system in less positive terms. They emphasize the negative features of American education.

PERPETUATION OF SOCIAL INEQUALITY

Conflict theorists do not suggest that an educational system automatically and inevitably contributes to the perpetuation of social inequality. However, they believe that the way education functions in the United States and most modern societies does in fact lead it to do so.

American schools are tied to residential communities. School systems are supported primarily by property taxes (only recently has this begun to change as a result of court orders to states to equalize the allocation of tax dollars to different communities). Richer communities have more funds to give to their schools. Thus they can hire better and more experienced teachers, provide better facilities, and buy more educational supplies and equipment than poorer communities. Even affluent city neighborhoods are apt to have better teachers and more resources because they have the political power to command a disproportionate share of the available funds. Thus the educational system mirrors and perpetuates the unequal allocation of resources of the existing stratification system.

The educational system perpetuates existing inequities in another way. Access to higher levels in the stratification system depends largely on the jobs people have. In American society, higher-level jobs are usually available only to people with higher levels of education. Furthermore, research has consistently shown a positive correlation between parents' education and the likelihood of going to college (e.g., Sewell, 1971; U.S. Bureau of the Census, 1987b). Even within this group, upper class families are more likely to be able to afford the elite, private universities that provide additional advantages in the occupational world. Children of upper class parents are likely to remain in the upper class, and the educational system is one of the mechanisms that facilitates this.

Tracking, assigning students to a particular educational program on the basis of ability, serves the same end. Theoretically, tracking is supposed to be based solely on ability, and thus should give all students the appropriate kind of education irrespective of background. In fact, however, research has shown that students' social backgrounds play a key role in the tracking process (Persell, 1977). The different tracks parallel wealthy and poorer communities: those in the higher tracks (who are more likely to be middle class) have better teachers and more resources than those in the lower tracks (who are more likely to be working or lower class); hence they receive a better education.

Finally, there is a clear positive correlation between amount of education and income as measured by lifetime earnings (U.S. Bureau of the Census, 1984). This connection is related to the occupations that people attain based on their level of education.

SOCIAL CONTROL

The major expansion of American public education occurred in the late nineteenth century, coinciding with industrial expansion and considerable growth in immigration. Bowles and Gintis (1976) argue that these factors are not unrelated. American capitalism needed a large, orderly, restrained, and moderately well-educated work force. Immigrants were just the pool of potential workers required, and laws requiring school attendance were used to draw them into the educational system. This point of view argues that education was not a benign, helpful mechanism aimed at helping people move up the social ladder but was designed to meet the needs of a capitalist economic system (see chapter 17).

CREDENTIALISM

Conflict theorists have tended to see education, particularly higher education, more as a social than an educational necessity. They use the word *credentialism* to point out that evidence of a certain level of education is often a requirement for a job whether or not the skills acquired through that education are necessary to perform the job well. Collins (1979) even refers to the United States as a "credential society"; in other words, diplomas are needed to certify levels of ability.

Credentialism might well be a democratizing factor, deemphasizing family background in favor of individual accomplishment. However, it has simply served as a marker or index of family background. Diplomas require not only intelligence and hard work but also time and money, and these are more likely to be available to those in the middle and upper classes. Also, the availability of time and money suggests the kind of background and training that would likely fit the requirements of the professions and higher levels of an organization. Thus credentialism serves as a screening process for the elite.

Credentialism has led to Americans' increasing desire to pursue a higher education. Large-scale federal aid for those wanting to continue their education, particularly the G.I. Bill for veterans and various grant and loan programs, has substantially increased the number of individuals going to college; ironically, it has also tended to increase the level of education needed to acquire job credentials. Jobs for which a high school education may have once been sufficient now require a college degree; jobs for which a B.A. was once acceptable often now require an M.A. or even a Ph.D.

THE TESTING CONTROVERSY

The testing of knowledge learned in a particular class is not controversial. What has generated considerable concern, however, is the use of various forms of intelligence and aptitude tests either as measures of "native ability" or as a screening device for colleges and universities.

Intelligence tests were developed at the beginning of the twentieth century and have been used extensively in the field of education. Initially intelligence tests were presumed to measure people's basic intellectual capacities. It has become clear, however, that they depend on a relatively detailed familiarity with the dominant culture. Many of the questions use the language of and often draw on examples from the white, middle class, urban experience. Recently, the use of the Scholastic Aptitude Test (SAT) as a screening device for entrance to schools of higher education has been attacked on precisely the ground that it does not measure basic intelligence but favors urban, white, middle class youth over others. It is also maintained that intelligence is only one important element involved in education and in social life and that these tests ignore or downplay creativity, intuition, and artistic or musical ability.

CHARACTERISTICS OF AMERICAN EDUCATION

The American educational system is unique in many ways. While many of its individual features are found in other systems, the particular combination of elements that makes up education in the United States is probably unduplicated anywhere else.

Mass Education

Americans take it for granted that free education for all youth is a natural part of the social landscape. In fact, though now most industrialized societies have similar systems, the United States pioneered this concept.

In 1900 only about 7 percent of youths had graduated from high school. By 1940 this number had risen to 50 percent; and currently about 80 percent of American youths and about two-thirds of the entire population have high school diplomas. Similarly, the percentage of the population going on to some form of higher education rose from 4 percent in 1900 to about 16 percent in 1940; about 40 percent now do so, in contrast to about 10 percent in Western Europe.

Elite systems of education, i.e., ones that are not open to all, have considerably higher standards for entrance and for academic performance. Academic standards are generally lower in systems of mass education than in restricted systems (e.g., Great Britain's) in order to accommodate the greater range of student abilities.

Education in the United States is not only free (financed through taxes for the public system), it is also compulsory. Though parents have some choice, except under special circumstances approved by the state, they must send their children to an accredited private, religious or public school. Students in the United States must attend school much longer than students in many other industrialized societies. Moreover, this public, compulsory education is financed through taxation of people whether or not they have children, and whether their children attend public or private schools. Not only does this widen schools' financial base of support, but it also signals the importance of education and the stake that the whole society has in this institution.

Pragmatic Orientation

American society has always seen education as a tool to serve both social and personal goals. It was clear to the founders that a free and democratic United States requires a reasonably well-educated citizenry. Thus, from the very beginning, education had the important practical purpose of educating people for democracy.

Earlier, we mentioned that schools help immigrants assimilate into American culture. We also noted education's usefulness in training immigrants and others in the skills necessary in an industrial society. This pragmatic emphasis of education continues today. Schools provide programs on driver education, family life and human sexuality, and drugs. Many states require students to attend these and other pragmatically oriented classes. Unfortunately, the common belief that the schools by themselves can solve many of society's social problems is probably mistaken. Many of the concerns thrust upon the schools (e.g., drug abuse and premarital sexuality) have their roots in other aspects of society and are not amenable to the "quick fix" some expect the schools to provide.

Decentralization and Community Control

In most societies, education is considered a national program and is controlled by the central government. In the United States education is decentralized. Each of the fifty states has responsibility for establishing and maintaining its own educational system, though the federal government contributes some modest funds for special programs.

Decentralization goes further than the states. Education is generally seen as a community responsibility, and most key educational policy decisions are made by the community through elected school boards. Through these boards, communities hire and fire their own teachers and administrators, establish curricula (subject to some state regulation), and generally choose their own textbooks.

Decentralization has resulted in an enormous diversity within the American educational system. This diversity is both a strength and a limitation. Responsiveness to community desires for pragmatic courses, for example, has reduced the available time for the more traditional academic subjects. What is gained on the one hand is lost on the other.

Community control also increases the political pressure on schools to include specific courses or programs in the curriculum or to eliminate them from it. Local community control has frequently led to considerable controversy over what books should be used in class or made available in school libraries. Thus community control both makes education more responsive to community needs and embroils it in community controversies.

It was pointed out earlier that the way education is financed leads to differences in the educational resources available in different communities. At the present time, a little less than half the cost of education is provided by the state and less than 10 percent by the federal government. Almost half comes from the community, and the wealth of the community influences the quality of its educational system.

Formal Structure of the School

Despite some diversity in school systems, the formal structure of schools tends to exhibit a clear bureaucratic form of organization (see chapter 5). A hierarchy of authority runs from the elected school boards through the chancellors or superintendents (and their deputies) to the school principals (and their deputies) to various department heads and then to the individual teachers.

Specialized organization also occurs. Students are generally organized by age into grade levels, though in some schools ability levels become the criterion for organization. In the elementary grades, teachers are often grouped according to the age levels of their students; in later grades they are grouped according to subject specialties.

Schools are run according to formal rules, which tend to be fairly consistent across school systems. These rules are intended to provide some degree of uniformity. Thus the individual has to adjust her or his needs to the general rules. Creativity and spontaneity are often seen as disruptive since they upset established routines.

School administrators keep detailed records of both teacher and pupil performances. The records are maintained for years and influence decisions about whether teachers should be promoted or recommended for other jobs and about whether students should go on to the next grade.

As in any bureaucratic organization, schools also have informal rules and relationships. These give American schools a greater informality and flexibility than might be apparent from looking solely at their formal structures.

Higher Education

A college degree is often essential for success in the modern world. It provides access to better jobs, leads to higher lifetime earnings, and exposes individuals to a wide range of cultural interests.

Colleges and universities, like other schools, are organized along bureaucratic lines. They have a clear authority structure and rules and maintain written records. Like other educational organizations, they possess considerable flexibility; in fact, there is often more openness at this level than in grade schools and high schools.

The clientele of higher education has been changing. The overall number of students at this level has been increasing, mainly in the junior and community colleges, and the composition of the student body is more diverse than before. A little more than half of all college and university students are women, and an increasing (though still small) number are from minority groups. The average age of these students has also increased. Also, a larger number of college and university students are combining work and study programs.

The phenomenal growth of higher education during this century, and especially from the 1950s on, has created a number of problems. Because high school and college are so different from one another many students have difficulty in making the transition from one to the other. There is increasing pressure on faculty, particularly in the large public universities, to do research in order to be promoted or to receive the grant funds that are necessary to carry out their research programs. This often encourages professors to divide their loyalty between teaching and research and between their institutions and their disciplines. There are also conflicting ideas about how to involve faculty and students in key institutional decisions that are usually made by administrators. And there is an increasing interest in specifically defining and measuring how colleges contribute to the intellectual, cultural, social, and personal development of their students. Finally, the economic climate has changed, and many institutions are having to learn to do more with less. Many of these problems are being addressed, but no easy solutions are in sight.

CURRENT ISSUES IN AMERICAN EDUCATION

Discipline and Violence

Reports of students using violence against other students and against teachers are increasing. Students in inner city areas occasionally bring guns, knives, and other weapons to school. Drug use and the sale of drugs in and around schools are increasing.

These problems are not limited to schools. In fact, the increasing violence in schools is but a reflection of the substantial increase in violence in society. What is different is that schools were often thought to be immune to these problems. Whether that was ever true is irrelevant; it is clear that it is not the case today.

Discipline is infrequently enforced either in the schools or in many families. Traditional lines of authority between generations have changed, in part as a consequence of the social and cultural upheavals of the 1960s and 1970s. A slogan sometimes seen on T-shirts and bumper stickers today spells it out: "Question Authority." However, there is increasing evidence that the key to success in schools lies in establishing clear goals and enforcing discipline firmly yet compassionately (Burns, 1985).

Effectiveness

THE PROBLEM

Deploring and denouncing organizations and institutions is a favorite American pastime. However, in the past decade serious examination of the American school system has set off a number of alarms. In a memorable phrase, the National Commission on Excellence in Education's 1983 report *A Nation at Risk* referred to a "rising tide of mediocrity" in American schools. In a more recent report of schools in large cities, the Carnegie Foundation for the Advancement of Teaching (1988) found them to be educationally bleak.

One of the bases for these discouraging assessments of American education is the continued decline of scores on standardized achievement tests and the increase in *functional illiteracy*, the lack of the reading and writing skills necessary to deal with the basic tasks of everyday life. Functional illiteracy is also demonstrated by the large sums many businesses and the military services spend to provide recruits with the remedial help they need to be able to do their jobs. Analyses of the academic performance of youths in various countries show American youths trailing their peers in almost all subjects, particularly science, mathematics, and geography.

PROPOSED SOLUTIONS

As a result of a massive study of American schools, Coleman (Coleman et al., 1966) concludes that schools themselves have very little effect on students' achievement. More important, Coleman argues, is the child's social background. This view is supported by Jencks (Jencks et al., 1972), who argues that the inequalities in students' social backgrounds are more important than what happens in the schools. However, this view is challenged by Rutter (Rutter et al., 1979), who studied inner city secondary schools in London, and by Winn (1981), who studied American schools.

These two views are not necessarily in opposition. Taken together, they argue that both the social environment outside the school and the school itself influence the quality of education. In his later work, Coleman (Coleman, Hoffer, and Kilgore, 1982) shows that schools can make a difference in academic performance.

All the research indicates that the school climate (orderliness and emphasis on achievement), good teachers, and adequate supplies and facilities are all important to academic performance. Clear educational goals are essential, as are order and discipline. A solid and supportive relationship with the community at large also contributes to a school's success in educating its students.

School-based management —where the school's staff cooperates with the administration in making decisions about curriculum, rules, supplies, and so on— may help improve the quality of schools by giving teachers more professional responsibility. This approach is supported by teachers and their union but has not found complete favor with many administrators or their union. It apparently has been tried successfully in several school systems and is currently being adopted by a number of others.

The voucher system is another proposed solution. In this approach, parents are issued vouchers that they can use toward the cost of educating their children in any accredited school they wish. In this manner, it is argued, market forces (schools' need to attract students) will lead schools to improve the quality of the education they provide. Critics have argued that the quality of education cannot be based on the short term fluctuation of funds that this system entails. For example, a school system cannot hire twenty-five teachers one year and only twenty the next, if the enrollment drops, and still expect to attract good staff. Teachers need longer commitments; equipment and supplies need a more stable funding base. Also, there is some danger that under this system schools could refuse to accept hard-to- teach students, all of whom would then end up in a limited number of public schools.

Race, Class, and Education

Perhaps the most complex and emotionally charged issue facing higher education in the United States is the relationship between race and class and the quality of education. It was pointed out earlier that social class affects the length and quality of education. There are several reasons for this. Middle and upper class children are socialized into values, attitudes, and practices that conform well to what schools expect of them. They are more likely to have been exposed to reading at an earlier age and to have greater access to books. They are taught to defer present gratification for more long term goals. They develop language facility earlier. Their teachers, who are generally from the middle class, share their values. And both the visible and hidden curricula are often based on these same class values and beliefs.

It was mentioned earlier that class and race are related (see chapter 11). Thus the class differences noted above apply also, by and large, to African Americans and Hispanic Americans. In particular there has been an ongoing debate about racial differences in intelligence that may restrict the educational achievements of African Americans. In short, the argument is that African Americans' consistently scoring from ten to fifteen points lower than whites on standardized intelligence tests (Jensen, 1969) may show that they are genetically inferior in intelligence. If this is the case, then educational differences between whites and African Americans may have nothing to do with the quality of schooling but rather be a function of heredity factors associated with race.

Recent research appears to refute these arguments. The standardized tests have been shown to be based on white middle class culture and hence to discriminate against those who do not belong to that group. Also, minority groups that scored low on these tests earlier in this century (e.g., Jews) now score at or above national levels (Sowell, 1977). Clearly, the genetic heritage of these groups has not changed in this short period of time, but their social environment has—and that must be the determining factor.

The issue of racial and ethnic segregation in education still faces the United States. Though the Supreme Court desegregated American schools in 1954, many still remain segregated because of residential patterns—particularly in the inner cities after the exodus to the suburbs of many middle class whites. Not only are inner city schools likely to be segregated but they are also typically underfinanced and, like the surrounding communities, challenged by problems of crime and drugs. Segregation based on residential patterns is difficult to deal with. Busing to achieve racial balance does work, but its appeal and legality are limited to areas where children will not have to spend excessive time being transported.

In short, the United States has not yet solved the problem of providing a good education to all its children, regardless of their race and class. While considerable desegregation has already taken place in the schools, much is still needed. Research indicates that the academic performance of minority students in desegregated schools tends to improve (Daniels, 1983). The task, therefore, is to change those social conditions that promote segregation both in communities and in their schools.

*F*unctionalists see the educational system as supplementing the family's role in socializing the young. Schools teach not only the necessary skills to function in society but also key norms, values, and behavioral traits. Schools facilitate the social integration of citizens and provide a setting for peer group interaction. They emphasize conformity and discourage deviance. The educational system is one of the main routes for social placement and social mobility. It also provides society with well-trained workers and allows mothers with *young children to work if they wish. Education is also an important element in cultural innovation and in scientific and humanistic advance.*

Conflict theorists have taken a less positive view of the educational system. They see it as perpetuating existing social inequality by linking social class to educational opportunities. They perceive education as a means of social control and as a way of meeting the labor needs of capitalist society. They decry the credentialist society that requires unnecessary educational certification for important societal and occupational roles. Conflict theorists also point to the controversy over standardized tests as supporting their argument that the educational system is biased in favor of the white middle class.

The American educational system is unique in its configuration. It is public and mandatory. It attempts to deal with a number of social problems (e.g., drugs and premarital sex). Decentralization of the U.S. educational system is another of its distinctive features. Education is a community responsibility and is community controlled. Schools and universities are, for the most part, bureaucratic organizations with clear patterns of authority, rules, and records.

Discipline and violence are increasing problems in the schools. American schools have been largely ineffective in providing the skills required in modern society; this is especially true when they are compared with schools in other countries. Several solutions to this problem have been proposed. One involves creating a more orderly and academically focused school climate. Another revolves around school-based management, which is intended to give more professional freedom and responsibility to teachers. The voucher system to let parents choose their children's school is another proposed solution, though there are several problems with this proposal.

Finally, the thorny issue of the intersection of race, class, and education was discussed. The question of racial and class bias in intelligence tests was considered, as was the argument that genetic factors account for racial differences in intelligence. The lingering effects on educational achievement of school systems segregated because of residential patterns were explored.

15

Religion

In this chapter, we will first describe what religion is and discuss some different forms it takes. We will then examine the functionalist perspective that argues that religion provides meaning in social life. We will also look at religion from the perspective of conflict theory, which sees it as a destructive social force. The relationship of religion to social change and how religion is organized in society will also be explored. Brief descriptions of some of the major world religions will be provided, along with an analysis of the role of religion in contemporary American society.

RELIGION: A DEFINITION

Since religion takes many forms, it is difficult to define it in a way that respects the different types. Durkheim (1954; original, 1912) provides a lead in his discussion of the sacred and the profane. The *sacred* involves anything that is considered supernatural beyond the ordinary. Any object or event can be invested with the aura of the sacred: a particular animal, a specific rock, the moon, a cross. The *profane*, on the other hand, is anything that is regarded as ordinary and routine. Rocks are rocks, and an animal is nothing special; in this case, these objects are seen as part of the profane rather than the sacred world. (Note that Durkheim does not use the term *profane* with its common meaning of anything that is offensive and vulgar.)

Another necessary element of religion is *ritual*, formal and stylized practices related to the sacred. These may include prayer, ceremonial purification, ceremonial dancing or incantation (a set formula of words or sounds often involving repetition). These actions enable the believer to approach the sacred in a careful and controlled manner.

With these definitions as background, *religion* may be defined as a system of shared beliefs and rituals that are concerned with the realm of the sacred. This definition is broad enough to allow a discussion of the diverse forms of religion noted throughout recorded history.

TYPES OF RELIGION

As far as can be determined, some form of religion has existed in all known societies. But the forms it has taken have varied considerably. Various people have worshiped all kinds of objects and beings and have engaged in a range of "religious" behavior.

Supernaturalism

Supernaturalism is a form of religion that assumes the existence of forces outside of the ordinary realm, in the supernatural, that influence human events both for good and for ill. No specific god or spirit is involved, just impersonal supernatural forces. While generally an element of preindustrial societies, some aspects of supernaturalism may be seen in the contemporary practice of carrying around a rabbit's foot or believing in luck.

Animism

Religion may also take the form of *animism*, a belief in the activity of "spirits" in the world. These spirits may exist in people or in any beings in the natural world, such as trees or animals. These spiritual forces may be either helpful, harmful or indifferent to human beings. They can be influenced by *magic*, ritual practices that allow people to use supernatural or spiritual power for their own ends. Animistic religion has been common among various tribes in Africa and elsewhere.

Theism

Theism is a belief in the existence of gods who are presumed to be both powerful and interested in the activities of human beings. These gods need to be worshiped or honored in some way. There are two major forms of theism.

POLYTHEISM

The most common form of theism is *polytheism*, the belief in the existence of many gods. Often one god is viewed as more powerful than the others, a god of gods.

MONOTHEISM

The second form of theism is the belief in one god. While *monotheism* is not as common as polytheism, the three monotheistic religions—Judaism, Christianity, and Islam—together have more members than any other form of religion.

Transcendent Idealism

Transcendent idealism, does not involve the worship of any god, spirit or supernatural force; it is based on sacred principles of beliefs and actions. Its goal is to enable human beings to achieve their highest potential. Forms of transcendent idealism are found mainly in Asia; Buddhism is an example.

RELIGION: A FUNCTIONALIST PERSPECTIVE

Functionalists generally see religion as a positive force in society. It fulfills important social functions and thus exists in some form in all societies.

Functions of Religion

SOCIAL COHESION

Religion acts as a cohesive force in society by providing a shared set of beliefs, values, and norms around which people can form a common identity. Religion becomes a unifier, a way of establishing common ground; it is the social glue that binds a group together by giving it a common set of values. For example, Jews, scattered around the globe in different cultures for centuries, have maintained their distinctive identity largely through their shared religious beliefs and practices.

It has been argued, however, that the cohesive aspects of religion are more apparent in societies that have only one religion. Such was often the case in preindustrial societies; it was to these societies that Durkheim was referring when he highlighted the cohesive aspect of religion.

PROVIDING MEANING IN LIFE

Religion generally provides emotionally satisfying answers to the "big" questions about human existence and purpose. In particular, it addresses the issues of life and death, outlines the kind of life people are expected to lead—their purpose in life—and explains what happens to them after they die. Religion is basically the only social institution that tries to deal with these critical questions.

SOCIAL CONTROL

The norms of society are often based on a set of religious beliefs. Most of the most important laws in American society (e.g., the law prohibiting murder) acquire a moral as well as legal force because they are embedded in religious values; they are given a sacred legitimacy. In the Middle Ages, kings were thought to rule by divine right, and the law in Islamic countries is justified by the Koran, the sacred book of Islam.

PSYCHOLOGICAL SUPPORT

Religion supplies many people with the emotional and psychological support they need to survive in a complex and uncertain world. It is especially useful in times of crisis, such as the death of someone close. It suggests some purpose in dying and provides a set of ritual practices for mourning (a "wake" for Christians or "shiva" for Jews, for example) that eases the grief of the survivors.

Secular Ideologies: Functional Equivalents of Religion

Religion pertains to the sacred realm of human experience. But what is considered sacred is socially constructed. Functionalists point out that there are *functional equivalents* (social or cultural features that have the same effect as and may be substituted for other social or cultural features) to religion. That is, secular (nonreligious) belief systems (e.g., science) can serve the same functions mentioned above for religion.

Many of the world's "isms"—fascism, socialism, communism, humanism—may be seen as secular religions. They all promote social solidarity and cohesion among their believers. They provide life with purpose and meaning and justify the behaviors required within the practicing group. And their ideological beliefs offer emotional support in times of difficulty and uncertainty. They even provide justification for death if it is in the service of a cause their believers define as noble. The difference between religion and secular ideologies is that religion is oriented to and draws its power from the realm of the supernatural. This belief in the supernatural increases religion's stability and inhibits it from changing drastically.

RELIGION: A CONFLICT PERSPECTIVE

Conflict theorists do not see religion as the positive social institution described by functionalists. They point out several negative features of society that are either directly traceable to religion or are maintained by it.

Religion as the "Opium of the People"

Religion, conflict theorists argue, supports and legitimates the existing system. It does so by diverting the attention of the oppressed away from their problems and any attempt to deal with them. In a memorable phrase, Marx (1964:27; original, 1848) called religion "the opium of the people." He meant that, like opium, religion makes people feel good but deflects their attention away from their miserable existence and the action necessary to change it.

Conflict theorists see religion as another element in societal power struggles. It is used by those in power both to justify their position and to dampen any attempt by the powerless to change their situation. It diverts attention from the problems and sufferings of the present world with the promise of rewards in the afterlife.

Religion and Inequality

The stability and cohesion that religion provides are seen by conflict theorists as examples of its destructive nature. Rather than put up with the inequities that conflict theorists believe exist in all modern societies, socially conscious people with a sense of history should be working to eliminate them. But religion often provides the moral legitimation for these inequities, discouraging social change. Kings rule and oppress their people by divine right and thus are immune from criticism. More generally, the existing economic conditions, which Marx and the conflict theorists take to be the fundamental forces in society, influence the shape, direction, and role of religion in society. Put differently, the underlying social and economic structure shapes values and belief systems, including religion.

Religion, from the conflict perspective, is a conservative force in the world. It derives from and preserves the *status quo*, the present social arrangements, and discourages social change. Recall the earlier discussion of the religious base of caste systems (see chapter 9). As another example, most religions are male-oriented and male-dominated, that is, patriarchal in form (see chapter 13). Even today many of the major religions have resisted to varying degrees increasing the power and authority of women in their hierarchies.

Religion and Social Conflict

In societies where there is more than one major religion, religion is more likely to create social division and conflict than to promote social cohesion. Northern Ireland and pre-Pakistan India are obvious examples. In the latter case, the Hindu-Muslim conflict became so acute that the country had to be divided on the basis of religion. In Northern Ireland the conflict between Catholics and Protestants seems unending, as does the conflict between Jews and Muslims in the Middle East.

Even across societies, conflict theorists point out, religion causes social conflict. The Crusades pitted Christians against Muslims and caused untold destruction. One of the major justifications for the European colonization of Africa, Asia, and South America was to convert the "heathen," people who worshiped idols or many gods.

RELIGION AND SOCIAL CHANGE

The relationship between religion and society is much more subtle and complex than conflict theorists believe. Contrary to their view, religion can promote social change, though not all this change is necessarily beneficial (e.g., European colonialism). One major example of the role of religion in supporting, if not instigating, social change involves the rise of capitalism. On the other hand, as the conflict theorists argue, religion often plays a conservative role, discouraging social change and reaffirming tradition. A case in point is the revival of Islamic fundamentalism.

The "Protestant Ethic" and Capitalism: Promoting Social Change

Marx insisted that belief systems, like religion, are a product of the economic structure of society and serve to reinforce and legitimate it. Weber disagreed. He argued that the relationship can work the other way; belief systems can influence the development of social and economic structures. In part to demonstrate this, Weber (1958; original, 1904) analyzed the role of Calvinist Protestantism in the early development of capitalism.

Weber notes that modern capitalism is a completely new mode of economic activity. In contrast to earlier economic forms, it emphasizes rational planning and accounting as well as the systematic and continual accumulation of wealth that can be used for development and expansion. The free-spending style of early times did not allow for the accumulation of capital that could then be used for investment and expansion. Thus, a whole new approach to economic activity and to life in general was necessary to the development of modern capitalism.

CALVINISM

This new approach, Weber points out, was provided by the early *Calvinists*, Protestants who base their beliefs on the views of John Calvin. Calvinists believe in *predestination*, the act by which God foreordains that certain souls will be damned and others will be saved, and that nothing they can do in this world will affect God's decision. Calvinists' earthly task is to be *ascetic* (abstain from worldly pleasure) and work for the glory of God. Though God's decision about their ultimate fate is unchangeable, Calvinists look for any clue to what it is and take the view that worldly success is a sign that God has marked them for a "successful" life in eternity.

In this manner, Weber argues, the frugal, hard-working, ascetic early Calvinists, looking for a sign of eternal salvation, engaged in just the kinds of actions that were necessary to the development of modern capitalism. They worked both hard and systematically. The money they accumulated by living frugally they invested in the expansion of capitalist enterprises.

OTHER RELIGIONS

Other religions did not provide the same base for the development of capitalism. Catholicism encouraged its followers to look for their reward in the next life rather than in this one. Asian religions (e.g., Hinduism) discouraged activities that would lead to personal advancement, discouraged the kind of hard work necessary for the development of capitalism (e.g., Islam) or stressed the afterlife rather than involvement in this world (e.g., Buddhism and Taoism).

Modern capitalism's dependence on the belief system of the early Calvinists is an example, Weber believed, of the way in which ideas and beliefs shape and direct society. While Calvinism did not cause capitalism, it certainly was an essential ingredient.

The Islamic Revolution: Reaffirming Tradition

The past decade or two has witnessed a considerable increase in *fundamentalism*, a rigid commitment to traditional religious beliefs and practices, among *Muslims* (believers in Islam). Islamic fundamentalism was instrumental in the assassination of President Anwar Sadat of Egypt and in the overthrow of the Shah of Iran, who tried to "westernize" the country.

Fundamentalism in many of the Islamic countries of the Middle East requires that women be submissive. In Iran women are required to cover their hair and most of their faces with veils. In Saudia Arabia women may not drive cars unaccompanied. Islamic fundamentalism is evident in Iran, where it is a total way of life for many people. It is a pervasive set of beliefs that specifies appropriate behavior in practically all areas of personal and social life. There has been considerable pressure to make Islamic law the law of the land and to authorize the clergy to interpret and dispense justice in accordance with it.

Fundamentalism appears to emerge during times of social change, when confusion and upsetting events erode familiar norms and values. A return to basic views offers stability and familiarity, a way of dealing with the turmoil and dislocating effects of change. Traditional beliefs and practices are understandable and soothing. By reaffirming the past and reinstituting tradition, religion can redirect social change from the future back to the past. While this section focused on Islamic fundamentalism, the conclusions would be equally applicable to an analysis of Christian fundamentalism.

THE ORGANIZATION OF RELIGION

Besides having a set of beliefs and rituals, religion, like other social institutions, has an organizational structure that takes different forms. The four most common forms of religious organization are described below.

The Church

The *church* is a stable religious organization that is well integrated into the surrounding society and that asserts a claim to be the only legitimate road to religious truth. It often has a well-defined hierarchy of officials and some form of bureaucratic organization. These officials are responsible for administering the relevant religious rituals. Among the world's religions Roman Catholicism, for example, has one of the most hierarchical and bureaucratic structures.

Churches tend to be conservative. They often accept the major goals of society and oppose change. This is evident, for example, in the opposition of the Vatican, the seat of authority of the Roman Catholic church, to *liberation theology*, which has its roots in Marxist ideology. Latin-American priests who subscribe to this theology dedicate themselves to promoting spiritual salvation but also to improving the material conditions of the poor through social and economic change.

The Sect

In some ways sects are similar to the church. Like the church, sects claim sole legitimacy for religious truth, but they do not fit as comfortably into the majority culture. They tend to be small and exclusive, often rejecting the norms and values of the dominant culture. Sects often form after a small number of individuals break away from a larger, more established church.

Sects are less formally organized than the church. Leadership is often based on *charisma*, extraordinary personal qualities that attract and hold followers. Whereas the church tends to focus on formal rituals, sects emphasize personal experience. Religious practices in sects tend to be more emotional than those in the church. Finally, sects often represent a form of dissent against some aspect of the larger culture or more traditional church. For example, the Anabaptists of the Reformation (the sixteenth-century movement that led to the establishment of Protestantism) denied the validity of infant baptism and practiced the baptism of adults.

The Denomination

A *denomination* is a churchlike organization that is generally integrated into society but does not claim exclusive legitimacy for its belief system. Acceptance of pluralism in religion is one of the marks of a denomination. In general, denominations have an established clergy and exhibit less emotional fervor in their religious rituals.

To some extent, denominations might be seen as sects that have grown larger and made some form of adjustment to society. Presbyterianism is a Calvinist denomination that is governed by its elders, called presbyters.

The Cult

The *cult* is a form of religious organization that has an antagonistic relationship with the surrounding society. Cults, like sects, often depend on charismatic leadership. They often tend to isolate their members from the larger society, which they see as corrupting.

Cults attempt to provide their members with a total lifestyle, that is often distinctly different from their earlier lives. Membership in a cult often involves considerable personal transformation. As a consequence, the past two decades have witnessed considerable concern about cults and their ability to *brainwash* —a popular term for what sociologists call "resocialization" (see chapter 6)—the young and alienated. Transcendental Meditation (TM), a movement led by the Maharishi Mahesh Yogi, and the Unification Church of Reverend Sun Myung Moon (the "Moonies") are two contemporary examples of cults.

MAJOR WORLD RELIGIONS

There are thousands of different religions in the world. In this section we will briefly describe the essential characteristics of six of the largest religions, roughly in the order of their size.

Christianity

Christianity is the most widely practiced religion in the world. About one billion people, approximately 20 percent of the world's population, identify themselves as Christians; more than half of them are Catholic. The central Christian belief is in the divinity of Jesus Christ, who is viewed as God's only child, the savior of the world, and the guarantor of life after death. Beyond this, Christians vary in their belief systems, ritual practices, and forms of organization.

DEVELOPMENT

Christianity grew out of Judaism. In the eleventh century, a religious division led to the establishment of two major Christian organizations: The Roman Catholic church and the Orthodox church in Constantinople (present day Istanbul). In the sixteenth century, the Reformation led to a further split with Rome; the result was the establishment of Protestantism. The religious pluralism of the Reformation in Europe resulted in the development of numerous denominations within Protestantism that continue to this day.

CHRISTIAN BELIEFS

The Bible is the most important source of beliefs for Christians. It is seen as divinely inspired, and some believe it contains the literal word of God. Through ritual and prayer Christians praise God, give thanks for what He has provided, and ask for His help in meeting important needs. Christ's crucifixion made the cross the main symbol of Christianity. To Christians, Christ's resurrection from the dead is proof of His divinity.

Most Christians live in Europe and the Americas. The large Christian populations in Asia and Africa stem from the colonization of these areas by Christian Europeans. In common with most religions, and despite the veneration of Mary, Christ's earthly mother through virgin birth, men have the more predominant role in Christianity. Recently, some denominations have allowed women a greater role in church rituals and leadership.

Islam

Islam, derived in part from ancient Judaism, is the second largest religion in the world, with about 500 million followers. It is the most popular religion in North Africa, the Middle East, and parts of Asia (e.g., Indonesia). Islam was founded by the prophet Muhammad in the seventh century A.D. Unlike Jesus Christ he is not considered a divinity but is believed to be Allah's (God's) messenger to the world; he transmitted Allah's word to the people.

HOLY SITES

The geographical center of Islam is the city of Mecca, in Saudi Arabia, Muhammad's birthplace. Two of Islam's holiest religious shrines, called mosques, are in the cities of Mecca and Medina in Saudi Arabia.

ISLAMIC RITUALS

Equivalent to the Christian Bible, the Koran contains the sacred writings of Muhammad, which are viewed as the word of God. The Koran teaches inner peace through submission to the will of Allah. Muslim ritual requires prayer five times a day and a pilgrimage to Mecca at least once in a person's lifetime. As in most religions, Islamic women are subordinated to men.

Hinduism

There are about as many Hindus in the world as Muslims. Hinduism, which began in the Indus Valley in India over 4,000 years ago, has been confined largely to the Indian subcontinent. Unlike Christianity and Islam, its founding is not linked to a particular person, nor does it have an officially sanctioned sacred book like the Bible or the Koran.

DHARMA AND KARMA

Though Hindu beliefs and practices vary widely, they share some common elements. Hindus believe that there is a moral force in society that requires the acceptance of certain responsibilities, called *dharma*. They also believe in *karma*, the spiritual progress of each person's soul, and that a person's karma is affected by the way he or she lives.

REINCARNATION

Hindus believe in *reincarnation*, rebirth into a different body after death and in the same spiritual state the person earned in the last life. By perfecting the soul in each new life, the person eventually achieves *nirvana*, a state of complete spiritual perfection that renders reincarnation no longer necessary. Besides private rituals, Hinduism embodies public rituals like *Kumbh Mela* in which millions of Hindus make a pilgrimage every twelve years to bathe in the ritually purifying waters of the sacred Ganges River.

Hinduism is a clear example of the conservative nature of religion. It upholds the existing stratification system in India by providing moral legitimacy for caste distinctions (see chapter 9).

Buddhism

Buddhism was founded in India by Siddhartha Gautama, a reformer called the Buddha (which means "the awakened one"), in the sixth century B.C.. His personal charisma attracted many followers, who spread his views to Central and Southeast Asia, China, Korea, and Japan. Buddhism has about 250 million followers today.

NOBLE EIGHTFOLD PATH

According to Buddhism, life is comprised of suffering. Misery is everywhere and originates in people's desires for pleasure. These desires can be curbed by systematically following the *Noble Eightfold Path*, which emphasizes right seeing, thinking, speech, action, living, effort, mindfulness, and meditation. Buddhism emphasizes the importance of sympathy and compassion for others and believes that the answer to the problems of the world lies in personal change and the development of a higher level of spirituality.

BUDDHISM AND HINDUISM

Buddhism's similarity to Hinduism is clear. However, Buddhism, unlike Hinduism, does not automatically support the caste system. In both Buddhism and Hinduism, action in doing good works and building spiritual communities is open equally to men and women. Buddhism also shares with Hinduism the lack of a personalized God and an origin in a charismatic leader.

Confucianism

Confucianism was founded in the fifth century B.C. by K'ung-Fu-tzu, more generally known as Confucius. For more than 2,000 years, until the beginning of this century, Confucianism was the official religion of China. While the 1949 revolution that established the People's Republic of China weakened religious observance in that country, over 150 million people still follow Confucianism, mainly in China.

JEN

Confucius shared Buddha's concern for the suffering of the poor. He taught the importance of attaining personal salvation through right action. The central concept of Confucianism is *jen*, being humane, according to which morality and loyalty to others should override self-interest. There is little occupation with the supernatural in these views, suggesting to some that Confucianism ought not to be classified as a religion. But because it has a central body of beliefs and practices, it is treated as a religion by many people.

Judaism

There are over 17 million Jews in the world, mainly in North America, Europe, and the Middle East, especially their newly established homeland in Israel. This number was much larger before World War II, when Hitler's "final solution" led to the deaths of about 6 million European Jews.

COVENANT

Begun several thousand years ago as an animistic religion, Judaism became the world's first monotheistic religion. Its God, Jehovah, established a *covenant* or special relationship with the Jewish people through Abraham, the founder of the religion. They were to be the "chosen people" to carry His word to the people of the world; in return, He would take special care of them.

THE OLD TESTAMENT AND THE TORAH

The major beliefs of Judaism are contained in the Bible (called by Christians the "Old Testament" to distinguish it from their body of beliefs, the "New Testament"). The first five books of the Bible, called the *Torah*, describe the early history and beliefs of the Jewish people. The Ten Commandments were handed down to Moses by God; they specify the key laws that all Jews are expected to obey. The beliefs of Judaism place special emphasis on learning and study, on conceptions of community, and on showing charity to those less fortunate.

RITUALS

Some of the rituals of Judaism include prayer twice a day, celebrations of holy days marking key events in Jewish history, and the maintenance of a set of dietary practices called the *kashruth* ("keeping kosher"). Like Christianity, Judaism has undergone some division because of differences in religious interpretation.

The Judeo-Christian Heritage

American cultural values rest squarely within the context of Judaism and Christianity. The first settlers from Europe brought with them their Christian beliefs, which emanated from Judaism. The Ten Commandments influenced American values and the legal system.

RELIGION IN THE UNITED STATES

Religious Affiliation

There is no official state religion in the United States. In fact, the First Amendment to the Constitution requires the separation of church and state. Despite that, however, the Judeo-Christian heritage is a major influence on American culture. About 90 percent of Americans identify with one or another of these religions; a somewhat smaller number, about 70 percent, actually belong to a particular religious organization (Gallup, 1984; U.S. Bureau of the Census, 1985).

Protestants are the clear majority in the United States. Of those indicating a religious affiliation, 65 percent are Protestant; the largest Protestant denomination, the Baptists, constitute about one-third of the category and is more than twice as large as any of the other Protestant denominations. Catholics comprise about 24 percent of religiously affiliated Americans, and a little over one percent are Jewish (National Opinion Research Council, 1987).

Church affiliation varies by regions of the United States. Catholics are most concentrated in New England, the Southwest, and urban areas of the Midwest. The Southern states are primarily Baptist, and most Lutherans live in the northern plains states. Jews are concentrated mainly in the urban centers of the East and West coasts.

Religiosity

Religious affiliation tells only part of the story of religion in American life. Another important issue is *religiosity*, the importance that religion plays in an individual's life. This importance can take many forms (Glock, 1959). It can refer to the emotional tie people feel with their religions (*experiential religiosity*), the extent to which they pray and attend religious services (*ritualistic religiosity*), the strength of their commitment to their religions' belief systems (*ideological religiosity*), how they integrate religion into their everyday activities (*consequential religiosity*), and the range and depth of their knowledge about the traditions, beliefs, and practices of their religions (*intellectual religiosity*).

While most Americans report believing in some supreme power (a form of experiential religiosity), fewer (about 70 percent) indicate that they agree with key elements of their religion's belief system (ideological religiosity). Still fewer demonstrate ritualistic religiosity. Only about one-half report praying at least once a day, and about 35 percent attend religious services approximately once a week (National Opinion Research Council, 1987). In short, Americans have extensive religious affiliation but demonstrate a lesser degree of religiosity.

Correlates of Religious Affiliation

If religion is important, it should make some difference in people's lives. This section examines the correlates of religious affiliation, the relationship between religion and other important social elements.

SOCIAL CLASS

In the United States, while members of all religions can be found in every social class, there is a measurable relationship between religion and social class. Jews have the highest class standing, followed by Protestants and then Catholics, though the latter two are not widely separated. Within the Protestant denominations, Episcopalians, Presbyterians, and Congregationalists rank just below Jews and above Catholics. Methodists and Lutherans are on about the same level as Catholics, with Baptists and the various sects below these three.

The relatively high standing of Jews is apparently due to the high values they traditionally place on education, which has led a higher proportion of them to acquire the education necessary to pursue high-level occupations and careers. The Protestant denominations at about the same social level as Jews are those whose members are from northern Europe, where they likely suffered less discrimination than members of some of the other Protestant denominations and Catholics whose origins are primarily in southern and eastern Europe.

ETHNICITY AND RACE

Religious groups in the United States show great internal racial and ethnic diversity. Among Catholics, for example, there are Irish Catholics, Italian Catholics, Polish Catholics, and Puerto Rican Catholics. All of their cultures—and some of their religious practices—are quite different from one another. Russian Jews are quite different from German Jews, and both can be distinguished from the Sephardic Jews of Spain and Portugal. In fact, in an interesting paper, Tyree (1991) shows that linking ethnicity to religion permits a more refined analysis of some aspects of American culture. For example, British Catholics have considerably higher household incomes than French Catholics, Polish Catholics, and Mexican Catholics.

Religion has always been important in the lives of African Americans. Many of the leaders of the African American community have been ministers: Martin Luther King, Jr., Adam Clayton Powell, Ralph Abernathy, and Jesse Jackson. The church generally plays a more important role in meeting the social and economic, as well as spiritual, needs of African Americans than it does for members of other groups.

POLITICAL ATTITUDES

Members of a number of Protestant denominations have higher class standing than Catholics, and they tend to be more politically conservative. Traditionally, Protestants have supported the Republican party and Catholics the Democratic party. Also, among Protestants there is a positive relationship between being conservative and ritualistic religiosity; that is, the more conservative people report more frequent church attendance. Jews have traditionally been quite liberal politically. They are strong supporters of the Democratic party, particularly its liberal wing.

In actuality, there are many factors that determine political attitudes. Religion influences but does not determine political attitudes.

Religion and politics have become more intertwined in American society in recent years. Though United States coins have long carried the inscription "In God We Trust," it is only relatively recently that the Pledge of Allegiance was amended to include the phrase "under God." Religious groups were quite active in the antiwar movement in the 1960s and 1970s. Today the political battle over abortion (see chapter 13) has religious overtones. The Roman Catholic church is strongly opposed to abortion and in favor of school prayer, while the other two major religions are split along the lines of their conservative and liberal adherents. Adding religion to politics sharpens political differences, often making compromise—the substance of politics—virtually impossible.

RELIGIOUS REVIVAL

The past few decades have seen a general decline in religious affiliation and certainly in various forms of religiosity. However, there is one exception. Protestant fundamentalism has been on the increase, becoming more vigorous and diverse. The number of fundamentalist sects is increasing. The label "born-again Christian" has passed into the American vocabulary. In large part, this increase has been caused by television, especially cable access, which is frequently used to transmit the religious, often fundamentalist, message to vast audiences. The result has been the development of what is called the *electronic church* (Hadden and Swain, 1981). It is estimated that about 60 million Americans watch religious programs at least monthly, and about 15 million are regular viewers (Gallup, 1982). As a consequence Oral Roberts, Billy Graham, Pat Robertson, Jimmy Swaggart, and, until recently, Jim and Tammy Bakker have gained a level of national attention that is unusual among the clergy.

Fundamentalism is especially strong in the rural areas of the United States. It is the backbone of the politically conservative movement called the "moral majority," led by the Reverend Jerry Falwell. This movement was quite influential in creating a more politically and socially conservative climate in the early and middle 1980s. Its power seems to have waned in the past few years, though there is still a large reservoir of fundamentalist fervor that permeates American society.

Religion deals with the sacred and the supernatural rather than with the ordinary realm of the profane. It has taken various forms. Supernaturalism and animism were among the earliest types of religion. Later forms were the belief in one God (monotheism) and in many gods (polytheism) and transcendent idealism.

From a functionalist perspective, religion is a positive force in society. It promotes social cohesion and gives purpose and meaning to life. It legitimizes social control and offers psychological support, especially in difficult times. Similar functions are performed by secular ideologies (e.g., humanism), which serve as the functional equivalents of religion.

Conflict theorists have a more negative view of religion. Marx saw it as the "opium of the people" in that it deflects people's attention from their earthly problems. Others have seen it as justifying and supporting social inequities and as the basis of social conflict. These people see religion as a conservative force in society.

There are different views of the relationship between religion and social change. Weber argues that Calvinist thought was essential to the development of modern capitalism. Calvinist belief in asceticism and predestination led to the kind of rationality, hard work, and capital accumulation that early capitalism needed. In another view the fundamentalist Islamic revolution is seen as resisting social change and reaffirming tradition.

Religious organizations take different forms. The church is the most organized and socially integrated; it tends to be somewhat conservative and believes it is privy to the ultimate religious truth. The sect is less integrated into society. It is often small and is based on charismatic leadership. It too believes it has sole religious legitimacy. The denomination is churchlike in its organization, but is much more accepting of different religions. The cult is usually antagonistic to the surrounding society and offers a total way of life to its members.

The largest religion, Christianity, is practiced by about one billion people. Its central feature is its belief in the divinity of Jesus Christ. It has split into several different churches: Roman Catholicism, the Orthodox Church, and Protestantism. Islam, with 500 million adherents, is the next largest. Founded by Muhammad, it is based on the holy Koran, the word of Allah as written down by his prophet Muhammad. Hinduism (roughly equivalent in size to Islam) and Buddhism (about half that size) are quite similar in that they also believe that individuals should live correct and dedicated lives that serve humanity. Confucianism, practiced mainly in China, is also dedicated to compassion and charity toward others. Judaism, the first monotheistic religion, has about 17 million members. They have distinctive practices that have often set them apart from members of other religious groups.

While religious affiliation in American society is quite common, various forms of religiosity are less so. Religion is linked to social class, with Jews, Episcopalians, Presbyterians, and Congregationalists generally having higher social status than Catholics, who similarly have higher status than Baptists and members of other sects. Religion is also connected to ethnicity and race, and these create differences within religious communities.

Political attitudes often differ by religion. Typically, Protestants are more likely to support the Republican party, while Catholics and Jews are apt to support the Democratic party. Politics and religion are often intertwined, as in the use of God in key American symbols like the Pledge of Allegiance. Social issues like abortion often get tied up with religion in ways that make them difficult to resolve. Finally, while religious activity has generally been declining, there has been somewhat of a fundamentalist revival. This is due in part to the use of cable television, which enables religious services to reach a much larger audience than previously. This fundamentalist response to various radical movements of the 1960s and 1970s had substantial influence in American society in the early and middle 1980s, though its effects seem to have waned in the last few years.

16

Politics and the State

*P*olitics deals with power, which will be examined in this chapter, along with the different bases of authority. Functionalist and conflict theory views of the state will be explored, as will different forms of government. Several aspects of the American political system will be discussed, and the various theories of power in the United States will be analyzed. A study of the exercise of political power through war, terrorism, and revolution will complete this chapter.

POWER AND AUTHORITY

Politics concerns power. It is the social institution that is responsible for how power is acquired, allocated, and used.

Power

All sociological discussions of power start with Weber's (1978; original, 1921) definition. *Power*, he said, is the ability to accomplish aims despite the resistance of others. Power may be derived from a number of sources. It may come from sheer physical force or from the use of economic resources. Such personal skills as being helpful and efficient may confer power. Some sociologists distinguish between legitimate and illegitimate power.

LEGITIMATE POWER

The use of power by those seen as having the right to it is considered to be *legitimate power*. In a democracy, elected official are conceded to have legitimate power; in a monarchy, it is the king or queen who exercises it. In a school, the teacher has the appropriate and legitimate power to schedule an examination. While any particular action based on legitimate power may be disliked, the right to the use of such power is not fundamentally questioned.

Legitimate power, then, is seen as appropriate both by those exercising it and by those over whom it is exercised. This form of power is often referred to as *authority*, which is discussed below.

ILLEGITIMATE POWER

Power that depends on coercion, which is the use or threat of force, to compel compliance is viewed as *illegitimate power*. Exercisers of illegitimate power are not granted the right to use force by those against whom they would use it. Instances of illegitimate power occur when, for example, employers use the threat of firing to secure sexual favors and when muggers force victims to yield their valuables.

Bases of Authority

Once more, Weber (1978; original, 1921) provides the key analysis of the bases of legitimate power or authority. He saw authority as deriving from three possible sources.

TRADITIONAL AUTHORITY

Perhaps the oldest base of justifying power is tradition. *Traditional authority* depends on custom or long-established cultural traditions. Monarchs rule, having inherited the right to do so through their families, on the basis of ancient and respected practices. Even if a particular monarch is seen as cruel and unfit to rule and is forced out, the traditional system is usually maintained because of tradition.

Industrialization tended to undermine traditional authority. Social change was so rapid and extensive that old ways seemed less appropriate.

RATIONAL-LEGAL AUTHORITY

Another source of authority, one that was more compatible with the bureaucratization that occurred with increasing industrialization (see chapters 4 and 5), was a system of laws or rules that invests legitimate power in a particular position. *Rational-legal authority*, then, is power that is justified by a system of socially accepted rules or regulations. Often called *bureaucratic authority*, it is tied to a particular position rather than to a person. While president of the United States, Ronald Reagan exercised considerable authority; for example, he could and did commit American military forces to armed conflict, call the Congress into session, and secure free time on national television. After he left office, he had no legitimate right to do any of these.

One important reason for locating rational-legal authority in positions rather than people is to ensure that those who occupy those positions exercise their authority only in the course of their official duties. Even as president, Ronald Reagan could not demand free products from stores, nor could he legitimately refuse to file a federal income tax return, because these actions have nothing to do with the duties of the president of the United States. At the college level, while faculty may legitimately demand that students demonstrate their knowledge of the course material in some form of examination, they cannot require students to wash their cars or babysit for them. Tests are a legitimate part of the educational enterprise, personal service is not.

CHARISMATIC AUTHORITY

The two forms of authority discussed above are impersonal; they are based on tradition and on position. *Charismatic authority*, on the other hand, derives from extraordinary personal qualities of the leader that inspire commitment and command obedience. There have been numerous charismatic leaders throughout history, though not all of them would be considered positive forces. Moses, Jesus Christ, Joan of Arc, Ghandi, Hitler, Martin Luther King, Jr., and Malcolm X are obvious examples of charismatic leaders whose unique personal attributes led to devoted and committed followings.

Most societies see charismatic leaders as dangerous because they are often less constrained by social and cultural norms. Thus they may undermine the more socially derived bases of authority: tradition and position.

Without tradition or position to sustain authority, the loss of a charismatic leader threatens the existence of the group. Weber argues that the continued survival of a charismatic movement depends on the *routinization of charisma*, the transformation of charismatic authority to either traditional or bureaucratic form or to some combination of the two. For example, the movement inspired by the charisma of Jesus Christ has survived for so long because its authority became traditional and bureaucratic.

THE STATE

The *state* is the principal organized political authority in a society. The modern state emerged in Europe during the sixteenth century. Functionalists and conflict theorists view the state quite differently.

A Functionalist Perspective

The English philosopher Thomas Hobbes saw life as chaotic and lacking order, saying that it was "solitary, poor, brutish and short." Functionalists insist that social order is absolutely essential to society and that the state is necessary to provide it. They believe that states flourish because they perform the following four essential functions that help create and maintain social order.

ENFORCEMENT OF NORMS

Norms are an important part of the social glue that holds a society together. In small, traditional societies, they were supported and enforced by the community. As societies grew larger and more complex and began to undergo rapid social change, informal social control was insufficient. Most modern societies developed formal, codified laws that needed to be enforced. The establishment of the system of laws, and of the organizational structure to enforce them, became the responsibility of the state—the ultimate political authority.

REGULATION OF CONFLICT

Conflict occasionally arises over the allocation of societal resources. The state is responsible for regulating any such conflict. It is supposed to act as an impartial umpire or arbitrator between the contending parties and to establish appropriate mechanisms for resolving these disputes. It will be successful to the extent that it is perceived as fair and unbiased.

PLANNING AND COORDINATION

Modern societies are complex. They require systematic planning and coordination in the allocation of societal resources. Air traffic, environmental protection, and highway construction are some of the tasks that cannot be handled easily by local authorities. They require some degree of planning and coordination at the national level; that is the function of the state.

CONDUCTING RELATIONS WITH OTHER SOCIETIES

Sheer chaos would result if individuals and the various local authorities were able to establish agreements and working relationships with other nations. Foreign policy, international economics, and defense strategy would be complex, confusing, and possibly contradictory. Alliances and agreements between nations are possible only because each of them is represented by a single political authority that can speak for it.

A Conflict Perspective

Not surprisingly, conflict theorists take an entirely different view of the state. They tend to focus on conflict and coercion in the state rather than on its social functions.

CLASS CONFLICT AND THE STATE

In the view of conflict theorists, the state is not a neutral arbiter of conflict over the allocation of societal resources. Following the example of the eighteenth-century French philosopher Jean Jacques Rousseau, they argue that the state serves the interests of the "ruling class," those wielding economic power, and that it protects and even extends their economic and social privileges at the expense of those already powerless.

For Marx the state was simply the political arm of those who owned the means of production (see chapters 1 and 9). In the beginning, societies took the form of *primitive communism*. In these societies private property was nonexistent, and thus there was no social class conflict. This was followed by *slavery*, which led to the development of two classes, one owning and exploiting the other. *Feudalism*, in which aristocratic landowners exploited the peasants, emerged next. That was followed by *capitalism*, in which those who own the means of production control those who do not; the state that evolved from this serves the interests of the capitalists. This situation will change, Marx argued, only when society evolves further. The last two stages of societal development, he believed, will be *socialism*, in which the proletariat will rebel and overthrow the capitalists, and *communism*, when all property will be jointly owned by every member of society, and no exploitation will occur. Under these conditions, the state will just "wither away."

STATE COERCION

The defense of ruling class interests has occasionally required the state to use its coercive power. Conflict theorists point to earlier laws that restricted the development of labor unions to protect the rights of workers and to the use of federal troops to break strikes, and of the use of the courts to order workers back to their jobs. The ruling class also uses its coercive power internationally to obtain markets for its goods and cheap labor for its manufacturing needs. In short, conflict theorists argue, the massive coercive power of the state has been used both domestically and internationally to serve the interests of the elite. It has not been the benign, neutral, and unbiased representative of every member of society that the functionalists describe.

Instrumental and Structural Marxists

There has been considerable disagreement with the views of conflict theorists. The state, some argue, has many more functions than just protecting the economic elite, even if it could justly be accused of doing that. Conflict theorists also differ among themselves. The critical view of the state described above is consistent with that of the *instrumental Marxists*. On the other hand, *structural Marxists* contend that the various aspects of the state apparatus (e.g., certain government departments) have independent histories that are not always tied to ruling class interests or even to the class struggle. While the state certainly provides a favorable climate for capitalism (the United States' economic system; see chapter 17), it must also promote social order and maintain some degree of internal harmony. Also, the capitalist class is not monolithic; there are differences between its members, and actions to help one group may be detrimental to others.

Forms of Government

While every society has a political structure, a *government*, its form varies. One way of analyzing the different types of governmental structures is to consider the relationship between the leaders and those they lead and the manner in which leadership is acquired.

MONARCHY

One of the oldest forms of government is the *monarchy*, in which the power to govern is passed from one generation to another within a single family with little or no input from the people governed. Early monarchies tended to be *absolute monarchies*, in which monarchs ruled with virtually no restrictions on their power. The few monarchies that exist today (e.g., in Great Britain and the Scandinavian countries) are *constitutional monarchies*. In these countries the monarch is the symbolic head of state, but real political power rests with a government that derives its power from some form of constitution.

AUTHORITARIANISM

In *authoritarianism*, the people are excluded from serious participation in political life, and the leader(s) generally cannot be removed from office by lawful means. *Dictatorship*, in which power is obtained and exercised by a single individual, is a type of authoritarianism. Papa Doc (and later his son Baby Doc) Duvalier of Haiti, Juan Peron of Argentina, and Ferdinand Marcos of the Philippines were dictators in the classic sense of the term. (Saddam Hussein of Iraq is a present-day example.) A *Junta* is a military dictatorship that results from the overthrow of a regime by military forces, who then place their own leader in power (e.g., until recently, the military junta headed by General Pinochet in Chile).

TOTALITARIANISM

An authoritarian government that recognizes absolutely no limit to its authority and seeks to intrude and regulate practically every aspect of social life is an example of *totalitarianism*. While authoritarianism has long existed, totalitarianism seems to be an invention of the past century. Only recently were the technological means created that allow a government to attempt to regulate rigidly and systematically the lives of its citizens. Nazi Germany and Stalinist Russia are often portrayed as totalitarian regimes. The pervasive aspects of totalitarianism are nowhere more clearly described than in George Orwell's novel *1984*.

DEMOCRACY

In a *democracy* the authority of the state rests ultimately with the people, who have the right to be involved in the political process, in national decisions, and in the selection and removal of their leaders.

Participatory democracy, in which all members of the population are involved directly in political decisionmaking, is limited to small societies or political units and is relatively rare in the modern world. The New England town hall meetings are a modest example of this form of government.

Representative democracy, in which the people periodically elect others to represent them in the political decision-making process, is more common.

Certain conditions create the climate for the development and maintenance of a democratic form of government.

Advanced stages of economic development often result in a literate, sophisticated, urban population that expects and even demands a significant role in the political process. Also, an advanced economy often has a large middle class that sees itself as benefiting from the existing system and thus is unlikely to support drastic political change; therefore, less control is required to maintain a democracy than the other forms of government described above.

Restraints on the power of government are built into democracies in the form of institutional checks and balances. Most democracies have an executive and a legislative branch, the former to carry out the laws enacted by the latter. Many also have a judicial system that serves as a check on both of the other two. In addition to these structural limitations are the cultural restraints in the form of norms and values that set limits on governmental action.

The absence of major divisions within a society provides a supportive cultural framework for the operation of a democracy. Minor differences between social groups and categories often serve to clarify acceptable social goals and means. But sharp differences can lead to a level of conflict that may be unresolvable within a democratic context. The abortion issue in the United States (see chapter 13) has that potential.

Tolerance for reasonable dissent is essential to the operation of democracy. In a democracy, people must respect everyone's right to hold opinions different from their own. In particular, those in power need to avoid the tendency to see their policies as the only appropriate ones and to brand those who disagree as disloyal and destructive to society. Just this kind of debate took place in the United States over the justification of the war in Vietnam. Thus democracy must continually be on guard against the "tyranny of the majority."

Access to information by the population is necessary to a democratic government. If the people are ultimately responsible for policy decisions, whether directly or through representatives, they must have the information on which to base those decisions. Denying necessary information or providing false or misleading information undermines the democratic process.

While government officials often try to ensure that only "appropriate" information is relayed to the public through the press, free access to information still remains an essential requirement of democracy.

The more diffuse the political power, that is, the more widely it is spread so that no single group can control it, the more democracy can flourish. Centralized control is a hallmark of authoritarian and totalitarian forms of government, not of democracies. Power can be distributed among various branches of the central government and also between the central government and regional or local governments. In the United States, both kinds of distribution occur: the executive, legislative, and judicial branches of government share central authority, and the federal government shares its authority with states and localities. One aspect of the recent problems in the Soviet Union revolves around the distribution of power between the central government in Moscow and the various constituent republics.

THE AMERICAN POLITICAL SYSTEM

The structure of the United States political system is based on the separation of powers both within the federal government and between the federal government and states and localities, periodic elections, a *bicameral legislature* (two different legislative bodies: a Senate having an equal number of representatives from each state and a House of Representatives, in which the number of members from each state is based on its population), and the Constitution and body of laws. This section gives a detailed examination of several other key elements of the United States political system.

Political Parties

Nowhere does the United States Constitution refer to *political parties*, (organizations made up of people who have a political philosophy), yet the issue of political parties was hotly debated by those writing the Constitution. Some argued that political parties could ensure that power would not become permanently concentrated in one group, while others countered that political parties would generate divisive conflict that would be destructive to the country. Apparently, neither side convinced the other, and the entire issue was omitted from the Constitution.

FUNCTIONS OF POLITICAL PARTIES

In the United States, political parties are seen as useful for several reasons.

Political pluralism is fostered by political parties. Different parties lead to different centers of power, reducing the likelihood that too much power will concentrate in the hands of the party. In Stalinist Russia, only the Communist party was recognized, and it held all political power. The political upheaval in the Soviet Union and the recent break up of Eastern European regimes have led to the establishment of additional political parties (e.g., in Czechoslovakia and Poland).

Increased political involvement on the part of the public often results from the activities of political parties, because their delineation of political positions helps Americans clarify their interests and how to pursue them. Political parties also help involve people directly in the political process by organizing activities such as voter registration drives and channeling citizens' views directly to political leaders.

Selection of candidates for political office is carried out through political parties, which choose appropriate candidates and define the platforms (sets of social and political views) on which they will seek election.

Forging coalitions among those with somewhat different views is carried out through political parties. These coalitions serve to increase the political power of those entering into them. In the United States, each of the two principal parties contains people with diverse interests who have, nevertheless, joined together to achieve their common goals.

Maintaining the stability of the political system is also accomplished through political parties. Each party defines positions on major issues that distinguish it from other parties. These positions remain remarkably stable despite changes in the people who make up the party.

POLITICAL PARTIES IN THE UNITED STATES

By and large, the United States has a two-party political system. While there are a number of small parties (e.g., Liberal party, Conservative party, and the Right to Life party) and people who define themselves as "Independents," the bulk of Americans see themselves as either Democrats or Republicans.

While there is considerable diversity of views within each of the major political parties, some general differences between them do exist. On the whole, Democrats tend to be more socially and economically liberal. They are in favor of greater rather than lesser governmental intervention to deal with society's social and economic problems. They tend to favor tax increases to support governmental action. Democrats are more likely to support affirmative action programs, a national health insurance program, and individual choice in abortion decisions and to oppose the death penalty. Democrats are frequently drawn from the middle and working classes.

Republicans, on the other hand, tend to be more conservative. They prefer the government to be less involved in economic activity, trusting more to the "market forces" that are presumed to better regulate this realm of activity. They tend to oppose the Democratic positions on the social issues mentioned above. They are more likely than Democrats to come from the upper and upper middle class.

Special Interest Groups

Political parties are not the only political organizations in the United States. *Special interest groups* are alliances or organizations of people with similar interests who try to influence the political process on behalf of those interests. Special interest groups abound in the United States. Labor unions, professional associations, business groups, and religious organizations become special interest groups when they attempt to influence legislation on their own behalf. Sometimes concerned individuals unite to promote their political and social interests (e.g., the nuclear freeze movement through SANE and the environmental movement through, among others, the Sierra Club).

LOBBYING

The major tactic of special interest groups is *lobbying*, trying to persuade the authorities to promote the groups' interests. Lobbying can take the form of providing information on a particular topic or by using the economic and other resources of the interest groups to influence the votes of legislators or the decisions of those in the Executive Branch. In 1986 there were 8,200 registered lobbyists in the United States; it is also believed that there are about another 20,000 lobbyists who are not formally registered (Thomas, 1986).

POLITICAL ACTION COMMITTEES

The most common form of special interest group today is the *political action committee (PAC)*, which raises and distributes funds to promote its goals. PACs use their funds to try to elect legislators who will support their interests and to defeat those who will not. In 1986 PACs contributed about $127 million to political candidates, and candidates for the House of Representatives received approximately one-third of their campaign funds from PACs.

There has been considerable debate about PACs. Some argue that PACs often operate in secrecy and buy legislative favoritism that may not promote the societal good. Others point out that PACs diffuse power, often provide information that may not be available to legislators and their staffs, and increase the political influence of otherwise powerless citizens. There has been no simple resolution of the question of whether PACs are a useful or a destructive element in the political process, though there are ongoing efforts to limit their ability to raise and spend funds.

Political Socialization

People learn about the political system and develop their political attitudes in the course of socialization. The schools teach the dominant norms and values of the culture, which often include the nature and advantages of the society's political system. Civics and history classes in junior high and high schools, and political science and history courses in colleges and universities often provide an introduction to the basic structure of the United States political system.

When it comes to political attitudes, however, the family is undoubtedly the most powerful influence. Children identify with the political party of their parents as early as elementary school. They learn to share their parents' political attitudes as well as their affiliations. Given residential segregation by class in American society, peer groups are likely to support the political views that children adopt from their parents. And the effects of the mass media are generally understood and interpreted through the prism of the already existing political attitudes. The analysis of the response of viewers to the 1960 televised presidential debate between John F. Kennedy and Richard M. Nixon (Lang and Lang, 1968) showed that by and large Nixon supporters thought he "won" the debate while Kennedy supporters thought he had; few people's minds were *changed*.

Theories about Political Power in U.S. Society

Theoretically, political power in a democracy is invested in the people. But a number of social scientists have pointed to the tendency of power to become concentrated in the hands of a few (e.g., Michels, 1949; original, 1911). Two competing explanations of the distribution of political power in the United States have been developed.

THE POWER ELITE MODEL

This view, advanced largely by conflict theorists, argues that political power in American society is concentrated in the hands of the rich. In an influential book, Mills (1956) asserts that U.S. politics is dominated by a small group of influential people who hold important positions in government, business, and the military; they constitute a *power elite*. While there may not be a conspiracy to effect such control, the complexity of the society requires coordination among these three institutional sectors that puts members of these small groups of leaders in constant touch with one another. Not only do they often have the same interests, but they often share a similar social background. Also, those in the power elite tend to circulate among the various institutional sectors. For example, Alexander Haig was an army general and then secretary of state under Ronald Reagan and has held top positions in a number of major corporations.

Empirical studies that assessed the validity of this model generally found supporting evidence. In studies of both the national level (Domhoff, 1967; 1983) and the local community level (Hunter, 1953; 1980), a small elite group was seen to dominate the political process. In fact, upon leaving the presidency, Dwight D. Eisenhower warned the country of the *military-industrial complex*, the link between weapons-producing companies and the military, and of its influence in national policy decisions. On the other hand, even Domhoff (1984), a forceful advocate of this model, shows that the elite does not always get its way.

THE PLURALIST MODEL

The power elite model is disputed by many social scientists (e.g., Dahl, 1961). They argue that rather than being concentrated in an elite, political power in the United States is actually widely dispersed among many interest groups. Each group seeks to influence rather than dominate the political process. Furthermore, there is considerable diversity of interests even among the powerful. Government action that might be beneficial to one major corporation may be detrimental to another. Thus the large number and diversity of competing interests serve to check one another and provide protection against domination by a power elite.

Relevant empirical research provides some measure of support for this view (Dahl, 1961; 1981). Also, antitrust legislation demonstrates that the economic elite, if it exists, does not control the political processes. The prosecution of a number of defense contractors for fraud similarly suggests the absence of an all-powerful elite.

In conclusion, both models seem somewhat simplistic, yet provide a useful way of examining the use of power in societies. Clearly, there is no dominant, small elite that controls the country. However, to believe that all individuals and organizations have equal influence in the political process would be naive.

WAR AS POLITICS

War

The waging of war is the ultimate expression of the political power of the state. The Prussian general Karl von Clausewitz was reported to have said that "war is the continuation of politics by other means." War is clearly an ancient political practice, dating at least from biblical times. However, the technology available to the modern state has dramatically changed conceptions of war and led to the formation of international bodies (e.g., the United Nations) to try to avoid war. Weapons of mass destruction like the atomic bomb have been developed and used, and others even more destructive weapons (such as the thermonuclear bomb) are now available in the arsenals of some countries. Moreover, the spread of these weapons has raised considerable concern that war may become an increasingly common way of settling international disputes.

Terrorism

Recently, the world has seen an increase in *terrorism*, the use or threat of violence to accomplish political aims. For example, the Palestine Liberation Organization (PLO) attempted to further its political aim to destroy the state of Israel by massacring Israeli athletes at the 1972 Olympics in Munich. Similarly, the Irish Republican Army (IRA) assassinated a member of the

British Parliament to further its political goal of getting Britain to withdraw from Northern Ireland.

Terrorism has been facilitated by the large-scale development and relatively wide distribution of all kinds of weapons. Plastic bombs have become very common, as have plastic guns that can escape detection from security devices. Hand-held rocket launchers and small "dirty" (with massive fallout effects on populations) atomic weapons have increased concern about terrorism. The mass media has unwillingly and inadvertently aided terrorism by giving the terrorists the public exposure that they often need to realize their political aims.

STATE TERRORISM

When states use terrorism to control their citizens or to intimidate other states they are practicing *state terrorism*. Totalitarian regimes frequently use terror to maintain internal control (e.g., Nazi Germany). Other states (e.g., Libya and Syria) use it to further their political goals in other locales. State terrorism tends to become a relatively enduring feature of a country's actions. Unless successfully opposed, it gets embedded in the country's political style; that was the argument the United States used to justify its bombing of Libya in 1987 after establishing that that country was involved in a terrorist attack on American soldiers in Germany.

Revolution

Political revolution is the overthrowing of the existing political system in the hope of establishing a new one. It differs from attempts at *political reform*, which seek to change the system from within, and from a *coup d'etat*, which aims to replace only the leader(s) of a political system. Several common elements have been identified in political revolutions.

RISING EXPECTATIONS

The historian Crane Brinton (1965) notes that contrary to what is usually assumed, revolutions do not occur under conditions of extreme oppression and miserable conditions. Quite the contrary, they are more likely to occur when social conditions are improving but not fast enough to meet the increasing demand for even better conditions.

INEQUALITY AND SOCIAL CONFLICT

Revolutions occur in highly stratified societies in which those who consider themselves disadvantaged and suffering see no way to reform conditions through the system.

AN UNRESPONSIVE EXISTING GOVERNMENT

Tilly (1986) points out that revolutions are more likely when increasingly powerful segments of the population see a lack of responsiveness on the part of the political structure to their needs and demands. The nonresponsiveness of the czarist regime in Russia to the growing demands of the peasants was a major factor in the Russian Revolution.

RADICAL LEADERSHIP BY INTELLECTUALS

Revolutions are fought by people, often the disadvantaged. However, they are inspired by symbols and principles that are often defined and illuminated by an intellectual elite. Lenin and Castro are but two examples of this type of leader.

ESTABLISHING A NEW LEGITIMACY

Overthrowing the old regime does not ensure the success of the revolution. When the revolution is over, revolutionaries must provide a justification for the new system and begin to address the grievances that inspired the change. Unless they are able to do that, they may be subject to a *counterrevolution*, led by the earlier leaders or their followers or by another group entirely. In the Philippines, first Ferdinand Marcos and then his followers (especially in the military) threatened to overthrow the newly established Aquino government practically from the moment of its inception in 1986.

In general, a revolution is neither automatically good nor bad. Which it is depends on what comes after the revolution—and what side a person is on. Many nations, including the United States, emerged from revolutions.

*P*ower, *which may not always be perceived as legitimate, is the ability to accomplish one's aims despite resistance. Authority is power that is legitimated either on the basis of long-standing custom ("traditional"), position in an organization ("rational-legal") or a leader's unique personal characteristics ("charismatic"). Charismatic authority needs to be routinized if the group is to survive the loss of the leader.*

From a functionalist perspective, the state—the political authority—is necessary to enforce social norms, regulate internal social conflict, provide the planning and coordination necessary to a modern state, and conduct relations with other states. Thus the state is seen as useful and necessary to society. Conflict theorists take another view. They see the state as a biased player in internal social conflict. It is under the control of the economically powerful and serves their interests. Marx tried to show how the evolution of society was moving toward the elimination of private property, which was socially divisive, and that once this was accomplished a state apparatus would no longer be required. Conflict theorists also point out the tendency of the ruling class to promote and defend its interests with the coercive power available to the modern state—including laws, judicial decrees, and physical force.

Four different forms of government were described. Monarchies, which transfer power within a family across generations, is one of the oldest forms. Authoritarianism, either in the form of dictatorships (Haiti) or juntas (Chile), excludes most people from serious political participation. Totalitarianism takes control a step further and intrudes into and regulates the daily lives of citizens, as in the case of Stalinist Russia. Democracy rests on the ultimate power of the people. It is facilitated by advanced economic development, structural restraints on governmental power, the absence of major social divisions, socially supported tolerance of dissent, access to relevant information by the people, and dispersal of political power in the society.

The American political system contains two major political parties, which help maintain political stability. These parties increase political pluralism and involvement. They are charged with the selection of political candidates and often find it necessary to forge coalitions to promote their interests. The Democratic party tends to be more liberal than the Republican party on social and economic issues and is more likely to support government involvement in dealing with social and economic problems. Special interest groups, especially PACs, engage in lobbying to try to effect their political agendas. Political socialization starts in the home and is complemented by the school, the peer group, and the mass media. Similar political affiliation and attitudes tend to be found in the same family.

There are two major theories about who wields power in American society. Conflict theorists argue that there is a small group of people, a power elite, who make all the key decisions in society. A contrasting view, the pluralist model, suggests that power is much more diffuse and that the many special interests groups check and balance one another so that no single one dominates the political process. Both models provide an important but partial glimpse into political power.

War is the ultimate expression of state power, and modern technology has changed the face of war dramatically. Terrorism, individual and state is an increasing problem in the modern world. Sophisticated weapons, ease of transportation, and the mass media have made terrorist activities easier to carry out. Revolutions result from rising expectations, perceived inequalities, a lack of responsiveness on the part of government to grievances, and radical leadership by an intellectual elite. They also need to establish and maintain legitimacy once the earlier government is overthrown.

17

Economics and the World of Work

The economy has been referred to frequently in previous chapters. In this chapter it will be examined in some detail. The nature of the economy in the evolution of societies will be explored, and different economic systems will be contrasted. The details of the American economic system will be discussed, as well as the nature of work and the professions in the United States. These will form the backdrop to a brief discussion of the world economy.

THE ECONOMIC ORDER

Every society has to ensure the availability of the resources necessary for human survival. To resolve this problem, each society has an *economy*, an institutionalized social structure for the acquisition, production, and distribution, and sale of necessary goods and services (see chapter 4). The economic structure of society changed as societies evolved from their preindustrial form to the present.

The Preindustrial Order

Before the Industrial Revolution, economies were dependent on either hunting and gathering or some form of agriculture. Production was initially limited to what people needed to exist; there was no surplus to distribute. The invention of the plow and the use of animal power substantially increased productivity, leading to a surplus of goods. These, in turn, led to the development of greater specialization and to larger, more permanent settlements. Contact between these communities resulted in the establishment of trade. These developments dramatically expanded the primitive economic system.

COTTAGE INDUSTRIES

In the later stages of agrarian societies, economic activity largely took the form of *cottage industries*. Goods were produced in the home and then typically sold in large outdoor markets. Production in the home involved not only family members but also nonfamily workers and apprentices (those learning the trade), who lived in the household. Industrialization changed all of this.

The Industrial Revolution

The Industrial Revolution began in England around the middle of the eighteenth century. The invention of machines, particularly the steam engine, substantially increased the energy power available for economic production. This new energy source led to the replacement of the cottage industry with the factory.

While previously most of the economy had been devoted to producing raw materials that people could then convert into finished products on their own, factories provided the basis for the large-scale manufacturing of finished goods. In the factory, it was clear that specialization of jobs would be more efficient than having a single person work on a product from start to finish. Specialization led to greater overall productivity but reduced the need for workers to develop the range of skills required in earlier times. Also, the equipment and organizational structure of the factory allowed for the mass production of manufactured goods.

The greater productivity that resulted from the Industrial Revolution changed the face of society. While living standards generally rose, economic inequities increased. Again, technological advance greatly altered the economic and social structure of society.

The Postindustrial Society

Rapid development of industrial society took place in the nineteenth and especially the twentieth centuries. Technology was developed at an ever-increasing rate, providing even greater sources of energy for production and distribution. In this situation, the emergence of the *postindustrial society*, in which the main economic activity is the production of information and services rather than material goods (see chapter 4), again transformed the economy.

When factories began to decline, so did the prominence of the large cities in which they were located. Information and service industries were more flexible in where they could be located. Especially in the United States, many of these industries moved to suburban areas and relocated from the urban Northeast to the Sunbelt in the South and Southwest.

Sectors of the Modern Economy

Modern economies are complex institutions. Generally, they involve three different sectors, each of which is defined by its principal activity. No sector is inherently more important than the other. Each is necessary to the economy, though each is more prominent in different stages of societal development.

PRIMARY SECTOR

The *primary sector* is the part of the economy that is involved in taking or generating resources from the natural environment. Fishing, mining, and agriculture belong to the primary sector. The economies of preindustrial societies were mainly of this kind. Only about 5 percent of today's labor force in the United States is located within this sector; however, it plays a more predominant role in developing nations such as India.

SECONDARY SECTOR

The *secondary sector* is the part of the economy that is involved in making manufactured goods from the raw materials generated by the primary sector. Factories that turn wood into furniture, build automobiles, and refine raw petroleum into heating oil are located in this sector. The economies of industrialized societies are dominated by this sector, which contains about one-third of the American labor force.

TERTIARY SECTOR

The *tertiary sector* is the part of the economy that provides services rather than goods. Medicine and teaching are examples of these kinds of activities. The tertiary sector increases throughout the process of industrialization and becomes the dominant economic sector in postindustrial society. In the United States, about 60 percent of the labor force is involved in this sector.

The Dual Economy

The economy can be looked at in another way: as a *dual economy* in which there is a core and a peripheral private sector. In addition, there is a governmental sector.

CORE SECTOR

The *core sector* contains economic organizations that are quite large; they have many employees, large total assets, branches that are widely dispersed, and very high profits. They employ advanced technology and dominate their markets. The major automobile companies, IBM, and Kellogg are examples of firms in the core sector. Unionization is often well developed, wages are high, and competition is somewhat restricted. Workers in this sector are often referred to as the *primary labor market*.

PERIPHERAL SECTOR

The peripheral sector involves relatively small firms that are usually located in one geographical region. They have less capital to invest, pay lower wages, are subject to substantial competition, and are generally less productive than firms in the primary sector. Auto supply firms, the textile industry, and small manufacturers are in this sector. Union organization in this sector tends to be weak; firms tend to employ large numbers of women, relatively young or old workers, and those from minority groups.

STATE SECTOR

The *state sector* refers to producers of goods and services, such as governmental agencies and companies under contract to the government. Productivity is generally lower in this sector than in the other two. Unions are not generally strong in this sector, and moderate wages are accepted as the cost of more long term security and adequate pension plans. Recent slowdowns in the economy have led to a shrinking work force in this sector.

COMPARATIVE ECONOMIC SYSTEMS

There are two major economic forms in the contemporary world: the market economy and the centrally regulated economy. In a *market economy* the state does not intervene in the economic activities of the society, believing that the "market," underlying economic forces, is the most natural and beneficial influence on economic activity and that it should be left to its own devices. In *centrally regulated economies*, the state plays the most prominent role in the economic activities of society. However, these are *ideal types* —abstract or "pure" models of concepts against which examples in the real world can be compared. Contemporary societies exhibit characteristics of both forms, although one may predominate. We shall explore each form separately and then discuss a case of a mixed arrangement.

A Market Economy: Capitalism

Capitalism is an economic system in which the natural resources as well as the means of production and distribution are privately owned. Adam Smith (1937; original, 1776) provided the theoretical outline of this economic system; his work suggests several defining features of capitalism.

PRIVATE OWNERSHIP OF PROPERTY

Though every society permits individuals or organizations to own some private property, the extent of such private ownership is considerably more extensive in a capitalist system. In pure capitalism, all property that generates or is capable of generating wealth is under the control of individuals and organizations, not of the state. This conception of property ownership provides the justification for making theft not only morally wrong but also a criminal act (see chapter 8).

MAXIMIZATION OF PROFIT

Pursuing maximum profit is strongly encouraged in a capitalist society. Such action is seen as benefiting both individuals and the society. For individuals, increasing profit permits the accumulation of wealth that can be used for personal pleasures, for investment, for business expansion or for any combination of these. For society, capital accumulation benefits the entire society by providing the necessary resources to expand and improve business.

ENCOURAGEMENT OF COMPETITION

In capitalism, unrestricted competition between economic enterprises is expected to lead to efficiency in the economy through self-regulation by market forces. The government can only upset these "natural" forces if it intervenes.

Consumers are in a better position than the state to decide what should be produced and at what price. If a product is inferior, or its price is too high, consumers will shun it as long as there is a competitive alternative. The original producer will then either go out of business or make the necessary modifications in the product or price to attract buyers away from the competition. In this way, Adam Smith argued, economic activity is appropriately guided by an all-knowing "invisible hand."

Thus capitalists view the unrestricted pursuit of personal gain as being in the interests of both consumers and producers. Ultimately, society benefits because of the efficiencies that competition introduces into the economy.

Centrally Regulated Economies: Socialism and Communism

In *centrally regulated economies*, the state plays a major role in making economic decisions. There are two major forms of such economies, socialism and communism.

SOCIALISM

In *socialism*, the natural resources, the means of production, and the means of distribution are owned collectively and the economy is centrally regulated by the state. Emphasis is placed on pursuing collective rather than individual goals. With collective ownership established, the profit motive is absent. Thus the defining features of this economic form are the reverse of capitalism's.

The basic thrust of socialism is to deny the validity of Adam Smith's assertion that when the people pursue their own narrow, individualistic self-interests they automatically benefit all of society. Socialism insists that there must be a guiding hand for the economy, one that looks out for the collective good. From this point of view, consumers often lack the necessary information to make the economic decisions that will ensure economic efficiency. Capitalists manipulate demand through false advertising; they seek to maximize profit, not to meet social needs.

Though often (until recently) termed communist states (see below), the Soviet Union and its former satellite countries in Eastern Europe, along with China, were the main examples of socialist societies. But there are a number of societies around the world—in Asia, Africa, Europe and Latin America—that are socialist in form.

COMMUNISM

Socialism was not the final stage Marx envisioned in the evolution of society. The ultimate stage he called *communism*, the evolution of socialism—with its collectivist orientation and structure—into a society of economic, political, and social equality. Marx considered socialism to be just a transitional form. Under socialism, private property would be abolished and inequalities based on them would disappear. Thus the state would no longer be required. Societal evolution would, paradoxically, come full circle back to its beginnings as "primitive communism" (see chapter 16), though at a higher level of technological and social advance.

No society has yet achieved the level of communism that Marx envisioned. In fact, even Marx was unclear about exactly how it would function. His description of communism served as an ideal type, defining a goal toward which people should and could strive.

Hybrid Economies: Democratic Socialism

Hybrid economies are those that combine features of market control with central government regulation.

DEMOCRATIC SOCIALISM

One example of a hybrid economy is *democratic socialism*, in which elements of both a market and a centrally controlled economy are used to reduce social inequalities. Another name for this form of economy is the *welfare state*. In these societies, the government owns and runs key sections of the economy (e.g., education, health care, transportation, and utilities) and strongly regulates other important parts of the private sector. Taxes are high, especially for the rich, in order to reduce individual accumulation of wealth, and the money is used to finance extensive social service programs.

Sweden is the prime example of a democratic socialist society, and to a lesser degree, so are Italy and France. Margaret Thatcher, the former prime minister of Great Britain, was determined to transform the country from its previous democratic socialist form under Labour party governments; she sold off a number of government enterprises (e.g., the airline company) to the private sector. Despite her extensive efforts, Great Britain still has a hybrid economy, especially in health care.

Comparison of Capitalism and Socialism

No simple comparison of these two systems is possible because the economy is only one element in a society's institutional structure. Other institutions often affect economic activities. However, two issues are seen as especially important by those arguing for or against either of these two economic forms: productivity and income equality.

PRODUCTIVITY

Capitalism claims that it is a more efficient and productive economic system than socialism. Allowing the market to regulate economic activities guarantees this superiority. There is considerable variability in productivity among both capitalist and socialist societies. For example, among predominantly capitalist societies, the United States has the highest *per capita Gross National Product (GNP)*—an accepted measure of productivity. Per capita GNP is the total value of all goods produced and services provided in the society divided by the number of people in the society (U.S. Arms Control and Disarmament Administration, 1986). However, Greece, another predominantly capitalist country, has only about 23 percent the per capita GNP of the United States. Similarly, the former East Germany had the highest per capita GNP among predominantly socialist countries, and Yugoslavia's was only about 21 percent of that level.

Despite the internal differences within each type of society, the average per capita GNP of capitalist countries far exceeds that of socialist states. In 1986 the per capita GNP of socialist societies was about two-thirds that of capitalist societies. Thus there is some supporting evidence for the capitalist claims of higher productivity.

INCOME EQUALITY

One of the goals of socialism is to reduce economic inequality. In capitalist societies, on the other hand, the market determines income. Any inequalities are perceived as an inevitable consequence of individual talent and skills, and it is felt that the state should not play any role in regulating this effect.

One way of exploring this issue is to look at the difference between the average incomes of people at the top and bottom of the income distribution. The greater the difference, the more income inequality exists. An examination of some available evidence demonstrates that income inequality is about two to three times as high in capitalist than in socialist societies, including democratic socialist countries like Sweden (Wiles, 1977). Though it is the most productive capitalist society, the United States exhibits the widest degree of income inequality.

In sum, it is clear that capitalist societies are more economically productive than socialist societies. However, one of the key goals of socialism is to reduce the income inequality found in capitalist societies. They demonstrate a considerable measure of success in achieving that goal.

THE AMERICAN ECONOMIC SYSTEM

The United States' economy is predominantly capitalist. It is highly productive and generates one of the highest living standards in the world. It also exhibits a high level of income inequality. We turn now to some of the key defining features of the American economic system.

Corporate Capitalism

Individual capitalism is overshadowed in American society by *corporate capitalism*, in which several dozen very large corporations dominate the economy. *Corporations* are formal organizations (see chapter 5) that have a legal existence, power, and liabilities that are separate from their owners or managers; they wield considerable power in society. The major oil companies such as Mobil and automobile manufacturers such as Ford are examples of the huge corporations that dominate the American economy.

Conglomerates, mammoth corporations that consist of a number of medium-sized to large corporations, are another major influence on the American economy. RJR Nabisco, whose holdings at one point included Delmonte Foods, Dr. Pepper, Kentucky Fried Chicken, and Bear Creek Mail Order Company, is one such conglomerate. The enormous size and organization of conglomerates endow them with great influence over the American economy.

CORPORATE CONTROL

Corporations became prominent toward the end of the nineteenth century. Some mechanism was required to provide the huge amounts of money needed to build the country at that time, and the corporation filled that need. It allows people to invest their money and acquire stock in a company. Theoretically, this gives investors a role in determining company policy through their ability to elect a board of directors or to vote directly on specific policy issues. In practice, however, individual stockholders generally have little control over a corporation, though institutional stockholders (e.g., union pension funds) often do.

Control of the corporation is split among stockholders, the board of directors, and managers, those hired to make the daily decisions needed to keep the company running. For most stockholders, the major if not sole responsibility of management is to maximize profits and hence provide a good dividend, or return, on their investment.

LINKS BETWEEN CORPORATIONS

Large corporations and conglomerates dominate the U.S. economy. The largest 100 own almost half of all manufacturing resources in the country. Some have budgets that are larger than those of most countries in the world. Many of these large corporations are linked to each other informally through *interlocking directorates*: social networks of individuals who sit on the boards of directors of several corporations. This network increases the concentration of economic power in the United States (Mintz and Schwartz, 1985).

CORPORATE TAKEOVERS

In recent years there has been a substantial amount of economic activity that is not geared to producing goods and services but to maximizing profits in other ways. Creative accounting to take advantage of changing tax laws, and sometimes influencing tax laws through economic power, is on the rise. So too is taking control of other corporations to seize their assets and then sell them to others at a profit or dismember them after keeping the productive parts.

There are a number of practices that are associated with takeovers. One is called *greenmail*, when a hostile investor (individual or corporation) acquires a large body of the corporation's stock and threatens to take control if the stock is not bought back at a higher level than its initial purchase price. Another is the *poison pill*, which is a defensive situation (such as having huge debts) that makes a corporation an unattractive target for an attempted takeover. Another is the *golden parachute*, an agreement to pay senior executives substantial severance in the event of a takeover.

All these practices have served to direct economic resources away from efficiency and productive capacity. They are focused on short term goals at the expense of long term planning and investment. This strategy has been viewed as contributing to the decreasing economic dominance of the United States in the world, especially in comparison with Japan.

MULTINATIONAL CORPORATIONS

One of the major effects of the technological advances in transportation and communications during the twentieth century has been the development of the *multinational corporation*, which has its headquarters in one country but operates in other countries through firms it either owns directly or controls. The major oil companies (e.g., Mobil), automobile manufacturers (e.g., Ford), and telecommunication companies (e.g., IBM) are examples of American-based multinational corporations.

Multinational corporations exert enormous economic and political influence. General Motors, for example, is active in almost forty countries and sells over $80 *billion* worth of products each year. Clearly, this amount of money makes GM a key part of the economy in many of those countries. Many of the largest multinational corporations have their headquarters in the United States. The economic importance of the United States and the sheer magnitude of their own economic resources give the multinational companies headquartered here enormous influence in world economic affairs. The economic leverage of multinational corporations may not always work to the advantage of their host countries. A number of these corporations have been accused of attempting to undermine governments (e.g, in Iran in 1953) and of bribing public officials (e.g., in Japan in the 1980s). On the other hand, they often provide useful resources and technology to developing countries that would not otherwise be available.

SMALL BUSINESSES

The United States is not all conglomerates and multinational corporations. In fact, almost half the labor force is employed in small firms of 100 or fewer employees. These include law firms, restaurants, grocery stores, dry cleaners, and video stores. Increasingly, these businesses are owned and operated by members of ethnic minorities, especially recent immigrants.

Hundreds of thousands of small businesses are started in the United States each year. Many of them lack sufficient capital to expand or to ride out difficult economic times. As a consequence, most of them fail—over half within two years of opening and most, 90 percent, within ten years (Aldrich and Auster, 1986). However, new ones continually arise. Small businesses play a key role in the American economy by serving the consumer more directly and by generating more new jobs in the economy than the large corporations.

Government and Business

The government is a key player in the economy in many ways. It supplies money and structures to encourage economic activity. It regulates to some degree the business enterprise, protecting firms against unfair competition, consumers against unsafe or ineffective products, and employees from dangers in the workplace. The government's monetary (the amount of money put into the circulation) and fiscal (tax) policies directly influence economic activity. The government also contracts with firms for goods (e.g., military weapons) and services; in fact, it is the largest consumer of goods and services in the country.

Conflict theorists' conception of a power elite was discussed in chapter 16. From their point of view, the government is but a tool of the economic elite; it protects the interests and serves the needs of this group. However, there is likely no small group that controls American society. Large business in the United States is made up of diverse companies that have no agreement on a particular governmental policy that would serve them best. Rather, government is generally responsive to diverse economic interests though their influence on governmental policy is not equal; greater economic power leads to greater, though not uncontrolled, political power.

WORK AND PROFESSIONS IN THE UNITED STATES

The Meaning of Work

Work is the central activity of many individuals. It not only provides them with necessary income but is also central to their concepts of self. While this has been traditionally true for men, the substantial increase in the number of women in the labor force (see chapter 12 and below) has by and large eliminated any earlier gender difference in this regard.

The jobs people hold are important indicators of their social class; thus jobs influence their life chances and life experiences (see chapter 9). Their jobs also play a role in how others define and interact with them. People have different conceptions of farmers and physicists and interact with them differently.

Jobs offer most people important personal satisfactions. The degree of satisfaction is often related to the characteristics of the job. Jobs requiring great skill and those that permit a fair amount of autonomy are often seen as more satisfying. People working in routine jobs under heavy supervision report less job satisfaction, though interpersonal relationships with peers at work provide an alternative avenue for job satisfaction. Marxists argue that work should be meaningful. However, in a 1985 Gallup poll, 70 percent of the respondents reported being satisfied with their jobs, and about the same number indicated that they would keep on working even if they won enough money to make them financially secure for life. Thus work is central to most Americans.

The Professions

Some jobs are considered more important than others (see chapter 9). One example is the *profession*, a job with great social prestige that requires extensive formal education and knowledge. Physicians, lawyers, and psychologists are examples of professional occupations. In general, people in professions control their own work situation; they are rarely closely supervised. They are supposed to be more interested in providing a necessary service than in personal profit or narrow self-interest.

Since a profession has high social standing, occupations often try to convert themselves into professions. They redefine their titles (e.g., from plumber to sanitary engineer), form professional associations that certify a certain level of skill (e.g., medical boards), adopt a code of ethics to define appropriate professional behavior, and seek to restrict through legal regulation the practice of the profession to members of the professional association.

Trends in the Workplace

At the start of the twentieth century, almost one-third of Americans were involved in agriculture, slightly less than one-third in white collar or service positions, and a little over one-third in blue collar and manufacturing jobs. That has changed dramatically over ninety years. Currently, about 3 percent of Americans work in agriculture, a fourth in blue collar or manufacturing jobs, and almost three-fourths in white collar and service positions.

Two major explanations have been offered to explain this dramatic change. Technological advances have increased the efficiency of agriculture and manufacturing, requiring substantially fewer workers in those fields. In addition, increasing numbers of women entered the labor force and were more likely to fill and expand jobs in the service sector than in either manufacturing or agriculture (see chapter 12).

These trends have significant social implications. They impact on education and family life. More education is required for white collar positions. Higher levels of education both provide the necessary technical skills for these positions and serve as a screening device for the attitudes and social habits that they require (see chapter 14). The family has had to adjust to the changes resulting from two working parents (see chapter 13).

Labor Markets

The white collar/blue collar distinction can be viewed in another way. Labor markets can be defined by the type and amount of benefits provided to workers rather than by the type of job involved.

PRIMARY LABOR MARKETS

The *primary labor market* refers to occupations that ensure considerable benefits to their practitioners. In the top layer of this category are people in the professions and in higher-level management. Below them is the "subordinate" primary labor market in which there are fewer extrinsic rewards (e.g., lower salary, less health insurance) and intrinsic rewards (e.g. more repetitive and supervised jobs). This labor market consists of lower-level management and skilled workers in office or blue collar positions.

SECONDARY LABOR MARKETS

The *secondary labor market* refers to jobs that provide minimal benefits to employees. Their income and job security are lower. They give little opportunity for advancement, and they are unlikely to be unionized. This level includes the least skilled among the blue collar jobs and low-level clerical positions. In general, the secondary labor market is likely to be populated by women and members of minority groups.

SELF-EMPLOYMENT

Initially, the United States was primarily a country of the self-employed, before urbanization and industrialization transformed the occupational landscape. Today, only about 7 percent of Americans are self-employed—and most of these are in agriculture (U.S. Bureau of Labor Statistics, 1988). The remaining tend to be in small businesses and a few in the professions.

Self-employment has always been highly valued. It eliminates the kind of supervision that many do not like. It provides a measure of freedom and flexibility often not available to those in the employ of others. On the other hand, the self-employed often lack adequate benefits —especially health insurance—and are quite vulnerable to economic downturns.

UNEMPLOYMENT

All societies face some degree of unemployment. However, technological developments in modern society tend to increase unemployment rates as workers become displaced by machines that can perform many jobs better, more consistently, and more cheaply. In socialist societies the government assumes the obligation of creating jobs, substantially reducing unemployment rates. In capitalist countries unemployment tends to range between 5 and 10 percent. In the United States a 5 percent unemployment rate is considered to be "full employment," a recognition that there is some irreducible number of people who will be unemployed.

Unemployment has varied in the United States. The highest rate of unemployment since the Great Depression of the 1930s occurred in 1982, encompassing just under 10 percent of the labor force. In 1988 about 7 million people (2 percent of the work force) were unemployed. Unemployment does not affect the population equally. It tends to be higher in the secondary labor market, which has a high concentration of women, teenagers, and members of minority groups. In fact, the recent unemployment rate for African Americans is more than double that for whites.

The official rate tends to underestimate unemployment. That rate is based on people who are actively looking for work; many people get discouraged, stop looking, and are no longer counted. Also, a number of unemployed take jobs requiring less skill and paying less money than their previous jobs. Thus while technically employed, they are actually *underemployed*.

A WORLD ECONOMIC SYSTEM

The economy of any modern society is linked to the economy of others. Wallerstein (1974; 1979) developed a *world system model* to examine the economic and political ties among societies. He argues that there is a *core* of highly industrialized societies and a much larger *periphery* of less-developed societies that are dependent on and exploited by the industrial core.

Wallerstein believes that the relationship between the two types is *neocolonial*, a new form of the old European colonialism. The periphery is exploited by the industrial world's control of prices for the commodities of the periphery, by the large debt incurred by the periphery because of insufficient capital accumulation, and by the power of multinational corporations headquartered in the core countries.

This view will be examined further in chapter 23.

The economic order of preindustrial societies was changed dramatically by the invention of the plow, by the use of animal power, and especially by technological improvements in energy provided by the industrial revolution. Consequently, the emphasis of the economy changed from producing raw materials to manufacturing them into usable products and later to producing information and providing services.

The modern economy consists of a primary sector that provides raw resources and a secondary sector that transforms those resources into finished products. The tertiary sector supplies necessary services to the economy. Looked at in another way, there is a dual economy in the private sphere: a core sector of large organizations with high profits that dominate their market and a peripheral sector of smaller firms that are more localized and more economically precarious. In addition to this private dual economy, there is a state sector that is controlled by the government; it is usually less productive than the private sector.

Two major kinds of economic systems were analyzed in ideal terms. Capitalism is a market economy with little state intervention. It stresses private ownership of property, the maximization of profit and the importance of free competition. The other type is the centrally regulated economy. In socialism property and resources are collectively owned, and the economy is controlled by the state to pursue collective rather than individual goals. Communism, a further development of socialism, aims at attaining social and economic equality. So far no society has reached this level. Most societies are combinations of the two major forms; democratic socialism is an example. Capitalism is generally more economically productive than socialism, whereas socialism is better able to reduce income inequality among its citizens.

The American economic system is dominated by corporations and conglomerates; it is a form of corporate capitalism. Multinational corporations have recently been on the increase; they play a major role in national and international economic activity. Still, small businesses are significant in the United States; they supply more than half of the new employment opportunities, though they tend to be economically unstable. The government also plays a significant role in the economy as a consumer and supplier of goods and as a regulator of economic activity.

Work is a significant aspect of most people's lives. It contributes to their identity and to their interactions with others. Most people generally derive considerable satisfaction from their jobs, especially those in higher status jobs. Professions require extensive education and have high status. There are constant attempts to upgrade jobs to professions through a variety of mechanisms. The American work force has shifted dramatically during the course of this century. Early on, there were roughly equal numbers of workers in agriculture, blue collar and manufacturing jobs, and white collar and service jobs. More recently white collar and service jobs have become considerably more numerous than the other types. This change was largely caused by technological developments and the entrance of increasing numbers of women into the labor market. Jobs in the primary labor market provide considerably more benefits to employees than jobs in the secondary labor market, which are more likely to be filled by women and minorities. While in the early history of the United States most people were self-employed, now most work for others. The self-employed enjoy a lack of supervision, but often they do not have adequate benefits and are more vulnerable to economic downturns. Unemployment in capitalist societies ranges from about 5 to 10 percent; it is considerably less in socialist countries because of the government's commitment to create jobs to maintain full employment.

Wallerstein argues that the economies of different societies are interconnected into a world system and that a core of industrial countries dominates and exploits a periphery of developing countries.

18

Medicine

In just a short time the field of medicine has grown into a vital and complex social institution. In this chapter, we will explore the medical institution, particularly patterns of health and illness, differences in response to illness, and medicine as a profession. Health and medicine will be examined from a functionalist, a conflict theory, and an interactionist perspective. A discussion of the relationship among health, the environment, and lifestyle will complete the chapter.

SOCIAL PATTERNS OF HEALTH AND ILLNESS

Health and Its Related Concepts

The World Health Organization (WHO) defines *health* as "a state of physical, mental, and social well-being and not merely the absence of disease or infirmity." *Illness* is a personal construct, a feeling that one is unwell. *Disease* indicates some medically diagnosed pathology that may be the cause of illness. And the term *sickness* refers to a social status that affects how people are treated because they are thought to have some disease.

Health and Human History

Health and its related concepts have been important factors in human history. Some anthropologists believe that half the members of hunting and gathering societies did not live beyond their teens and that only a very few lived past forty. Though advances in agriculture provided a more plentiful food source, the growing urbanism that accompanied societal evolution before the Industrial Revolution—with its environmental pollution, poor sanitation, and widespread infectious diseases—apparently did not significantly lengthen people's lifespan. The life expectancy in medieval times was not much different than it had been during the period of hunting and gathering societies.

The onset of the Industrial Revolution brought more pollution and industrial accidents. Sanitation problems resulted from inadequate sewage and large concentrations of people in urban settings. Only in the early part of the nineteenth century did the situation begin to improve. Though often attributed to advances in medicine, improvement in health actually started before any scientific breakthroughs; improved living standards had led to better nutrition and housing (McKeown, 1979). The latter part of the nineteenth century was marked by significant medical advances, and the recognition of the clear relationship between health and the physical environment led to improved sanitation.

World health today varies by type of society. People in Third World societies (the developing countries) have a life expectancy of about sixty years, about ten years less than the average of people in industrial societies (Mahler, 1980). In Africa the life expectancy is about fifty. Poverty, poor sanitation, poor nutrition, widespread infectious diseases, and the high rate of infant deaths caused by these conditions account for these figures.

Epidemiology

Sociologists are interested in patterns of health in populations and the social structures that are devised to promote health. *Epidemiology* is the study of the origin, distribution, and transmission of disease within a population. Originally epidemiology focused mainly on the origin and distribution of disease. Today it has a wider, more social focus; it traces the link between patterns of health on the one hand and the social and physical environment on the other.

Differential Patterns of Health in the United States

PATTERNS BY AGE

The life span of Americans has been consistently increasing, and the death rate has been reduced for practically all age groups. The one major exception is young adults, who are more likely to die from accidents, often automobile crashes. Also, the United States has a higher infant mortality rate than would normally be expected in a society with its resources. This rate is linked to social class.

PATTERNS BY GENDER

Women appear to be healthier than men. As was pointed out earlier, while there are more males conceived than females, more of them die before birth, during infancy, and throughout life (see chapter 12). The gender difference in death rates before and just after birth is likely a result of biological rather than social factors. However, the continuing gender difference suggests the influence of social factors.

The stress resulting from emphasis in the masculine role on aggressive and competitive behavior, along with men's greater involvement with riskier jobs (e.g., military service, mining, and construction) undoubtedly contributes to the greater rate of death by accidents, violence, and suicide among boys and men. Smoking and alcohol consumption is higher among men than among women, and both contribute to poorer health. Paradoxically, as women attain increasing equality with men, their rates of smoking and alcohol consumption have been rising and are likely to reduce gender differences in health. At the present time, the average life expectancy of those Americans born in the mid-1980s is 71.2 years for men and 78.2 for women.

PATTERNS BY SOCIAL CLASS

Middle and upper class Americans report better health than those below them in the class structure (U.S. National Center for Health Statistics, 1987). The relatively high infant mortality rate referred to above is almost entirely a result of poverty. Moreover, at every age level the health of the poor is worse than the health of those economically better off (Doyal and Bennett, 1981). For example, the number of sick days claimed by those earning $10,000 or less is two and one-half times greater than for those earning $35,000 or more (U.S. National Center for Health Statistics, 1987). African Americans have a life expectancy of 67.2 years for men and 75.2 for women, considerably less than for whites, and their general health is poorer as well.

In large part, these social class differences in health and life expectancy reflect the substantially inferior living conditions of the poor, who tend to live in more crowded and less sanitary housing conditions and to have insufficient income to maintain an adequate and nutritious diet. Consequently, they have a higher rate of tuberculosis and infectious diseases than the wealthy. Also, they are more subject to the social stresses and violence that occur in the inner cities, and they have a higher rate of death by homicide, especially among young African American men. Obviously, middle and upper class Americans also get sick and die. However, their disorders result largely from their affluent lifestyle. Their relatively rich diet and lack of physical activity result in their deaths by a variety of heart diseases.

Cultural Differences in Response to Illness

People respond differently to illness. Some of these differences are due to cultural and subcultural background. The pain a person feels might be attributed to an illness by someone from a Western culture and to voodoo by someone from the West Indies. Devout Christian Scientists believe that illness is given by God and that only God, and not medicine or physicians, can cure it. People's culture and ideology orient them to different kinds of explanations for events, including those related to health.

Zborowski (1969) found that American ethnic groups differ in their reactions to pain. Italian Americans see pain in terms of fate, *il destino,* and are concerned about its current manifestation; they want the pain relieved as soon as possible and are less concerned with how that is accomplished. Jewish Americans, on the other hand, are more future oriented. They want to know the long-term implications of both their pain and the mode of prescribed treatment. White Anglo-Saxon Protestants complain less than the other two ethnic groups about their pain and take a less emotional view of what happens to them.

Chinese Americans who are tied to the Chinese culture view illness differently than other Americans; they use more culturally traditional remedies instead of or in addition to "modern" medicine. They stress the importance of a balance of natural forces that can be gained through the use of special foods and herbs. Pain is controlled through acupuncture, needles inserted and at very specific parts of the body. Native Americans follow traditional practices based on their conception of the sacred relationship between humans and nature. They tend to use special herbs and drugs, spiritual rituals, and various forms of physical actions to improve or maintain their health.

MEDICINE AS A PROFESSION

Physicians enjoy high social status in American society. This is the result not only of scientific advances in medicine but also of the organized attempts of physicians to promote their own interests. They have done so by making medicine a profession (see chapter 17).

Profession- alization

In earlier days, physicians did not need formal qualifications to practice medicine. Anyone could set up a medical practice and advertise his or her services. Thus there were many unqualified practitioners as well as dedicated, trained physicians. In 1846 a group of physicians formed the American Medical Association (AMA). They lobbied state governments to require licensing and certification for those providing medical advice and treatment. Medical schools were closed down if they did not attain satisfactory standards. This reduced the number of physicians and gave the remaining ones more economic control over an expanding market. By the early twentieth century the AMA controlled the certification process and established itself as the dominant force in American medicine.

Establishing medicine as a profession requiring rigorous training and specialized knowledge increased both the social position and incomes of physicians. It also gave them considerable power within the medical field.

They were not supervised, nor were they responsible to anyone except their colleagues for their actions. Any complaint of medical malpractice needed to be validated by other physicians, making it unlikely that such a charge would be sustained upon review. Medicine often served as a model for other occupations wishing to gain independence and prestige as a profession.

In recent years, however, the bureaucratization of American society has reached even to the medical profession (Starr, 1982). The increasing cost of medical training, research, and equipment requires the assistance of government and industry, whose policies and practices influence the activities of doctors and other health care specialists. In addition, the rising costs of health care systems has allowed the government, labor unions, corporations, and consumer groups to intrude into the medical arena. Each seeks to devise ways to contain rising costs, and many of their actions reduce the lack of oversight that physicians had enjoyed in the past (Light, 1991).

Medical Socialization

Medical education is long, rigorous, and costly. Consequently, those who go to medical school are mainly white men from affluent families. They not only have the resources necessary to pay for medical school, but they are also socialized to defer immediate gratification in the interests of longer term goals (see chapter 9). They are also more likely to have physicians in their family who serve both as role models and as important sources of professional contacts. Recently, women and minority groups have increasingly been entering medical schools.

Becker and his colleagues (1961) found that those attending medical school begin their education with idealistic views of the profession and of their ability to serve others. They are enthusiastic about learning everything they might need to know as physicians. However, they find medical school an overwhelming experience. Since they are expected to learn more than they believe is possible, they gradually reduce their educational goals and become satisfied with merely passing their examinations. Medical students develop some emotional distance from the human body and disease to enable them to deal with the difficult aspects of both. They increasingly become aware of the gaps in their knowledge and of the amount of uncertainty that exists in medicine. They come to understand the need to deal with these uncertainties and with their ignorance in certain areas by using educated guesses; they also learn to expect and to tolerate errors. Physicians-in-training learn the professional norms about relationships with patients: emotional, sexual, and financial ties are seen as inappropriate. In short, they gradually develop a more realistic understanding of both the possibilities and the limitations of modern medicine.

Medical socialization continues beyond medical school. Since most physicians tend to become specialists, they often must take further training. They need to stay current with rapidly changing medical technology and practice; some do so through continuing education programs offered by hospitals and medical boards.

A similar socialization process occurs for other key professionals in the field of medicine. Nursing schools share many of the same characteristics of medical schools. Recently, two new positions have developed in the medical field: The *physician's assistant* and the *nurse practitioner*. The intensity of the training for these positions is somewhere between that of a physician and that of a nurse. These professionals provide medical diagnosis and treatment under the supervision of a licensed physician. The roles have emerged because of the reduction in the number of physicians being trained and the rising costs of medical care. People holding these jobs provide important medical care at a reduced cost. However, both these new statuses and the more traditional nursing role have less power and prestige both in medicine and in society.

The Medicalization of Society

The growth of the medical profession has correspondingly increased its impact on society, leading in turn to what some have called the *medicalization of society*, the extension of medicine and the medical model into nonmedical areas of social life (e.g., Freidson, 1970; Zola, 1972). Several factors attest to the validity of this view.

THE GROWTH OF MEDICINE

The phenomenal growth in the number of medical practitioners and hospitals, along with the development of massive pharmaceutical and health insurance industries, has given medicine an increasingly large role in the economy. Expenditures for health constitute about 10 percent of the United States' gross national product (GNP), and about 7 percent of the work force is associated with the field of medicine.

EXTENSION TO "NATURAL" ACTIVITIES

Many activities that were once seen as natural are now seen through the lens of medicine. Childbirth is such an activity. Before this century most children were born at home without the involvement of trained medical personnel (Aries, 1962). This too was the case with death (Aries, 1974). Today, birth and death make up the first and the ultimate medical experiences. They generally take place in a hospital, requiring the involvement and certification of a physician. Other typical human problems such as difficulties in sleeping, weighing too much, and eating too little have become medical issues (insomnia, obesity, and anorexia nervosa, respectively). It is not that medical attention is inappropriate in these cases; however, it should be pointed out that they were dealt with in other ways before they became appropriated by medical practitioners.

THE MEDICALIZATION OF DEVIANCE

Perhaps nowhere is the increasing influence of medicine seen more clearly than in the area of deviance (see chapter 8). Acts of deviance are increasingly explained as physical or mental disorders rather than as, in previous times, sin, immorality or criminality. "Sick" has replaced "bad" as a description of the deviant. This is clearly seen in the case of drug abusers, who are defined as addicted and therefore as not really responsible for their "condition." Psychiatrists (medical doctors who specialize in mental disorders) are routine participants in many trials; they often testify to the sickness and level of responsibility of those charged with criminal acts.

WIDE ACCEPTANCE OF THE MEDICAL MODEL

The problems of everyday life are seen as amenable to medical treatment. Aspirin is prescribed for a headache, one kind of pill for depression, and another kind of pill for excitability. There is a medical basis for all sorts of feelings and behaviors, and, therefore, a medical treatment for them when necessary. The medical model is often applied even to attitudes and social behaviors. Psychiatrists are typically asked to explain all sorts of behavior: aggressiveness, timidity, laziness, and ambition.

CHALLENGES TO THE MEDICALIZATION OF SOCIETY

The intrusion of medicine and the medical model of explanation has not gone unchallenged. The number of consumer rights groups, particularly those focusing on the medical field, has mushroomed in recent years. For example, several groups have organized to challenge physicians' powerful role in deciding whether to use or withhold life-supporting technology (the issue of the right to die with dignity). Also, review boards that certify the technical adequacy and appropriate ethics of medical research financed by the federal government, which is most such research, now include individuals outside the medical and scientific professions.

The sharpest attacks, however, have come from within the medical profession itself. Szasz (1970), a psychiatrist, and others (e.g., Torrey, 1974) argue that medicine in general and psychiatry in particular are being extended to inappropriate areas of social life, where they can do little but add confusion.

THEORETICAL PERSPECTIVES OF HEALTH AND MEDICINE

A Functionalist Perspective

The functionalist view of health and medicine examines the functions medicine performs in society and the key elements of health and illness.

THE FUNCTIONS OF MEDICINE

Functionalists see the growing importance of the institution of medicine in terms of three functions: the maintenance of health, research and the providing of innovative treatment, and social control.

Maintaining the health of the population, the central function of medicine, is obviously essential for any society. In the modern world, many individuals cannot provide all that they need to be healthy because they lack technical knowledge or adequate resources or both. The medical profession assumes the responsibility of keeping people healthy. It not only seeks to restore health to the ill through appropriate treatment but also to promote those activities that will prevent illness in the first place: good nutrition, good health practices, regular checkups, and necessary public health measures.

Scientific medical research and innovative treatment are carried out by the medical profession. Research into illness and disease and the modes of treating them can only be carried out by those with medical knowledge. Medical and pharmaceutical research is carried out primarily in universities, university-affiliated hospitals, and government and corporate laboratories. Recent developments in biotechnology and genetic engineering have led to an increase in the number of specialized companies carrying out research in these fields.

The social control function of society (see chapter 8) often requires the participation of medical practitioners, who are frequently required to certify people's health and thus their availability for certain duties ranging from factory work to military service. Physicians also certify the health of subscribers to health insurance programs and carry out the mandates of public health policy (e.g., in providing vaccinations).

KEY ROLES

Functionalists point to two key roles having to do with health and illness: the sick role and the physician's role.

The sick role involves expectations that permit variation from typical behavior because of illness. Playing the sick role allows individuals to avoid their usual responsibilities and to be granted certain privileges (Parsons, 1951). They can be absent from their jobs or from school, for example. In general, people are not held responsible for being sick, though they are expected to want to get healthy and to seek out appropriate assistance, usually from physicians, to regain their health.

Critics of the functionalist approach to medicine (e.g., Arluke, et al., 1979) have argued that the functionalist argument is geared to acute diseases and the role adjustments they require rather than to the more common and frequent experience of temporary illness. Also, it tends to focus on treatment rather than prevention and overemphasizes the need for professional medical attention in contrast with other forms of dealing with illness (e.g., ignoring it and carrying on normally). Finally, certain illnesses (e.g., AIDS) carry a social stigma whether or not people seek proper medical attention.

The physician's role is also central to the functionalist position. The patient's sick role implies that there is a reciprocal role (see chapter 4), that of the physician, the primary provider of required medical care. For the functionalists, physicians have some measure of authority over patients because of cultural norms that require ill people to seek out and cooperate with the trained medical practitioner. This view is more appropriate to treatment-oriented physicians and less appropriate to those involved in promoting good health (e.g., in public health or holistic medicine), where a more equal relationship is seen as beneficial.

Physicians too are bound by norms. They must treat their patients with respect and protect the confidentiality of the information they receive in the course of treatment, though not all do. While the first cannot be guaranteed, the second is enshrined in the law with rare exceptions (e.g., recently physicians—along with nurses and teachers—have become obligated to report cases of suspected child abuse to the police).

A Conflict Perspective

Conflict theorists take a less positive view of the medical profession. They focus on the inequities in the system and on the less altruistic side of medical practice.

UNEQUAL ACCESS TO HEALTH CARE

Health care is expensive. While many people have some form of health insurance through their jobs, they often do not have complete coverage. Also, the discussion of the peripheral sector in the private labor market (see chapter 17) pointed out that many in this sector—mainly women and minorities—have little or inadequate health insurance coverage.

Conflict theorists argue that the poor have unequal access to adequate health care. Health and life expectancy vary by race and social class. The poor and African Americans have shorter life expectancies than other Americans, and they report being less healthy. There has been continual political debate over establishing a national health care program, as in Great Britain and Canada, to provide universal access to adequate health care regardless of ability to pay. However, the strong opposition of the American Medical Association has killed all such legislative efforts to date. Nevertheless, two government programs have been established to cover some of the costs of medical care for the poor (*Medicare*) and the elderly (*Medicaid*).

Some conflict theorists take a more radical view. They argue that even a national health care program would be less useful than a complete redistribution of economic resources in society to eliminate poverty and to let all citizens, not the state, define and take care of their own needs.

THE PROFIT MOTIVE IN MEDICINE

Despite the idealistic assertions of the medical profession, conflict theorists argue that medicine is just another large business enterprise. Collectively, the medical and pharmaceutical industries generate hundreds of billions of dollars of business each year. Conflict theorists maintain that the pursuit of profit rather than the treatment of illness is the primary goal of medicine. This leads physicians to prescribe more drugs, require more tests, and perform more surgery than is medically necessary.

The growing role of health insurers has led to increasing demands for the reduction of the costs of medical care, and with it of the profits involved. Reviews of medical and surgical decisions by professional review boards (PRBs) and the establishment of rates by "diagnostically related group" (DRG) are steps in that direction.

An Interactionist Perspective

Interactionists look at health differently, focusing on perceptions and definitions of health and illness.

PERCEPTIONS OF HEALTH

Interactionists emphasize that perceptions of health and illness are often subjective. People often have "symptoms" of illness such as a cough, a runny nose, and body aches; they do not, however, always decide that they need medical attention. The translation of feelings of discomfort or pain into perceptions of illness is a social process that is related to cultural or subcultural conceptions of health (Zola, 1966). Hispanics in the Southwest, for example, treat diarrhea as an everyday occurrence; though the frequency of groin pain is about equal in both groups, Americans with a Southern European background are more likely to seek medical help for this problem than those from Eastern European backgrounds.

SOCIAL DEFINITIONS OF ILLNESS

Different cultures have different definitions of illness. Only recently have *psychosomatic disorders* been seen as actual physical illnesses that are caused or aggravated by a person's state of mind. For example, some forms of asthma exhibit this quality, as do some stress-related illnesses.

The label society places on a set of symptoms has a powerful effect on people. Many people are terrified of cancer. Although many forms of cancer are treatable, especially if diagnosed early, the label strikes terror in most people's hearts and a feeling of fatalistic resignation to the inevitability of death. To label someone as having AIDS is to identify the person as a deviant: a homosexual or a drug abuser. However, the person with cancer is not held responsible for the disease; the person with AIDS is. Our responses to the two people are likely to be quite different, independent of the issue of the communicability of the disease.

Social and political factors sometimes play a role in defining a condition as an illness. In the Soviet Union several years ago, political dissenters were labeled as psychopaths (having psychological disorders) and were confined in mental hospitals. Only sustained political pressure by the International Psychiatric Association forced a change in that policy.

Social situations also play a role in defining illness. College students are more likely to ignore symptoms of ill health that occur just before a vacation than they are for those that occur before an important examination. Likewise, those in military service are less likely to complain of a symptom when they are about to go on leave than when they are immersed in their regular duties.

In short, interactionists stress the subjective definitions and social construction of health and illness. However, there are occasions where there is clear and unambiguous evidence of poor health, whether the person subjectively realizes it or not. Constant poor nutrition will at some point cause ill health, whether the person is aware of it or not. Continual pain is often a signal of some underlying problem, even if the person chooses to ignore it.

HEALTH, THE ENVIRONMENT, AND PERSONAL LIFESTYLES

Medical knowledge and technology have grown tremendously during this past century. Nevertheless, there has been no significant change in the general death rate in the United States and in most industrial societies as a consequence. The most dramatic improvements in public health took place before these developments, largely because of improvements in nutritional practices and public health policies.

Medical advances have been more effective in treating physical ailments than in preventing them. In modern societies death is less likely than in the past to result from the spread of infectious disease—with the exception of AIDS. People are more likely to die from chronic diseases of middle and old age that have a clear relationship to environmental and lifestyle factors: heart disease, stroke, and cancer. These disorders are created or aggravated by unsanitary living conditions, hazardous jobs, stress, pollution, poor nutrition, and lack of exercise. Lung cancer and automobile accidents are major causes of death, which is usually preceded by long term and expensive medical care. Prevention of deaths from smoking and dangerous driving is less amenable to medical than to social intervention.

In short, environment and lifestyle are major contributors to health and well-being. These factors reflect social issues more than medical treatment alone. Increasingly, members of the medical profession are placing emphasis on these social factors along with scientific and technological improvements in the field of medicine as the way to achieve the goal of improved public health (e.g., Dubos, 1969; McKeown, 1979).

In the United States, patterns of health vary by age, gender, and social class. The United States has a higher infant mortality rate than would be expected in a country of its wealth and resources. This is in part explained by the higher rate of disease among the poor, which is often implicated in infant mortality rates. Women appear to be healthier than men, and they live longer. Both biological and gender role behavior contributes to these differences. The masculine role emphasizes aggressive and competitive behavior as well as more risky occupations; these are not conducive to good health or long life. The poor report less good health than those more socially and economically advantaged. They are more likely to live in unsanitary conditions and polluted environments and to be subjected to considerable stress. Moreover, they lack the financial resources to get appropriate and preventive medical attention.

How people conceive of and deal with illness often depends on their cultural or subcultural background. Similarly, reactions to pain and what is deemed an acceptable mode of treatment varies by ethnic groups. The medical profession enjoys substantial social prestige and accompanying economic benefits. In part, this is the result of the professionalization of medicine that began in the middle of the nineteenth century. The establishment of the AMA helped secure physicians' control over the definition of health and the treatment of illness. Recent trends in American society, particularly efforts to control the rapidly escalating costs of health care, have increased the bureaucratization of medicine and reduced the autonomy of physicians.

Medical education tends to be lengthy and costly, leading to an overrepresentation of the middle and upper classes as medical practitioners. The difficulties and complexities of medical training transform the initial idealism of medical students into a more practical view of what they can learn and use in practice.

The increasing influence of medicine has led to the medicalization of society, extending medicine and the medical model of human behavior well beyond areas of physical health. Activities previously considered "natural"—like birth and death—and requiring little or no medical inter-

vention are now routinely within the province of physicians. Deviance is often defined by physicians and psychiatrists, both on the job and in the courts, though this practice is increasingly being challenged from within the profession itself.

The three major theoretical perspectives see health and medicine differently. Functionalists see the medical profession as maintaining the quality of health in society, forging scientific advances in understanding and treating illness, and serving a useful social control function in certifying illness. They focus on appropriate roles for patient and physician. The sick role allows patients to avoid their normal responsibilities as long as they indicate that they want to get better and seek out appropriate medical help to do so. While physicians have considerable authority over patients, they are bound by norms of respect and confidentiality even though some may violate these norms by being rude and arrogant or talking to others about their patients on occasion.

Conflict theorists emphasize the unequal access to health care. The poor often cannot afford the ever-increasing cost of medical care despite the growth of health insurance programs and the government programs Medicare and Medicaid. They live in conditions that are not conducive to good health, and they typically cannot afford adequate preventive care or treatment programs. Conflict theorists also point out that far from being an idealistic profession, medicine is a big business that is bound up with the quest for profit.

Interactionists point out that perceptions of health and illness are often subjective. These perceptions are influenced by cultural and subcultural backgrounds and by society's definitions of illness.

Finally, environmental factors and lifestyle were shown to affect health. Stress on the job, environmental pollution, smoking, and aggressive driving habits all contribute to poor health and a shorter life.

19

Science and Technology

Science and technology play central roles in the institutional structure of modern societies. We will examine the growth of modern science and look at science as a social process. The norms governing science, deviance from those norms, and the modes of scientific advance will be discussed. Technology's relationship to modern society, its influence in social change, and public policy regarding technology will be explored.

MODERN SCIENCE

One of the hallmarks of contemporary society is the important role that science and technology play in its institutional structure. *Science* is the systematic pursuit of reliable knowledge about the physical and social world through empirical (using the human senses) observation. By means of science, we can obtain a detailed understanding of the nature and operation of physical and social phenomena. *Technology*, though closely related, is different from science; it refers to the application of scientific or other forms of knowledge to the solution of practical problems.

Technology is older than science. Early humans built tools, shelters, and weapons through trial and error before they acquired detailed scientific knowledge. Even today many people use modern technology without necessarily understanding its scientific base. For example, not all people who fly in airplanes understand why planes rise and stay up in the air; few understand the nature of the electric current and circuits they use when they flip a light switch in their homes.

The Growth of Modern Science

THE BEGINNINGS OF SCIENCE

Science is a powerful force in modern life. Some form of it exists in all societies. The early Greeks, Arabs, and Mayans acquired detailed scientific knowledge, especially in astronomy and mathematics. Little of this knowledge spread to other societies. However, the Italian Renaissance in the fifteenth century uncovered a good deal of early Greek scholarship, including scientific documents. Furthermore, the invention of the printing press by Gutenberg in 1439 allowed new and existing scientific and cultural works to be more widely distributed, thereby increasing the circle of people with cultural and scientific knowledge.

Sixteenth- and seventeenth-century Europe was the birthplace of modern science. The increasing desire to explore new lands and waterways heightened the need to deepen scientific knowledge to accomplish those ends. Sixteenth-century philosophers like Bacon and Descartes revised existing conceptions of nature. The surrounding world became less mystical and supernatural, making it more amenable to systematic observation and analysis.

During this period, few specialized scientific roles existed. Science was carried out primarily by a small group of relatively well-to-do individuals, and only a few universities provided any systematic education in science. The Royal Society in London was established in 1662 as the first scientific society. It served as a place where scientific observations could be shared and discussed. The Royal Society also provided legitimacy for claims of credit for scientific advances. Much of the scientific study of the time was centered in Europe and focused on the technology needed for practical problems of society: beginning industry, navigation, and warfare (Merton, 1970, original, 1938).

THE MORE RECENT PERIOD

In the nineteenth century Germany created a major university system with some focus on laboratory science; in fact, the first psychology laboratory was established by Wilhelm Wundt in 1879 at the University of Leipzig. Many American scientists at that time received their training in Europe, especially in Germany; the German university became the model for the developing system of higher education in the United States. By the end of the nineteenth century scientific knowledge had advanced to the point that it could serve as the basis for Thomas Edison's invention of the electric light and Alexander Graham Bell's invention of the telephone.

The Institution-alization of Science

SCIENCE AS AN INSTITUTION

Science has become a social institution (see chapter 4). It has organized structures (e.g., professional societies, review boards, funding sources), career lines, and a set of norms (discussed below). Most scientists work in teams in universities or in government or corporate laboratories. Often they work together in research centers or institutes that make it easier to share ideas and analyses. The lone scientist is a rare occurrence today.

BASIC AND APPLIED SCIENCE

A conceptual distinction can be made between basic and applied research. *Basic scientific research* seeks to generate new knowledge irrespective of any immediately recognizable practical use. Attempts to understand how a human cell undergoes division is an example of basic research. *Applied scientific research*, on the other hand, focuses on developing new knowledge for some identifiable purpose or on how to use existing knowledge. For example, in studies of the causes of cancer, applied researchers explore why cells start to divide and reproduce after maturity. Scientists involved in "research and development" (R&D) tend to be applied scientists.

There is not always a clear separation of the two forms of research. Basic researchers try to understand fundamental processes. Applied researchers want to find out how these fundamental processes produce certain results, like cancer, that they wish to change. Both approaches, and the results they uncover, are necessary to scientific progress; they nourish one another.

OCCUPATIONAL PATTERNS

Scientists have high social prestige in American and other industrial societies. Among scientists, those who carry out research programs and publish their findings have the highest prestige (Cole and Cole, 1973). The proportion of scientists working in the variety of institutional settings has remained relatively constant over the past quarter of a century. Approximately three-quarters of all R&D scientists and engineers are employed by industry. Of the rest, about 15 percent have college or university positions, 8 percent work for the government, and another 4 percent are employed in free-standing research centers and institutes.

The Functionalist Perspective

Functionalists see science as a useful tool in understanding the physical and social world, and thus in dealing with the problems society faces. It provides a reliable body of knowledge on which to base social decisions. It is through science, the functionalists argue, that questions about the origin and fate of the universe can be adequately addressed; or, closer to home, it is through science (in the form of a census) that society determines changes in the size or composition of its population and the necessary allocation of economic, political, and social resources.

Science is also an important cause of social change (see chapter 23). Improvements in science and technology often change social norms. For example, improving knowledge about human reproduction and the development of improved contraceptive technology has had a major effect on sexual norms and practices.

The relationship between science and other social institutions is reciprocal. Not only does science influence social norms and practices but it is also influenced by them. Merton's (1970; original 1938) research into seventeenth-century England demonstrates the influence on science of military needs, trade patterns, industrial development, and religious concerns as well as science's influence on them.

The Conflict Theory Perspective

Conflict theorists focus less on the benefits of science. They emphasize how the unequal distribution of resources and power in society affects science. Science is not neutral, they argue. It is in the service of those who have the resources needed to sustain it and therefore serves these narrow interests. For example, they point out, more scientific effort goes into military research than into ways of helping the homeless and the economically disadvantaged. And large corporations are able to guide significant amounts of scientific research into areas that will maximize their profits rather than into those that would be of more general social benefit.

Even the federal government, conflict theorists argue, takes advantage of the powerless in the name of science. There has been a growing body of evidence that the federal government sponsored medical research on some prison inmates, on some poor African Americans in rural regions, and on some in military service without providing them with adequate, detailed information about what was being done to them and what were likely to be the short and long term effects.

Conflict theorists make it clear that science is not neutral; it serves the interests of those who can pay for it. Far from science being a tool to promote the general good, it is a weapon in the hands of the powerful. Science's sponsorship, rather than its general benefits, explains its development and influence.

SCIENCE AS A SOCIAL PROCESS

Science is not simply a method of acquiring knowledge or the accumulation of verifiable facts. It is a social process that can be examined.

The Norms of Science

Taking a functionalist perspective, Merton (1957) describes four key norms as necessary to continued scientific advance. They constitute the very essence of science as an ongoing social process.

UNIVERSALISM

Scientific research must be evaluated on its technical merit alone and not on the basis of who carried it out. Science is committed to valuing the contribution of all scientists irrespective of their race, religion, ethnicity, gender, religion or notoriety. A proposal for scientific research undergoes review by others in the same or a comparable field without information about the proposal's author. In this way, the technical value of the research, not the characteristics of the proposer becomes the basis for accepting or rejecting a particular project for funding.

COMMUNALISM

Scienowledge is the property of everyone. It is owned in common, and even those for whom certain principles and laws are named (e.g., Einstein's theory of relativity) cannot claim them as their exclusive private property. On the other hand, a technological invention can be patented in the name of an individual, who then may hold the sole legal rights to its use.

Science is communal in another sense. All scientific information is presumed to be public knowledge. Secrecy is not seen to be in the interests of science and of scientific advance. Scientific work is expected to be shared fully and freely with others who are interested in the topic. It is this norm that occasionally causes conflict, when scientists working for the military are not always free to share their findings with colleagues in civilian institutions.

DISINTERESTEDNESS

Scientists are expected to be more interested in the pursuit of valid knowledge than in any personal fame or fortune that may result from their activities. Science should be an altruistic pursuit, engaged in for the benefit of others (including society as a whole) rather than for personal ambition.

ORGANIZED SKEPTICISM

Scientists are hard to please. They examine all evidence carefully. They are expected to be skeptical, to withhold judgment until all the relevant data are in. Even then they often expose research results to a series of alternative explanations. Science, in short, is a search. Because of the high status that society places on scientific "truth," all such claims need to be carefully scrutinized. No theory and no scientist is too sacred to avoid such examination. Einstein's theory of relativity is still undergoing continual tests of its validity, despite the esteem in which he is held, the intense examination of various aspects of the predictions derived from it.

The requirement that scientific evidence be reviewed before it is published in a reputable scientific journal derives from this norm. Furthermore, the very act of publishing scientific research is intended to result in even more knowledgeable scrutiny. Thus, publication is as important for science as it is for the reputation of the individual scientist.

Deviance in Science

VARIATIONS FROM SCIENTIFIC NORMS

The norms of science specify appropriate behavior, but they cannot guarantee it. Though they are less likely to violate professional norms, scientists are not immune from deviant behavior (see chapter 8).

Variation from the norms of science does occur. Because Einstein was Jewish, some Nazi scientists did not take his theories seriously, despite the norm of "universalism." Military scientists engage in work that is not always open to other scientists, even though they generally subscribe to the norm of "communalism." Some scientists are very much interested in personal recognition for their work (Watson, 1968). Though organized skepticism is the norm, the work of scientists who have been accorded great honor by their colleagues (e.g., Nobel Prize winners) does carry more weight in scientific deliberations because of their reputation (Merton's "Matthew Effect"; see the last section of chapter 9).

SCIENTIFIC FRAUD

Some practices go beyond variation from established norms; they constitute actual fraudulent behavior, involving the deliberate falsification or fabrication of data.

For example, the work of Sir Cyril Burt, one of the mainstays of psychological research on the issue of nature versus nurture in human intelligence, was determined to be a fraud (Kamin, 1974). In addition to inconsistencies in the reported data, investigators discovered that Burt had apparently created evidence to back up his views. He then published these data under the made-up names of two nonexistent researchers and used this "independent" source to support his theory of the dominance of genetic over cultural factors in intelligence. More recently, other examples of the use of fraudulent data in medical research have come to light (Broad and Wade, 1982).

As dramatic as these examples of scientific fraud are, deviant behavior in science is relatively uncommon (Zuckerman, 1977). The professional socialization that scientists undergo emphasizes the importance of honesty and is a counterforce to the desire to cheat. Also, the need to subject research findings to the scrutiny of the public and of other knowledgeable scholars serves as a deterrent to fraud. While these and other mechanisms are not foolproof, they keep deviance to a much lower level than occurs in other areas of society and assure that deviance will likely be brought to light when it does occur.

Merton (1957) argues that such deviance is less attributable to the personal characteristics of the scientist than to the structural conditions within which scientists work. In particular, the tremendous pressure on scientists to produce new discoveries is seen as playing an important role; this pressure exists despite how difficult it is to produce original knowledge. This conclusion is consistent with Merton's general approach that sees deviance as a response to the absence of or difficulty of using legitimate means to attain culturally valued goals (see chapter 8).

Scientific Development

Thomas Kuhn (1962) studied the process of scientific innovation in a number of different fields. He came to the conclusion that there are two different types of innovation: normal science and paradigm shifts.

NORMAL SCIENCE

Since science is a social process, it advances in perceptible ways. Rarely does a scientific discovery come "out of the blue." In general, science builds on previous knowledge. Often this previous knowledge is the cumulative work of many people, each of whom adds different pieces to the puzzle until it is ultimately solved. The hallmark of science is that these pieces of information are the result of systematic research and are often linked in some organized way. Scientific development is also a product of its time. Both the conceptual and technological bases must be present for science to proceed. Watson and Crick could not have discovered DNA in the eighteenth or nineteenth century (or even in the first half of the twentieth century) because neither the necessary conception of nucleic acids and genetic structure nor the appropriate laboratory tools existed.

Normal science, then, involves collecting data to examine current theories about the world. It describes the important but routine activity of most scientists. It is the route through which most science develops and grows.

SCIENTIFIC REVOLUTION: PARADIGM SHIFT

Normal science takes place within a *paradigm*, a general set of shared assumptions, concepts, and methods about a certain area of human experience. This paradigm gives shape and direction to normal science. It helps define the questions to be addressed and the mode of investigating them. It brings order to what would otherwise be a chaotic pursuit. The system of astronomy dating from the Greek mathematician Ptolemy in which the earth was regarded as the center of the universe, was just such a paradigm.

At some point, however, research within a particular paradigm begins to raise questions that cannot be answered using science's existing assumptions, concepts, and methods. Patchwork answers are provided rather than the more systematic knowledge to which science usually leads. At that point, a new approach—a new paradigm—seems to be the only way to systematically address these new questions. For example, because astronomical information accumulated that could not be explained by the Ptolemaic view of the universe, Copernicus developed a new paradigm. It put the sun at the center of the solar system, and the earth as one of the planets orbiting it.

This reconceptualization was more consistent with known facts and advanced scientific knowledge.

Kuhn calls this replacement of one scientific paradigm with another a *scientific revolution.* The replacement of Newton's conception of the physical universe with Einstein's was a similarly dramatic *paradigm shift.* Freud's conception of the mind and personality, and particularly of the operation of the unconscious, defined another scientific revolution, this one in the understanding of human behavior.

Scientific Knowledge as a Social Construct

It is generally believed that scientists go about "discovering" or "uncovering" scientific truths. A realistic view of science suggests that scientific knowledge is more likely to be constructed than discovered (Knorr-Cetina, 1981). The discussion about paradigms points out the importance of the framework with which scientists approach their task. The kinds of questions they ask substantially influence what they are likely to come to believe.

Scientists develop certain ideas about the nature of reality. They then define and seek the kind of evidence that would shed light on the validity of their ideas. For example, physicists were speculating about subatomic particles (elementary particles that make up the atom, once thought to be the smallest unit of matter) well before they were able to "see" or trace the consequences of these particles. Scientists then developed techniques to locate and examine the characteristics and effects of these particles.

The social process of constructing scientific knowledge also requires convincing the community of scientists of the validity of a particular theory or set of research findings. Presentations at scientific meetings, informal circulation of draft reports, and publication in scientific journals are all part of the social process of constructing scientific knowledge.

In short, science is often less "cut and dried" than it seems to be from viewing its end product: scientific knowledge. What is known scientifically has undergone an intensive process of social construction, as a series of field studies of scientific laboratories has demonstrated (e.g., Knorr-Cetina, 1981; Latour and Woolgar, 1983).

TECHNOLOGY AND SOCIETY

Technology and Social Change

As with science, technology and society influence each other. Technological innovation affects social life; the automobile and the telephone are obvious illustrations. However, societal concerns also affect technological development.

PROBLEMS OF TECHNOLOGICAL ADVANCE

Technology deals with practical problems. Often, however, while solving or easing one problem, technology may generate new ones. For example, the automobile gave people more mobility and freedom. It made it easier to separate work from home. However, more Americans die from automobile accidents each year than were killed in the Vietnam War. The availability of the car led to the growth of the suburbs, causing the consequent financial problems faced by cities. The mobility and freedom provided by the automobile also reduced community constraints on people's behavior. Thus the invention of the car solved some problems and created others.

Technology can lead to social change through *automation*, the replacement of workers by machines. Machines do many of the routine operations on factory assembly lines; increasingly, automated bank teller machines are replacing human tellers. To employers, such automation makes economic sense. It generally costs less and leads to greater productivity. However, automation displaces quite a few trained workers, who often have to settle for new jobs that demand less skill and pay lower wages. Consequently, automation often results in an increase in those earning less than poverty-level incomes as well as in an increase in governmental expenditures for unemployment payments and social services for displaced workers who cannot find new employment.

Technology is not foolproof. Occasionally there are severe disasters caused by inadequate or faulty technology. The explosion aboard the space shuttle *Challenger* that killed all seven crew members is a case in point. More subtle negative consequences of technology may be seen in the environmental effects of the chlorofluorocarbons that are used in refrigerants and in many household products.

CONTROL OF TECHNOLOGY

Despite appearances, technology is not without social constraints. While technology influences social change, it does not determine it (see chapter 23). Social, political, economic, and even ethical factors play a role in creating the climate for technological development and in operating as a restraining force. The current computer revolution has raised fears about the creation of centralized personal files on all citizens. There is currently a web of legislation that restricts the linking of all the various sources of information about individuals into just such a centralized network.

Technology, like other social institutions, does not operate in a societal vacuum. The diversity of various social forces makes it virtually impossible for any institution to operate without some restraint.

Science, Technology, and Social Policy

The highly technical base of modern society gives science and technology an important role in the formulation and implementation of social policy. Defense and economic policies, for example, depend on scientific knowledge and technological tools. Even social policies, such as former President Johnson's so-called war on poverty, require social-scientific knowledge and technology to establish the necessary programs and then to assess their results.

RELIANCE ON TECHNICAL EXPERTS

As scientific and technological knowledge becomes both more complex and more applicable to societal life, society is forced to rely increasingly on technical experts. The new field of genetic engineering, derived from advances in molecular biology, has enormous implications for the future of human life. Some changes in humans that may have taken evolution millions of years to effect can potentially be accomplished almost immediately through genetic engineering. These new powers are largely in the hands of experts in the field of genetics. Similarly, issues of military disarmament are largely entrusted to military and scientific experts, who advise experts in the political sphere.

The complexity of modern science and technology has increased the influence on public policy of relevant experts. For example, when an Arkansas law mandating a "balanced treatment" of evolution and "creation science" (which argues the Biblical view that the world was created by God at one point in time) was challenged in the courts, biological scientists successfully argued that there is no scientific foundation for "creation science"; in effect, they argued that it is not really a science at all, but merely religion dressed up as science. Their perceived technical expertise was extremely influential in the court's decision.

CITIZEN'S ROLE IN SCIENCE POLICY

The increasing influence of experts on public policy, especially science policy, has diminished somewhat the role of the ordinary citizen. Recently, however, the public has become increasingly forceful in its insistence on participating in public policy decisions. Organizations representing the gay community, for example, forced a change in the procedures for testing new drugs in order to speed up delivery of those drugs with potential benefit to AIDS sufferers. Nonscientists are currently represented on review boards evaluating scientific research at universities and government-supported research facilities. And increasingly, hospitals have on their staffs "bioethicists" who help patients, families, and physicians analyze the impact of modern medical treatment on the quality of life; solely technical considerations are seen as insufficient bases for key "medical" decisions.

As American society has become more reliant on science and technology, there has been a groundswell of concern that general societal needs be not overlooked. The ethical issues involved in the use of medical technology to prolong life have been seized upon by citizens, legislatures, and the courts to broaden the bases of such decisions beyond the medical; to take into account human concerns like the quality of life. There has been a growing public debate about the level of funding for science and, equally important, about the priorities for such funding. This debate is taking place not only among scientists but also among the educated public at large.

One of the most important educational issues in modern society is how to produce a scientifically and technologically literate public that can play an important role in creating and carrying out public policy in an increasingly science- and technology-driven world. Since the Russians placed Sputnik in orbit in 1957, the United States has been trying to improve its teaching of science and mathematics. As has been pointed out (see chapter 14), it has been somewhat less successful in this endeavor than countries like Japan.

Science and technology play an important role in modern society. The growth of science can be traced to the early Greeks, Arabs, and Mayans, whose accomplishments were picked up and amplified during the European Renaissance of the sixteenth and seventeenth centuries. During this period, science had few specialized roles and was generally carried out by a few well-to-do individuals. In the nineteenth century, science became a more prominent part of the curricula of European, and especially German, universities, and this rapidly increased its growth.

Science has become an important social institution. It has an organized structure, specialized roles, and a set of norms. Basic science aimed at some theoretical problems can be distinguished from applied science, which uses "pure" or basic science for some identifiably practical purpose. Most research scientists are employed in industry, with universities constituting the next largest group of employers.

Functionalist theorists argue that science has been useful in helping people to understand and control the physical and social world; it provides a reliable base of knowledge with which to deal with societal concerns. It also facilitates social change that improves the quality of life. These theorists see the relationship between science and society as reciprocal. Conflict theorists point out that science is not a neutral tool for societal advance. It generally serves the interests of its funding sources, and those are likely to be the political and economic elite.

Science is a social process and has a set of norms. First, it is universal, committed to valuing scientific contributions solely on technical merits. Second, scientific knowledge is communal, considered public knowledge, available to all those who have an interest in it. Third, science is a disinter-

ested or an altruistic pursuit. Science is to be engaged in because of a desire to pursue valid knowledge and not for personal gain. Fourth, science is a form of organized skepticism. All scientific knowledge is subject to close examination and is not to be routinely accepted.

These norms do not eliminate deviant scientific behavior. Some scientists are interested in personal gain; others take into account the characteristics of the scientist in assessing scientific work. There are some scientists whose work is not open to public scrutiny. Outright fraud is not unknown in science. Kuhn describes scientific advances as building on past knowledge; this is what he called "normal science." However, sometimes the "paradigm" proves to be inadequate, and a new paradigm must be created. This paradigm shift, or scientific revolution, occurred in the change from Ptolemaic to Copernican astronomy, from Newtonian to Einsteinian physics, and from conceptions of human personality before and after Freud.

Science can also be viewed as a social construct. Scientists go about the difficult task of creating explanations of what they "see." Presentations at scientific meetings, informal circulation of draft reports, and publications in reputable professional journals are aimed at persuading colleagues of the validity of scientific research.

Technology and society influence each other. Social conditions direct attention to certain issues requiring technological solutions, and developing technology influences social activities. Sometimes technology developed to solve one problem creates another. For example, the invention of the automobile facilitated mobility and freedom, but it also weakened central cities and community control and increased the death rate from accidents. Automation is an example of how technological developments can be beneficial to one group (employers) and harmful to another (workers displaced by machines).

While technology influences social change, it does not determine it. There are social, political, economic, and ethical restraints on the development and use of technology, as is evident from the restrictions impeding the creation of a centralized computer data file on all citizens.

The heightened importance of science and technology has increased reliance on experts rather than on ordinary citizens in the formulation and implementation of public policy. Recently, however, there has been increasing concern that experts may not reflect the values and judgment of the general public. Consequently, educated nonexperts are increasingly playing an important role in creating and executing public policy (e.g., drug testing for AIDS vaccines, bioethicists in hospitals, and nonscientists on review boards for scientific research). Another approach to this problem has been to seek to improve the quality of scientific and technological education. Evidence discussed in chapter 14 suggests that the United States has been less successful in this than have countries like Japan.

20

Population

A society's population is a key defining element of its social structure and culture. This chapter will focus on the science of demography, which studies the growth, movement, decline, and composition of population. World population trends will be explored, along with various explanations of these trends and population policies. The focus will then turn to the population of the United States, its current and future trends.

POPULATION DYNAMICS

The Science of Demography

Populations are not static; they grow, decline, and move. They have a structure, and that also changes. *Demography* is the study of population trends. It involves more than calculating numbers of births, deaths, and movers. Demography raises questions about the consequences of population changes and how these affect the quality of human life. It must take into account social, cultural, and environmental factors that influence population changes, not all of which are precisely known. Demography is a complex and inexact science. Demographers seek to understand population changes through the use of a set of important conceptual tools.

Components of Population Change

FERTILITY

There are two related concepts that are necessary to understand population growth. *Fertility* refers to the actual number of children born to the average woman over her childbearing years (ages fifteen to forty-four); it determines long term population changes. *Fecundity* denotes the potential number of children that could be born to the average woman of childbearing age. Actual fertility rates tend to be lower than fecundity rates because of economic, health, and cultural considerations.

The *crude birth rate*, the number of live births in any given year for each 1,000 people in the population, determines short term population change. In 1987 the crude birth rate for the United States was 15.3 (U.S. Bureau of the Census, 1987b). This rate is "crude" because it is based on the total population, including men, women, and children. Thus comparisons of crude birth rates may be misleading if the compositions of the populations being considered are different. However, it is a useful index of a society's overall fertility. Birth rates can also be calculated for specific segments of the population; for example, they can be determined for different racial and ethnic groups.

MORTALITY

Populations also change because people die; that is, because of *mortality*.

The *crude death rate*, the number of deaths in any given year per 1,000 population, is an index of mortality. In 1986 the crude death rate for the United States was 8.7.

The *infant mortality rate*, the number of deaths within the first year of life for each 1,000 live births in a given year, is another index of mortality. In 1986 the infant mortality rate in the United States was 10.3; this is somewhat higher than might be expected in a country with such great wealth and is largely caused by the relatively high death rate of infants born in poverty (see chapter 18).

Life expectancy reflects how long, on average, a person born in a particular year is likely to live (see chapter 18). The life expectancy of boys born in the United States in 1985 was 71.2 years, and for girls it was 78.2 years; these reflect about a 60 percent increase in life expectancy in this century. In contrast, the human *life span* (the maximum length of life possible) has hardly changed at all over the same period. Very few people live beyond the age of 100 because of the degenerative diseases of old age.

MIGRATION

Populations change not only because people are born and die but also because they move around. *Migration* refers to the movement of people from one geographical location to another so as to establish a new residence. Such movement takes place both within (*internal migration*) and between (*international migration*) societies. The *migration rate* of a society is the annual difference between the number of people entering the society (*immigrants*) and the number of people leaving (*emigrants*).

People migrate voluntarily for two basic reasons, often termed "push-pull" factors. In one case, the new location exerts a *pull* that induces them to come. The promise of religious freedom or economic advantages are examples of pull factors that lead to migration. People also migrate because of the *push* exerted by the area they are leaving. Where they are is not hospitable, so they leave. Famine, war, and plague are examples of push factors. Often, migration involves both push and pull factors.

Population Growth

NATURAL GROWTH RATE

Populations grow because of high fertility, low mortality, and high immigration, though the first two factors are often more important than the last. In measuring population growth, then, demographers examine the *natural growth rate*, which is the crude death rate in a particular year subtracted from the crude birth rate in the same year.

In 1986 a crude death rate of 8.7 subtracted from a crude birth rate of 15.3 led to a natural growth rate in the United States of 6.6 percent. In contrast, the average natural growth rate in the world at that time was more than double the figure for the United States The growth rates in industrialized countries are typically under 1 percent, while they are often over 2 percent in the less developed countries (LDCs). The LDCs often lack the resources necessary to provide an adequate standard of living for their populations; the high growth rate compounds the problem.

DOUBLING TIME

Though a growth rate of even 2 percent seems small, its cumulative effect is substantial. If a society maintains a 2 percent growth rate for thirty-five years, it will *double* in size. This *doubling time,* the number of years it takes a population to double itself can put a staggering burden on societal resources. (To discover the doubling time of any population, simply divide seventy, the number of years it takes a population with a 1 percent growth rate to double itself, by the growth rate of that population.)

ZERO POPULATION GROWTH

Population dynamics that results in a stable size is called *zero population growth* (ZPG). Global ZPG requires an average fertility rate of 2.1 per woman; this figure provides for the parents reproducing only themselves, while also taking into account those parents who die too young to do so or, for whatever reason, do not have two children. The United States actually had a growth rate just below ZPG (2.02) in 1979, but the population still grew. It did so because immigration exceeded emigration (see below) and because ZPG has to be maintained consistently for at least twenty-five years to result in a stable population.

Population Composition

Sociologists and demographers are interested not only in changes in population but also in its structure. Among the most important structural elements of a population are sex and age.

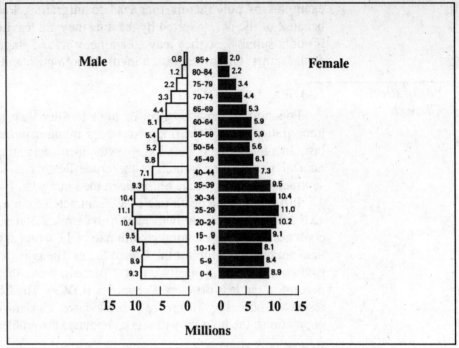

Fig. 20.1 Age-Sex Population Pyramid for the U.S., 1986

SEX COMPOSITION

The sex composition of a society is determined by its *sex ratio*, the number of males per 100 females. As was pointed out earlier (see chapter 12), there are more males conceived than females (a sex ratio of 140 at conception in the United States). However, from that point on, more males die than females at every age interval. The sex ratio at birth is 105. By about age twenty-one, there are more females than males, leading to an average sex ratio of 95 for the United States over all ages.

AGE COMPOSITION

The *age structure* of a society, the relative proportions of people in the different age categories in the total population, is extremely important to demographers. The larger the proportion of young people, the greater the population growth is likely to be. Also, the youngest and oldest age categories are the least economically productive. Therefore, the economy of a society that has most of its members in these categories will be quite different from that of another that has the bulk of its population in the middle categories.

POPULATION PYRAMIDS

Demographers often use a population pyramid showing both age and sex categories, to illustrate the shape of the population (see figure 20.1). The age categories are arranged along the rising vertical axis; the percent of the

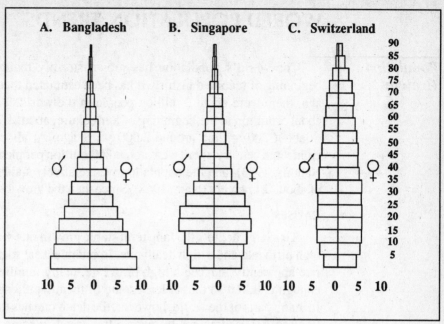

Fig. 20.2 Population pyramids

population that belongs in each of these are given along the bottom horizontal axis. The resulting "pyramid" is split so that one side shows relevant figures for males and the other side shows those for females. The value of such population pyramids is that they permit a clear visual comparison of the age composition of different societies (figure 20.2) or of the same society at different points in time (figure 20.3).

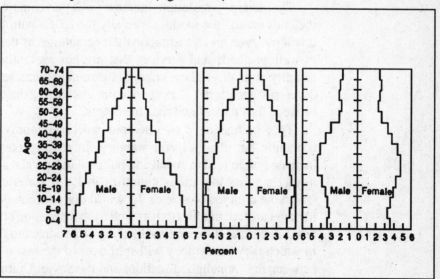

Fig. 20.3 Population pyramids, U.S.

WORLD POPULATION TRENDS

*Population
Growth*

The world's population has grown steadily though slowly from the beginning of recorded history. It has been estimated that about 40,000 years ago, there were about 3 million people in the world. That number grew to about 5 million at the beginning of agriculture, about 10,000 years ago, and to about 200 million around 2,000 years ago. At about the middle of the eighteenth century, there were about 800 million people in the world (United Nations, 1973), and the population was relatively stable with a growth rate of about 0.1 percent (Nam, 1968). Since then the growth rate has speeded up.

CAUSES

To a large degree, the long term stable growth rate was due to a relatively high birth rate and a high death rate. In preindustrial societies the high death rate apparently induced a high birth rate; many families hoped to produce enough children so that at least some of them would survive to adulthood. In many parts of the world, however, the death rate has dropped dramatically (though AIDS threatens to reverse this trend in some areas, especially in parts of Africa), and this has led to a sharp increase in population. The present world population stands at a little over 5 billion people. It has been estimated that at the present annual growth rate of 1.7 percent, the world population will double to over 10 billion by the year 2031 and reach more than 30 billion by the year 2100.

CONSEQUENCES

This sharp population increase will have major consequences for societies around the world, especially the LDCs with their high birth rates. It will put even greater stress on their economies as they try to provide jobs as well as goods and services that are not presently sufficient in either quantity or quality. These changes threaten to increase the gap between the developed and the developing societies, increasing the economic differences between the "haves" and the "have-nots."

This increasingly two-layered world economy threatens not only economic but also political stability. Increasing poverty and population increases often lead to social and political upheavals, as has been witnessed in recent years in various countries in Latin America, Africa, and Asia. Given the diminished size of the world due to technological developments in travel and communication as well as to increasing economic and political ties, these instabilities are not likely to be localized to the particular country in which they occur; they will spill over to the rest of the world. The link between the "nonaligned" nations and the Soviet Union during the cold war era and the attempt to establish a new world economic order of relationships between the poor and the rich nations demonstrate this interrelationship.

Another consequence of rapid population increase, particularly in LDCs, is the sharp increase in migration. Images of large numbers of "boat people" from Southeast Asia migrating to the United States and other Western countries for economic as well as political reasons are still vivid—and such migration continues. The continual flow of legal and illegal immigrants from Latin America has been a constant source of concern to the United States, as has the number of Asian and African immigrants to many Western European countries. In most cases these immigrants come from societies with high population growth; they leave because the economies of their home countries often cannot support their rapidly increasing population at an adequate standard of living.

Theories About Population Growth

THE MALTHUSIAN THEORY

The major theory of population growth and its consequences was put forth by the English clergyman and economist Thomas Malthus (1926; original, 1798) at the end of the eighteenth century. He argued that the natural passions of men and women would lead to a "geometrically" increasing birth rate, by which he meant that the rate would increase very rapidly (as in multiplication); at the same time, food production would increase only "arithmetically" (as in addition) because of the technological limitations on agricultural production and the limits of available arable (usable) land. Thus, population would shortly outstrip the available food to support it.

Malthus believed that *checks on population* are required, or misery, hunger, and poverty will be the inevitable consequences. He stated that there are only two ways to check this disastrous population explosion: through *positive checks* and *preventive checks*. The former are "natural" ways of preventing excessive numbers of people in the world, such as famine, disease, and war. Malthus personally favored preventive checks on population increase: the use of "moral restraint." He advocated sexual abstinence, birth control (though his religious beliefs did not allow him to support "artificial means"), and delayed marriage.

Since he believed that most people would not engage in such moral restraint except in the face of extreme famine, he was pessimistic about the world's ability to check the excessive and harmful increase in population. Such pessimism earned Malthus the nickname "dismal parson." He also argued for the elimination of relief for the poor (what today we call welfare) so as to reduce their numbers, since they had a much higher birth rate than the wealthy.

Malthus underestimated several developments that later undermined his basic argument. First, new birth control techniques came into use, along with a greater cultural emphasis on smaller families; these reduced the rate of population growth. Also, technological improvements in agriculture and irrigation vastly increased the food supply and promise even further advances. Thus the substantial reduction that is possible in the rate of population growth and the sharp increase that is possible in the amount of available food are considered major rebuffs to the Malthusian position.

However, some of Malthus's ideas are still relevant. We have pointed out the sharp increase in population among LDCs that threatens available resources. As an added danger, it is conceivable that there is a finite limit to the technological developments necessary to increase both the available arable land and food supplies. Thus the concern over population growth—especially in countries that can least support it—remains alive for two main reasons: (1) population growth leads to the paving over of arable land and (2) the required resources strain the *ecosystem* —a system created by the interaction of a community of organisms with its environment.

THE MARXIAN RESPONSE

Karl Marx took issue with Malthus from a different angle. He believed that excess population was less a matter of a restricted food supply than of limited economic opportunities, especially for the working class. Marx contended that Malthus was living in the midst of the Industrial Revolution and witnessing the problems of capitalist forms of organization rather than the laws of "human nature." "Excess" population meant that there were more workers than were required by the capitalist system at the time, not that there were too many people in the world. A more efficient economic system would be able to make better use of the available population. In the collectivist economy he envisioned (see chapter 17), Marx argued that population growth would be seen as a social advantage leading to greater economic production and improved well-being.

Marx and Malthus differed in another way in their orientation to the type of solution required. Malthus focused on the individual's ability to exercise moral restraint. Marx, on the other hand, emphasized the importance of collective action to effect change in the basic social and economic structure of society.

The Malthus-Marx debate continues today. Ehrlich (1968) has advanced a modified version of the Malthusian argument about the devastating consequences of unchecked population growth. This view received support from the influential report of the Club of Rome (Meadows, et al., 1972), *The Limits to Growth*. The contemporary argument that "small is beautiful" reflects this position. Simon (1986) rejects the notion of finite, nonrenewable resources. He argues that the earth has ample space and resources to support a vastly increased population; the difficulties are political, not biological.

A more intermediate position has emerged in an analysis by the National Research Council (Holden, 1986). In this view, the earth's resources will probably be able to support a vastly increased population. In fact, some scarcity is useful to motivate the development of appropriate technology and economic strategies to deal with the problem. However, beyond a certain level of population increase, that situation may change.

The Demographic Transition in Industrial Society

The reduction in the rate of population increase that occurred in Europe is seen as largely attributable to the consequences of industrialization. This phenomenon is called a *demographic transition* and denotes a change in the birth and death rates, which affects population growth. In this theory, the change occurs in three stages.

1. *Stable population with high potential growth.* In early societies there was a high birth rate *and* a high death rate. Because of the high death rate, people wanted to have many children to ensure that at least some of them would live to adulthood. Typically, the number of births roughly equaled the number of deaths so that the population was stable or increased only modestly. However, this foreshadowed potential population growth once a society was able to reduce its death rate.

2. *Transitional growth.* As societies shift to industrial modes of economic production and distribution, standards of living, sanitary conditions, nutrition, and medical care improve. These changes substantially reduce the death rate while the birth rate remains high. Consequently, these societies experience substantial and rapid population growth. It was in this period of British history that Malthus lived; his experiences under these conditions led him to the view he subsequently developed. He was not, however, able to envision the next stage.

3. *Population stability with low growth.* Changes in technology and cultural norms lead to a reduction in the birth rate. Contraception improves, and cultural norms support smaller families. The increase in economic standards makes it more expensive to raise large families, and having many children is seen more as a liability than as the asset it was in previous times as "old age insurance" for parents. Once more the population becomes relatively stable; however, the low birth and death rates lead to relative stability with slow population growth, in contrast to the situation in preindustrial times.

The Contemporary Relevance of the Demographic Transition Theory

Many social scientists have questioned whether the demographic transition is an appropriate model for all societies undergoing industrialization. The developing countries have generally reduced their death rates while maintaining high birth rates, the transitional growth stage of the demographic transition. However, it is not clear that the conditions in Europe and the United States during the eighteenth and nineteenth centuries that led those societies to the third stage exist today in societies currently undergoing modernization. The population pyramids of these societies are different, with a much higher proportion of children, resulting in a different pattern of economic production and distribution. Further, capital accumulation in these countries is less likely to be used for economic expansion and improvement in material conditions than it is for simply accommodating the most fundamental needs of their continually and rapidly increasing populations. In some parts of the world it is not even clear that the second stage of reduced death rates has occurred.

In short, many have questioned the automatic operation of the demographic transition as the answer to the problems in these societies. Further, there are substantial differences within the LDCs that need to be taken into account. The exploitation of these countries that is explicit in Wallerstein's world systems model (see chapters 17 and 23) suggests that contemporary economic forces are different from those that led to industrialization and the demographic transition in Europe and the United States. Consequently, whether such a process is automatic and only a matter of time is neither clear nor accepted by all students in this field.

Population Policies

FERTILITY REDUCTION

Clearly, one major strategy to deal with a rapidly increasing population is to directly reduce its rate of growth. "Family planning" programs are a major part of any such policy. These programs range from providing information on human reproduction and human sexuality to distributing contraceptives to the people. These programs often run up against ingrained beliefs that children are an insurance policy for old age and there should be no effort to reduce their number. Also, religious beliefs about contraception and ignorance about the actual process of human reproduction often need to be overcome. The systematic and organized personal behavior that effective contraception requires is not common in many LDCs, posing formidable problems for family planning programs.

Some societies go beyond educational family planning programs. They engage in various forms of coercion. In India, for example, the government in the 1970s initiated a program of forced sterilization. And in recent years, China has instituted a vast program of population control by punishing those families that have more than one child. Families that have more than one child are subject to social ridicule. The parents are fined, and they may lose their jobs and certain social benefits. Women pregnant with subsequent children are pressured to have abortions.

ECONOMIC DEVELOPMENT

Deliberate strategies to improve economic conditions are often part of an overall attempt to reduce population growth. Economic improvement betters the chances of lowering death rates and hence invalidates the requirement for high birth rates to maintain the family. Also, there is ample evidence that economic growth leads to social approval of smaller families.Children are less of an economic asset in industrial societies than they are in agricultural ones. Thus economic development is not only beneficial for the economy but is also seen as having a positive effect on population growth.

FOOD PRODUCTION AND DISTRIBUTION

The *green revolution*, the development and use of new agricultural practices, has led to substantially increased food production. It is seen as one answer to the Malthusian problem because it allows a society to focus on providing the necessary food for an increasing population rather than on reducing its growth. New high-yield grains that have resulted from this approach have reduced to some degree the nutritional difficulties in certain areas of the world.

Policies to improve the distribution as well as the production of food is another important strategy in dealing with population growth. The United States is one of the most efficient agricultural producers in the world. In recent years it has developed a variety of programs to distribute its agricultural products to needy societies. Much of this activity is carried out through private companies whose need for profit means that these goods are often sold rather than given to other societies. Many countries that sorely need such goods may not be in a position to pay for them. While there are some programs to distribute necessary food at reduced or no cost, the world faces a moral dilemma about whose responsibility it is to feed the hungry of poorer societies. Also, even when food is provided to some countries (e.g., Ethiopia), political turmoil may prevent it from being distributed to those who most need it. Discussions on these issues continue in the recent debate about a "new economic world order."

PRONATALIST POLICIES

Some societies are worried more about having too few people than too many. Several European countries (e.g., Denmark, Switzerland, and Italy) have experienced a birth rate below replacement levels (less than ZPG). In some of these societies, the government has sought to encourage more births (a *pronatalist* policy) by providing financial subsidies for each additional child. Others (e.g., the Soviet Union) have given public recognition to those women who have had a number of children and provide paid maternity leave with a guaranteed return to the same job each time a woman gives birth.

Pronatalist policies are often about power and control. Both within and between societies, strength is assumed to be based on large populations. Thus populations of societies that wish to increase their power adopt pronatalist attitudes and strategies (Wattenberg, 1987).

POPULATION TRENDS IN THE UNITED STATES

Current Population Trends

FERTILITY AND GROWTH

The population in the United States has been steadily increasing, currently exceeding 250 million people. Despite this growth, the birth rate is low and has been declining since the middle of the nineteenth century when it stood at about 55 per 1,000 population. The birth rate reached its lowest level, 17 per 1,000, during the Great Depression of the 1930s. The next major change came after World War II; the "baby boom," which resulted from delayed marriages, began in about 1946 and lasted until the early 1960s. This led to a birth rate that rose to about 25 per 1,000 before declining to another low of 15 per 1,000 in 1970. Though the birth rate has stabilized since then at a little under 16 per 1,000, the birth rate of the children of the "baby boomers" (the "baby boom echo") will likely lead to higher birth rates than of their parents.

MORTALITY

Mortality rates are favorable for most Americans. The death rate is quite low, about 9 per 1,000. At the same time the life expectancy of most Americans is extremely high at about 75 years, though this varies by social characteristics, especially sex and race. For women, average life expectancy is 78.5 for whites and 73 for African Americans; for men, it is 71.1 for whites and a much lower 64.4 for African Americans.

The United States has recently experienced a graying of its population (see chapter 12). The median age is about thirty-one, somewhat higher than that of many other countries and even than earlier U.S. populations. This graying is due in part to the reduction in death rates and to declining fertility; these have increased the number of elderly as a proportion of the population.

IMMIGRATION

The United States has been called a country of immigrants. The country was initially transformed by European immigrants and later became a haven for those from all over the world who sought political and economic betterment. Immigration was quite high until the enactment of restrictive immigration laws in the early and middle 1920s. Immigration picked up after World War II, essentially doubling in the past quarter of a century. In 1986 a little over 600,000 legal immigrants entered the United States. It has been estimated that many more illegal immigrants have entered. Currently most immigrants come from Latin America and Asia.

Sources of the Declining Birth Rate

ECONOMIC FACTORS

Though people often point to the economic consequences of the Great Depression to explain the historically low birth rate in the United States, the birth rate had already been declining and continued to decline after economic recovery. Objective economic conditions themselves are unable to account fully for birth rates.

Another way of looking at the effects of the economy on fertility is to understand the importance of *expectations*. It is not so much the actual economic conditions that are important but rather the expectations and standards that couples set for their lives. For example, according to this view the "birth dearth" of the post baby boom was caused by the high standard of living of the 1960s and 1970s that led couples to reduce the number of children they had in order to maintain that standard. Thus economic conditions and the expectations they create influence fertility rates.

LIFESTYLES AND VALUES

Expectations are related to the kind of lifestyle people wish to have. In addition to these economic influences on lifestyle, social factors play an equally important role. The women's movement of the past thirty years has had an enormous impact on women's roles in society (see chapter 12). The opening up of greater economic and educational opportunities to women has changed people's ideas about family and parenthood. One consequence of this is that couples are reducing and more carefully scheduling conception so as to provide for the economic and educational needs of women.

As a direct result of urbanization and industrialization, the value of large families declines as children are no longer the same economic asset they were in an agrarian society with a high death rate. Smaller families allow greater freedom for the two adults and cause less strain on family resources. In addition, the opportunity to spend more time with fewer children is seen as an appropriate social value.

BIRTH CONTROL

Technological developments in contraception played a major role in reducing fertility. It provided the technical means to accommodate the new ideas about family size that resulted from new values and lifestyles. The birth control pill and the intrauterine device (IUD) became widely available and affordable. The number of married women who use some form of contraception has about doubled in recent years, leading both to fewer children and to more careful spacing.

Abortion, which became legal in 1973, also contributes to a declining birth rate (see chapter 13). Despite the attention that pro- and anti-abortion forces give to its use by the unmarried, substantial numbers of married women as well use abortion to help regulate fertility.

Future Trends

It appears that the American population will continue to age. Death rates as well as birth rates continue to be low and life expectancy high. This combination of factors will probably cause senior citizens to become an increasing proportion of the population. There will be a large "bulge" in the middle years for a while as the "baby boomers" age; the base of the population pyramid, the young, will continue to shrink. Thus the population pyramid of the United States will diverge further and further from the actual pyramidic shape it had at the beginning of this century. Internal migration from the Frostbelt of the Northeast to the Sunbelt of the South and Southwest will probably continue, following economic activity. Internal migratory shifts will also change the political and economic power of the different regions.

Demographic analysis of population trends reveals much about the nature of a society. Its fertility is indexed by its crude birth rate, and the mortality of any society is described by its crude death rate. The infant mortality rate is a useful measure of the quality of life in society. Mortality can also be viewed in terms of the life expectancy in society, which has generally been increasing (substantially in industrial societies). Life span, another index of mortality, has remained relatively stable over the past century. Societies also change because of internal and international migration. In general, people migrate because the new area has certain advantages (a "pull" factor) and/or because the old area becomes unbearable (a "push" factor).

Every society has a natural growth rate, which is determined by subtracting its crude death rate from its crude birth rate. Even small population growth rates have large cumulative effects. At a growth rate of 1 percent, a population will double in size in seventy years; at a 2 percent growth rate, a population will double in thirty-five years. Zero population growth (ZPG), which amounts to an average of 2.1 children per woman, leads to a stable population if it is maintained for at least 25 years. The United States reached a level just below ZPG (2.02) in 1979.

The composition of a population is also important. The sex ratio, the number of males per 1,000 females, changes from a higher proportion of males at conception to a higher proportion of females by age twenty-one and thereafter. Population pyramids are used to portray graphically the composition (age and sex structure) of a society's population and make it easier to compare it with the composition of other societies or with its own composition at different points in time.

The world's population grew steadily though slowly until the eighteenth century because of a high birth rate coupled with a high death rate. Industrialization reduced the death rate, while the birth rate initially continued at a high level, leading to a sharp increase in population. The present high growth rate is concentrated in the less developed countries (LDCs). This puts great strain on their economic resources and threatens to increase the gulf between them and the more highly developed industrial societies with consequent economic and political instability and increased emigration to the more developed countries.

In the eighteenth century, Thomas Malthus argued that the natural passions of humans would lead to a geometrically increasing birth rate and that the technological and space limitations would limit the growth of agricultural production and cause the population to outstrip its necessary food base. Malthus favored "moral restraint" in the form of sexual abstinence and late marriages (preventive checks) but was pessimistic about people's capacity to exercise these restraints. He believed that only war, disease, and famine (positive checks) would be able to control excessive population growth. Malthus underestimated the social and cultural changes that, along with technological developments in contraception, would reduce population growth. He also failed to anticipate the dramatic technological innovations taking place in agriculture (the green revolution) that would sharply increase the available food supply.

Marx took issue with Malthus's view that there was a restricted food supply. He argued that the insufficient economic base of Malthus's era was more a reflection of limited economic opportunities caused by capitalistic forms of organization. A collectivist economy would solve that problem, Marx believed. The Marx-Malthus debate continues today with discussions about the limits of growth and the notion that "small is beautiful."

The changing rate of population growth in industrial societies is explained by reference to a three-stage demographic transition. In the first stage, the population was relatively stable because of simultaneously high birth and death rates. In the second, populations grew dramatically because of a continued high birth rate and a sharply reduced death rate resulting from improved nutrition, sanitation, medical care, and standards of living. The final stage ("population stability with low growth") was achieved when technology and changing social norms resulted in lowering the birth rate, producing a relatively stable population with slow growth.

Though the demographic transition theory has been proposed as an appropriate model for contemporary LDCs, it has been argued that the population composition and economic conditions of LDCs differ substantially from those of eighteenth and nineteenth century Europe. In short, it is not clear that the LDCs can or need to follow the same model of economic development and population dynamics.

Direct control of population growth through governmental policies is common. Four different strategies have been used. Many LDCs have adopted some form of fertility reduction policies, ranging from educational campaigns and distribution of contraceptive devices to coercive forms of control. Economic development has been increased both to provide for the growing population and to induce the social and cultural changes that are associated with lower fertility rates. Insufficient food supply has been attacked directly by increasing production and improving distribution (the green revolution). Finally, some industrial societies have become concerned about low growth and have developed pronatalist policies, one of which is to provide monetary and social rewards for higher fertility.

The United States has a low growth rate because of its low birth and death rates, which are characteristic of advanced industrial societies. The baby boom of the post World War II period was a minor exception. Life expectancy is high, though higher for women and whites than for men and African Americans. The elderly constitute an increasingly larger fraction of the population because of the reduction in death rates and the low birth rate. Initially high immigration slowed after restrictive legislation in the 1920s and picked up again during the past twenty-five years. The long term decline in the birth rate is due to economic conditions and the higher expectations they exert on standards of living. Also, changes in lifestyles and values caused by the women's movement, among other factors, have led to lower fertility rates. The substantial improvement in contraceptive technology and the legalization of abortion provides technical means to reduce the number of births. The future seems to hold a continuation of these trends: low fertility and a graying of the American population.

21

Urbanization

Urbanization is the hallmark of modern societies. This chapter will trace the growth of cities from preindustrial times to the present. It will also examine the three major theories that have been put forth to explain urban growth. Contemporary urban life in the United States will be explored through a comparison of urban and rural life. The problems of urban America, including crime, drugs, and financial difficulties, will be discussed, along with recent attempts at rational city planning and development.

URBAN GROWTH

Human beings emerged between 5 and 15 million years ago, with the current form (*homo sapiens*) developing some 50,000 to 60,000 years ago. On that scale of time, *urbanization*, the concentration of populations in a limited area called a city, is a remarkably recent phenomenon; cities began to appear about 6,000 years ago. This gap between human and urban development resulted from societies' need to achieve a certain level of social and technological development before they are able to create and maintain cities (Reissman, 1964).

Cities are permanent concentrations of a relatively large number of people who do not grow their own food. They emerged in the Middle East, in the "fertile crescent" between the Tigris and Euphrates rivers in Iraq, as a consequence of climatic changes and technological developments. As glaciers melted, the water flow in certain areas increased the amount of warmer and more fertile soil. In addition, techniques were developed to raise crops and animals. Horticultural and pastoral societies emerged, which required more permanent settlements than did the earlier hunting and gathering societies (see chapter 4). At some point these societies also produced the surpluses needed to support growth and role specialization (see chapter 4).

The Preindustrial City

ANCIENT CITIES

About 4,000 B.C. cities developed along the Indus River in what is now Pakistan and in several locations in China. About 1,000 years later cities evolved in Central and South America and recent research indicates that there was significant urban growth in North America.

These early cities were quite small by today's standards. The earliest cities contained fewer than 10,000 people (Gist and Fava, 1974). Cities grew during the classical period; Athens had 150,000 people during its Golden Age and Rome had just under a million. With the fall of the Roman Empire in the fifth century A.D., cities declined in Europe for several centuries. However, one of the results of the Crusades was the opening of trade with the Middle East, which revived urban life in southern Europe, particularly Florence and Venice. The pace of urbanization increased, and by the fourteenth century many parts of Europe as well as the Middle East and Asia had begun to urbanize.

The cities of this time remained relatively small because transportation was limited and slow. Also, frequent conflicts between cities and the surrounding rural areas threatened the stability of the urban food supply. Medical and sanitary conditions were primitive and could not sustain large, dispersed populations.

MEDIEVAL CITIES

The typical medieval city was enclosed by a wall for protection from invaders but had little separation between different districts within the city. Streets were narrow, winding, and filthy. They were frequented by people from all walks of life, from peddlers, merchants, and artisans to priests, nobles, and servants. There was considerable social heterogeneity (variation), with clear stratification patterns among the different occupations. The Christian church dominated these cities. Women and minorities had few rights, and the latter were often restricted to certain areas of the city called ghettos.

The pace of life in the medieval city was faster than in rural areas but considerably slower than in today's cities. The relatively compact nature of cities led to considerable social interaction. Most people had some knowledge of, if not direct acquaintance with, one another. Social control was more personal than in the modern city.

The Industrial City

THE EUROPEAN CITY

The Industrial Revolution of the eighteenth century quickened the rate of urbanization. New sources of power enabled the development of factories, which resulted in increased production. To fill factory jobs it was necessary to bring together people from diverse locations. These factories were located in the urban centers, which already had a good-sized labor pool to draw from. The success of this new economic form drew people from rural areas to the city. As a result, between 1700 and 1800 most European cities grew substantially; some, like Vienna, more than doubled in size. Between 1800 and 1900 the cities again grew rapidly. The smallest growth was registered by Lisbon with more than a 50 percent increase in population; London grew the most, to almost eight times its earlier size (Chandler and Fox, 1974).

Many of the early urban settlements became "city-states" like Athens and Rome. (Later, many of them served as the nucleus for the creation of nations.) Urban centers became the focus of economic and political life. The earlier chaotic pattern of narrow, winding streets was replaced by wider and straighter streets to facilitate transportation and commerce.

Social life became more complex. Because of the large concentrations of people, individuals had less direct knowledge of each other. City life became more impersonal and more crime-ridden. Some cities attracted more people than they could support. The early stages of industrialization also caused substantial environmental pollution in cities. In short, urban growth in industrial Europe was a mixed blessing.

The cities are still growing today, though at a much slower rate than during the nineteenth century. However, the number of urban areas has risen dramatically. At the beginning of the nineteenth century there were fewer than 50 cities in the world that had a population of more than 100,000. Today over 2,000 do.

THE AMERICAN CITY

The earliest settlements by Europeans in the United States were established by the Spanish in 1565 in St. Augustine, Florida, and by the English in 1607 in Jamestown, Virginia. The first major urban area was established by the Dutch in New Amsterdam (New York) in 1624; this was soon followed by Boston, which was settled by the English Puritans in 1630.

Essentially, these settlements were small villages whose design was patterned on that of European cities prior to industrialization. (The resulting helter-skelter arrangement of streets still exists today in lower Manhattan and parts of central Boston.) Most urban expansion took place during the nineteenth century, paralleling developments in Europe. The building of railroads provided necessary transportation, which opened up both the West to expansion and the East to urban growth.

By the middle of the nineteenth century, about one-third of all Americans lived in urban areas. The city played an increasingly important role in economic, political, and social life. Differences between the urban and rural areas became more pronounced, particularly in lifestyles. Differences also widened between a largely rural South and an increasingly urban North.

The Metropolis

A number of large cities grew even larger and became more central to the society. They became *metropolises*, urban areas that contain a large central city with its surrounding suburbs and related satellite cities. Examples are New York City, Chicago, London, Paris, Mexico City, and Tokyo. Metropolises form relatively integrated economic and geographical units. Major growth of metropolitan regions took place from about the middle of the nineteenth century to the middle of the twentieth century. For example, in 1860 New York City had under a million residents; by 1900 it had about 4 million, and in 1950 the population had increased to almost 8 million. Since then, the growth of metropolises has been slower (some have even experienced a slight population decline) because of the growth of the suburbs (see below).

Metropolitan growth was made possible by technological developments, especially increased use of electric power, improved communication, and modern modes of transportation. Electricity made possible the construction of the large skyscrapers that are the hallmark of the metropolis. The widespread availability of telephones, cars, and mass transportation permitted the city to spread and still maintain easy connection between its central areas and outlying sections.

METROPOLITAN STATISTICAL AREAS

The importance of the social, economic, and communication links between a central city and its surrounding communities led the U.S. Bureau of the Census to develop the concept of the *Metropolitan Statistical Area* (MSA) for analytic purposes. An MSA is an urban area that contains a city with at least 50,000 residents and has a total population of at least 100,000. At present there are almost 300 MSAs in the United States; they contain about three-quarters of the population. The federal government's Office of Management and Budget also defines a *Consolidated Metropolitan Statistical Area* (CMSA), an urban area that has at least a million population and meets several other criteria.

The economy of a metropolis depends on close ties among its residential, industrial, commercial, and recreational areas. Good transportation facilities are necessary to move workers from their residences to their places of employment and to move goods from where they are made to where they are needed. Recreational and educational facilities are required to attract and hold the work force. Commercial and industrial firms that depend on one another for goods or services are often located within metropolitan regions for convenience and efficiency.

MEGALOPOLIS

Metropolises have spread to such an extent that some flow directly into other metropolises. The corridor in the northeastern United States from Boston to Washington, D.C., is just such a *megalopolis*. The importance of these megalopolises to each other is evident from the transportation system that has grown up between them. The train and airline shuttles that connect Boston and New York City and New York City and Washington, D.C. are testimony to the economic relationship between these metropolitan regions.

The Suburbs

One of the most dramatic events of the mid-twentieth century was the growth of the *suburbs*, which are relatively small urban areas that surround a city. The increased number of commuter railroads and automobiles, aided by massive federally funded highway construction, made suburban growth possible.

The development of the suburbs created the commuter, the person who could live in one location and work a considerable distance away. Thus suburban communities began to surround central cities. People began to move from the cities to the suburbs, where they were often able to afford their own homes and where they hoped to escape the problems of urban life. The number of suburbanites in the United States doubled between 1940 to 1980; suburbs now accommodate about 40 percent of the population.

Suburban growth contributed to urban decentralization. Large firms began to locate branch offices in the suburbs, and small businesses sprang up to handle the needs of the suburban population. The oil crises of the 1970s had a much greater effect on the suburbs than on the cities because of their considerable dependence on automobiles for basic transportation. Today, an increasing number of companies are locating their headquarters, not just their branch offices, in the suburbs because of tax advantages, lower costs, and more hospitable social and educational environments. The suburban shopping mall is a recognized feature of the American landscape. Medium- and even some highrise buildings have begun to find their way into suburban communities. Increasingly, the line between the city and the suburbs is becoming blurred.

THEORIES OF URBAN GROWTH

The explanations of urban growth grow out of an ecological approach, which is concerned with the interplay between people and their physical environment. This view predominated at the University of Chicago during the 1920s and 1930s and led to a series of studies and to a theory of how urban areas develop. Subsequent analyses resulted in other explanations of urban growth.

The Concentric Zone Model

The earliest view of city growth was put forth by a group of University of Chicago sociologists: Burgess, Park, and colleagues (Park, et al., 1925). In studies of Chicago they noted that it consisted of a series of concentric circles, with a different land-use pattern for each ring. At the center is the *central business district*, which contains financial firms, theaters, good restaurants, retail and department stores, and other businesses that cater to the shopper. This is encircled by a *zone of transition* that had originally been a residential area for the wealthy but later evolved to a mixed land-use pattern of marginal businesses and slums. The next areas are *residential zones*, with working class homes closest in and the more affluent residences radiating out in circular fashion from the center.

This theory was based on a dynamic conception of urban growth. Land-use patterns of the inner areas would "invade" the adjacent zones and transform them. This model seemed to adequately portray the development of Chicago but was less effective as a general model of urban growth. The physical terrain of the city, the amount of governmental planning, the widespread availability of the automobile and mass transportation all influence urban growth, and these vary for different cities.

The Sector Model

Analysis of urban growth in a larger number of cities led Hoyt (1939), an urban ecologist, to see a different pattern. He believed that cities grow in wedge-shaped sectors from the center of the city out, often along some transportation route (for example, railroad lines or waterways). The land in each sector is used for different purposes; there is a residential sector, an industrial sector, a central business sector, and a suburban sector. Hoyt, however, understood that the particular topography—rivers and hills, for example—would shape each city's development in unique ways.

The wedge or pie shape of a sector means that different land-use patterns exist side by side. Some parts of the residential sector are adjacent to the industrial sector; these would likely be working class neighborhoods. On the other hand, the most desirable residential neighborhoods need not be far away from the central business district, as is evident in the case of Nob Hill in San Francisco.

**The
Multiple-Nuclei
Model**

Later technological developments that made automobiles more widely available and improved communication also influenced urban growth patterns. Harris and Ullman (1945) point out that cities have several "nuclei," or separate centers devoted to specific activities. For example, many cities have a centralized entertainment district, such as the Times Square theater and restaurant area in New York City.

There are several factors that influence the development of these specialized nuclei. First, certain activities need specialized facilities. Entertainment and shopping areas, for example, need to be easily accessible using the available public transportation. Second, some enterprises often benefit from being close to certain other ones. The clustering of financial companies around the Wall Street area in New York City is no accident. Their proximity to one another eases communication among them; this was especially the case when they initially congregated in that area. Third, certain districts do not adjoin one another because their activities are inherently uncongenial. For example, industrial sectors are not next to high rent residential districts.

**Comment on
the Different
Theories**

It is clear that the models described above are more descriptions than analytic theories. Each describes a particular pattern of urban growth that was a consequence of technological and ecological factors at a particular time and in a specific location.

SOCIAL AREA ANALYSIS

Some ecologists use *social area analysis* to examine urban residential patterns (Shevky and Bell, 1955). This approach seeks to find the common characteristics of people living in the same residential area. In general, it appears that three factors influence people's choice of neighborhoods. The first is *family status*: married or not married, and the size of family if married. The second is *social standing* as indicated by income and social prestige. The third is *race and ethnicity*.

AN INTEGRATED APPROACH

Each of the above models describes urban growth in particular locations. Berry and Rees (1969), two social ecologists, have provided an integrated explanation. They argue that the structure of families leads them to spread in concentric zones around the central city, with smaller families closer to the center and larger ones further out. However, social status characteristics exert pressure for sector growth. Racial and ethnic residential segregation, on the other hand, leads to the creation of a number of central areas as described by the multiple-nuclei model.

In short, Berry and Rees have combined the various models of urban growth with social area analysis to offer an explanation of the growth patterns of American cities. Their work supports the validity of each of the models under a particular set of social conditions that are illuminated by social area analysis. While some research has supported this analysis in another society, Tel Aviv in Israel (Borukhov, Ginsberg, and Werczberger, 1979), it is unlikely that any single model or analytic scheme will be able to account for the variety of patterns of urban growth around the world. Even within the United States, conflict theorists have pointed to the way big business interests have affected urban growth to increase profits (e.g., Molotch, 1976).

URBAN LIFE IN THE UNITED STATES

Urban Life vs Rural Life

The classical view of urban life was quite pessimistic. Toennies and Simmel, two German sociologists, emphasized the difference between urban and rural life. This view was taken up by Wirth, whose ecological comparison of urbanism was an important element in the "Chicago school" of urban analysis.

GEMEINSCHAFT UND GESELLSCHAFT: FERDINAND TOENNIES

Toennies (1963; original, 1887) distinguishes between what he calls *Gemeinschaft*, a "community" based on strong social ties, tradition, and personal relationships, and *Gesellschaft*, an "association" of people with weak social ties resulting from considerable social diversity and characterized by impersonal relationships. The first, he indicates, is more descriptive of rural life while the second characterizes the city.

In *Gemeinschaft* communities, people know one another, share interests, and are oriented toward the collective community interests. They have a strong sense of common fate and shared identity. Family ties are strong, and life often centers around these ties. *Gesellschaft*, on the other hand, is descriptive of communities where people are largely motivated by self-interest and have few common values or shared identities. Tradition and custom are no longer binding forces.

THE URBAN PERSONALITY: GEORG SIMMEL

Simmel (1950:635-640) adds a social psychological dimension to the study of cities by focusing on how urban life influences the personalities of city dwellers. The stimulation and fast pace of city life requires some "defensive" reaction by urbanites. He argues that the impersonal and apparently unfriendly manner of city dwellers is a necessary protection against the confusion and disorientation of constant stimulation.

The centrality of a money economy in the city tends to transform potentially intimate relationships into rational encounters. Calculating the cost of any transaction, actually or implicitly, is an important part of the daily life of the urbanite; in a way, this is similar to the later formulation of "exchange theory" (see chapter 1). The city dweller is often likely to act "with his head instead of his heart," Simmel indicates.

There are positive aspects of city life as well. City life grants the individual a good deal of personal freedom. The stimulation of the city is exciting, as long as it is not overwhelming, and its sheer variety of activities and opportunities offers an array of social and personal choices unavailable elsewhere.

ECOLOGY AND INTERACTION IN THE CITY: LOUIS WIRTH

Whereas Toennies focuses on forms of association and Simmel on the urban person, Wirth devotes his attention to how social interaction in the city and differs from social interaction in rural areas. He argues that three important factors distinguish the interaction patterns of urbanites from those living in rural areas.

Population size affects social interaction. The sheer size of a city's population renders impossible the intimacy that was common in rural life. Interaction among city dwellers is more likely to be based on secondary group characteristics such as segmented relationships (for example, knowing somebody only on the job). Interaction of those living in rural areas is more similar to primary group contact, involving more rounded and complete relationships; for example, knowing persons because of working with them, socializing with their families, and going to the same church (see chapter 5).

Population density is another element affecting patterns of interaction. As the number of people living in residential neighborhoods increases, life becomes more difficult and strained. Additional problems arise in dense communities when there is considerable diversity in values and norms. Establishing smaller residential communities or populating them with people of similar cultural beliefs can reduce potential conflict over incompatible values and social norms. Thus, Wirth apparently sees some value in voluntary residential segregation.

Social diversity in city life tends to break down rigid class and race boundaries and permit more social mobility. It also allows for considerable diversity in lifestyles. These characteristics of urbanism make it difficult for city dwellers to form lasting relationships and result, Wirth believes, in urban alienation (a sense of loss of intimate connection to others).

Criticism of Wirth's View. Wirth's analysis of urban life has been criticized for not being clear about how the three factors he outlines relate to one another and operate jointly. Urban alienation is not as common or as strong as Wirth assumes (Fischer, 1976), and ease of communication and transportation has allowed for the development of primary relationships over wide geographical areas. Population density is seen more as an indicator of difficulties than their cause (Choldin, 1978). Finally, Gans (1962) points out that Wirth underplays the importance of social homogeneity within urban neighborhoods in providing social anchors for the urban dweller.

Despite these criticisms, Wirth's views shed light on some important ecological variables that distinguish city from rural life. They have directed considerable research to the important task of specifying the concrete effects of these variables.

THE CITY AS AN "URBAN VILLAGE": HERBERT GANS AND CLAUDE FISCHER

Gans (1962; 1965) and Fischer (1976) have studied urban life and conclude that urbanites do in fact experience considerable personal interaction and maintain intimate social ties. Gans sees the city as composed of neighborhoods that are, in his words, "urban villages." Suttles (1970) analysis of urban slums has provided further support for Gans's view that these are marked by strong community identification and feelings of social solidarity, qualities often thought to be found only in rural communities. While people may know fewer of their immediate neighbors in a large apartment house, for example, they have wide-ranging social contacts and relationships through their jobs, voluntary organizations to which they belong, and recreational pursuits they follow. The quality of life does not significantly differ between urban and rural areas, then, even though their styles are different.

Fischer argues that the large and dense population of the city leads to the creation of numerous and varied subcultures (see chapter 3), which are relatively internally homogeneous (composed of people with similar characteristics and outlooks). Thus the unconventional person can find others who are similar, forming a "critical mass" of like-minded people. The city, then, becomes a breeding ground for social diversity and creativity.

In short, both Gans and Fischer believe that earlier views of urban life overemphasize its negative aspects. While they recognize that city life is not without its problems, as is also the case for rural life, it offers many advantages as well.

Even the strongest proponent of city life recognizes the many problems that the urban environment generate.

Problems of the City

CRIME AND DRUGS

Cities are centers for criminal activity and drug use. The concentration of people in the city makes it a natural breeding ground for both. Even if the *rate* of crime were relatively low, the sheer number of people in cities is likely to result in high *numbers* of crimes being committed. Also, the intermixing of wealth and poverty in the city brings the haves and the have-nots into close proximity, increasing both the motivation and the opportunity for crimes against property (see chapter 8). The relative degree of anonymity of the city affords greater opportunity to commit crimes without detection.

The sharp increase in drug use has made the crime problem worse. While drugs are also used in rural and suburban areas, they are linked to crime primarily in inner city areas, where the hopelessness and despair generated by poverty have made drug use epidemic and drug-trafficking a major urban industry. Turf battles between drug lords have become increasingly violent. Petty street crimes to obtain the money to feed a drug habit have similarly become part of the urban landscape.

FISCAL PROBLEMS

When the United States suffers a general economic decline, cities are often affected more than other political units. In addition to loss of federal funds, three other factors play a major role in the financial problems faced by most cities.

Suburban flight of the middle class that started in the 1950s reduces both the tax base in cities having an income tax and the level of routine and consistent spending on which cities have come to depend.

High concentrations of poor people remain in the city. While they contribute less to the city's economy, they require extensive services that draw on reduced municipal resources. Because of national economic problems, the cost of providing welfare as well as health and unemployment benefits for the disadvantaged falls disproportionately on the largest cities. As a consequence, many cities have had to reduce police and fire protection and sanitation services and limit the repairing or rebuilding of their aging infrastructures (bridges, roads, and utility facilities).

Businesses have begun to relocate away from cities because of a decline in municipal services and technological improvements in transportation and communication. This relocation has resulted in a further and substantial reduction of the city's tax base, in turn reducing its attractiveness to other firms that otherwise might have established themselves there.

TRANSPORTATION

The city is seen as a mass of snarling traffic. Driving into the central city is a frustrating experience for many commuters and a frequent source of complaint for the occasional visitor. Parking is either nonexistent or expensive. Mass transportation is inadequate, dirty, unreliable, and dangerous. Many urban roads and bridges are in terrible states of decay, and there is not enough money to make the necessary repairs on a reasonable schedule.

Traffic congestion is seen as seriously undermining the economic viability of urban areas. Gridlock alerts, which warn motorists of traffic paralysis, are becoming commonplace in central cities. Traffic problems that make it difficult to get to recreational areas also make urban life less attractive. The combination of problems, not the least of which is traffic congestion, have influenced corporations to move out of large cities to the suburbs or to smaller cities.

OTHER PROBLEMS

Environmental pollution is a growing urban problem. So too is population loss, which leads to a further reduction in federal funds and of congressional seats. Deteriorating water mains, gas and power lines, and transportation equipment aggravate the problems of city life. Cities' ability to deal with these problems is limited by their political and economic subordination to states and to the federal government.

Urban Planning

While urban planning dates back to the ancient Greeks, it has generally been fragmentary and inconsistent and usually limited to areas of the city that are considered showcases. The public buildings in central Washington, D.C., were planned with both functionality and aesthetic beauty in mind, but the plan for the rest of the city did not receive the same kind of effort and attention.

URBAN RENEWAL

Considerable "urban renewal" took place in the 1950s and 1960s. Large public housing projects built in many cities were intended to provide adequate housing and to improve the lot of the poor. Many of these projects turned out to be social disasters. The Pruitt-Igoe project in St. Louis is a prime example. The buildings and apartments were unattractive. Decisions about important issues like the kind of paint that could be used, the schedule for use of the laundry rooms, and the length of time a visitor could stay in an apartment were all made by a remote housing authority. As a result, the project had more than its share of burglary, murder, rape, and robbery.

In some cases urban renewal led to the poor being displaced to make room for middle class housing. Some called this form of urban renewal "black removal." Tightly structured neighborhoods were destroyed and people were scattered, though many preferred not to move despite the promise of better housing.

GENTRIFICATION

A more modern form of urban renewal is less a consequence of deliberate governmental planning than of changing economic and social conditions. *Gentrification* involves the taking over of formerly working class neighborhoods by white collar professionals, who buy older buildings, lofts, and former warehouses and renovate them. These gentrifiers tend to be white and young (usually between 25 and 45); they are typically single, cohabitating, or married but childfree.

Buildings undergoing gentrification are restored inside and out. The old neighborhood stores, usually of the mom-and-pop variety, are replaced by higher-status enterprises: boutiques, gourmet food shops, and upscale chain stores. The cost of living in these areas rises considerably, sometimes forcing any remaining working class residents to move.

By and large, gentrification takes place in and around important nuclei of cities: Soho and the Upper East Side in Manhattan, the Mission district in San Francisco, and Inman Park in Atlanta are some examples. Those moving into these areas are similar in many ways to those who initially moved to the suburbs. The "gentrifiers," though, are trying to remake the city—at least their portion of it—rather than to escape from it. This renewal, however, does nothing to solve the massive problems of the urban poor.

Urbanization, or concentrations of populations into cities, began about 6,000 years ago. Preindustrial cities were relatively small; Rome, for example, grew from less than 10,000 people to just under one million. The Industrial Revolution in Europe led to improved transportation, enabling large numbers of people to move to the cities to work in the factories. City life became more hectic and impersonal; crime and pollution increased.

The first urban settlement in the United States was established in New Amsterdam (New York). Urban growth generally followed the European pattern. By the 1850s about one-third of all Americans lived in urban areas. Small cities grew into large cities, and these grew further into metropolises.

The development of the suburbs was one of the major events of the 1950s; it was made possible by the growth of commuter railroads, the increasing availability of automobiles, and an extensive highway-building program. Suburban growth led to decentralization as people and firms began to move out of the central cities.

There are three major theories of urban growth. According to the concentric zone model, cities grew in concentric circles around a central business district. The sector model suggests that cities grew through the development of sectors of pielike wedges of different land-use patterns that radiated out from the center of the city. The multiple-nuclei model theorizes that rather than a single central district, a city has many "central" business districts (or nuclei) with adjacent sectors showing other land-use patterns. Social area analysis explains the pattern of urban residence in terms of the family status, social standing, and race and ethnicity of the residents. Like the other theories of urban growth, it suggests that family status leads to concentric ring development. Social status characteristics, on the other hand, encourage sector development; racial and ethnic segregation promote multiple nuclei.

Gemeinschaft ("community") and Gesellschaft ("association") describe rural and urban life, respectively. Rural life is based on personal relationships and collective identification, while urbanism emphasizes the reverse. Simmel argues that the impersonality, emphasis on rationality, and presumed unfriendliness of cities are a defensive reaction to the confusion and disorientation of city life. However, he also points out that the city provides a degree of freedom and social diversity that is unavailable in the rural environment. According to Wirth, urban interaction is affected by the size, density, and social diversity of the population.

Gans, a more contemporary researcher of the city, has a more positive view. He sees it as composed of many "urban villages" within which people are linked in relatively homogeneous subcultures with strong personal ties and commitments to collective interests. He also sees the city as fostering social diversity and creativity.

Cities have many problems. Crime and drug use is rampant in many cities; their financial problems have become worse; and city traffic has become increasingly congested.

Ambitious urban renewal projects of the 1950s and 1960s were not as effective in "renewing" cities as had been anticipated. They often merely disrupted existing communities and displaced the poor. More recently, "gentrifiers" have tried to reclaim areas of the city by renovating older buildings and upgrading neighborhood facilities. Gentrification has been carried out primarily by young, white, urban professionals and has not dealt directly with the massive problems of the urban poor.

22

Collective Behavior and Social Movements

Collective behavior is an important subfield of sociological analysis. In this chapter, we will examine some of the typical forms of collective behavior. These will include crowds, rumor, public opinion, fads and fashions, and panics and mass hysteria. Special attention will be paid to the various types, characteristics, and explanations of social movements—a more organized and more durable form of collective behavior.

THE FIELD OF COLLECTIVE BEHAVIOR

In one sense, any form of "collective" behavior is the subject of sociological analysis. There is, however, a difference between the actions that define the special subfield of "collective behavior" and the forms of collective action that have so far been the focus of this book. *Collective behavior* refers to the somewhat spontaneous and short-lived social actions of a relatively large number of people in ambiguous situations. A large antiwar demonstration and the activities of the audience at a rock concert are examples of the kind of "crowds" that are analyzed by students of collective behavior. So too are the latest crazes in fads and fashions, changes in "public opinion," and the panic or hysteria that may result from some disaster (like a fire or tornado that destroys a community). Finally, the creation and maintenance of social movements (e.g., the civil rights movement) are also appropriate subjects for collective behavior analysis.

Elements of Collective Behavior

RESTRICTED, SHORT-TERM SOCIAL ACTION

In collective behavior the participants engage one another only temporarily. Their interaction is relatively restricted to the particular situation at hand—a concert, a demonstration, escaping from a fire—and tends to last only as long as that situation. Thus their interaction is more limited in range than that of social groups and organizations and is likely to be similarly restricted in scope and time.

AMBIGUOUS IDENTIFICATION AND SOCIAL BOUNDARIES

The exact boundaries of participants in any form of collective behavior is not always clear. For example, while there are usually many people congregating around the site of a demonstration, some are not participants but spectators wanting to find out what is going on. Nor do participants in collective behavior (such as a crowd at a rock concert) necessarily know or identify with each other.

WEAK OR NEWLY DEVELOPED SOCIAL NORMS

In collective behavior, standard norms are not sufficient guides to appropriate actions. As a consequence, collective behavior is more likely to be relatively more spontaneous and unpredictable than behavior in clearer and more socially regulated contexts.

CROWDS

Types of Crowds

The most obvious and dramatic form of collective behavior is the *crowd*, a temporary and unorganized collection of individuals in close proximity to one another who have a common focus. Blumer (1969) has identified four different types of crowds.

CASUAL CROWDS

A *casual crowd* is a collection of individuals who form spontaneously because some common event captures their attention, but who engage in little if any interaction with each other. The casual crowd is exemplified by the passersby who stop to look at a car accident. Their commonality is unplanned and does not lead them to collective action.

CONVENTIONAL CROWDS

Participants in a *conventional crowd* have gathered for some specific purpose. Their actions are guided to some extent by existing social norms. There is generally little interaction among the participants. Individuals attending a lecture or a movie are examples of a conventional crowd. They share a common goal, but pursue it as individuals.

EXPRESSIVE CROWDS

Expressive crowds develop around emotionally charged events. The participants at the annual Mardi Gras in New Orleans, the Woodstock Festival in New York in 1969, and the annual New Year's Eve celebration in Times Square are examples of expressive crowds. This form is less organized than the conventional crowd. The level of emotions expressed by this type of crowd is often unacceptable in ordinary circumstances.

ACTIVE CROWDS

Perhaps the form that has captured the most attention from sociologists and the general public is the *active crowd* (mob), an excited and emotional collection of individuals that often vents emotion through violent and destructive action. The active crowd seeks not only to discharge the strong emotions that have been built up but also to take action against some perceived wrong. The violence of fans of the losing team at a European soccer match and the actions of a lynch mob are examples of the behavior of an active crowd.

PROTEST CROWDS

Recently, McPhail and Wohlstein (1983) have suggested a fifth type of crowd, the *protest crowd*, which has elements of both the conventional and the active crowd. This form is moderately organized, like the conventional crowd, but destructive, like the active crowd. McPhail and Wohlstein point to the violence that occurs during labor disputes as an example of the behavior of the protest crowd.

Theories of Crowd Dynamics

CONTAGION THEORIES

Initially advanced by Le Bon (1960; original, 1895), *contagion theories* explain crowd behavior as a result of a "collective mind," the loss of individual identity because of the "contagious" spread of emotions aroused in the situation. In the anonymity and emotionality of the moment, individuals transfer their judgments and responsibility to the collective. The crowd has a life of its own, independent of the personalities of the participants or of existing social norms.

This social psychological view has been amplified by Blumer (1951), who argues that the emotional states created in a crowd result from people "milling" around. These emotions are accepted without serious reflection and spread through a "circular reaction" that raises the emotional level and focuses action toward some common goal.

This view has been criticized for assuming that emotions are uncritically accepted and automatically contagious. Critics argue that crowd behavior is not unique; it differs little from the reasonably well-studied effects of the presence of others on behavior (see Chapter 5). Furthermore, the dynamic explanative processes seem unable to account for the termination of crowd behavior. These criticisms are in part responsible for the development of emergent-norm theory, discussed below.

CONVERGENCE THEORIES

In a more psychological approach, *convergence theories* explain crowd behavior as the actions of like-minded individuals who are drawn to a situation and then act in common because of existing similarities of personality. Early convergence theorists (e.g., Martin, 1920) argue that the crowd releases primitive emotional impulses, like hate, from the social constraints that have held them in check. Others (e.g., Allport, 1924) insist that "social facilitation" (see chapter 5) rather than contagion is the major mechanism that leads to crowd behavior.

Convergence theories have difficulty explaining crowd behavior because they rely heavily on factors (like pre-existing personality characteristics) that are independent of the situation. Also, this view cannot explain why certain impulses (fear and hate) are released in crowd situations rather than others (love and affection). Finally, though convergence theories assume that specific situations determine which personality predispositions will be released, and despite the fact that how the situation is viewed depends on its collective definition, they do not address this issue.

EMERGENT-NORM THEORY

Turner and Killian (1957; Turner, 1964) do not believe that crowds are irrational collections of individuals pushed by the emotions of the moment or by their personality predispositions. Their view is that crowd behavior can be explained by social norms that arise out of the interaction among participants in a collective event. This explanation is called *emergent-norm theory*.

Turner points out that careful studies of various types of crowds reveal that participants are not single-minded; they vary considerably in their motives, attitudes, and behavior as well as in their commitment to what is occurring. Also, since behavioral conformity in the presence of others is a well-established fact (see chapters 5 and 7), no special mechanism such as contagion need be invoked. The only difference between behavior in crowds and in other social situations, Turner and Killian argue, is that in crowds the appropriate norms emerge from the situation rather than being imposed on it. These emergent norms then guide the behavior of the participants.

Rumor

Norms are communicated through participants' interaction. Occasionally communication takes the form of *rumor*, unsubstantiated information from anonymous sources that is spread informally. Rumors may be true or false, but their origin and validity are hard to establish. They thrive in situations of ambiguity and in the absence of official or trusted channels for disseminating information.

Rumors are attempts to make sense out of an unclear situation. Often, rumors change as they are being spread, much as information does in the children's game of "telephone." The final story transmitted by rumor is often quite different from the original. Once begun, rumors are quite difficult to stop.

Rumors may initiate crowd behavior or focus its action once formed. The behavior of a lynch mob is an example of crowd behavior in which rumor may play both roles. Rumors are often the primary or even only means of information in ambiguous situations; they result from a collective effort to clarify what is going on. Shibutani (1966) points out that this collective process includes different contributions. Some participants are "messengers" who pass along rumors. Others serve as "interpreters" by trying to provide an appropriate context for the information and examining its implications. Some are "protagonists" who argue for a particular interpretation, and still others are "decision makers" who attempt to initiate some form of action on the basis of the rumors. Most participants, however, are part of the "audience" for rumors. This collective effort may, on occasion, clarify the situation by establishing the validity or lack of it of the rumored information.

OTHER FORMS OF COLLECTIVE BEHAVIOR

Collective behavior need not take place in a confined space, as is the situation in crowds. *Mass behavior* takes place when people respond similarly to an event though they may be physically scattered. Two particular forms of mass behavior are "public opinion" and "crazes." A third, "panic and mass hysteria," may occur among people who are separated or in close proximity.

Public Opinion

In the field of collective behavior, a *public* refers to a substantial number of individuals who share an interest in an issue on which opinion is divided. Most people are members of several publics: a person may be part of the "pro-choice" public, the "peace movement" public, the "save the environment" public, and the "antihandgun" public.

Public opinion is made up of the collective views of a public on a specific issue. Since opinions not only vary but also change with new circumstances, public opinion refers to a particular point in time. *Public opinion polls*, surveys to determine and measure public opinion, testify to the shifting views of publics. In democracies, where the people's support for public policy is required, politicians frequently use such polls in assessing the views of relevant publics.

OPINION LEADERS

The views of various publics are often influenced by *opinion leaders*, high-status individuals who play an important role in shaping the views of a public. Sometimes this role is based on presumed expertise; scientists, for example, are influential in shaping public opinion on disarmament and environmental concerns. At other times influence is based primarily on social status; innumerable research has demonstrated the influence of husbands/fathers on the political views of their wives and children. Finally, those in key positions in the media also serve as opinion leaders. Television commentators like David Brinkley, Walter Cronkite, and John Chancellor— as well as prominent print columnists like William Safire, Evans and Novak, George Will, and Tom Wicker—significantly influence public opinion.

PROPAGANDA

Many people attempt to influence public opinion, including politicians, lobbyists, and special interest organizations. In the course of doing so, they may use *propaganda*, information or points of view that deliberately attempt to influence and shape public opinion. Commercial advertising, political speeches, and the publicity generated by some organizations are to some degree forms of propaganda.

Propaganda is not necessarily false; however, it is not neutral information. Its purpose is to support a particular point of view and thus to persuade people of the correctness of the desired opinion. Propaganda becomes a problem when it is defined as informational or educational; when its clear agenda to persuade rather than to enlighten is not acknowledged.

Crazes

Crazes are temporary forms of expressive mass behavior. Two particular forms are noteworthy: fads and fashions.

FADS

Fads are forms of behavior that are followed enthusiastically by large numbers of people for a relatively short time. People typically engage in fads because it has become the "thing to do." In recent years a number of fads have come and gone: "streaking" (running naked in public), hula hoops, Rubik's cubes, disco dancing, and Cabbage Patch dolls. Klapp (1969) believes that fads offer ways of emphasizing personal identity and of highlighting individuality. Thus it is not surprising that fads are common among the young, who are still firming up their identity. However, this view ignores the *lack* of individuality that results from engaging in a fad, from doing what many other people are doing.

After some period of time, most people get bored with fads and abandon them. For example, while there are still some children who demand Cabbage Patch dolls and play with hula hoops, these objects no longer command the same level of interest or attention they did earlier.

FASHIONS

Fashions are the particular styles of behavior or appearance that are in vogue at a particular time. The very word *fashion* implies temporariness, though fashions are usually more long-lasting than fads. Fashions are a product of modern society's emphasis on change. The stability of traditional societies made fashion unnecessary and even undesirable.

Fashions are often created for commercial reasons: they sell products. New dress styles require people to get rid of their present clothes and buy the latest fashions. New styles of grooming likewise require the use of products or services (such as hairdressers and barbers) to achieve the "new look."

Not all fashions have an economic intent or effect. Some derive from status concerns. To engage in the latest form of behavior (for example, to adopt the particular style of speech of the "Valley Girls" in California) marks the person as a member of the "ingroup" (see chapter 5) and provides status points. Fashions are more central to social life than fads. They often reflect important social concerns rather than "passing fancies." It has been argued that the language adopted by white youths from African American culture during the 1960s and 1970s was a deliberate attempt to connect with an oppressed group.

Panic and Mass Hysteria

These related forms of mass behavior involve fear. The response to that fear is often individualistic and unguided by social norms.

PANIC

Panic is the disorganized flight from some actual or perceived danger. It occurs when people experience a sense of overwhelming fear that reduces their ability to seek reasonable solutions. Their vision is narrowed and alternative courses of action go unrecognized. Behavior in such situations tends to be irrational, self-centered, and often counterproductive. Shouting, screaming, and general confusion are common in panic situations. There are few clear lines of communication through which adequate information about possible courses of action can be provided. In innumerable cases of panic caused by fires in crowded places, most of the deaths resulted from people piling up at a single exit or leaping prematurely out of windows.

MASS HYSTERIA

Mass hysteria involves the rapid spread of fear and frantic activity in response to the perceived threat of some powerful force. These perceived dangers are communicated to others, who similarly respond with equal fervor. The scare about the witches of Salem, Massachusetts, in 1692 provides a vivid example of mass hysteria (Erikson, 1966). The more recent "Red Scare" involving alleged communist activity in government and the entertainment industry during the McCarthy era of the 1950s is another example of mass hysteria. In both cases, many innocent people were hounded and persecuted because of the belief that they were in the service of a "foreign" power (Satan in the case of the "witches," and an "international communist conspiracy" in the McCarthy episode). Even more recently the mass hysteria produced by the fear of AIDS has led to similar persecution of homosexuals in some communities.

Perhaps the most dramatic example of mass hysteria involves the famous broadcast describing an alleged invasion from Mars. On the night before Halloween in 1938, Orson Welles broadcast a dramatization of H. G. Wells's novel *The War of the Worlds*. Though he stated that it was a dramatization several times during the broadcast, thousands of Americans believed that what they were hearing was a live report of an invasion of Martians. Mass hysteria and panic led many to call to warn relatives and friends; some people in the part of New Jersey where the landing was supposed to be taking place simply fled. It was difficult to reassure many of the most panic-stricken that no invasion was occurring.

Mass hysteria feeds on itself. Once begun, it spreads like wildfire and is difficult to extinguish. In Salem, it gradually faded away as increasing doubts arose as to the validity of the testimony of some of the young girls involved. In the case of the Red Scare, the television program exposing "McCarthyism" by a respected journalist (Edward R. Murrow) and a deeply emotional televised defense in a relevant trial (by lawyer Joseph Welch) were major factors in changing public opinion and reducing the hysteria.

SOCIAL MOVEMENTS

One form of collective behavior is somewhat more long-lasting, more organized, and wider in scope than those discussed above. This form is called a *social movement*. It is a collection of individuals who have organized to promote or resist some cultural or social change.

Types of Social Movements

FOCUS ON INDIVIDUALS

Some social movements focus on individuals in an attempt either to promote or resist change in their behavior. There are two kinds of social movements that focus on individual change: alternative and redemptive.

Alternative movements encourage individuals to change their own behavior. Typically, they attempt to get individuals to discard particular attitudes or forms of behavior and to replace them with other behaviors that they see as more desirable. The Women's Christian Temperance Union, for example, sought to convince people that drinking alcohol in any form was wrong and they should abstain from doing so.

Redemptive movements attempt to bring about sweeping and radical changes in individuals. For example, the Hare Krishna movement is essentially a redemptive movement. Movements such as this seek to remake the individual completely; some refer to this process as being "born again."

FOCUS ON THE SOCIETY

Other social movements focus on trying to make changes in the overall society rather than in individuals. Four types of movements focus on the society: regressive, reform, revolutionary, and utopian.

Regressive movements aim to resist social change and to return society to an earlier state. They wish to turn back the clock of progress. Fundamentalist religious movements whose goal is to change society and not just the individual are often regressive. Islamic fundamentalism and the "moral majority" in the United States (see chapter 15) are examples of regressive social movements.

Reform movements, though basically satisfied with the existing society, seek limited change in some specific areas. Reform movements generally work within the existing political system to promote moderate change. The environmental movement, the feminist movement, and the consumer movement exemplified by the work of Ralph Nader are instances of reform movements.

Revolutionary movements arise from strong dissatisfaction with the existing society. They seek to apply a specific ideological program to radically alter society's fundamental structure or practices. The revolutions that lead to the creation of China, Cuba, France, the Philippines, the Soviet Union, and the United States are examples of this form of movement. Revolutionary movements exist on the political left (e.g., SDS and Weatherman of the 1960s and 1970s) and on the political right (e.g., the John Birch Society).

Utopian movements also seek a radical restructuring of society, but they lack a specific blueprint to do so. Utopian movements differ from revolutionary movements in their unwillingness to use violence to achieve their goals. The word *utopia* has come to convey a pleasant but vague image of an impossibly perfect society. To some extent, the "counterculture" movement of the 1960s and 1970s was a utopian movement. It espoused the goal of making this society more humane and better connected to its natural environment but offered no specific program to accomplish this goal.

Characteristics of Social Movements

IDEOLOGY

All social movements have an *ideology*, a set of beliefs that justify a particular social arrangement or action. These beliefs typically define the situation that the movement wishes to influence and the consequences that are likely to occur if the movement is not successful. Though the ideology is often vague, it often serves as a recruiting device and rallying cry for the movement. *The Communist Manifesto* (Marx and Engels, 1955; original, 1888) outlined communism's ideology as a revolutionary social movement.

ORGANIZATION

Social movements are more organized than other forms of collective behavior. They often have a small core group of leaders and a larger group of devoted members. Beyond them there is frequently a larger group of supporters who are sympathetic to the movement's aims and can often be counted on for financial and moral support. Successful movements may become so highly organized that they turn into formal organizations (see chapter 5). The Communist party in the Soviet Union started out as a revolutionary social movement; after overthrowing the czar it became a formal governmental structure.

Large social movements often involve a number of organizations. The environmental movement, for example, includes organizations such as the Sierra Club, Friends of the Earth, and the Wilderness Society. The problem of organization thus becomes more complicated, because not only must the activities of the members of each particular organization in the movement be coordinated, but the action of each of the various relevant formal organizations must also be usefully connected if they are to accomplish their common purpose.

TACTICS

All social movements engage in *tactics*, specific activities aimed at accomplishing a particular goal. Tactics often have several different specific purposes. For the movement's aims to be accomplished, tactics are used to mobilize the support of those who are sympathetic to but not directly involved in the movement. Tactics are also important in trying to change the attitudes of those who do not support the movement's efforts. For example, the tactics of the environmental movement are to get more people to separate different forms of waste; to encourage the recycling of papers, bottles, and cans; and to promote appropriate legislation at the local, state, and federal levels.

Tactics vary by type of movement. Utopian movements are not likely to use violence as a tactic, whereas revolutionary movements might and often do. Movements that are well established and have relatively easy access to the political process (the consumer movement, for example) are less likely to use mass public demonstrations and more likely to lobby the political structure to attain their ends. On the other hand, those with little political access, such as the anti-Vietnam War movement in the 1960s, often require the publicity that mass demonstrations and controversial activities (such as burning draft cards) generate. Violence is more likely to be used as a tactic when all other ways of changing society are blocked.

The "Natural History" of Social Movements

Each social movement is different. However, sociologists (Blumer, 1969; Tilly, 1978) have noted four common stages in the life cycles of many social movements.

STAGE 1: EMERGENCE

Social movements emerge in response to some felt need. A number of people become increasingly dissatisfied with some element in society or with a recent change. The women's movement started with a growing dissatisfaction over the subordinate role of women in society. The Moral Majority reacted to the increasing sexual permissiveness and what they perceived as moral decay in American society. In the emergence stage, then, a small group of activists identify the problem and agitate for change.

STAGE 2: COALESCENCE

As a result of the agitation, more individuals become interested in the activities of the original small group. They coalesce, or join together, to organize the activities required to achieve their goal. Typically, a small leadership group develops. Policies and tactics are adopted and plans to encourage participation in the movement are set in motion. Often, some form of collective action, such as a rally or demonstration, is used to increase public awareness of the movement and its aims. Organizations sharing similar views may link up to strengthen the overall movement.

STAGE 3: BUREAUCRATIZATION

When a movement becomes firmly established, it often acquires many of the characteristics of a bureaucratic organization (see chapter 5). It develops a set of rules and procedures, maintains files, and has specialized roles and often a hierarchical structure of leadership. Sometimes the bureaucratic requirements siphon off energy that would otherwise be directed to accomplishing the movement's aims (Piven and Cloward, 1977).

STAGE 4: DECLINE

Most social movements end at some point. There are several reasons why this occurs (Miller, 1983). In some relatively rare cases the movement accomplishes its goals and has no reason for continuing. This was the case with the suffragette movement that in 1920 won women the right to vote. A movement may decline because its leadership is coopted by those in power or because it does not effectively mobilize the resources and support necessary to accomplish its aims. Splits within a movement, especially within the leadership group, caused by different views of tactics and strategies are not uncommon and may result in the movement's decline. Other reasons include society's loss of interest in the goals of a movement or its suppression by those in power. Finally, overbureaucratization may cause a social movement to lose its energy and focus.

Explanations of Social Movements

DEPRIVATION THEORY

Deprivation theory argues that social movements occur when a relatively large number of individuals feel deprived of what they believe is necessary for their well-being and happiness (Morrison, 1978). Marx's theories appealed to poor workers who felt economically deprived by the capitalist system. Marx's analysis demonstrates the importance of *relative deprivation*, feelings of disadvantage based on a comparison with some standard. Workers, Marx argued, would always be deprived relative to capitalists, who use worker labor to accumulate more profits than they pay out in wages.

Brinton (1965) points out that revolutions are more likely under conditions of "rising expectations" (see chapter 16). Feelings of deprivation combined with rising expectations of an improving situation lead to the formation of social movements to hasten the change.

While sociologists generally accept deprivation theory as a reasonable explanation of social movements, it has attracted some criticism. There are always segments of a population that feel deprived, and this theory is not able to explain why social movements arise in one situation rather than another.

MASS SOCIETY THEORY

According to this theory, social movements arise because of the social isolation and feelings of insignificance experienced by large numbers of people in modern mass society (Kornhauser, 1959). These feelings of powerlessness are overcome when people join others in a social movement. The sense of being part of a group that people get from participating in a social movement is often as important as the particular goal of the movement. Social movements are much more likely to arise among individuals in weakly integrated communities, some of whom may be manipulated by movement leaders.

This theory is valuable because it points out the characteristics of people who are likely to join a social movement. However, it is undermined somewhat by empirical research showing that several social movements have attracted people with extensive community ties (e.g., Tilly, Tilly, and Tilly, 1975).

STRUCTURAL STRAIN THEORY

Smelser's (1962) structural strain theory argues that there are six factors that contribute to the rise of a social movement. The more of these factors that are present, the higher the likelihood that a social movement will develop.

Structural conduciveness refers to particular social patterns that are likely to lead to significant social problems. The environmental movement grew up because of the perceived threat to the environment and its resulting effect on the quality of human life.

Structural strain is a social condition brought on by strains within a society. These may be caused by patterns of conflict within society. For example, the civil rights movement grew out of the increasing strain of racial conflict in the South.

The growth and spread of an explanation of the source of a social problem and of a particular program to remedy it can transform a disorganized rumbling of discontent into an organized social movement. The antiwar movement of the 1960s provided political analyses of the implications of massive military build-up and of the escalation of the war in Vietnam; it also developed a strategy of massive protest and communicated the strategy to large numbers of youths in universities.

Precipitating factors, or particular sparks, often serve to get individuals to commit themselves to collective action. While people may have perceived a problem and begun to consider some action to address it, a dramatic event is often required to crystallize things. Rosa Parks's refusal to sit at the back of the bus in Montgomery, Alabama, was just the dramatic event needed to put the civil rights movement into high gear.

Mobilization for action is required for a social movement to get off the ground. This hard and often unglamorous work includes raising funds, writing letters, calling people, and arranging for meetings or rallies.

Lack of social control over a budding social movement by responsible authorities can allow it to flourish. On the other hand, severe repression can undermine its existence or at least weaken its effect for some time. Such was the case when the South African government jailed key leaders of the African National Congress, such as Nelson Mandela.

Smelser's structural strain theory has been used to explain other forms of collective behavior, such as crowd formation. However, it has been criticized for omitting any serious analysis of the role of necessary resources (see below).

RESOURCE MOBILIZATION THEORY

This theory, developed by McCarthy and Zald (1977), fills in the gaps noted in several of the other approaches. It asserts that social movements arise in response to deprivation and structural strains only when the resources necessary to sustain them are available, organized, and effectively used. The resources they point to include money, office space, communication facilities, contacts, and people willing to do the necessary work. By and large, most of these resources are acquired from those not directly participating in the social movement.

This theory is generally accepted as a useful explanation of the rise and likely success of social movements. It has been criticized, however, for the emphasis it places on "outside" help. Morris (1981), for example, has shown that the civil rights movement among African Americans in the 1960s and 1970s was sustained largely by the African American community itself, especially through its churches.

SOCIAL MOVEMENTS AND SOCIAL CHANGE

Social movements are directed toward social change. The success or failure of a social movement affects the nature and extent of social change within society. The rights of minority groups and others with little social power are often advanced only through the actions of social movements. Women's right to vote and legislation to improve the conditions of workers, to protect the environment, and to grant and enforce the civil rights of minorities are all examples of the consequences of social movements. Social movements and social change, then, are inextricably linked.

Collective behavior is the somewhat spontaneous and short-lived action of a relatively large number of people that arises in ambiguous situations and that stands in contrast to the behavior of groups and organizations. The social boundaries of collective behavior are fuzzy, and the actions of participants are regulated by relatively weak or newly developed social norms.

Crowds are one type of collective behavior, and they take different forms. The casual crowd is made up of people who happen to respond to an event but engage in little social interaction. The conventional crowd forms when people gather for a particular purpose. Its members also engage in little interaction. The expressive crowd exhibits an emotional level that is usually not acceptable in other circumstances. Active crowds show excited and emotional behavior that is often violent and destructive. A protest crowd combines elements of the conventional and active crowds; they are moderately organized and are likely to be destructive or violent.

Three major theories explain crowd behavior. Contagion theories argue that in a crowd people lose their individual identities and succumb to the "collective mind." The "milling" of people and the easy and uncritical acceptance and transmission of the emotions that develop in the anonymity of the situation contribute to the "herd" mentality. Convergence theories assert that crowd behavior can be explained by the simultaneous presence of large numbers of like-minded individuals who act in common because of these predisposed similarities. Emergent-norm theory suggests that crowds are regulated by the social norms that also regulate other forms of social behavior, though in crowds the norms emerge within the situation itself. This theory finds more diversity in the actions, motivations, and commitments of participants in crowds than the other two theories.

Rumors are made up of unsubstantiated information from anonymous sources that spreads informally. They are attempts to clarify ambiguous situations, and may lead to the formation of crowds. In the rumor mill, people participate as messengers, interpreters, protagonists, decision makers or audiences.

Public opinion is the collective view of a public, a number of individuals who share an interest in an issue on which opinion is divided. Opinion leaders, high status people, play an important role in shaping public opinion. Propaganda is information that is deliberately used to influence public opinion.

Fads and fashions refer to short-lived forms of behavior. Fads are often followed enthusiastically for a short time and then fade away. Fashions are particular styles of clothes, grooming or behavior that, while longer-lasting than fads, are in vogue for a short time. They result from society's emphasis on change.

Panic and mass hysteria occur when people are overwhelmed with fear of threat and there are few channels of communication to assess the degree of danger or to suggest alternative courses of action. In such circumstances, people tend to behave in irrational and counterproductive ways.

Social movements are a more organized and more stable form of collective behavior. Some social movements try to change individuals' behavior. Two kinds of social movements are alternative movements, which seek limited change in behavior; and redemptive movements, which seek sweeping and radical change. Other social movements focus on changing society. Regressive movements wish to turn back the clock on progress. Reform movements seek limited change within a system that in other ways is basically satisfactory. Revolutionary movements, on the other hand, attempt a radical restructuring of what is perceived to be an unsatisfactory society. Utopian movements are guided by an ideal of the future but lack a specific program to accomplish their aims.

All social movements are organized to some degree and are guided by an ideology. They develop tactics to achieve their aims. The type of tactics varies with the particular form of social movement. Typically, social movements emerge in response to some felt need and then coalesce by bringing together like-minded individuals. A leadership group emerges to guide the activities; many social movements become bureaucratized. Most social movements end at some point— some because they accomplish their aims; others because of poor leadership, suppression by those in power, society's loss of interest in the relevant issue or overbureaucratization.

Four major theories attempt to explain the rise of social movements. Deprivation theory argues that movements occur when large numbers of people feel relatively deprived of what is important to their well-being. Deprivation and rising expectations of relief often combine to create social movements. Deprivation theory, however, is unable to explain why some deprived segments of society form social movements while others do not.

Mass society theory is based on the notion that modern society creates conditions of social isolation and feelings of insignificance. Joining together with others in a social movement alleviates those feelings. However, this theory is not adequate as a general explanation since research has shown that a number of social movements involve people with extensive community ties.

Structural strain theory cites six factors that lead to the emergence of a social movement. One factor is structural conduciveness, the existence of social patterns that lead to significant social problems that a movement wishes to address. Structural strain involves stresses and patterns of conflict within society that give rise to a movement. The growth and spread of an explanation for a particular social problem and of a program to remedy it is another important element in this theory, as is a specific precipitating factor that energizes individuals into collective action. Finally, the movement needs to mobilize its members for necessary action and escape social control by those in authority. Some sociologists feel that this theory does not adequately address the issue of necessary resources.

The final explanation, resource mobilization theory, asserts that deprivation and strain result in social movements only if there are adequate resources to sustain them. This theory assumes that much of these resources come from outside the movement. However, research on the civil rights movement shows that this is not always the case.

Finally, it is clear that social movements and social change are inextricably linked. The success or failure of social movements affects the nature and extent of social change in society.

23

Social Change and Modernization

Change is a part of social life. In this chapter, we will examine the sources of social change, the processes through which it occurs, and the theories that have been developed to explain it. In particular, we will explore the nature of modernity. Finally, we will describe trends in development in the Third World and some theories that explain them.

SOURCES OF SOCIAL CHANGE

Change is a constant element in social life. All societies experience *social change*—a significant alteration in patterns of culture and social structure that are reflected in social behavior. Some societies, like small tribes in the remote parts of South America change slowly; others, like the United States, change more rapidly. Societies change in different directions, so that while political liberalization, for example, may be taking place in one country (such as Poland), political repression may be happening in another (such as China). Some social changes are planned, as when governments regulate and deregulate industries; others are unplanned, as when a country's losing a war results in changes in the structure of its government. Some changes are of short duration, as in the case of fads or fashions (see chapter 22); others are more long-lasting, such as the effects of the invention of the automobile. Some change is readily accepted by society, as in improved health care programs. Most, however, are at least mildly controversial (such as feminist attempts to equalize power between men and women), because change upsets comfortable and familiar patterns.

Change doesn't just happen. A number of factors contribute to social change. Several of the most significant causes of social change are discussed below.

The Physical Environment

Societies and their physical environments are intimately interrelated. For example, societies situated near large bodies of water (for example, Great Britain) become seafaring nations, whereas those that are landlocked (such as Poland) do not. Urban settlements initially occurred at geographical crossroads: rivers, mountain passes, oceans, and seas.

Similarly, the surrounding environment is a major source of social change. The receding ice age about 13,000 years ago led to the growth of forests and to the development of various animal forms that influenced the evolution of different types of societies. There is a major debate at present about the *greenhouse effect* — an increase in average world temperature resulting from carbon dioxide emissions from cars, many industrial factories, and chlorofluorocarbons in refrigerants. There are differences in opinion about the extent and cost of social change necessary to reduce the threat this effect poses to human existence. Global warming may melt polar ice caps to some degree, causing a rise in sea level. This change, along with the temperature changes themselves, may force some communities to relocate (away from the higher tides that will occur along some coasts) and other communities to change their patterns of agriculture.

Cultural Processes

Culture is rarely static; both its material and nonmaterial aspects (see chapter 3) change. The car and the airplane, not to mention modern indoor plumbing, changed the nature of social life. Similarly, norms of "civility" (courtesy and manners) are quite different today than they were in the Middle Ages (Elias, 1978). There are several cultural processes through which these changes take place: discovery, invention, and diffusion.

DISCOVERY

The uncovering of some existing idea or principle is called a *discovery*. In this process of cultural innovation, something new is found. The principle of gravity is a discovery; it was always there, and at some point in time scientists were able to understand what it is and how it works. Similarly, the realization that some chemical elements are subject to radioactive decay was a discovery.

INVENTION

The new use or new combination of existing knowledge is called an *invention*. The automobile was an invention; it used existing knowledge about controlled combustion and gears, among other things, to produce something new. Airplanes, computers, and skyscrapers are examples of material inventions. However, nonmaterial aspects of a culture are also capable of being "invented." The alphabet, for example, is such a cultural invention; so are bureaucracy, social norms, and all social institutions.

Rarely is an invention the result of a single creative act. Typically, inventions occur over a period of time as a consequence of the accumulation of knowledge. Also, inventions lead to other inventions. The greater the number of existing inventions, the more rapid the growth of new inventions.

DIFFUSION

In addition to discoveries and inventions, societies change through cultural *diffusion*—the spread of cultural traits from one society to another. Diffusion occurs because of migration, trade or travel between societies. It also results when one society conquers another. In the modern world, diffusion may result from the array of available communications facilities (phone, mail, cable, satellites, fax machines, teletypes, and computers).

Both material and nonmaterial aspects of a culture can diffuse from one society to another. Values such as freedom and democracy have spread in this manner, as have tools and weapons. In general, the diffusion of material artifacts occurs more readily; norms, values, and cognitive beliefs are embedded in a cultural framework and are slower to spread to other societies.

Social Structure

Sometimes the source of change is in the social structure. Marx insisted that the structural arrangements between social classes would lead inevitably to social change. This source of change also springs from other kinds of inequalities. Differences among racial, ethnic, and religious groups are also potential engines of social change, as are gender differences. Sometimes competition between and within segments of the economy promotes social change, as when a country's trade policy is formulated to help one industry (textiles) at the expense of another (sugar).

Population

Significant changes in population are likely to produce social change. Fast-growing populations strain societal resources and require some accommodations in existing practices. They also force changes in the patterns of social life. The growing urban population changed the slow pace of small town social interaction into the hectic pace of modern city life (see chapter 21). The "baby boom" beginning in the 1940s led to the expansion of educational facilities. Population growth that is too slow, on the other hand, may threaten a society's long term viability; there may be too few workers to produce the necessary resources.

Dramatic shifts in population also lead to social change. Migration from the Frostbelt to the Sunbelt led to changes in congressional representation (and therefore in political power) and in the allocation of federal funds (and therefore in economic power). Similarly, the substantial migration of rural southern African Americans to the urban centers of the North earlier in this century (see chapter 11) had a significant influence on racial and economic relations in the United States.

The shifting age composition of the United States, especially the graying of the population (see chapters 12 and 20), is having a significant effect. The economics of social security has changed, as has the political impact of an aging population with more voting power than before.

Science and Technology

Scientific knowledge leads to technological advances that result in social change. The development of the automobile revolutionized social relationships. People became more mobile; they were less tied to their immediate neighborhoods and communities. They could now live and work in different areas. The automobile transformed relationships between men and women and influenced dating practices.

Medical technology and public health improvements have significantly changed the life expectancy of people in most societies. Machines and changing energy sources transformed preindustrial societies. Modern communication technology (satellites) instantaneously send information all around the world.

Ogburn (1922) takes the position that technology is a primary driving force in social and cultural change. He argues, for example, that the invention of the cotton gin was instrumental in making slavery in the South economically advantageous. He also notes that change is not equal in all segments of the culture. Ogburn coined the term *cultural lag* to refer to the tendency of the material culture to change more rapidly than the nonmaterial culture. For example, most office workers rarely use computers to their full potential, perhaps because of the so-called "fear of technology" caused by inadequate training.

Human Action

Individuals and the collective activities of many individuals also cause social change.

INDIVIDUAL ACTION

Many historians subscribe to what has been called the "great man [sic] theory of history," which holds that the actions of key individuals make history. They point to people like Jesus Christ, Julius Caesar, Karl Marx, Adolph Hitler, Albert Einstein, among others, as unique individuals whose actions changed history. If these men had not been born, this view asserts, the world would be considerably different.

Sociologists, on the other hand, generally take a different position. While recognizing the distinct contributions to history that key individuals make, sociologists point out that each of these notable individuals is a product of a distinct social and cultural milieu. Each is, in effect, a product of his times. Further, the changes instigated by these key individuals often tap deeper social processes that were already underway. Germany's social and economic strains resulting from World War I and Allied demands for reparations provided the context for Hitler's rise to power and for the changes he effected.

Also, sometimes significant social change results from the actions of relatively obscure individuals. Consider how recent United States history would have been different if a security guard had not noticed that a door lock in the offices of the Democratic party in the Watergate complex in Washington, D.C., had been taped to keep it from closing. There probably would not have been a "Watergate" scandal, and former President Richard Nixon would not have been forced to resign the presidency in favor of Gerald Ford. It is highly likely that these events resulted in a quite different set of foreign and domestic policy actions and in a different political context for the next presidential election.

Collective Action

Social change is often the result of the actions of large numbers of people. The actions of social movements in effecting social change was discussed in chapter 22. Social revolutions, it was pointed out, led to the present forms of many of the world's societies. The birth of many of the world's religions resulted from various forms of social movements; these religions, in turn, transformed human history (see chapter 15). Collective as well as individual action, then, is an important source of social change.

THEORIES OF SOCIAL CHANGE

Evolutionary Theories

Early sociological thinking focused on social progress and on whether there are any underlying laws of social change (see chapters 1 and 4). Spencer, for example, took the position that change always progresses from simpler systems to more complex ones. Adopting the evolutionary theories of Charles Darwin as his model, Spencer argued for limited governmental intervention in societal functioning so as to allow these natural evolutionary laws of social progress to be played out. In keeping with Darwin's concept of the "survival of the fittest," those activities and institutions that can manage in this type of competitive environment will continue and even flourish; others will simply die out. Natural laws, not human intervention, will be the determining factor.

This somewhat simplistic evolutionary theory of social progress fell into disrepute. Gerhard and Jean Lenski developed a more sophisticated version of sociocultural evolutionary theory that did not assume the inevitability of "progress" (see chapter 4). They believe that the driving mechanism in social change is changing technology, which leads to changes in economic production, social organization, and social behavior. These changes are not the result of an underlying law of social change but can be traced to specific actions in the sociocultural context of societies. These sociologists also saw change as "multilineal," taking place in different social spheres, at different rates, and in different directions.

Cyclical Theories

Some theorists of large scale social change viewed it as cyclical. Spengler (1926), for example, argued that like the human organism, societies are born, develop, and then decay. The cycle is inevitable. The vigor of early development slows down in its middle period. Society then becomes more materialistic and eventually begins to decline. Toynbee (1946), on the other hand, believed that societies could learn from the experience of history. Decay was not inevitable, though societies have to take specific actions to arrest it. Civilizations develop in response to challenges that arise from the environment (geographical or climatic conditions) or from human action (threat of war by a neighboring society). Societies flourish if the challenges are relatively mild or if they take appropriate action and establish effective institutions to meet them.

Recently, this view has been argued vigorously by Kennedy (1987). He notes that great powers tend to overextend themselves in military pursuits and thus weaken their economic base. Their impoverished economic structure leads to an overall societal decline. Kennedy sees the contemporary United States in just such a circumstance.

Functionalist Theory

Parsons (1937) views society as a social system of interrelated and interdependent parts. This system seeks equilibrium or balance. Change occurs when this essential stability is disturbed; the system is then forced to react to reestablish its equilibrium. Societies are conservative, resisting social change. Change is an irritant, something that upsets the relatively smooth functioning of society.

Social change is introduced by external forces (such as a war), or it arises from internal strains (such as a recession). Society adjusts to the changes and establishes a new balance. In this view change still leads to stability as a new equilibrium arises from the adjustments that are made.

DIFFERENTIATION AND INTEGRATION

When change is acknowledged, it is from an evolutionary perspective. Societies grow through a process of *differentiation*, the creation of different social institutions to deal with recurrent societal problems, and *integration*, or the relative coordination of the activities of these institutions. Stability and change both occur, but functionalists traditionally tend to emphasize the former. However, some functionalists devote attention to the issue of social change (Cancian, 1960) and to the way it is stimulated by internal societal strains (Merton, 1968).

Conflict Theory

In classic Marxian theory, social change arises from the class struggle between the economic exploiters and the economically exploited. The tensions between unequal groups in society force changes in the structure of society. Change is a consequence of the need to reconcile contradictions in structure and actions. The result of resolving these contradictions is not compromise but the creation of something entirely new—social change.

Marx focused primarily on economic contradictions as the engine of social change. Other conflict theorists have attempted to broaden this view. Dahrendorf (1958), for example, sees various kinds of *social* conflict as causes of social change. Ethnic, racial, and religious group conflict may be the basis of important changes in society (laws and practices regarding affirmative action; see chapter 11). The battle between "pro-choice" and "pro-life" activists are having dramatic effects on social policy in the United States and elsewhere (see chapter 13).

A Proposed Synthesis

None of the theories fully account for social change. Evolutionary theory provides little explanation for many internal social changes, such as migration patterns and political realignments. Cyclical theories seem rooted in explanations that are appropriate to social change in Western societies but less relevant to societies in other parts of the world. Functionalist theories place too heavy an emphasis on stability and equilibrium; change is often grudgingly studied, and then as an irritant. Conflict theorists focus almost exclusively on social, mainly economic, strain and generally ignore other sources of social change, such as advancing technology and external pressures.

Whatever their limitations as *comprehensive* explanations of social change, the various theories discussed above do provide useful analyses of specific types and particular circumstances of change. Most of the theories use some form of sociocultural evolution as a starting point, either explicitly or implicitly. Also, Merton's model of social change blends elements of functional and conflict theory. His introduction of elements of tension into the social system and Coser's (1956) examination of the "functions of social conflict" demonstrate that functionalist and conflict theories of social change can be integrated to some degree.

In short, evolutionary and cyclical theories provide the general framework for understanding the underlying dynamics of social change. They alert the analyst to the importance of both external pressures and internal strains in producing social change. Conflict theories highlight the specific forms of internal stress that are often involved. Functionalist theories point to the idea that in response to change, societies adjust in ways that attempt to preserve their balance and equilibrium, so that, paradoxically, change and stability are not always mutually exclusive. These theories of social change are complementary, though a fully comprehensive theory of social change is still not available.

MODERNIZATION AND DEVELOPMENT

Modernity

As a consequence of social change, many societies around the world have been characterized as "modern." *Modernity*, in sociological terms, refers to a pattern of social organization and social life that is linked to industrialization. It implies the replacement of tradition by rationality as a way of viewing the world and an emphasis on efficiency as a guiding principle of social action (Weber, 1978; original, 1921).

The early theorists of modernity (Toennies, Durkheim, Weber, and Marx) had a complex view of modernity. They were aware that it brought certain benefits to society; it led to improved health and longevity and to a better quality of life for most people. But they were equally aware of its possible negative consequences. They understood the problems modernity poses for personal identity, particularly its potential for increasing alienation and dehumanizing social relationships.

Third World Development

Modernity has not reached all corners of the world equally. The developed countries have a higher standard of living, a longer life expectancy, and a different residential pattern than Third World countries. The average per capita GNP in developed countries is about $9,500, but only about $700 in the Third World. While people in the developed countries can expect, on average, to live to about age seventy-three, those in the Third World have a life expectancy of about fifty-eight years. Though almost three-quarters of people in the developed countries live in cities, more than two-thirds of Third World citizens live in rural areas. There is also a considerable difference in the literacy rate in developed and Third World countries.

These differences are largely a result of the varying degrees of change that have occurred in these societies. In large part, change has been a consequence of technological developments leading to industrialization. The question of why these changes have occurred in some societies but not in others has led to several explanatory theories. The four most common are discussed here.

MODERNIZATION THEORY

This model focuses attention on *modernization*, a cultural, economic, and social process that transforms a preindustrial society to an industrial one. These changes were caused largely by technological developments that increased economic productivity and greatly altered the style of social life. Together, these factors are responsible for the modern industrial societies of the United States, Western Europe, and Japan, and to a lesser extent, the Soviet Union.

In this theory, modern societies have developed economic structures that promote development, encourage innovation, and use technology to improve efficiency and productivity. Extensive banking, transportation, and communication facilities are created. Religious institutions and kinship ties become less powerful, and government plays an increasing role in social life. The nuclear family system of modern society permits greater social and geographical mobility than the extended family structure (see chapter 13) in many Third World countries. Tradition is replaced by rationality as a guiding social principle (Weber, 1978; original, 1921), and heavy emphasis is placed on formal schooling to acquire the technical skills needed in a modern society.

The psychology of individual behavior is seen as transformed by modernization (Inkeles and Smith, 1974). Individuals in the developed countries have a stronger drive for individual achievement and are willing to defer immediate gratification to attain longer term personal goals. They feel a greater sense of control over their own lives and have a highly developed work ethic. In contrast, those in Third World countries are seen as fatalistic, believing they do not control their own fate. They are oriented to the present and lack the driving ambition that characterizes modernity.

Modernization theory implies that Third World countries need only follow the model of Western societies to achieve the same end. The driving forces are said to be internal, and Third World countries are urged to establish those necessary policies. In particular, they are encouraged to promote higher levels of education to reduce illiteracy. Further, they are encouraged to revise their economic and political institutions to provide incentives and encouragement for individualism while reducing social inequalities.

This model presents a relatively optimistic picture of the ability of Third World societies to modernize. However, these countries face considerably different conditions than those that were faced by the currently developed societies at a similar stage of development. Population pressures are greater and the world has become so interconnected that societies are less able to pursue isolated, independent change. Also, the simple diffusion of technology does not automatically guarantee progress without the considerable social and cultural changes that often must accompany it, and that takes time and effort (Ogburn, 1922).

CONVERGENCE THEORY

In a variant of modernization theory, *convergence theory* suggests that modernizing societies become increasingly similar as a result of that process (Rostow, 1960; 1962). They share a similar level of technological development and have a similar structure to their labor force and political institutions. These societies gradually "converge" around a general model of modern society.

Third World countries are seen as working to imitate the more developed societies, whether it is appropriate or not. This view underplays the degree to which the interconnectedness of the modern world pushes Third World societies in this direction. The developed countries have the capital funds and technological knowledge that the LDCs require, and the transference of both involves the Third World countries' acceptance of economic and political changes designed by the developed countries, even if these might not be appropriate to their culture or social circumstances.

DEPENDENCY THEORY

Many scholars, unhappy with the assumptions of modernization and convergence theories, argue that the LDCs exist in a world dominated by the developed countries (Frank, 1969). They framed a different explanation, *dependency theory*, that points out that the reason Third World countries did not modernize was that they were dependent on the more developed countries to whom the LDCs present state was more useful economically and politically. The industrialized nations found it useful to keep the Third World countries as suppliers of the raw materials they needed and as outlets to sell their finished products. They did not need further industrial competitors in an already highly competitive world.

Typically, Third World countries have one major crop (sugar or coffee) or raw material (tin or rubber) that is the center of their economy. These countries often do not have the economic and technological resources needed to improve this centerpiece. Therefore, these resources must come from outside—from more modern societies or from international agencies dominated by Western nations (e.g., the International Monetary Fund or the World Bank) on whom they then become dependent.

Dependency theory argues that Third World countries cannot simply follow the earlier modernizing process because their economic and technological needs are linked to their dependent status in a world economy. Dependency theory, however, has not adequately defined a more appropriate model to improve the situation of Third World countries. Originally this theory suggested socialist policies as the appropriate mechanism to improve the quality of education and health care in Third World countries. However, it has become apparent that while socialist economies may provide better education and health care, they are less productive than capitalist economies (see chapter 17). The economic and political upheavals of the Soviet Union and the socialist societies in Eastern Europe has thrown further doubt on the prescription for change offered by dependency theory.

WORLD SYSTEMS THEORY

In a further elaboration of the perspective of dependency theory, Wallerstein (1974; 1979; 1980) developed the *world systems theory*, which explores the relationship between the developed and less developed countries in the context of economic, geographical, historical, and political factors. In brief, this view suggests that the LDCs have little chance of ever catching up with the developed countries because they are so far behind and because their particular economic structure is useful for the dominating societies.

The world economy, Wallerstein argues, is essentially run on capitalist principles (see chapter 17). The nations in the world belong to one of three tiers.

Core states, the powerful military and industrial societies like the United States, most of Western Europe, and Japan, dominate the world economy by controlling most of its technology and capital. They serve as the world's industrial power source.

Periphery states supply the necessary raw materials to the industrialized core and are subservient to them. The economies of these countries are generally organized around agriculture or some limited mineral development. Many of them are in Africa or Latin America. In the past, the relationships between these and the core states was characterized as colonial. Wallerstein believes that a similar relationship still exists in "neocolonial" form, a new and modern version of the older colonialism.

Semiperiphery states are somewhere between the core and periphery and move up and down between them. These societies are partly in control of their own economic and political destiny but still are heavily influenced by the core states. These include such countries as South Korea, Spain, and Iran.

Three reasons for the dependency of Third World countries. First, the world economy has led these countries to narrow an earlier, more diversified, and self-maintaining economy to one that is *export dependent*. They are no longer able to control the prices for their goods, which are set by the industrialized countries of the core. Second, most of the Third World countries find themselves in a *debt trap*; they owe enormous sums of money to the core countries as a result of having borrowed to develop their economies. These debts make them increasingly dependent on the core states and less able to control their own economies (Dalmaide, 1984).

Third, there has been a tremendous increase of *multinational corporations* (see chapter 17), which are based in core countries and operate in the Third World countries. While these corporations have often provided the capital and technology that Third World countries need for development, they also accumulate considerable economic and political power in these countries and exert tremendous independent influence (Kumar, 1980).

World systems theory argues that a country's development cannot be seen in isolation from its relationship to other societies. Development is *inter*national, not just *intra*national as modernization theory emphasized. The core industrial societies will continue to dominate a world economic system. However, the ability of OPEC (the Organization of Oil Producing Nations, most of which are part of the periphery) to influence the world economy by altering production rates and prices of oil demonstrates that the periphery is not always completely powerless. Also, world systems theory has not been able to fit the Soviet Union and the socialist countries of Eastern Europe easily into any of the tiers, nor is it able to explain the rapid and successful modernization of Third World countries like Taiwan, South Korea, and Venezuela.

MODERNITY AND PROGRESS

Americans typically equate modernity with social progress. While it is clear that modernization has brought enormous benefits to many people, it also has had it negative side. Better health, nutrition, and human rights are among the many advances made possible by modernization. But these benefits have not reached all people, even in the most modern societies. Poverty, poor health, and high infant mortality still exist in the United States—probably the richest, most powerful, and most modern society on earth.

Moreover, the technological developments that led to modern society are not always beneficial. For example, nuclear power and modern weapons have made war more destructive. Modern communications technology has the potential to reduce personal freedom and invade privacy. Also, linking modernity to progress assumes that social change always moves in a straight line toward improvement; such is not always the case (Toffler, 1981). On balance, though, most sociologists believe that modernization has brought sufficient progress and benefits to justify the positive view most people hold of it.

Societies are not static; they are constantly changing, though not uniformly or at the same rate or in the same direction. The physical environment is one factor that affects social change. For example, societies adjacent to large bodies of water are likely to develop a maritime culture, while landlocked societies are likely to change slowly because of lack of frequent contact with the outside.

Certain cultural processes also produce change. Innovation, whether through discoveries or inventions, instigate change. Change also occurs through a process of diffusion. Migration, trade, travel, and conquest result in the spread of ideas and technology. Strains within the social structure, such as gross social inequalities, also force change. One of the most powerful factors in change is shifting populations. Large and rapid changes in birth rates, death rates or migration force societies to adapt.

Human action, both individual and collective, promotes social change. Key individuals may play an important role in initiating social change because of the context of the time in which they live and the preparatory work that has already been done. Collective human action through social movements is another engine of social change.

Several theories have been developed to explain social change. Evolutionary theories are grounded in a view that societies "naturally" change from the simple to the more complex. Governments should not intervene in this natural process of change and progress. Cyclical theories explain social change by analogy to the human life cycle of birth, maturity, and death. Some cyclical theorists hold that decline is not inevitable if society learns from history and takes specific, effective action to meet the challenges it faces. Functionalist theories see societies as stable social systems that are upset by social change. Change is an irritant, and adjustments to it allow society to return to a state of equilibrium or stability. When societies change, their institutions become more differentiated (distinct and separate) and require closer integration and coordination. Conflict theories see change as arising from internal strains within society.

Evolutionary and cyclical theories provide a useful framework and starting point for understanding social change. Conflict theories highlight the internal strains that may cause social change; functionalist theory points to the ways societies respond to change to preserve their equilibrium.

Modernity did not occur uniformly across the globe. Third World societies have a lower standard of living, poorer health conditions, a shorter life expectancy, and a lower literacy rate than the more developed countries. Four theories attempt to explain this variation in modernity around the world. Modernization theory emphasizes the technological development that led to tremendous economic advance. This theory suggests that Third World countries need only follow the model of the United States, most of Western Europe, and Japan to achieve the same level of modernization. Convergence theory, a variant of modernization theory, stresses the convergence or growing similarity of all industrial states.

Dependency theory, on the other hand, argues that modernization and convergence theories underestimate the changed nature of the world; they point in particular to the domination of the world economy by the developed industrial societies. The model of change of the developed societies is seen as inappropriate for Third World countries because of different economic circumstances. World systems theory develops this notion further, arguing that the present capitalist-oriented world economy is composed of a three-tiered system. A core group of industrial societies dominates a periphery of poorer societies. The core-peripheral connection is, in essence, a neocolonial relationship. The third tier is made up of the semiperiphery of states that move between the core and the periphery; they have some control over their own economies but are still subject to substantial influence by the core. The peripheral states' problems are rooted in their dependency on exports and prices controlled by the core, the staggering amount of debt they have accumulated, and the growing influence of multinational corporations on their economic and political structures. The inability of this model to locate the socialist countries of Eastern Europe in a suitable tier and the rapid modernization of some Third World countries have raised questions about its adequacy.

Finally, modernization does not always mean progress. Though bringing undoubted benefits, modernization has not uniformly benefited all societies. Some of the technological advances that led to modernization have increased the destructive power of nations and resulted in possible limitations on freedom and personal privacy. Also, social change—and progress—does not always move in a straight line. On balance, however, most sociologists believe that the world has benefited from modernization.

Glossary

absolute monarchies	Kings and, less frequently, queens rule with virtually no restrictions on their power.
achieved status	Statuses that depend on qualities over which the individual has some control.
acquaintance rape	Forced sexual intercourse by someone who is known or engaged in a social activity such as a date with the victim.
active crowds	An excited and emotional collection of individuals that often vent emotions through violent and destructive action.
activity (substitution) theory	Points out the importance of a high level of social activity to the personal satisfaction and sense of self among the elderly.
adversarial legal system	Lawyers for the defense and for the government (the prosecution) battle to establish the legitimacy of their position on the guilt or innocence of the accused.
affirmative action	Setting goals and timetables for increasing the number of minority group members in such organizations as business establishments, government offices, and educational institutions.
ageism	A belief that one age category is inherently inferior to other age categories and thus unequal treatment is justified.
agrarian societies	Societies based on the cultivation of large-scale agriculture using the technology of the plow driven by various draft animals.
altercasting	The other (alter) is presented with (cast into) a particular identity that will constrain behavior.
alternative movements	A form of social movement that seek limited change by individuals in their own behavior.
animism	A belief in the activity of "spirits" in the world.
anomie	A situation where the typical norms that guide behavior are no longer appropriate or effective.
applied scientific research	Focuses on developing new knowledge or on how to use existing knowledge for some identifiable purpose.

ascetic Abstain from worldly pleasures.

ascribed status Conferred on a person by society or some group without the specific individual's input, and for qualities over which the individual has little control.

assimilation When a minority group modifies its distinctive characteristics and ways of life to conform to the pattern of the dominant group.

audience effects Individuals working on their own but with the knowledge that they are visible to others.

authoritarian personalities Having a distinctive set of traits—conformity, intolerance, and insecurity—that result in their being prejudiced.

authoritarianism A political system in which people are excluded from serious participation in political life and the leader(s) generally cannot be removed from office by lawful means.

automation The replacement of workers by machines.

basic conflict Conflict over the fundamental norms of the situation.

basic scientific research Seeks to generate new knowledge irrespective of any immediately recognizable practical use.

beliefs Ideas that have not as yet gained sufficient empirical support to be seen as unequivocally true.

bicameral legislature Two different legislative bodies.

bilateral descent Traces descent equally through both the men and women on the father's side and both the men and women on the mother's side.

bilocal residence Residential rule that allows the new couple to choose between living with or near the bride's family or the groom's family.

blended family Two parents, at least one of whom brings to this new family unit one or more children from a previous marriage (see **reconstituted family**).

blue collar occupations Those occupations that involve considerable manual labor and are often closely supervised.

bureaucracy Formal administrative structure that is responsible for planning, supervising, and coordinating the work of the various segments of an organization.

bureaucratic authority Authority that is tied to a particular position rather than to a qerson.

capitalism An economic system in which the natural resources and the means of production and distribution are privately owned.

capitalists Those who own the means of production.

caste system "Closed" stratification system in which position is determined by the family into which a person is born; change in that position is not usually possible.

casual crowd A collection of individuals that forms spontaneously because some common event captures their attention, but who engage in little if any interaction with each other.

centrally regulated economies The state plays the major role in the economic activities of society.

charisma Extraordinary personal qualities of a particular person that attracts and holds followers.

charismatic authority Authority that derives from the extraordinary personal qualities of the leader that inspire commitment and command obedience.

church A religious organization that is well integrated into the surrounding society, and asserts a claim to be the only legitimate road to religious truth.

cities	Permanent concentrations of a relatively large number of people who do not grow their own food.
class system	Form of "open" stratification in which the position a person has at birth is capable of being changed.
closed-ended questionnaire	A questionnaire containing a set of possible answers from which the respondent is asked to choose an answer.
co-action effects	Influence on people's behavior of the fact that others are involved with them in a similar activity.
cohabitation	An intimate relationship in which an unmarried couple share a household.
cohesiveness	The degree to which members of a group feel bound to one another.
collective behavior	The somewhat spontaneous and short-lived social actions of a relatively large number of people in ambiguous situations.
communism	The evolution of socialism—with its collectivist orientation and structure—into a society of economic, political, and social equality.
community	A social group that not only shares an identity and structured pattern of interaction, but also a common geographical territory.
concentric zone model	Theory of the growth of cities through a series of concentric circles, with a different land use pattern for each ring.
conflict theory	Theory that focuses on the conflict and competition between various elements in society (emanates from the work of Karl Marx).
conglomerates	Mammoth corporations that consist of a number of medium to large corporations.
consequential religiosity	The degree of integration of religion into everyday activities.
consolidated Metropolitan Statistical Area (CMSA)	An urban area with a population of at least a million that meets several other criteria.
constitutional monarchies	Monarch is the symbolic head of the state but real political power rests with a government that derives its power from some form of constitution.
contagion theory	An explanation of crowd behavior as a result of a "collective mind", the loss of individual identity as a result of the "contagious" spread of emotions aroused in the situation.
control group	A group that is identical to an "experimental group" except that it is not subject to the experimental variable.
control theory	A theory that argues that criminal behavior results from a lack of internal control by the individual or appropriate and effective external social control mechanisms by society.
controls	Various techniques of eliminating other factors that may confuse the relationship between the variables being studied.
conventional crowd	People who have gathered for some specific purpose and whose actions are guided to some extent by existing social norms.
convergence theories	An explanation of crowd behavior in terms of like-minded individuals who are drawn to a situation and then act in common because of the existing similarities of personality. Also used to suggest that modernizing societies become increasingly similar as a result of the modernizing process.
cooptation	Bringing people into the system who might threaten its continuity or very existence.
core sector	The sector of the economy that contains quite large organizations.

core states   In world systems theory, these are the powerful military and industrial societies.

corporate capitalism   An economic system in which several dozen very large corporations dominate the economy.

corporations   Formal organizations that have a legal existence, power, and liabilities that are separate from their owners or managers and wield considerable power in society.

correlation   A link between variables.

cottage industry   An economic system in which goods are produced in the home and then typically sold in large outdoor markets.

counterculture   A pattern of beliefs, values, norms, and lifestyles that are in direct opposition to the larger, societal cultural patterns.

Coup d'etat.   The replacement of leader(s) though the same political system continues.

crazes   Temporary forms of expressive mass behavior.

credentialism   Refers to the fact that evidence of a certain level of education is often a requirement for a job whether or not the educational skills are necessary to perform well in that position.

crime   Violations of those cultural norms that have been enacted into law.

crowd   A temporary and unorganized collection of individuals in close proximity to one another who have a common focus.

crude birth rate   The number of live births in any given year per each 1,000 people in the population.

crude death rate   The number of deaths in any given year per 1,000 population.

cult   A form of religious organization that has an antagonistic relationship with the surrounding society, though it accepts the legitimacy of other religious forms.

cultural diffusion   Spread of inventions, technology or aspects of the nonmaterial culture from one social group to another.

cultural lag   The tendency of the material culture to change more rapidly than the adjustments necessary in the relevant nonmaterial culture.

cultural relativism   The idea that no cultural practice is inherently good or bad; each has to be judged in the context of its overall configuration.

culture   The learned, socially-transmitted heritage of artifacts, knowledge, beliefs, values and normative expectations that provides the members of a particular society with the tools for coping with recurrent problems.

data   Observable information such as facts and statistics.

debt trap   Countries who owe enormous sums of money to the core countries as a result of necessary borrowing to develop their economies.

defer gratification   To put off the need for immediate pleasure for more long term benefits.

definition of the situation   Attributed meaning in a social context.

democracy   A political system in which the authority of the state rests ultimately with the people.

democratic socialism   Elements of both a market and centrally controlled economy are used to reduce social inequalities. (See also **welfare state**.)

demographic transition   A change in the birth and death rates, which affect population growth.

demography   Study of population trends.

denomination   A church-like organization that is generally integrated into society but does not claim exclusive legitimacy for its belief system.

dependency theory A theory that points out that Third World countries did not modernize because they were dependent on the more developed countries to whom their present state was more useful economically and politically.

dependent variable A variable that is influenced by another variable.

deprivation theory An explanation of the initiation of social movements due to a relatively large number of individuals who feel deprived of what they believe is necessary for their well-being and happiness.

detached observation An observation in which the researcher remains outside of what is being observed.

deterrence The view that punishment will prevent future crime either by the specific criminal or by others for whom it will serve as a warning.

developmental socialization Socialization after childhood that is continuous with that which took place before.

dharma In Hindu society, the belief that there is a moral force in society that requires the acceptance of certain responsibilities.

dictatorship A political system in which power is obtained and exercised by a single individual.

differential association Theory that criminality is learned in the course of socialization. Through interaction with "significant others" individuals develop the kinds of beliefs, attitudes and values that make them more or less willing to conform to social norms, including deviance.

differentiation The creation of different social institutions to deal with recurrent societal problems.

diffusion The spread of cultural traits from one society to another.

diffusion of responsibility Presence of co-actors leads to a shared obligation for any action and a lessening of individual responsibility.

discovery The uncovering of some existing idea or principle.

discrimination The unequal treatment of people based on their membership in a group or social category.

disease A circumstance that occurs when some medically-diagnosed pathology is seen as the cause of illness.

disengagement theory A theory which argues the need for the elderly to disengage gradually from positions of social responsibility for the orderly transition required in society.

distributive justice The view that people expect to receive benefits in social interaction that are roughly proportional to the costs they have incurred.

domination The dominant group uses its power to maintain control over minority groups, granting them little power or freedom.

double descent A straight linear combination of the matrilineal and patrilineal descent systems. Heritage is traced through the men (but not the women) on the father's side and the women (but not the men) on the mother's side.

doubling time The number of years it takes a population to double in size.

dramaturgical approach Use of the language and conceptual framework of the theater to examine social interaction.

dual-earner family A family in which both partners work outside the home.

dysfunctions Negative consequences.

ecological approach A perspective that focuses on the interplay between people and their physical environment.

economy The social institution responsible for distributing the necessary goods and services required in collective life.

ecosystem	A system created by the interaction of a community of organisms with its environment.
egalitarian	Family authority is vested in both the man and the woman.
ego	In psychoanalytic theory, that part of personality that is in contact with reality.
emergent-norms theory	A theory that explains crowd behavior in terms of social norms that arise out of the interaction among participants in a collective event.
emigrants	The number of people leaving a society.
endogamy	The rules specifying the class of persons with whom marriage is both permissible and encouraged.
epidemiology	Study of the origin, distribution, and transmission of disease within a population.
eros	In psychoanalytic theory, the "life instinct".
ethnic group	Those who share a common cultural heritage that marks them as distinct.
ethnocentrism	The tendency to view one's culture as morally superior to others and to judge the others by one's own culture's standards.
ethnomethod-ology	A social psychological perspective that directs attention to the often unanalyzed rules that guide and structure our interactions with others.
eufunctions	Positive consequences.
exogamy	The rule that defines a class of individuals who are not acceptable as marriage (or sexual) partners.
experiential religiosity	The degree of emotional tie people feel toward their religion.
experimental group	A group of subjects that is exposed to some experimental variable.
experiments	Collection of data under controlled conditions in order to establish whether there is a cause and effect relationship among the relevant variables.
export dependent	Countries that are no longer able to control the prices for their goods, which are set by the industrialized countries of the core.
expressive crowds	A type of crowd that develops around emotionally-charged events.
expressive leadership	Leader who creates harmony and solidarity within the group.
extended family	Consists of two or more nuclear families linked by the parent-child tie, which includes the bonds of siblings.
fads	Forms of behavior that are followed enthusiastically by large numbers of people for a relatively short period of time.
family	A relatively permanent social group of individuals connected by ancestry, marriage or adoption.
fashions	Particular styles of behavior or appearance that are in vogue at a particular time.
fecundity	The potential number of children that could be born to the average woman of childbearing age.
feminism	A social movement organized to eliminate sexism against women.
fertility	The actual number of children born to the average woman over her childbearing years.
folkways	Routine conventions of everyday life.
formal organizations	Large secondary groups deliberately created to accomplish a specific goal or set of goals.
functional equivalents	Social or cultural features that have the same effect and may be substituted for other social or cultural features.

functional illiteracy	The lack of basic reading and writing skills to deal with the necessities of every day life.
fundamentalism	A rigid commitment to traditional basic religious beliefs and practices.
gemeinschaft	A "community" based on strong social ties, tradition, and personal relationships.
gender	The social and cultural traits that different societies assign to males and females.
gender roles	The patterns of behavior, rights and obligations defined as appropriate for each sex.
general theories	Theories that attempt comprehensive explanations.
genocide	The extermination of one class of people by another.
gentrification	The taking over of formerly working class neighborhoods by white collar professionals.
gesellschaft	An "association" of people with weak social ties resulting from considerable social diversity and characterized by impersonal relationships.
gestures	Movements of the body (or parts of the body, like facial expressions) that have socially agreed-upon meaning.
golden parachute	An agreement to senior executives of substantial severance pay in the event of a takeover.
green revolution	The development and use of new agricultural practices to improve food production.
greenmail	The threat of a hostile investor (individual or corporation) to acquire a large body of the corporation's stock and to take control if the stock is not bought back at a higher level than its initial purchase price.
group	Two or more individuals who have a shared sense of identity and who interact with one another in structured ways on the basis of a common set of expectations for each other's behavior.
group marriage	Two or more men are collectively married to two or more women.
health	A state of physical, mental, and social well-being and not merely the absence of disease or infirmity.
horizontal social mobility	Movement from one social position to another of approximately equal status.
horticultural societies	Type of society based on the cultivation of plants.
hunting and gathering societies	Type of society based on foraging for edible foods, hunting animals, and fishing using simple technologies of primarily wood and stone.
hypotheses	Statements about how two or more variables are connected or about how one or more variables will or will not change as certain specified conditions are altered.
I	In symbolic interaction theory, the novel, creative, unpredictable phase of the self.
id	In psychoanalytic theory, the storage bin of universal biological drives, which often demand immediate satisfaction.
ideal type	Purified model of a concept against which a real world example can be compared.
ideological religiosity	The strength of commitment to a religious belief system.
ideology	A set of beliefs to justify a particular social arrangement or action.
illegitimate power	Power that depends on coercion, the use or threat of force, to compel compliance.
illness	Personal construct, a feeling that one is unwell.
immigrants	The number of people entering the society.
incarceration	A method used to confine, lock up, and restrict criminals from the normal activities of ordinary citizens.

incest taboo A rule that excludes close relatives from marriage to one another.

income Salaries, wages, and investments.

independent variable A variable that influences other variables.

industrial societies Type of society based on the use of complex, power-driven machinery to produce material goods.

infant mortality rate The number of deaths within the first year of life for each 1,000 live births in a given year.

ingroup Groups that persons belong to and with which they have a sense of identity and loyalty.

innovation A form of adaptation in which a person accepts the standard cultural goals but does not accept the socially-sanctioned means of obtaining those goals.

institutional discrimination Actions that may not have been intended to be discriminatory but have that effect nonetheless.

institutional racism Practices that have the effect of treating one racial group as less worthy than another, deserving less equal treatment.

institutional sexism The belief in the inherent superiority of males that is woven into the social fabric and affects the social and economic opportunities of women whether personally intended or not.

instrumental leadership Leader who moves the group toward accomplishing the goals of the group.

integration The relative coordination of the activities of social institutions.

intellectual religiosity The range and depth of knowledge about the traditions, beliefs, and practices of a religion.

intergenerational social mobility Change in the social position of children relative to their parents.

interlocking directorates Social networks of individuals who sit on the Boards of Directors of several corporations.

interview A technique of data collection that asks a set of general questions of respondents, allowing them to answer freely in their own words.

intragenerational social mobility Change in the social position of individuals within their lifetime.

invention The new use or new combination of existing knowledge.

jen The central concept of Confucianism of being humane.

juntas Military dictatorships that result from the overthrow of a regime by military forces, who then place their own leaders in power.

juvenile delinquency The violation of legal norms by those who are below the age at which the law treats them as adults.

karma The Hindu belief in the spiritual progress of each person's soul.

knowledge Ideas for which there is some measure of empirical evidence.

kumbh Mela The obligation of Hindus to make a pilgrimage to bathe in the ritually purifying waters of the sacred Ganges River.

labelling theory A theory of deviance that some people have the power to categorize certain actions as appropriate or not, thereby creating deviants.

language A socially constructed set of significant symbols.

latent functions Unintended or unexpected consequences.

laws	Norms that have been established by the political authority of the society and are enforced by them.
legitimate power	The use of power by those seen as having the right to do so.
liberation theology	The belief of some priests that their role is not only to work for spiritual salvation, but also to promote social and economic change that will improve the material conditions of the poor. Its roots lie in Marxist ideology.
life expectancy	How long, on average, a person born in a particular time is likely to live.
life span	The maximum length of life possible.
lobbying	Activities engaged in to affect the legislative process and executive decisions by trying to persuade the authorities to promote the groups' interest.
looking glass self	A conception we have of ourselves that is derived from our reaction to the imagined perceptions that others have of us.
lower class	Individuals who either do not work at all or whose income is such that it needs to be supplemented by the government.
macro-level theories	Theories that focus mainly on large scale social units.
manifest functions	Consequences that are known or expected.
(The) Market	Underlying economic forces.
market economy	Economic systems in which the states do not intervene in the economic activities of the society.
marriage	The socially approved arrangement by which a family is created.
mass behavior	Situations in which people respond similarly to an event though they may be physically scattered.
mass hysteria	The rapid spread of fear and furious activity in response to the perceived threat of some powerful force.
mass society theory	An explanation of social movements as a consequence of the social isolation and feelings of insignificance experienced by large numbers of people in modern mass society.
master status	A key status that has great weight in social interactions and in social identity.
material culture	All the tangible creations of society, those that have a concrete existence
matriarchy	Family authority is vested in the woman.
matrilineal descent	The rule that traces heritage only through the female line.
matrilocal residence	The rule that requires the new couple to situate near or with the woman's family.
matthews effect	The tendency of those with already established reputations to reap rewards in science more easily than those less well known.
me	In symbolic interaction theory, the social phase of the self that is the internalized social order that promotes stability.
mechanical solidarity	A form of societal cohesiveness based on the sameness of qualities and activities of individuals.
medicalization of society	The extension of medicine and the medical model into nonmedical areas of social life.
megalopolis	Metropolises that have spread to such an extent that they flow directly into other metropolises.
meritocracy	A society based on the relationship between the qualities of individuals and the rewards they earn.

methodology   A set of generally accepted procedures that directs empirical investigations and provides a way for others to verify the results.

metropolises   Urban areas that contains a large central city with its surrounding suburbs and related satellite cities.

metropolitan Statistical Area (MSA)   An urban area that contains a city with at least 50,000 residents, and a total population of at least 100,000.

micro-level theories   Theories that focus on small-scale social units.

middle class   Individuals of reasonable wealth from business and the professions, and, at the low end, in white collar clerical or service jobs.

middle range theories   Special theories applicable to limited ranges of data.

migration   The movement of people from one geographical location to another to establish a new residence.

migration rate   The annual difference between the number of people entering the society (immigrants) and the number of people leaving (emigrants).

military-industrial complex   Link between weapons-producing companies and the military, and their influence in national policy decisions.

minority group   People who share a common set of cultural or physical characteristics that mark them as different from the dominant group, and for which they often suffer social disadvantages.

mixed motive conflict   Conflict in which neither person wants to win all or lose all.

modernity   A pattern of social organization and social life that is linked to industrialization.

modernization   A cultural, economic, and social process that transforms a preindustrial society to an industrial society.

monarchy   A political system in which power is passed from one generation to another within a single family with little or no participation of the people.

monogamy   Marriage between one man and one woman at a time.

monotheism   The belief in one god.

mores   Norms that are seen as central and significant to the functioning of society and to social life.

multinational corporations   Corporations that have their headquarters in one country but operate in other countries through firms they either own directly or control.

multiple-nuclei model   A theory of city growth based on the view that cities had several "nuclei," separate centers devoted to specific activities.

natural growth rate   The crude death rate in a particular year subtracted from the crude birth rate in the same year.

natural signs   Representations in which there is an inherent, built-in relationship between the sign and that which it is representing.

negative correlation   When the value of one variable increases (or decreases) as the value of the other decreases (or increases).

nirvana   In Buddhism, a state of complete spiritual perfection of the soul so that further reincarnation is no longer necessary.

noble Eightfold Path	In Buddhism, a manner of controlling desires for earthly pleasures by emphasizing right seeing, thinking, speech, action, living, effort, mindfulness, and meditation.
nonbasic conflict	Conflict involving the application of the agreed-upon norms to a specific situation.
non-material culture	The abstract creations of society that are transmitted across generations.
non-unilineal descent	The rule of tracing inheritance through both the male and female side.
normal science	Collecting data to examine current theories about the world.
norms	Social rules and guidelines that prescribe appropriate behavior in particular situations.
nuclear family	A social group consisting of two adults of the opposite sex who maintain a socially sanctioned sexual relationship, with their own or adopted children.
nuclear family of orientation	The family into which we are born and in which we occupy the status of child.
nuclear family of procreation	The family we create through marriage and in which we hold the status of adult.
objective method	A technique to measure social class as a statistical category into which people are placed by the researcher based on some objective indicators presumed to reflect class position.
observational study	A way of examining the actions of individuals or groups by scrutinizing them, often intensively.
oligarchy	A political system of the rule of the many by the few.
open-ended questionnaire	A questionnaire that does not have a predetermined set of possible answers.
opinion leaders	High status individuals who play an important role in shaping the views of the public.
organic solidarity	A form of social cohesiveness in which society is bonded through mutual support and interdependence of its members.
organization	A type of group that is specifically created to carry out a particular task and has a formal structure through which it attempts to accomplish that task.
outgroups	Groups to which persons neither belong nor to which they have any sense of identity or loyalty.
panic	The disorganized flight from some actual or perceived danger.
paradigm	A general set of shared assumptions, concepts, and methods about a certain area of human experience.
parole	The release of prisoners from prison before the end of their maximum sentence on the condition that they behave themselves and remain under the guidance and custody of a parole officer.
participant observation	A method in which a researcher is an active participant in the groups or situations being studied.
participatory democracy	All members of the population are directly involved in political decision-making.
pastoral societies	Type of society based on the domestication of animals.
patriarchy	Family authority is vested in the man.
patrilineal descent	Traces descent only through the male line.
patrilocal residence	A rule that requires a new couple to establish residence near or within the residence of the man.

per capita Gross National Product (GNP)	Total value of all goods produced and services provided in the society divided by the number of people in the society.
peripheral sector	The sector of the economy that involves relatively small firms that are usually located in one geographical region.
periphery states	In world systems theory, the societies that supply the necessary raw materials to the industrialized core and are subservient to them.
personality-based conflict	Conflict due to the personal differences between the individuals involved.
plea bargaining	A negotiation prior to trial to reduce the level of a criminal charge in return for an admission of guilt to a lesser charge.
pluralism	The pattern in which all racial and ethnic groups retain their distinctive identities and enjoy relatively equal social standing.
poison pill	A defensive situation (such as having huge debts) that makes a corporation an unattractive target for an attempted takeover.
political action committee (PAC)	An organization that raises and distributes funds in the political process to promote its goals.
political parties	Organizations of those with similar attitudes and interests who attempt to gain control of political authority.
political reform	A mode of seeking to change the system from within.
political revolution	The attempt to overthrow the existing political system in the hope of establishing a new one.
polity	The political institution of a society.
polyandry	Marriage of a woman to two or more men.
polygamous family	Consists of two or more nuclear families linked by the marital tie.
polygyny	Marriage of a man to two or more women.
polytheism	The belief in the existence of many gods.
population	The total group of people in whom the researcher is interested.
population transfer	The forced removal of one of the contending parties as a solution to intergroup differences.
positive correlation	When the value of one variable increases (or decreases) as the value of the other variable increases (or decreases).
postindustrial society	Type of society in which the main source of subsistence is in the production of information and services rather than material goods.
power	The ability to influence the actions of others.
power elite	Small group of influential people who hold important positions in government, business, and the military.
predestination	The view that God has already selected people for salvation or eternal damnation and nothing the person does in this life can change their fate.
prejudice	An unsupported generalization, a prejudgment, about a group or category of people.
presentation of self	Identity that persons project and for which they attempt to gain agreement from the others in the situation.
prestige	People's social standing or the amount of "social honor", "esteem", or respect they are accorded.

primary deviance	Acts that are defined by society (or a social group) as deviant, but that are not observed or are seen as temporary.
primary group	Small groups in which members have close, personal, and enduring relationships.
primary labor market	Occupations that insure considerable benefits to their practitioners.
primary sector	Part of the economy that is involved in taking or generating resources from the natural environment.
primary sex characteristics	Genitals that are necessary for human reproduction.
principle of cumulative advantage	The maintenance and even strengthening of existing differences in the allocation of societal resources—the essential underpinnings of a system of social stratification.
probation	Allowing convicted criminals to remain outside of prison but subject to a number of restrictions on their activities for a defined period of time.
profane	Anything that is regarded as ordinary and routine.
profession	A job with great social prestige that requires extensive formal education and knowledge.
proletariat	Those who provide the labor necessary to run the factories and other forms of economic enterprise.
pronatalist policy	A policy in which the government seeks to encourage more births.
propaganda	Information or points of view that deliberately attempt to influence and shape public opinion.
protest crowd	A form of crowd that has elements of both the conventional and the active crowd.
psychosomatic disorders	Physical illnesses that are caused or made worse by a person's state of mind.
public	A substantial number of individuals who share an interest in an issue on which opinion is divided.
public opinion	The collective views of a public on a specific issue.
public opinion polls	Surveys to measure public opinion.
questionnaire	A technique to collect data that uses a series of specific questions or issues to which a person is asked to respond.
race	Category of people who they and others consider to be similar because they share some common physical attributes.
random sampling	A sampling procedure that requires that every member of the population has an equal chance of being selected for the sample.
rational-legal authority	Power that is justified by a system of socially accepted rules or regulations.
rationality	An emphasis on the relationship between means and ends.
rebellion	Mode of adaptation that not only fails to accept culturally-approved goals and means, but actually substitutes other goals and means.
reconstituted family	Two parents, at least one of whom brings to this new family unit one or more children from a previous marriage (see **blended family**).
redemptive movements	A form of social movement that attempts to bring about more sweeping and radical changes in individuals.
reference group	Individuals, groups, ideas that are used by people to formulate, compare, and evaluate their behavior.

reform movements	A form of social movement that, though basically satisfied with the existing society, seeks limited change in some specific areas.
regressive movements	A form of social movement that aims to resist social change and to return society to an earlier state.
rehabilitation	An attempt to reform offenders and make their behavior conform to general social norms.
reincarnation	In Buddhism, the belief that after death persons are reborn into a different body in the same spiritual state they earned in the last life.
relative deprivation	Feelings of disadvantage based on a comparison with some standard.
reliability	The belief that if the same study was repeated it would yield similar results.
religion	A system of shared beliefs and rituals that are concerned with the realm of the sacred.
representative democracy	A political system in which the people periodically elect others to represent them in the political decision-making process.
reputational method	A technique to measure social class by asking individuals in a community to identify its social class structure.
resocialization	Uprooting and restructuring of basic attitudes, values or identities.
retreatism	Mode of adaptation by abandoning both the culturally-approved goals and means.
retribution	A view of incarceration as a punitive act to make criminals suffer for their illegal behavior.
retrospective label	Labelling of a person's past identity to make it conform to the present identity.
reverse discrimination	Providing special advantages to members of minority groups.
revolutionary movements	A form of social movement that arises from strong dissatisfaction with the existing society and seeks radical change in terms of specific ideological program to alter society's fundamental structure or practices.
ritual	A formal and stylized set of practices related to the realm of the sacred.
ritual pollution	Rendering the members of the higher caste "unclean" because of the contact with those of a lower caste.
ritualism	A form of adaptation in which persons who do not accept or seem to understand appropriate cultural goals still act in socially-approved ways.
ritualistic religiosity	The extent to which people engage in prayer and attend religious services.
role conflict	A situation in which the role prescriptions for a person's performance have contradictory requirements.
role performance	The actual behavior of the incumbent of a particular role.
role prescriptions	The social norms that are appropriate to a particular status.
role set	The set of relationships a person has as a consequence of occupying a particular social status.
role strain	The result of attempts to meet one or more role prescriptions, which causes stress in efforts to meet other prescriptions embodied in the same social status.
routinization of authority	Transformation of charismatic authority to either traditional form or bureaucratic form or some combination of the two.
rumor	Unsubstantiated information from anonymous sources that is spread informally.
sacred	That which is considered supernatural, beyond the ordinary.
sample	A smaller group of individuals who are selected to be representative of the population.

scapegoating   Placing blame for one's own failings and limitations onto others less powerful.

school-based management   An administrative practice in which the staff in each school cooperates with the administration in making educational decisions.

science   The systematic pursuit of reliable knowledge about the physical and social world through empirical (using the human senses) observation.

scientific revolution   Replacement of one scientific paradigm by another, also referred to as a paradigm shift.

secondary sex characteristics   The different physical attributes of males and females that are not directly related to reproduction.

secondary labor market   Jobs that provide minimal benefits to employees.

secondary sector   Part of the economy that is involved in making manufactured goods from the raw materials generated by the primary sector.

secondary analysis   Analysis of previously collected data.

secondary group   A group which is temporary, being brought together for some specific purpose or task, and in which the relationships are relatively impersonal.

secondary deviance   Public labelling as deviant and the acceptance by the person of the correspondent deviant identity.

sector model   A theory of urban growth that argues that cities grow in wedge-shaped sectors from the center of the city out, often along some transportation route.

sects   An organized form of religion that claims sole legitimacy for religious truth, but does not fit as comfortably with the majority culture.

segregation   The physical and social separation of the different ethnic and racial groups.

self-placement method   A technique to measure social class that involves subjective judgement by asking individuals to identify the class to which they believe they belong.

semiperiphery states   In world systems theory, the states that are between the core and periphery, and move up and down between them.

sex   A biological concept that is used to divide the human species into females and males.

sex ratio   The number of males per 100 females.

sexism   The view that one sex (usually females) is inherently inferior to the other (usually males).

sick role   The expectations that permit variation from typical behavior because of illness.

sickness   A social status that affects how others treat people because of their view that they have some disease.

situational conflict   Conflict that is due to the social context the two people are in.

social aggregates   People who share a common characteristic, a similar status or the same situation (see also social categories).

social area analysis   An approach to urban analysis that seeks to find the common characteristics of people living in the same residential area.

social categories   People who share a common characteristic, a similar status or the same situation (see also social aggregates).

social change   A significant alteration in a society's patterns of culture and social structure that is reflected in social behavior.

social construction of reality   The view that people create and shape the nature of the social world in which they find themselves.

social deviance   Actions that violate social norms but are not part of the legal code.

social differentiation	Distinctions made not between individuals but between entire social categories of individuals.
social dynamics	The examination of social change in society.
social exchange theory	A theory of social interaction as a series of exchanges that have certain costs attached and may bring some benefits.
social institutions	Relatively stable cultural and structural configurations that evolve or are specifically designed to meet the recurrent problems faced by society.
social interaction	The mutual and reciprocal influence that person's exert on one another.
social mobility	The movement of individuals up or down in the class structure.
social movement	Collection of individuals who have organized to promote or resist some cultural or social change.
social network	Social relationships of differing degrees of intimacy and connection.
social statics	The examination of problems of order and stability in society.
social stratification	The ranking of different social categories in some hierarchical order that leads to differing access to social resources.
social structure	The recurrent pattern of relationships among the elements of society.
socialism	An economic system in which the natural resources, the means of production, and the means of distribution are owned collectively and the economy is centrally regulated by the state.
sociobiology	The systematic study of the biological basis of human behavior.
socioeconomic status	A person's position in the class system based on some combination of factors including wealth, power, and prestige.
sociology	The scientific study of human social behavior and human association, and the results of these actions.
special interest groups	Alliances or organizations of people with a similar interest who try to influence the political process on behalf of that interest.
spurious correlation	A correlation that is just coincidental.
state	Principal organized political authority in a society.
state sector	That part of the economy in which goods and services are produced by governmental agencies or under contract to the government.
status	A person's position in a network of social relationships.
status attainment model	An explanation that highlights the individual factors that contribute to a person's social mobility.
status inconsistency	A situation in which there are individuals who experience differences in the various criteria of class.
stereotypes	An inflexible view of a class of people that resists change even in the face of evidence that suggests its falsity.
stigma	A potent negative view that substantially changes a person's sense of self.
structural strain	Results from a lack of clear relationship between culturally supported goals and societally provided means to attain those goals.
structural strain theory	A theory that argues that there are six factors that contribute to the rise of a social movement.

structural-functional perspective	A macro-level theory that focuses on the structural aspects of organisms, their interrelations, and the functions they perform for the organism as a whole.
subculture	Cultural patterns that differ from those of the over-all society of which they are a part, and which have a distinctive flavor and identity.
suburbs	Relatively small urban areas that surround a city.
superego	In psychoanalytic theory, a part of the personality that is similar to what we call our conscience.
supernaturalism	Assumes the existence of forces outside of the ordinary realm, in the supernatural, that influence human events both for good and for bad.
survey	A data collection technique in which people are asked to respond to a series of questions about their characteristics, attitudes, values, perceptions of a situation or events, or behavior.
symbolic interaction	A theory based on the premise that interaction is the primary social process and takes place through symbols.
symbols	Arbitrarily created representations, such as words, gestures, objects, visual images, that acquire meaning through social convention.
system	The idea that the various elements of society are related to one another such that a change in one lead to changes in the others.
taboos	Mores that are proscriptive, defining what should not be done.
tactics	Specific activities designed to accomplish a particular goal.
technology	The application of scientific or other forms of knowledge to the solution of practical problems.
terrorism	The use or threat of violence to accomplish political aims.
tertiary sector	Part of the economy that provides services rather than goods.
thanatos	In psychoanalytic theory, the "death instinct".
theism	A belief in the existence of gods who are presumed to be both powerful and interested in the activities of human beings.
theories	Systematic ways of explaining how two or more phenomena are related to one another.
Torah	In Judaism, the first five books of the Bible.
totalitarianism	An authoritarian government that recognizes no limit to its authority and seeks to intrude and regulate practically every aspect of social life.
tracking	Assigning students to a particular educational program on the basis of ability levels.
traditional authority	Authority based on custom or long-established cultural traditions.
transcendent idealism	A form of religion that focuses on sacred principles of beliefs and actions rather than worship of supernatural forces or beings.
unilineal descent	The rule of tracing descent through only one parental line.
upper class	Individuals whose families have had wealth and prestige, and occasionally power, over several generations.
urbanization	The process of concentrating populations in a limited area called a city.
utopian movements	A form of social movement that seeks radical restructuring of society but lacks a specific blueprint to do so.
validity	Measurements that represent an accurate portrayal of reality.
values	Abstract ideas of what a society believes to be good, right, and desirable.

variable	A trait or characteristic that changes or has different values under different conditions.
vertical social mobility	Change from one social position to another of either higher or lower rank.
wealth	Total value of the money and valuable goods that a person or family controls.
welfare state	Elements of both a market and centrally controlled economy are used to reduce social inequalities. (See also **democratic socialism**.)
white collar crime	Criminal activities by high status, seemingly respectable people who are well integrated into their communities.
white collar occupations	Those occupations that involve mental activity more than manual labor and are relatively free from extensive supervision.
working class	Those earning a living in manual labor.
world systems theory	A macro-level theory that explores the relationship between the developed and less developed countries in the context of economic, geographical, historical, and political factors.
zero population growth	An average fertility rate of 2.1 children per woman.
zero-sum conflict	Conflict in which a person either wins everything or loses everything.

Bibliography

Adler, Freda and Herbert M. Adler. 1979. "Female Delinquency: Minor Girls and Major Crimes." Pp. 523–53 in *Deviant Behavior: Readings in the Sociology of Deviance*, edited by Delos H. Kelly. New York: St. Martin's Press.

Adorno, Theodor W., Else Frenkel–Brunswik, Daniel J. Levinson,and R. Nevitt Sanford. 1950. *The Authoritarian Personality*. New York: Harper.

Aldrich, Howard and Ellen R. Auster. 1986. "Even Dwarfs Started Small: Liabilities of Age and Sex and their Strategic Implications". *Research in Organization Behavior* 8:165–198.

Allport, Floyd H. 1924. *Social Psychology*. Boston: Houghton.

Ariés, Philippe. 1962. *Centuries of Childhood: A Social History of the American Family*. New York: Knopf.

Ariés, Philippe. 1974. *Western Attitudes Toward Death: From the Middle Ages to the Present*. Baltimore, MD: Johns Hopkins University Press.

Arluke, Arnold, Lorianne Kennedy and Ronald C. Kessler. 1979. "Reexamining the Sick Role Concept: An Empirical Assessment". *Journal of Health and Social Behavior* 20:432–439.

Asch, Solomon. 1952. *Social Psychology*. Englewood Cliffs, NJ: Prentice–Hall.

Bales, Robert F. and Philip E. Slater. 1955. "Role Differentiation in Small Decision-Making Groups". Pp. 259–306 in *Family, Socialization and Interaction Process*, T. Parsons and R.F. Bales. New York: Free Press.

Bales, Robert F., Fred L. Strodtbeck, Theodore M. Mills, and Mary E. Roseborough. 1951. "Channels of Communication in Small Groups". *American Sociological Review* 16:461–468.

Baltes, Paul B. and K. Warner Schaie. 1974. "The Myth of the Twilight Years". *Psychology Today* 7:35–39.

Barash, David. 1977. *Sociobiology and Behavior*. New York: Elsevier.

Becker, Howard S., et al. 1961. *Boys in White: Student Culture in Medical School*. Chicago: Chicago University Press.

Belkin, Gary S. and Norman Goodman. 1980. *Marriage, Family, and Intimate Relationships*. Chicago: Rand McNally.

Bell, Daniel. 1977. *The Coming of Postindustrial Society*. New York: Basic Books.

Bendix, Rinehart and Seymour Martin Lipset (eds.). 1966. *Class, Status and Power*. 2nd Edition. New York: Free Press.

Benedict, Ruth. 1934. *Patterns of Culture*. Boston: Houghton Mifflin.

Berger, Joseph, Bernard P. Cohen, and Morris Zelditch, Jr. 1972. "Status Conceptions and Social Interaction". *American Sociological Review* 37:241–255.

Berger, Peter and Thomas Luckmann. 1963. *The Social Construction of Reality*. New York: Doubleday.

Bernard, L.L. 1924. *Instincts*. New York: Holt, Rinehart and Winston.

Berry, Brian L. and Philip H. Rees. 1969. "The Factorial Ecology of Calcutta." *American Journal of Sociology* 74:445–491.

Blau, Peter M. and Otis Dudley Duncan. 1967. *The American Occupational Structure*. New York: Wiley.

Blood, Robert O. and Donald Wolfe. 1960. *Husbands and Wives: The Dynamics of Married Living*. Glencoe, IL: Free Press.

Blumer, Herbert G. 1969. "Collective Behavior". Pp. 65–121 in *Principles of Sociology*, 3rd edition, edited by A. M. Lee. New York: Barnes and Noble Books.

Blumstein, Philip and Pepper Schwartz. 1983. *American Couples: Money, Work, Sex*. New York: Morrow.

Bock, Kenneth. 1981. *Human Nature and History: A Response to Sociobiology*. New York: Columbia University Press.

Borukoo, Eli, Yona Ginsberg, and Elia Werczberger. 1979. "The Social Ecology of Tel Aviv–A Study in Factor Analysis". *Urban Affairs Quarterly* 15:183–205.

Bowlby, John. 1969. *Attachment and Loss*. Vol. 1. New York: Basic Books.

Bowles, Samuel and Herbert Gintis. 1976. *Schooling in Capitalist America: Educational Reforms and the Contradictions of Economic Life*. New York: Basic Books.

Brim, Orville G., Jr. 1960. "Personality Development as Role Learning". Pp. 127–157 in *Personality Development in Children*, edited by Ira Iscoe and Harold Stevenson. Austin: University of Texas Press.

Brim, Orville G., Jr. and Stanton Wheeler. 1966. *Socialization After Childhood: Two Essays*. New York: Wiley.

Brinton, Crane. 1965. *The Anatomy of a Revolution*. New York: Vintage.

Broad, William and Nicholas Wade. 1982. *Betrayers of the Myth*. New York: Simon and Schuster.

Brownstein, Ronald and Nina Easton. 1983. *Reagan's Ruling Class: Portraits of the President's Top One Hundred Officials*. New York: Pantheon.

Burns, James A. 1985. "Discipline: Why Does it Continue to be a Problem? Solution is in Changing School Culture". *National Association of Secondary School Principals Bulletin* 69:1–47.

Busby, Linda J. 1975. "Sex Role Research on the Mass Media". *Journal of Communication* 25:107–131.

Callaway, M.R. and J. K. Esser. 1984. "Groupblink: Effects of Cohesiveness and Problem-Solving in Group Decision Making". *Social Behavior and Personality* 12:157–164.

Calmore, John O. 1986. "National Housing Policies and Black America: Trends, Issues, and Implications". Pp. 115–149 in *The State of Black America 1986*, edited by Janet Dewart. New York: National Urban League.

Cancian, Francesca. 1960. "Functional Analyses of Change". *American Sociological Review* 25:818–827.

Carnegie Foundation for the Advancement of Teaching. 1986. "Report." *Change: The Magazine of Higher Learning*, May–June.

Chandler, Tertius and Gerald Fox. 1974. *3000 Years of Urban History*. New York: Academic Press.

Choldin, Harvey M. 1978. "Urban Density and Pathology".*Annual Review of Sociology* 4:91–113.

Clark, Curtis B. 1986. "Geriatric Abuse: Out of the Closet". Pp. 49–50 in *The Tragedy of Elder Abuse: The Problems and the Response*. Hearings before the Select Committee on Aging, U.S. House of Representatives, July 1, 1986.

Cole, Jonathan and Stephen Cole. 1973. *Social Stratification in Science*. Chicago: University of Chicago Press.

Coleman, James C., Thomas Hoffer, and Sally Kilgore. 1982. *High School Achievement: Public, Catholic, and Private Schools Compared*. New York: Basic Books.

Coleman, James S., et al. 1966. *Equality of Educational Opportunity*. Washington, DC: U.S. Government Printing Office.

Collins, Randall. 1974. *Conflict Sociology: Toward an Explanatory Science*. New York: Academic Press.

Collins, Randall. 1979. *The Credential Society: An Historical Sociology of Education and Stratification*. New York: Academic Press.

Collins, Randall. 1985. *Sociology of Marriage and the Family: Gender, Love, and Property*. Chicago: Nelson Hall.

Cooley, Charles Horton. 1902. *Human Nature and the Social Order*. New York: Scribners.

Coser, Lewis A. 1956. *The Functions of Social Conflict*. Glencoe, IL: Free Press.

Coser, Lewis A. 1967. *Continuities in the Study of Social Conflict*. New York: Free Press.

Coser, Lewis A. 1977. *Masters of Sociological Thought* (2nd edition). New York: Harcourt, Brace, Jovanovich.

Crosbie, Paul. 1975. *Interaction in Small Groups*. New York: Macmillan.

Cummings, Elaine and William E. Henry. 1961. *Growing Old: The Process of Disengagement*. New York: Basic Books.

Curtis, Susan. 1977. *Genie*. New York: Academic Press.

Dahl, Robert. 1961. *Who Governs?* New Haven, CT: Yale University Press.

Dahrendorf, Ralf. 1958. "Toward a Theory of Social Conflict". *Journal of Conflict Resolution* 11:170–183.

Dalmaide, Darrell. 1984. *Debt Shock*. New York: Doubleday.

Daniels, Lee A. 1983. "In Defense of Busing". *New York Times Magazine*, April 17:34–37.

Darley, John and Bibb Latane. 1968. "Bystander Intervention in Emergencies: Diffusion of Responsibilities." *Journal of Personality and Social Psychology* 8:377–383.

Davis, Kingsley. 1940. "Extreme Social Isolation of a Child". *American Journal of Sociology* 45:554–564.

Davis, Kingsley. 1947. "Final Note on a Case of Extreme Isolation."*American Journal of Sociology* 52:432–437.

Davis, Kingsley. 1948. *Human Society*. New York: Macmillan.

Davis, Kingsley and Wilbert Moore. 1945. "Some Principles of Stratification". *American Sociological Review* 10:242–249.

Dennis, Wayne. 1960. "Causes of Retardation Among Institutionalized Children". *Journal of Genetic Psychology* 96:47–59.

Dennis, Wayne. 1973. *Children of the Creche*. New York: Appleton-Century-Crofts.

Dollard, John, et al. 1939. *Frustration and Aggression*. New Haven, CT: Yale University Press.

Domhoff, William. 1967. *Who Rules America?* Englewood Cliffs, NJ: Prentice-Hall.

Domhoff, William. 1983. *Who Rules America Now? A View of the 80s*. Englewood Cliffs, NJ: Prentice-Hall.

Domhoff, William. 1984. "The Growth Machine and the Power Elite: A Theoretical Challenge to Pluralists and Marxists Alike". Paper presented to the American Political Science Association, Washington, D.C.

Doyal, Lesley and Imogen Pennell. 1981. *The Political Economy of Health*. London: Pluto Press.

Dubois, Rene. 1969. *Man, Medicine and Environment*. New York: Mentor.

Durkheim, Emile. 1938 (original, 1895). *The Rules of Sociological Method*. Chicago: University of Chicago Press.

Durkheim, Emile. 1954 (original 1912) *The Elementary Forms of Religious Life*. Joseph W. Swain (trans.). Glencoe, IL: Free Press.

Ehrlich, Paul. 1968. *The Population Bomb*. New York: Ballantine.

Elias, Norbert. 1978. *The Civilizing Process: The History of Manners*. New York: Urizen.

Emerson, Richard. 1962. "Power-dependence Relations".*American Sociological Review* 27(1):31–41.

Engels, Friedrich. 1902 (original 1884).*The Origins of the Family*. Chicago: Charles H. Kerr and Company.

Erikson, Kai T. 1966. *Wayward Puritans: A Study in the Sociology of Deviance*. New York: John Wiley.

Festinger, Leon, Stanley Schachter, and Kurt Back. 1950. *Social Pressures in Informal Groups: A Study of Human Factors in Housing*. New York: Harper and Row.

Fischer, Claude. 1976. *The Urban Experience*. New York: Harcourt Brace Jovanovich.

Forbes, Malcolm. 1987. "The 400 Richest People in America". *Forbes*. Special Issue (October 26, 1987).

Fox, Thomas G. and S.M. Miller. 1965. "Economic, Political and Social Determinants of Mobility: An International Cross-Sectional Analysis." *Acta Sociologica* 9:76–93.

Frank, Andre Gunder. 1969. *Dependent Accumulation and Underdevelopment*. New York: Monthly Review Press.

Freidson, Eliot. 1970. *Professional Dominance*. Chicago: Aldine.

Friedman, Eugene A. and Robert J. Havighurst. 1954. *The Meaning of Work and Retirement*. Chicago: University of Chicago Press.

Gallup, George H. 1982. *Religion in America*. Princeton, NJ: Princeton University Press.

Gallup, George H. 1984. "The 16th Annual Gallup Poll of the Public's Attitudes Toward the Public Schools". *Phi Delta Kappa* 66:23–38.

Gans, Herbert J. 1962. "Urbanism and Suburbanism as Ways of Life: A Reevaluation of Definitions". Pp. 625–648 in *Human Behavior and Social Processes*, edited by Arnold Rose. Boston: Houghton Mifflin.

Gans, Herbert J. 1965. *The Urban Villagers*. New York: Free Press.

Garfinkel, Harold. 1967. *Studies in Ethnomethodology*. Englewood Cliffs, NJ: Prentice-Hall.

Gergen, Kenneth J. 1969. *The Psychology of Behavior Exchange*. Reading, MA: Addison-Wesley.

Gilligan, Carol. 1982. *In a Different Voice*. Cambridge, MA: Harvard University Press.

Glock, Charles Y. 1959. "The Religious Revival in America". Pp. 25–42 in *Religion and the Face of America*, edited by Jane Zahn. Berkeley: University of California Press.

Glueck, Sheldon and Eleanor Glueck. 1950. *Unraveling Juvenile Delinquency*. New York: Commonwealth Fund.

Goffman, Erving. 1959. *The Presentation of the Self in Everyday Life*. Garden City, NY: Anchor.

Goffman, Erving. 1961. *Asylums: Essays in the Social Structure of the Mental Patient and Other Inmates*. Chicago: Aldine.

Goffman, Erving. 1963. *Stigma: Notes on the Management of Spoiled Identity*. Englewood Cliffs, NJ: Prentice-Hall.

Goffman, Erving. 1976. *Gender Advertisements*. New York: Harper and Row.

Goode, William J. 1959. "The Theoretical Importance of Love". *American Sociological Review* 24:38–47.

Goodman, Norman and Gary T. Marx. 1978. *Society Today* (3rd Edition). New York: Random House.

Goodman, Norman and Gary T. Marx. 1982. *Society Today* (4th Edition). New York: Random House.

Goodman, Norman and Richard Ofshe. 1968. "Empathy, Communication Efficiency and Marital Status." *Journal of Marriage and the Family* 30:596–603.

Goring, Charles. 1913. *The English Convict*. London: His Majesty's Stationery Office.

Gouldner, Alvin P. 1960. "The Norm of Reciprocity". *American Sociological Review* 25:161–178.

Gove, Walter R. (Editor). 1980. *The Labeling of Deviance: Evaluating a Perspective*. Beverly Hills, CA: Sage.

Granovetter, Mark S. 1973. "The Strength of Weak Ties". *American Journal of Sociology* 77:1360–1380.

Hadden, Jeffrey K. and Charles E. Swain. 1981. *Prime Time Preachers: The Rising Power of Televangelism*. Reading, MA: Addison-Wesley.

Harlow, Harry F. 1958. "The Nature of Love". *American Psychologist* 13:673–685.

Harlow, Harry F. and Margaret K. Harlow. 1965. "The Affectional System". Pp. 287–334 in *Behavior of Nonhuman Primates: Modern Research Trends*, edited by A. M. Schrier, H. F. Harlow, and F. Stollnitz. New York: Academic Press.

Harris, Chauncey D. and Edward L. Ullman. 1945. "The Nature of Cities". *The Annals* 242:7–17.

Hartley, Eugene L. and Ruth E. Hartley. 1961. *Fundamentals of Social Psychology*. New York: Knopf.

Hauser, Robert M. and David L. Featherman. 1978. *Opportunity and Change*. New York: Academic Press.

Hirschi, Travis. 1969. *Causes of Delinquency*. Berkeley: University of California Press.

Hochschild, Arlie Russell. 1989. *The Second Shift: Working Parents and the Revolution at Home*. New York: Viking.

Homans, George. 1950. *The Human Group*. New York: Harcourt Brace Jovanovich.

Homans, George. 1961. *Social Behavior: Its Elementary Forms*. New York: Harcourt, Brace and World.

Hoyt, Homer. 1939. *The Structure and Growth of Residential Neighborhoods in American Cities*. Washington, DC: U.S. Government Printing Office.

Hunter, Floyd. 1953. *Community Power Structure*. Chapel Hill, NC: University of North Carolina Press.

Hunter, Floyd. 1980. *Community Power Succession: Atlanta's Policy-Makers Revisited*. Chapel Hill, NC: University of North Carolina Press.

Hyde, Janet S. 1985. *Half the Human Experience: The Psychology of Women*, 3rd edition. Lexington, MA: Lexington Books.

Jensen, Arthur. 1969. "How Much Can We Boost IQ and Scholastic Achievement." *Harvard Educational Review* 39:273–274.

Kamin, Leon. 1974. *The Science and Politics of IQ*. Hillsdale, NJ: Erlbaum.

Kanter, Rosabeth Moss. 1977. *Men and Women of the Corporation*. New York: Basic Books.

Kennedy, Paul. 1987. *The Rise and Fall of Great Powers*. New York: Random House.

Kessler, Ronald C. and Paul D. Cleary. 1980. "Social Class and Psychological Distress". *American Sociological Review* 45:463–478.

Klapp, Orin. 1969. *Collective Search for Identity*. New York: Holt, Rinehart and Winston.

Kluckhohn, Clyde. 1949. *Mirror for Man*. New York: McGraw–Hill.

Knorr–Cetina, Karen. 1981. *The Manufacture of Knowledge: An Essay on the Constructivist and Contextual Nature of Science*. New York: Pergamon.

Kohlberg, Laurence. 1969. "Stage and Sequence: The Cognitive Developmental Approach to Socialization". Pp. 347–480 in *Handbook of Socialization Theory and Research*, edited by D.A. Goslin. Chicago: Rand MacNally.

Kohn, Melvin L. 1963. "Social Class and Parent–Child Relationships: An Interpretation." *American Journal of Sociology* 68:471–480.

Kohn, Melvin L. 1969. *Class and Conformity: A Study in Values*. Homewood, IL: Dorsey.

Kohn, Melvin L. 1976. "Occupational Structure and Alienation". *American Journal of Sociology* 82:111–130.

Kohn, Melvin L. 1977. *Class and Conformity: A Study in Values*. (2nd Edition). Homewood, IL: Dorsey.

Kohn, Melvin L. 1978. "The Benefits of Bureaucracy". *Human Nature* 1:60–66.

Kohn, Melvin L. and Carmi Schooler. 1983. *Work and Personality*. Norwood, NJ: Ablex.

Kornhauser, William. 1959. *The Politics of Mass Society*. New York: Free Press.

Kuhn, Thomas S. 1962. *The Structure of Scientific Revolutions*. Chicago: University of Chicago Press.

Kumar, Krishna (ed.). 1980. *Transactional Enterprises: Their Impact on Third World Societies and Cultures*. Boulder, CO: Westview.

Landry, Bart. 1987. *The New Black Middle Class*. Berkeley: University of California Press.

Lane, David. 1984. "Social Stratification and Class". Pp. 563–605 in *The Soviet Polity in the Modern Era*, edited by Erik P. Hoffman and Robbin F. Laird. New York: Aldine.

Lane, Harlan. 1976. *The Wild Boy of Aveyron*. Cambridge, MA: Harvard University Press.

Lang, Kurt and Gladys Engel Lang. 1968. *Television and Politics*. Chicago: Quadrangle.

Latour, Bruno and Steven Woolgar. 1986. *Laboratory Life*. (2nd edition). Princeton, NJ: Princeton University Press.

LeBon, Gustave. 1960 (original 1895). *The Crowd: A Study of the Popular Mind*. New York: Viking.

Lenski, Gerhard. 1966. *Power and Privilege: A Theory of Social Stratification*. New York: McGraw–Hill.

Lenski, Gerhard and Jean Lenski. 1987. *Human Societies: An Introduction to Macrosociology*. (5th Edition). New York: McGraw–Hill.

Lever, Janet. 1978. "Sex Differences in the Complexity of Children's Play and Games." *American Sociological Review* 43:471–483.

Lewontin, R.C., Steven Rose and Leon Kamin. 1984. *Not in Our Genes: Biology, Ideology and Human Nature*. New York: Pantheon.

Light, Donald. 1991. "Role Protection in an Era of Accountability." In *Social Roles and Social Institutions: Essays in Honor of Rose Laub Coser*, edited by Judith R. Blau and Norman Goodman. Boulder, CO: Westview.

Linton, Ralph. 1936. *The Study of Man*. New York: Appleton-Century-Crofts.

Linton, Ralph. 1945. *The Cultural Background of Personality*. New York: Free Press.

Lombroso, Cesare. 1896–97. *Uomo Delinquente*. Torino, Italy: Bocca.

Luker, Kristin. 1985. *Abortion and the Politics of Motherhood*. Berkeley: University of California Press.

Mahler, Halfdan. 1980. "People". *Scientific American* 243:67–77.

Major, Brenda. 1981. "Gender Patterns in Touching Behavior". Pp. 15–37 in *Gender and Nonverbal Behavior*, edited by Clara Mayo and Nancy M. Kenley. New York: Springer-Verlag.

Malinowksi, Bronislaw. 1948. *Magic, Science and Religion*. Glencoe, IL: Free Press.

Malson, Lucien. 1972. *Wolf Children and the Problems of Human Nature*. New York: Monthly Review Press.

Malthus, Thomas Robert. 1926 (original 1798). *First Essay on Population*. London: Macmillan.

Martin, E. D. 1920. *The Behavior of Crowds*. New York: Harper.

Marx, Karl. 1964 (original 1848). *Selected Writings in Sociology and Social Philosophy*. T.B. Bottomore and Maximillian Rubel (eds.). Baltimore, MD: Penguin.

Marx, Karl and Frederick Engels. 1955 (original 1848) *The Communist Manifesto* (S.H. Beer, Editor). New York: Appleton-Century-Crofts.

McCarthy, John D. and Mayer Zald. 1973. *The Trend of Social Movements in America: Professionalization and Resource Mobilization*. Morristown, NJ: General Learning Press.

McCarthy, John D. and Mayer Zald. 1977. "Resource Mobilization and Social Movements: A Partial Theory". *American Journal of Sociology* 82:1212–1241.

McDougall, William. 1908. *An Introduction to Social Psychology*. London: Metheun.

McKeown, Thomas. 1979. *The Role of Medicine: Dream, Mirage or Nemesis?* Princeton, NJ: Princeton University Press.

McPhail, Clark and Ronald T. Wohlstein. 1983. "Individual and Collective Behaviors Within Gatherings, Demonstrations, and Riots." *Annual Review of Sociology* 9:579–600.

Mead, Margaret. 1935. *Sex and Temperament in Three Primitive Societies*. New York: Morrow.

Meadows, D.H., D. L. Meadows, J. Randers, and W. Behrens III. 1972. *The Limits to Growth*. New York: New American Library.

Merton, Robert K. 1938. "Social Structure and Anomie." *American Sociological Review* 3:672–682.

Merton, Robert K. 1957. *Social Theory and Social Structure* (Revised and Enlarged Edition). Glencoe, IL: Free Press.

Merton, Robert K. 1968. "The Matthew Effect in Science". *Science* 159:56–63.

Merton, Robert K. 1970 (original 1938). *Science, Technology, and Society in Seventeenth Century England*. New York: Howard Fertig.

Michels, Robert. 1949 (original 1911). *Political Parties*. Glencoe, IL: Free Press.

Middlebrook, Patricia Niles. 1974. *Social Psychology and Modern Life*. New York: Knopf.

Milgram, Stanley. 1967. "The Small World Problem". *Psychology Today* 1:61–67.

Miller, Frederick D. 1983. "The End of SDS and the Emergence of the Weatherman: Demise Through Success". Pp. 279–297 in *Social Movements of the Sixties and Seventies*, edited by Jo Freeman. New York: Longman.

Mills, C. Wright. 1956. *The Power Elite*. New York: Oxford University Press.

Mills, C. Wright. 1959. *The Sociological Imagination*. New York: Oxford University Press.

Mintz, Beth and Michael Schwartz. 1985. *The Power Structure of American Business*. Chicago: University of Chicago Press.

Molotch, Harvey. 1976. "The City as a Growth Machine". *American Journal of Sociology* 82:309–333.

Money, John and Anke A. Ehrhardt. 1972. *Man and Woman, Boy and Girl*. Baltimore, MD: Johns Hopkins University Press.

Morrison, Denton E. 1978. "Some Notes Toward Theory on Relative Deprivation." Pp. 202–209 in *Collective Behavior and Social Movements*, edited by Louis E. Genevie. Itasca, IL: F.E. Peacock.

Murdock, George P. 1949. *Social Structure*. New York: Macmillan.

Murdock, George Peter. 1937. "Comparative Data on the Division of Labor by Sex." *Social Forces* 15:551–553.

Nam, Charles B. 1968. *Population and Society*. Boston: Houghton Mifflin.

National Center for Health Statistics. 1987. "Current Estimates from the National Health Interview Survey, United States: 1986." *Vital and Health Statistics*. Series 10, No. 164. Washington, DC: U.S. Government Printing Office.

Neugarten, Bernice L. 1977. "Personality and Aging". Pp. 626–649 in *Handbook of the Psychology of Aging*, edited by James E. Birren and K. Warner Schaie. New York: Van Nostrand Reinhold.

Newcomb, Theodore M. 1961. *The Acquaintance Process*. New York: Holt, Rinehart and Winston.

N.O.R.C. 1987. *General Social Surveys, 1972-1987*. Chicago: National Opinion Research Center.

Ogburn, William Fielding. 1922. *Social Change*. New York: Viking.

Park, Robert E., et al. 1925. *The City*. Chicago: University of Chicago Press.

Parsons, Talcott. 1937. *The Structure of Social Action*. New York: McGraw-Hill.

Parsons, Talcott. 1951. "Illness and the Role of the Physician: A Sociological Perspective". *American Journal of Orthopsychiatry* 21:452–460.

Parsons, Talcott and Edward A. Shils (Editors). 1951. *Toward a General Theory of Action*. New York: Harper.

Parsons, Talcott and Robert F. Bales (eds.). 1955. *Family, Socialization and Interaction Process*. Glencoe, IL: Free Press.

Persell, Caroline Hodges. 1977. *Education and Inequality: A Theoretical and Empirical Synthesis*. New York: Free Press.

Pescosolido, Bernice A. and Robert Mendelsohn. 1986. "Social Causation or Social Construction of Suicide? An Investigation into the Social Organization of Official Rates". *American Sociological Review* 51:80–101.

Pines, Maya. 1981. "The Civilization of Genie". *Psychology Today* 15:28–34.

Piven, Frances Fox and Richard A. Cloward. 1977. *Poor People's Movements: Why They Succeed, How They Fail*. New York: Vintage.

Pomer, Marshall I. 1986. "Labor Market Structure, Intragenerational Mobility, and Discrimination: Black Male Advancement Out of Low-Paying Occupations, 1962–1973." *American Sociological Review* 51:650–659.

Quinney, Richard. 1974. *Criminal Justice in America*. Boston: Little, Brown.

Quinney, Richard. 1980. *Class, State, and Crime*. New York: Longmans.

Reckless, Walter C., Simon Dinitz, and Ellen Murray. 1956. "Self Concept as an Insulator Against Delinquency". *American Sociological Review* 21:744–746.

Reissman, Leonard. 1964. *The Urban Process*. New York: Free Press.

Robertson, Ian. 1987. *Sociology*. (3rd edition). New York: Worth.

Roethlisberger, Fritz and William J. Dickson. 1939. *Management and the Worker*. Cambridge: Harvard University Press.

Rosenberg, Morris. 1979. *Conceiving the Self*. New York: Basic Books.

Rostow, Walt W. 1960. *The Stages of Economic Growth*. New York: Cambridge University Press.

Rostow, Walt W. 1962. *The Process of Economic Growth*. New York: Norton.

Rothschild-Witt, Joyce. 1979. "The Collectivist Organization". *American Sociological Review* 44:509–527.

Rutter, Michael. 1974. *The Qualities of Mothering: Maternal Deprivation Reassessed*. New York: Aronson.

Rutter, Michael, et al. 1979. *Fifteen Thousand Hours*. Cambridge, MA: Harvard University Press.

Sapir, Edward. 1929. "The Status of Linguistics as a Science". *Language* 5:207–214.

Sawhill, Isabel and John Palmer. 1984. *The Reagan Record*. Washington, DC: Urban Institute.

Scanzoni, Letha and John Scanzoni. 1976. *Men, Women and Change: A Sociology of Marriage and Family*. New York: McGraw–Hill.

Schaie, K. Warner. 1980. "Intelligence and Problem Solving". Pp. 262–284 in *Handbook of Mental Health and Aging*, edited by James E. Birren and R. Bruce Stone. Englewood Cliffs, NJ: Prentice–Hall.

Schutz, Alfred. 1962. *Collected Papers, I: The Problem of Social Reality*. M. Natanson (editor). The Hague: Nijhoff.

Schutz, Alfred. 1964. *Collected Papers, II: Studies in Social Theory*. A. Brodersen (editor). The Hague: Nijhoff.

Selznick, Philip E. 1948. "Foundations of a Theory of Organizations." *American Sociological Review* 13:25–35.

Sewell, William H. 1971. "Inequality of Opportunity for Higher Education". *American Sociological Review* 36:793–809.

Shaw, Clifford R. and Henry D. McKay. 1942. *Juvenile Delinquency and Urban Areas*. Chicago: University of Chicago Press.

Sheldon, William H., Emil M. Hartl, and Eugene McDermott. 1949. *Varieties of Delinquent Youth*. New York: Harper.

Sherif, Muzafer. 1966. *The Psychology of Social Norms*. New York: Harper and Row.

Shevky, Eshref and Wendell Bell. 1955. *Social Area Analysis*. Stanford, CA: Stanford University Press.

Shibutani, Tamotsu. 1966. *Improvised News: A Sociological Study of Rumor*. Indianapolis: Bobbs–Merrill.

Simmel, Georg. 1950. *The Sociology of Georg Simmel*. Kurt H.Wolff (tr.). New York: Free Press.

Simon, Julian. 1986. *Theory of Population and Economic Growth*. New York: Basil Blackwell.

Simpson, George E. and J. Milton Yinger. 1985. *Racial and Cultural Minorities: An Analysis of Prejudice and Discrimination*, 5th ed. New York: Plenum.

Simpson, Ida Harper, David Stark and Robert A. Jackson. 1988. "Class Identification Processes of Married, Working Men and Women." *American Sociological Review* 53:284–293.

Singh, J.A.L. and Robert M. Zingg. 1942. *Wolf Children and Feral Man*. New York: Harper and Row.

Smith, Adam. 1937 (original 1776). *An Inquiry into the Nature and Causes of the Wealth of Nations*. New York: Modern Library.

Sowell, Thomas. 1977. "New Light on the Black IQ Controversy". *New York Times Magazine* March 27:56–63.

Spanier, Graham B. and Linda Thompson. *Parting: The Aftermath of Separation and Divorce*. Beverly Hills, CA: Sage.

Spengler, Oswald. 1926. *The Decline of the West*. New York: Knopf.

Spitz, Glenna. 1988. "Women's Employment and Family Relations: A Review". *Journal of Marriage and the Family* 50:595–618.

Spitz, Rene A. 1945. "Hospitalism: An Inquiry into the Genesis of Psychiatric Conditions in Early Childhood." Pp. 53–75 in *The Psychoanalytic Study of the Child*, V.1, edited by Anna Freud, et al. New York: International Universities Press.

Spitzer, Steven. 1980. "Toward a Marxian Theory of Deviance". Pp. 175–191 in *Criminal Behavior, Readings in Criminology*, edited by Delos H. Kelly. New York: St. Martins Press.

Starr, Paul. 1982. *The Social Transformation of American Medicine*. New York: Basic Books.

Stein, Peter J. 1976. *Single*. Englewood Cliffs, NJ: Prentice–Hall.

Stoner, J.A.F. 1961. "Comparison of Individual and Group Decisions Involving Risk." Unpublished Master's Thesis, Massachusetts Institute of Technology, School of Industrial Management.

Strodtbeck, Fred L., Rita M. James, and Charles Hawkins. 1957. "Social Status in Jury Deliberation." *American Sociological Review* 22:713–719.

Stryker, Sheldon. 1980. *Symbolic Interactionism: A Social Structural Version*. Menlo Park, CA: Benjamin Cummings.

Sumner, William Graham. 1906. *Folkways*. Boston: Ginn.

Sutherland, Edwin. 1940. "White Collar Criminality". *American Sociological Review* 5:1–12.

Suttles, Gerald. 1970. *The Social Order of the Slum*. Chicago: University of Chicago Press.

Szasz, Thomas. 1970. *The Manufacture of Madness*. New York: Dell.

Taylor, Frederick W. 1911. *Principles of Scientific Management*. New York: Harper.

Thomas, Evan. 1986. "Peddling Influence". *Time* March 3:26–36.

Thomas, W. I. 1931. *The Unadjusted Girls*. Boston: Little, Brown and Co.

Tilly, Charles. 1978. *From Mobilization to Revolution*. Reading, MA: Addison-Wesley.

Tilly, Charles. 1986. "Does Modernization Breed Revolution?" Pp. 47–57 in *Revolutions: Theoretical, Comparative, and Historical Studies*, edited by Jack Goldstone. New York: Harcourt Brace Jovanovich.

Tilly, Charles, Louise Tilly and Richard Tilly. 1975. *The Rebellious Century, l830-1930*. Cambridge, MA: Harvard University Press.

Tocqueville, Alexis de. 1969 (original 1835). *Democracy in America*. Garden City, NY: Doubleday Anchor Books.

Toennies, Ferdinand. 1963 (original 1887). *Community and Society*. New York: Harper and Row.

Toffler, Alvin. 1981. *The Third Wave*. New York: Bantam.

Torrey, E.F. 1974. *The Death of Psychiatry*. New York: Penquin.

Toynbee, Arnold. 1946. *A Study of History*. New York: Oxford University Press.

Tumin, Melvin M. 1953. "Some Principles of Stratification: A Critical Analysis". *American Sociological Review* 18:387–394.

Tung-Sen, Chang. 1970. "A Chinese Philosopher's Theory of Knowledge." Pp. 121–140 in *Social Psychology Through Symbolic Interaction*, edited by Gregory P. Stone and Harvey A. Farberman. Waltham, MA: Ginn-Blaisdell.

Turner, Jeffrey S. and Donald B. Helms. 1988. *Marriage and Family: Traditions and Transitions*. New York: Harcourt, Brace Jovanovich.

Turner, Ralph H. 1964. "Collective Behavior". Pp. 382–425 in *Handbook of Modern Sociology*, edited by R.L. Faris. Chicago: Rand McNally.

Turner, Ralph H. and Lewis M. Killian. 1957. *Collective Behavior*. Englewood Cliffs, NJ: Prentice-Hall.

Tylor, Edward B. 1871. *Primitive Culture*. 2 vols. London: Murray.

Tyree, Andrea. 1991. "Town Mass Migration to the Transformation of an Ethnic Hierarchy: The U.S. in the 20th Century". In *Social Roles and Social Institutions: Essays in Honor of Rose Laub Coser*, edited by Judith R. Blau and Norman Goodman. Boulder, CO: Westview Press.

U.S. Arms Control and Disarmament Agency. 1986. *World Military Expenditures and Arms Transfers*. Washington, DC: U.S. Government Printing Office.

U.S. Bureau of the Census. 1984. *Projections of the Population of the United States by Age, Sex, and Race: 1983 to 2080*. P–25. No. 952. Washington, DC: U.S. Government Printing Office.

U.S. Bureau of the Census. 1985. *Statistical Abstract of the United States 1985*. 105th ed. Washington, DC: U.S. Government Printing Office.

U.S. Bureau of the Census. 1986. "Household Wealth and Asset Ownership: 1984." *Current Population Reports*. Washington, DC: U.S. Government Printing Office.

U.S. Bureau of the Census. 1987a. *Money, Income and Poverty Status of Families and Persons in the United States: 1986*. P–60, No. 157. Washington, D.C.: U.S. Government Printing Office.

U.S. Bureau of the Census. 1987b. *United States Population Estimates and Components of Change: 1970-1986*. P–25, No. 1006. Washington, D.C.: U.S. Government Printing Office.

U.S. Bureau of Labor Statistics. 1987a. *Employment and Earnings*. Vol. 34, No. 10. Washington, DC: U.S. Government Printing Office.

U.S. Bureau of Labor Statistics. 1987b. *Statistical Abstracts of the United States 1987*. 107th ed. Washington, DC: U.S. Government Printing Office.

U.S. Bureau of Labor Statistics. 1988. *Employment and Earnings*. Vol. 35, No. 1: Washington, DC: U.S. Government Printing Office.

U.S. Federal Bureau of Investigation. 1987. *Crime in the United States, 1986*. Washington, DC: U.S. Government Printing Office.

United Nations. 1973. *Determinants and Consequences of Population Trends*. (2nd edition). New York: United Nations.

Vander Zanden, James. 1990. *The Social Experience: An Introduction to Sociology*. (2nd Edition). New York: McGraw- Hill.

Veblen, Thorstein. 1934 (original 1899). *The Theory of the Leisure Class*. New York: Modern Library.

Wallerstein, Immanuel. 1974. *The Modern World System*. New York: Academic Press.

Wallerstein, Immanuel. 1979. *The Capitalist World- Economy*. New York: Cambridge University Press.

Warner, W. Lloyd. 1949. *Democracy in Jonesville*. New York: Harper and Row.

Warner, W. Lloyd and Paul S. Lunt. 1941. *The Social Life of a Modern Community*. New Haven, CT: Yale University Press.

Warner, W. Lloyd and Paul S. Lunt. 1942. *The Status System of a Modern Community*. New Haven, CT: Yale University Press.

Watson, James D. 1968. *The Double Helix*. New York: Atheneum.

Wattenberg, Ben J. 1987. *The Birth Dearth*. New York: Pharos.

Weber, Max. 1946. *Max Weber: Essays in Sociology*. H.H. Gerth and C. Wright Mills, eds. and trans. New York: Oxford University Press.

Weber, Max. 1958 (original 1904-1905). *The Protestant Ethic and the Spirit of Capitalism*. New York: Scribner's Sons.

Weber, Max. 1978 (original 1921). *Economy and Society*. G. Roth and C. Wittick, Editors. Berkeley, CA: University of California Press.

Weinstein, Eugene A. and Paul Deutschberger. 1963. "Some Dimensions of Alter-casting." *Sociometry* 24:454–466.

Weitman, Sasha R. 1973. "National Flags: A Sociological Overview." *Semiotica* 8:328–367.

Weitzman, Lenore. 1985. *Divorce Revolution: The Unexpected Social and Economic Consequences for Women and Children in America*. New York: Free Press.

White, Ralph and Ronald Lippitt. 1953. "Leader Behavior and Member Reaction in Three 'Social Climates'". Pp. 586–611 in *Group Dynamics*, edited by D. Cartwright and A. Zander. Evanston, IL: Row, Peterson.

Whorf, Benjamin Lee. 1956. *Language, Thought and Reality: Selected Writings of Benjamin Lee Whorf*. John B. Carroll (Editor). Cambridge, MA: MIT Press.

Whyte, William Foote. 1943. *Street-Corner Society: The Social Structure of an Italian Slum*. Chicago: University of Chicago Press.

Whyte, William H., Jr. 1957. *The Organization Man*. New York: Anchor.

Wiles, P.J.D. 1977. *Economic Institutions Compared*. New York: Halsted Press.

Williams, Robin M. Jr. 1970. *American Society: A Sociological Interpretation*. New York: Alfred A. Knopf.

Wilson, William Julius. 1978. *The Declining Significance of Race*. Chicago: University of Chicago Press.

Wilson, William Julius. 1987. *The Truly Disadvantaged: The Inner City, the Underclass, and Public Policy*. Chicago: University of Chicago Press.

Winn, Edward A. 1981. "Looking at Good Schools". *Phi Delta Kappan* 62:377–381.

Wrong, Dennis. 1961. "The Oversocialized Conception of Man in Modern Sociology". *American Sociological Review* 24:183–195.

Yankelovitch, Daniel. 1978. "The New Psychological Contract at Work". *Psychology Today* 11:53–66.

Zajonc, Robert B. 1965. "On Social Facilitation". *Science* 149:269–274.

Zborowski, Mark. 1969. *People in Pain*. San Francisco: Jossey-Bass.

Zelditch, Morris, Jr. 1955. "Role Differentiation in the Nuclear Family: A Comparative Study." Pp. 307–352 in *Family, Socialization and Interaction Process*, edited by T. Parsons and R.F. Bales. Glencoe, IL: Free Press.

Zerubavel, Eviatar. 1981. *Hidden Rhythms: Schedules and Calendars in Social Life*. Chicago: University of Chicago Press.

Zola, Irving K. 1966. "Culture and Symptoms—An Analysis of Patient's Presenting Problems". *American Sociological Review* 31:615–630.

Zola, Irving K. 1972. "Medicine as an Institution of Social Control". *Sociological Review* 20:480–504.

Zuckerman, Harriet. 1977. "Deviant Behavior and Social Control in Science". Pp. 87–138 in *Deviance and Social Change*, edited by E. Sagarin. Beverly Hills, CA: Sage.

Index